MW01282517

THE ENDURING HOLD OF ISLAM IN TURKEY

DAVID S. TONGE

The Enduring Hold of Islam in Turkey

The Revival of the Religious Orders and Rise of Erdoğan

HURST & COMPANY, LONDON

First published in the United Kingdom in 2024 by
C. Hurst & Co. (Publishers) Ltd.,
New Wing, Somerset House, Strand, London, WC2R 1LA

A Cataloguing-in-Publication data record for this book is available from the British Library.

ISBN: 9781911723837

www.hurstpublishers.com

Printed and bound in Great Britain by Bell and Bain Ltd, Glasgow

To my parents,
who never knew how much I loved them,
and my shining son, who does.

CONTENTS

LIST OF ILLUSTRATIONS

Every effort has been made to trace and acknowledge copyright, but in some cases this has not been possible. We would be pleased to rectify any omissions in subsequent editions should they be drawn to our attention.

ACKNOWLEDGEMENTS

My research was triggered by an article on the political role of the Nakşibendis in Turkey in 2018.[1] I had just finished an analysis of the social engineering being carried out by Erdoğan's party, and sensed that this paper raised more questions than it answered. The changes were clear, but the motivation for them was not. The article left me asking how Islam had come to Turkey, what type of Islam had reigned through the long Ottoman centuries before the Republic, how the Nakşibendis had risen to their current pre-eminence, and how durable the change might prove.

This book sets out to explain what I discovered. The process taught me, *pace* Sir Hugh Foot on Cyprus, that "Anyone who says he understands Turkey has been misinformed." It has led me to reconfigure my half-century relationship with a country I thought I knew. Some of the protagonists were familiar to me—though I sense how far I had remained from them. Others, reviled by Kemalists and adulated in the New Turkey of Erdoğan, were fresh on my horizon. It has also caused me to adjust my values. I was from a generation that looked on religion and nationalism as atavistic aberrations. But the twenty-first century has seen their revival. Today's Turkey shows how vigorous they can be, and how intertwined.

Old friends and new acquaintances who have contributed much and to whom I give my thanks include Francis Bennett, Doğan Bermek, Kenan Gürsoy, Kimberly Hart, Gülten Karagöz, the late Şerif Mardin, Giles Merritt, Christopher Roper, Şükran Vahide, and Hasan Şükrü Yayıntaş.

I have benefitted from the fine libraries of İstanbul, particularly the Research Center for Anatolian Civilizations (ANAMED), the Orient Institute, the American Research Institute in Turkey (ARIT), and other members of the Bibliopera network, in particular the Institut Français d'Études Anatoliennes (IFEA) and İstanbul Araştırma Enstitüsü (İAE), as well as the libraries of the Foundation for Sciences and Arts (BİSAV) and İstanbul Municipality. Good online resources include the *İslam Ansiklopedisi* of the *Türkiye Diyanet Vakfı*, the foundation of the Directorate of Religious Affairs; YÖK's thesis database, the *Ulusal Tez Merkezi*; and the national book catalogue, *Ulusal Toplu Katalog*.

I would also like to thank Isis Press, İstanbul Bilgi University, İletişim Publishing, the Persian Heritage Foundation, Saqi Books, Sözler Neşriyat and *Yeni Şafak* for permission to cite from their works.

NOTE ON SPELLING

For names and titles, I have used Turkish spellings as in the current online edition of *İslam Ansiklopedisi*. In most cases, the Turkish names of religious orders are used, for example Mevlevi(yye) rather than the spelling Mawlawi(yya) often used outside Turkey. If these significantly differ, at first reference I also give between brackets the alternative spellings.

I have generally used Turkish terms for religious matters, and append a glossary setting these out, along with their Arabic equivalents (transliterated) and their translation. Exceptions to this practice include Wahabbism, where the Turkish Vehhabilik would seem egregious.

With a few exceptions, such as faith communities, e.g. Alevis and Bektaşis, no letter 's' is added to Turkish nouns when used in the plural, for instance many *tarikat* (the Arabic word for way), rather than many *tarikats* or (the Turkish plural) *tarikatlar*. Turkish political parties are usually referred to by their Turkish acronyms, e.g. AKP and CHP.

In Ottoman times and during the first years of the Republic, İstanbul was known to its Muslim inhabitants as Kostantiniyye, a variant of Constantinople. I have used the current names of İstanbul (formally adopted in 1930), İzmir, and Ankara for the major cities, and the current spellings of other cities, for example Diyarbakır. In May 2022, the Turkish government requested that the United Nations and other international bodies term the country Türkiye. I have reflected this in the description of the newly declared "Century of Türkiye."

I generally refer to Mustafa Kemal as Atatürk (Father of the Turks) only for his acts after he was awarded the honorific surname in November 1934. Years cited are Common Era (traditionally known as AD in the West). All dates are according to the Gregorian calendar, though in Turkey this was first used in the country's *Official Gazette* in January 1926.

The alphabet in force in Turkey since 1928 consists of twenty-nine letters. It is based on a late Latin one, with the following modifications (*pace* the philologists) for phonetic purposes:

- C and c are pronounced as the j in juniper.
- Ç and ç are pronounced ch as in beech.
- Ğ and ğ lengthen the vowel that precedes them, like the final w in willow.
- I and ı are pronounced as the i in fir.
- İ and i are pronounced as the i in ginkgo.
- Ö and ö are pronounced as the oa in oak.
- Ş and ş are pronounced as the sh in ash.
- Ü and ü are pronounced as the ew in yew.

The official alphabet does not include Q, W, and X, though these increasingly crop up in loanwords.

I have omitted the circumflexes put over vowels in a few Turkish words, usually to increase their length, and most of the diacritics used in transliterations from Arabic.

PREFACE

There is no issue in Turkey that is not related to religion.

İsmail Kara, contemporary Turkish theologian,
Medyascope TV, 20 June 2016

Ahead of us lies the century of Türkiye. So assures us the re-elected president of the country, Recep Tayyip Erdoğan. Already he has won his country a geopolitical veto in his region. Now, foreign tutelage shaken off, it will become one of the top ten countries in the world "in politics, economy, technology, military, diplomacy, all fields." As he told a massed party meeting in October 2022: "We pray to our God every day, every moment, for granting us the honour of being a member of such a nation."[1]

Nationalism and religion are the governing forces in this second century of the Republic of Turkey. Long buried are the hopes, burnished in the anguish of the post-September 11 world, that the Republic moulded by Atatürk would be a textbook example of Islam blending with modernity—modernity as defined by the country's Western allies. To cold warriors and liberals, it was a model for how Islam could and should be marginalized from politics, offering a forward-looking alternative to the discourse of al-Qaeda and ISIS, the Islamic State of Iraq and the Levant.

But the premise was wrong, for the secularism of the Republic was in retreat, and by 2001 had been so for half a century—from before Turkey even joined the Council of Europe and NATO at the start of the 1950s. In the post-war period, governments have come and gone, but one constant has been that Islam has advanced. Between 1947 and 2018, when the office was abolished, twenty-three people (caretakers excluded) served as prime minister. Three quarters of these took measures that, intentionally or not, furthered the profile of religion in Turkey. Rather than initiate, Erdoğan accelerated an ongoing process.

That is not what the Western chancelleries have been proclaiming, or even understanding, as they have sought to enhance the south-east flank of NATO. Long casting the "moderate Islam" of the conspiratorial Fethullah Gülen, inspirer of the coup attempt of 2016, as a pivot in this process is an indication of the practised ease with which Western diplomacy surfs.[2] But the reality of the post-war period is the inexorable return of Sunni Islam in general, and the mystical religious orders in particular, to their integral role in the culture of the Turks.

Islam was slow to come to Anatolia. It was not until the early twelfth century CE that Islam began to take hold in Anatolia, and the Islam that came was no longer dominated by the Hijaz and the Arabs but by distant Khorasan and the Persian mystics.

As the Seljuk Sultanate of Rum was succeeded in Anatolia by the Ottomans, religious orders, shaped by these eastern origins and more mystical than military, developed to carry, spread, and protect the faith. The Ottoman Emperors proved among the most faithful servants that the Prophet has known. In imperial times, almost every Ottoman family would have at least one member with a connection to one of these orders, whose 3,000 or more lodges stretched from the Danube to the Tigris.

The attacks on that world engendered a febrile debate on how Islam should rebuff an expansionist Europe. The early Republic had no time for such ideas. It declared itself secular and launched a major exercise in social engineering, with its ruling generals seeking to create a new identity for the Turks that linked them to the folk traditions and history of the early Turkic tribes.

This endeavour to excise six centuries of Ottoman glory and struggle, all inextricably tied to the Empire's role as the *Dar al-Islam* (Abode of Islam), was soon to be challenged. Hand-in-hand with this challenge was a resurgence of a brand of nationalism that has given space to extremism and, at times, to antisemitism.

In the world of the Turks, many Islamic fraternities have risen and faded. However, one in particular stands out, as it does in many troubled parts of the world. That is the Nakşibendis (often spelt Naqshbandis), whose intrinsic distrust of the West was forged by the intrusions of the British and French into their spiritual home in India and the Russians into Central Asia. Followers of this tradition include three of the last five presidents of

Turkey, a reflection of the durability of the Nakşibendis' message, and the impact it may have in the years ahead.

The Nakşibendis' name comes from the fourteenth-century Transoxianan saint, Muhammed Bahâeddin Şah-ı Nakşibend. His teaching inspires the main orders active in Turkey, half a dozen in number, all coloured by the later Halid el-Bağdadi, a Kurdish preacher from the time of Napoleon. The latter's vision was of an Ottoman Empire strong enough to resist the West. It is a message that, adapted to modern commercial life, resonates through the halls of power in Ankara and the breasts of many of Turkey's citizens. So robust has this order become that one sociologist suggests it is "a possible candidate for the slot of a 'world historical development.'"[3] The rise in Turkey's Islamic parties reflects and encourages this thrust.

Erdoğan's New Turkey is old Ottoman rather than neo-Ottoman, with Sunni Islam today restored to its role as a central part of the people's cultural identity, a position it had held for half a millennium and more. With its leavening of nationalism, this is the Turkish model of the 2020s.

In this, the dervishes are back—with a difference. The communities of the past included mystical communities of learning, tolerance and great artistic creativity. The saints of today are buoyed by social media and masonic-like solidarity, creating commercially vibrant communities that permeate the state and mobilize to colour party politics.

The enigmatic Fethullah Gülen is no outlier in this process. As a young man, he was influenced by Said Nursi, a Turkish saint of Kurdish origin and part-Nakşibendi formation. From early on, Gülen focused on temporal power, turning education into a multi-million-dollar business, developing newspapers and television outlets to attack his opponents, and infiltrating his followers into the key arms of the state—the judiciary, the military, and the police.

The crackdown since the failed coup attempt of 2016 has weakened but not destroyed his following. It has led to the authorities encouraging other orders, all of them more overtly Nakşibendi in teaching, to replace the Gülenists in the state machinery. The new establishment includes the Erenköy, İskenderpaşa, İsmailağa, and Menzil branches of the Nakşibendi, and all are well entrenched in the governing institutions of Turkey. Operating in parallel, though often at odds with the state, is the covert Süleymancı community, another Nakşibendi grouping.

Erdoğan's own career draws on all these orders, while his green mantle of faith is now interwoven with the vivid red of the Turkish flag, as nationalism bolsters his offer.

Economic vigour has led Turkey to cast off the robes cut for it by the protagonists of the Cold War. With its regional competitors less threatening than for several centuries, Turkey has cast aside the caution of three generations and sought to raise its profile in many of the lands from which it was driven a century ago. It has openly backed the Muslim Brotherhood in Egypt and Hamas in Gaza, and gave more support to the ISIS in Syria than it cares to admit. It has troops in Iraq, Libya, and Syria, bases in Albania, Qatar, and Somalia, dares the world to challenge its oil and gas exploration vessels in the Eastern Mediterranean, fought in the civil war in Libya, equipped the Azeris in their recapture of most of Nagorno-Karabakh, and largely supports the Ukrainians in their resistance to Russia.

And it is at frequent odds with Saudi Arabia. The murder of the journalist, Jamal Khashoggi, in the Saudi consulate in İstanbul was hardly a signal of respect to Turkey. Erdoğan retaliated in kind, his officials drip-feeding details of the dissident's grisly dismemberment. Only in April 2022, with an improbable embrace of Erdoğan and Prince Mohammed bin Salman, did some tentative olive branches begin to appear.

While living the schizophrenia shared by most Western countries as they try to square strategic and economic dependence on Riyadh with the Kingdom's despotic reality, the Turks are differentiated rather than united with the Saudis by Islam. The Wahhabi tradition of the Saudis holds that there should be no human intermediation between the believer and God. By contrast, in Turkey, the Nakşibendis look to living saints to help the believer follow the true path.

I have worn three cloaks in Turkey before today. When I first came to the country in the 1960s, I was an expatriate, living amidst a Bosphorus community of foreigners in an İstanbul of crumbling wooden houses, gas streetlights, duck eggs when chicken eggs fell short, cobbles, and 2.5 million people; working in the garden city of Ankara; and travelling in a pristine country sedate in its long-worn traditions. A decade later, I was a foreign correspondent in a city where a first bridge linked its Asian and European shores, but which was divided by the civil strife of a people on the move from village to town. Come the 1980s I was an economic consultant. Cement and motorways ruled, İstanbul had two bridges for its 6 million inhabitants, and Turgut Özal was helping Turks find their Ottoman past and Islamic roots while questing for a consumerist future. Now, as I quest the past, three bridges link Europe to Asia Minor, and over 16 million people live in a metropolis bespoiling 70 kilometres of the shores of the Sea of Marmara.

I had set off on my travels with a sense that Christianity did not fit me well. Like many of my generation, I wondered whether the mysticism that flourished in Islam might fill the void as I questioned my Anglican upbringing. I warmed to the Islamic vision of brotherhood portrayed by Wilfred Thesiger in his portraits of the Arabs. It was a world before the hijackings by Black September and the Taliban.

I read a little on the universal wisdom of the Sufis and watched the whirling of dervishes, who were again allowed to perform in public. I left unconvinced and then put religion aside. Five years living under the Colonels' 'Greece of the Christian Greeks' stifled my quest for faith, and, when I returned to Turkey, I embraced the Republic's professed secularism. I was the partner of a modern Turk. Our friends were the breezy, self-confident heirs to the Republic, one of them the grandson of the last Ottoman Caliph.

Then suddenly, they were yesterday's people. The casebook experiment of burying Islam to build a modern society had failed. Secularism weakened and withered, just as it has in so many countries in the face of resurgent fundamentalism of all hues, Buddhist, Christian, Hindu, Judaic, and Muslim.

I turned back to the Sufis and came to know dervishes of a dozen orders, not because of an urge to join their communities, but because of the belated conviction that without approaching them, I would not be able to understand the forces shaping Turkey and its future.

Erdoğan may go. The orders, though now misshapen, will continue, as they have for half a millennium and more, as will the fateful appeal of Turkish nationalism. This book describes my quest to understand the reality that I, and many, have long denied.

INTRODUCTION

Oh Solomon, I have surpassed Thee!

The words attributed to Justinian the Great as he opened Hagia Sophia on 27 December 537 CE

Rebuilding the nation

"As for those who are bent on denying the truth... God has sealed their hearts and their ears, and over their eyes there is a covering. They will have a terrible punishment." With these words, Recep Tayyip Erdoğan closed his recital from the *Kur'an*, with the *imam* at his side proclaiming "Amin" on behalf of the tens of thousands of faithful gathered in Ayasofya and the streets and spaces surrounding what for a millennium had been the premier church of Christianity.

That hot July midday in 2020, the Great Church was being reopened for Muslim worship. To mark the occasion, kneeling where the altar once stood, Erdoğan incanted a dozen verses, doing so in the original Arabic with an evident learning and elegance—and what Christians would call musicality. His recital resonated far and wide among the fifth of humankind who follow the Prophet. "At last, an Islamic President" viewers from the Caucasus, Pakistan, and Indonesia commented on a YouTube recording of the event.

Apart from faith, there was a second message in the richly staged ceremony, and that was to the Turkish people and their standing in the world. In 1453, Mehmed the Conqueror had converted Justinian's creation into what became the premier imperial mosque of the Ottomans—and so it had stayed until it was recast as a museum by the secularizing Republic of the 1930s. That change appalled the nationalists of the time. For over 475 years, the great dome had resonated with the Muslim call to prayer. Reviving its hallowed role was the dream of the poets who inspired Erdoğan's youth.

The Turkish president had now made their clarion calls a reality, addressing head-on many Turks' sense of grievance over their lost grandeur—and such was the theme of the sermon delivered that day by Ali Erbaş, Turkey's top cleric.

Mehmed the Conqueror had entrusted Ayasofya as a mosque to be protected by believers until the end of time. So Erbaş proclaimed. Reopening it to worship would serve as a blessing to oppressed believers and troubled mosques throughout the world, especially the Dome of the Rock in Jerusalem. It was a fulfilment of the dreams of the giants of Ottoman lore: the Seljuk Sultan Alp Arslan who opened Anatolia to the Turks; the Conqueror himself, who had oxen drag his fleet over a ridge to imperil the besieged Byzantines; the dervish Akşemseddin who inspired the conquering troops and led the first Friday prayers on 1 June 1453; and the renowned architect, Mimar Sinan, whose buttresses sustain one of the great monuments of mankind.

Erbaş underlined the Ottoman import of all this by delivering his sermon sabre in hand. The weapon had helped him work his way up the precipitous minbar, at this point being in his right hand. But for preaching, he moved it to his left, indicating that his message was one of peace rather than a summons to religious war. For nigh five centuries, preachers in Ayasofya had girded a sword. Today, they continue to do so.

With the service over, Erdoğan left to pay his respects at the thrice-rebuilt tomb of Mehmed the Conqueror, flanked, as he had been throughout, by the leader of the ultra-right party whose votes sustain his presidency, Devlet Bahçeli.

Past and present were as blended that day as faith and chauvinism. This heady combination is fomented relentlessly by Erdoğan as he stakes an increasing place in the sun for what he long called the New Turkey. This New Turkey was nothing less than "a new politics, a new economy and a new sociology," he asserted when he launched it in August 2014, the day before taking over as Turkey's first popularly elected president. It has since proved to be a nation-rebuilding project, atavistically harking back to an idealized past. Those who dared to close the premier mosque of the Empire—and they included Mustafa Kemal Atatürk, revered leader of Turkey's War of Independence—were condemned as liable to the curse decreed by Mehmed the Conqueror on those who interrupted its prayers.

In October 2022, Erdoğan rebranded his project the Century of Türkiye, this time casting himself as the successor to Atatürk and the great figures of the Republic's first century who had freed Turkey from foreign tutelage. In the next 100 years, following Erdoğan's path, Turkey would become one of the ten great states of the world. The 10,000 invitees gave him the appropriate standing ovation for what proved to be the unleashing of his 2023 election campaign. Seven months later, he won, health permitting, a further five years at the country's helm.

The lesson of the tombstones

One mile to the north-west of Ayasofya lies a second mosque also central to Erdoğan's vision of the nation. This is the great Süleymaniye, erected by Mimar Sinan for Süleyman the Magnificent, and today a haven of relative peace. Its esteemed schools of learning now serve the university of a foundation established by Turkey's current leader, and its graveyard hosts one of his ministers.

This graveyard contains the tombs of the Sultan and his favourite wife, Roxelana, a former slave from Ruthenia, with early engravings showing them surrounded by gardens so well tended that their flowers provided funds for the complex of which they were part. That income withered away as the gardens were invaded by eighteenth-century notables jostling for space beside the illustrious couple. But the imperial mausolea stand as sumptuous as ever.

That of the Sultan is octagonal with a piece of the black stone of the Kaaba of Mecca in the entrance tympanum. That of Roxelana is sixteen-sided, its tiles a vision of the gardens of Paradise. Yet it is the simpler tombs beside them that draw the local faithful today. For in this quiet corner, south-east of the mosque commanding the skyline of old İstanbul, lie six of the last nine masters who headed one of the most powerful religious orders of Turkey. And here the visitor finds not only the graves of these saints, but also those of figures linking this order to two recent presidents of Turkey, Turgut Özal, president from 1989 to 1993, and Erdoğan himself, leader of the country since 2003.

In Islam, the choice of grave is as symbolically significant as in many religions. From the late 1920s, the generals ruling a secular Ankara closed the precincts of Süleymaniye to burials, but in 1980 Özal persuaded the junta which had just seized power to end the ban. This was to allow the burial of Mehmet Zahit Kotku, *şeyh* (master) of a *tarikat* (religious order) now known as the İskenderpaşa *tarikat*, after the İstanbul mosque where he long served as *imam* (incumbent prayer leader). Three years later and confirming the closeness of his family to this *tarikat*, Özal arranged for his mother, Hafize, to be buried there. Özal himself was entombed in a spacious site outside the city walls, but in January 2001 his youngest brother, Yusuf Bozkurt, also chose to be buried close to Kotku. Fifteen years later, Erdoğan's Minister of Finance, the late Kemal Unakıtan, joined the departed.

It is not only in death that politics and religion are so intertwined but also in life. All thirty-three Ottoman Sultans from 1389 had connections with one of the *tarikat* that spread through their lands.[1] Indeed, the last, Mehmed VI Vahdeddin, was a follower of the tradition that spawned, and was invigorated by, Kotku.[2]

Today, these religious orders and the communities of over 1 million that they mobilize—at election times, in ministries and business, in towns and countryside—play a critical role in the governance of Turkey. *Tarikat* offer the individual a route to communion with the divine, through their teaching and practices assisting the believer to accommodate the austere precepts of Islam. All trace their origins to a holy man whose teachings became ritualized by his followers and transmitted through a line of *şeyh*, a figure taught and nominated by his predecessor, with a chain of authority tracing back to the saint who inspired them. The principle of apostolic succession is not confined to the Christian church.

The religious orders helped the Ottomans carry Islam into the Balkans, and were integral to the faith during the six centuries that the Ottoman Empire was its devoted manifestation on Earth. One *tarikat*, the Bektaşi, inspired the Emperor's long-feared infantry, the Janissaries; a second, the Mevlevi with its whirling dervishes, inspired courtly art as it operated huge estates; and others moved seamlessly in the chambers of the Sultan.

The new Republic, casting the orders as nests of sedition and idleness, closed their lodges in 1925 and banned their activities. But a number survived, particularly those focusing on the individual's relationship with God and making limited use of public ceremony. Such is the tradition of the Nakşibendis, and it is this order that dominates the Islamist discourse in twenty-first-century Turkey—as it does in Russia where Muslims long faced persecution.

Today, six main Nakşibendi groupings influence the governance of Turkey, some generally termed as *tarikat* (even though all *tarikat* have been formally proscribed since 1925) and others termed *cemaat* or community, a word indicating a break in the line of duly trained and anointed *şeyh*.[3]

- Erenköy, now a *cemaat* rather than a *tarikat*, appealing to the wealthy of İstanbul and, though eschewing political activism, long appreciated by Erdoğan.
- İskenderpaşa, which has targeted the state, inspiring the generation of politicians that opened the way for the Islamist Necmettin Erbakan and Erdoğan, initially his follower.
- İsmailağa, a *tarikat* that has reached out to the urban and rural under-privileged and prides itself on its adoption of the clothes worn at the time of the Prophet, an approach that scandalizes secularists.
- The various Nurcu *cemaat* of followers of Said Nursi, of which Fethullah Gülen's *Hizmet* (Service) community is notorious for its involvement in the abortive coup on 15 July 2016.
- Menzil, a *tarikat* offering redemption to all, stepping into posts in the state machinery from which Gülenists have been cleared.
- The Süleymancı, a *cemaat* distrustful of state secularism that has inculcated conservative religious attitudes among millions.

Several of these have been buffeted by splits. One, the Gülen *cemaat*, is now on the run, and that its traces continue to be a factor in post-coup Turkey is an indication of the extent to which it had infiltrated the country's fabric.

While in a practical sense competing for the loyalty of the believer, these groupings have an underlying commonality of purpose. In this sense, Erdoğan's own trajectory is symbolic. Born in 1954, he received his initial education from the Süleymancı. In his early political days, he linked himself to İskenderpaşa. He visited the leaders of İsmailağa seeking their political backing, and could count on the financial support of Erenköy. He long allied himself with the *cemaat* of Fethullah Gülen with its infiltration of security services and judiciary, benefitting from the support of its newspapers, television, and ubiquitous discussion groups. After he and Gülen spectacularly fell out in the middle of the last decade, he turned to Menzil to fill the gaps in the state machinery.

As for his own eventual grave, Erdoğan is said to favour being laid either in the peaceful Karacaahmet graveyard beside the inspirer of the Süleymancı, as his parents have been, or in Süleymaniye mosque in the İskenderpaşa corner of the imperial graveyard.[4]

PART ONE

ORIGINS

Cet animal est très méchant. Quand on l'attaque il se défend.
La Ménagerie, a burlesque song from 1868

Islam is astoundingly diverse, with its contours responding to local cultures and experience. The Ottoman Empire was one of its most durable manifestations. It is thus with the forces shaping the emergence of the Turkish Republic that this book begins.

1

ABDÜLHAMID II
RELIGION AND POWER

The best of rulers is he who keeps company with men of learning, and the worst of learned men is he who seeks the society of the king.

Sufyan al-Thawri (d. c. 778), *The Book of Government or Rules for Kings, The Siyar al-Muluk or Siyasat-nama of Nizam al-Mulk*, tr. Hubert Darke, Yale University Press, 1960, p. 63[1]

Collapse in Europe, stifled reform at home

In summer 1867, Prince Abdülhamid visited Paris and London as part of the entourage of his uncle, the stocky, bearded, and profligate Sultan Abdülaziz. He was then twenty-four years old, taciturn and awkward, the younger of the Sultan's two nephews in the retinue, attracting little attention from his hosts. A decade later, he was pitchforked to the throne, being declared "Sultan of Sultans, Khan of Khans, Successor and Faithful Warrior of the Prophet of the Lord of the Worlds, Guardian of the Holy Cities of Mecca, Medina, and Jerusalem."[2] For the next three decades, he was to combine these temporal and religious roles, absolute in his powers until the Young Turk revolution of 1908.

His reign was dominated by loss of empire, and foreign reverses and his protective conservatism were to colour his approach to Islam. From the start, he was caught up in what became the Great Eastern Crisis and a devastating war with Russia. The Ottomans found themselves largely on their own. British press reports of massacres of Christians in Bulgaria—the most wanton violence in the region since both sides' atrocities during the Greek War of Independence—led to Gladstone's tract condemning the Ottomans' "fell Satanic orgies." Public opinion and splits within his cabinet constrained Disraeli's ability to restrain the empires to the Ottomans' north.

Russian forces surged down the western coast of the Black Sea to the approaches to Constantinople. They also seized Kars, the Ottomans' fortress town for the Caucasus. A humiliating armistice led to the crippling Treaty of San Stefano of 3 March 1878. Under this, Montenegro, Serbia, and Romania were to become independent, while Bulgaria—tripled in size to stretch from the Black Sea to the Aegean—would become autonomous, with only token suzerainty to the Sultan. The Ottomans were to pay a war indemnity equivalent to four times their annual revenues, partially reduced by their ceding coastal regions on the Black Sea, islands on the Danube, and eastern provinces of Anatolia. The Sultan's Orthodox subjects were to come under Russian protection, with reforms promised in areas inhabited by the Armenians, who had provided some support to Russian forces.

Central European concerns over this dramatic increase in the sway of Russia led to the Congress of Berlin. Here the Great Powers reduced the new Bulgaria in size but confirmed İstanbul's losses of Montenegro, Serbia, and Romania. They obliged Russia to return parts of eastern Anatolia but not Ardahan, Kars, and Batum, and they authorised the Austro-Hungarians to occupy Bosnia and Herzegovina. The run-up to the Congress also cost the Ottomans the strategic island of Cyprus, Britain demanding this purportedly in order to safeguard the integrity of Ottoman Anatolia.[3]

For the Ottomans, it was a disaster. The Empire had lost one fifth of its population and two fifths of its territory, was beset by the millions of Muslim refugees fleeing the Christian armies in the Balkans, and was financially ruined. That was only the beginning. In 1881, the French seized control of Tunisia. In 1882, the British invaded Egypt, a country of particular symbolic and material importance to the Ottomans. In 1885, the southern half of today's Bulgaria broke away. A decade later Crete gained autonomy.

It was the misfortune of Abdülhamid to rule through this cataclysm.

Table 1. The Last Seven Sultans

Sultan	Born	Reign	Death (if deposed)
Mahmud II	1785	1808–1839	
Abdülmecid	1823	1839–1861	
Abdülaziz	1830	1861–May 1876	June 1876
Murad V	1840	May–August 1876	1904
Abdülhamid II	1842	August 1876–1909	1918
Mehmed V Reşad	1844	1909–1918	
Mehmed VI Vahdeddin	1861	1918–1922	1926

In parallel with these disasters, two other great tides were swirling. One was that created by the struggle between centre and periphery, between a state needing control to develop its defences and its fringes, riven by the stirring of local autarchs, separatism, and nationalist revolt. The second was the inexorable chiding of modernity and the changes this required in ruling structures, economic actors, and reconciling religion with scientific progress.

The Sultan's predecessors had embarked on a series of reforms, the *Tanzimat-ı Hayriyye*, or the Auspicious Reorderings. Read out in November 1839 to an assemblage of dignitaries, both religious and civil, local and foreign, in a park beneath Topkapı Palace, these committed the Empire to ensuring transparency of justice and equal treatment for all citizens, whether they be Muslims or others. The reforms aimed at modernizing all levels of Ottoman society, civilian and military, exempting only the religious hierarchy.

The ensuing changes affected almost all state institutions. New ministries were added, creating a semblance of the structures that had emerged in much of Western Europe. A commercial code was introduced in 1850 and rendered secular in 1860. This was based on a code drawn up by Napoleon, as was the final reorganization of the penal code in 1858. Also dating back to that period were regulations authorizing private sector publishers and printing firms and the appearance of the first translations of French literature. Before long, Ottomans had access in their own language to many of the works that provided the intellectual background for the French Revolution.

Education lagged behind. Secondary schools for engineering, medicine, and military studies were established, but primary education remained as it had been for centuries. Muslim children were sent to school around the age of five or six, and were taught verses and short chapters from the *Kur'an* and certain prayers, learning the sounds rather than the meaning of the words involved. From eight to twelve, they learnt the rules of ablution, prayer, and other religious obligations and rituals. The study of maps was banned as tantamount to the proscribed practice of drawing. New adolescence and middle/preparatory schools were opened, but by 1890 these only accounted for 4 per cent of the student body. Even then, their curricula were controlled by commissions involving the *ulema* (the religious hierarchy), and their textbooks were firmly rooted in Islam.[4]

Initially, only boys proceeded to secondary education.[5] The year 1870 saw the opening of a teachers' training college for women—one for men had been opened in 1848. The year 1870 also saw the launching of a short-lived university. However, the *şeyhülislam*, the senior religious official, viewed the latter as a challenge, and it soon closed. Today's İstanbul University did not open its doors until 1900.

Conceived as core to the process was a constitution limiting the ruler's absolute authority. Soon after taking office, Abdülhamid duly promulgated a constitution. His text fell far short of reformist demands, safeguarding the rights of the sovereign rather than those of the people. Fourteen months later, he suspended it. Restoration of this inadequate charter was to become the rallying cry of his opponents.

The Caliph and his sufis

During this implosion, the spiritual leader of the Empire was Abdülhamid himself. In his role as Caliph, successor of the Prophet, he was also acknowledged as the religious guide of Sunni Muslims throughout the world.

The Ottomans had inherited this role from the Abbasids when they took control of Mecca and Medina in 1517 and adopted the title of Servant of the Two Holy Cities. However, it was not until two centuries later that they began to project their claims to be leaders of the Muslim community worldwide. These claims became of international import as European powers, followed by the U.S., took over countries with large Islamic populations and the embattled Muslim communities looked to the Caliph in İstanbul for support.

They knew Abdülhamid to be a devout believer. He was also deeply involved with the great religious orders of the time. An early and enduring influence was Ahmet Ziyaeddin Gümüşhanevi, a scholarly figure who had also been the teacher of his father and uncle, Sultans Abdülmecid and Abdülaziz. Gümüşhanevi was a *şeyh* of the Nakşibendi fraternity, following the activist anti-Western tradition of Halid el-Bağdadi. He was author of a classical scholarly work on the *hadis* (*hadith*), the traditions of the Prophet. He was also a political activist, organizing protests in 1838 against the opening of Ottoman lands to Western economic interests, and sending disciples to the Caucasus, the Crimea, Tataristan, and even China.[6] His standing with Abdülhamid was such that the Sultan allowed him to be buried in the hallowed rose garden beside the tomb of Süleyman the Magnificent.

Apart from this doughty figure, three other dervishes influenced the Sultan—*Şeyh* Muhammed Zafir el-Medeni, his spiritual adviser for a quarter of a century and an advocate of the unity of Islam; the fierily anti-British Cemaleddin Efghani, who also aspired to reconcile the two main sects of Islam; and Ebü'l-Hüda es-Sayyadî, a young member of the Rifai *tarikat* who affirmed that the whole of Islam was looking to the Caliph for leadership.[7]

Born in Tripolitania, *Şeyh* Zafir was a member of the Medeni branch of the Şazeliyye (Shadhiliyya), an austere order dominant in North Africa and present from Syria to Malaysia. He insisted that religious orders transcended political boundaries and could unite Islam, a message that resonated with the Sultan as he anguished over the West's encroachment into the Empire. Abdülhamid endowed three *tekke* (lodges) in İstanbul for him, which prepared emissaries to go out and win recruits in Algeria, link up with the powerful Senusiyye (Sanusiyya) of Libya, and become active in Syria and the Levant.[8]

The Şazeliyye were relatively open to Shiites, but the stormy Cemaleddin Efghani went further, seeking to end the division at the heart of Islam. Brought up in Persia and Afghanistan, he briefly and precociously served as a minister—some reports say chief minister—under Muhammed Azam Khan, Emir of Afghanistan in 1867 and 1868, before falling into a welter of family, tribal, and British intrigue. He left for India, where he urged: "Oh Muslims! If you were not humans but flies, your buzzing would deafen the ears of the English. Oh Hindus! If you were water turtles, you would have ripped the British Isles from their place and sunk them under the ocean."[9]

From India, he went to Cairo and then visited İstanbul for the first time in 1870. He was welcomed by the Young Ottomans and other reformists and invited to speak at the capital's embryonic university. His suggestion that philosophy and religion conveyed the same truths led to outrage and calls for the execution of those holding such views.

Back in Cairo, Efghani resumed teaching, railing against the British presence there and in India, and was expelled from both. He moved to Paris and linked up with the Egyptian scholar, Muhammed Abduh, and the two launched the newspaper, *el-'Urvetü'l-vüs̱ḳā*, which helped inspire the movement in Egypt dedicated to Muslim reform and, initially, unity against the British.[10] The Shah, Nasser-al-Din, invited him to Tehran and appointed him as a personal adviser before falling out with him due to his calls for popular resistance to misgovernment. Between 1886 and 1889, Efghani became interested in the Muslims in Russia, a restive community of some 15 million stretching from the Black Sea to the Tien Shan.

In around 1892, he was invited to İstanbul, where he was given a house, an allowance, and a horse and carriage, and offered a bride from the palace. He was a passionate advocate of what Muslims called the unity of Islam and the West referred to as Pan-Islamism. He argued that, if united, Muslims from Morocco to Afghanistan were strong enough to counter Britain and other Western invaders. In his view, by weakening the Muslim world, corrupt local rulers had allowed outsiders to take control. He began to call for diplomats to resolve the situation, supporting the Ottomans as the one power with the ability to stand up to the West.[11]

At this point, with the British putting pressure on the Sultan over Efghani's activities in India and Afghanistan, Efghani making contact with the Young Turks (a loose coalition of opponents of the Sultan), allegations of his involvement in the murder of the Shah, and the Sultan wishing to avoid criticism of being pro-Shiite—all these led to Efghani becoming distanced from the ever-distrustful Abdülhamid.[12] He was placed under house arrest, dying of cancer in 1897 at the age of 58.

While the influence of Efghani waxed and waned, a consistent presence was maintained by Ebü'l-Hüda es-Sayyâdî, a young member of the Rifai *tarikat*, who brought the message that the whole of Islam was looking to the Caliph for leadership. The Rifais are known for their antinomian practices, which include self-piercing.[13]

When he was just twenty-four years old, Ebü'l-Hüda was appointed guardian of the honour of the Prophet at Aleppo. Before long, he appeared in Istanbul, where his singing and extraordinary powers in the Rifai tradition attracted the attention of the youth who was shortly to become Sultan.[14] He was swiftly nominated to head the Council of *Şeyh*, the body designed to control the *tarikat*. Despite his lack of experience, he then became chief military judge first of Anatolia and later of Rumelia, the European provinces of the Empire. Esteemed for his astrological and divinatory powers, he remained close to Abdülhamid for thirty years. A prolific writer, he was constantly arguing that the authority of the Caliph was binding upon all Muslims. He was sought after by Arab visitors to the capital, some of whom suggested using the Rifais to promote Abdülhamid's role through the extended Muslim world.

The tarikat and the inspirational Islam of Khorasan

For Abdülhamid, as for many Muslims, the *tarikat* were important to him as an individual, as well as for their role in society.

For the individual, the *tarikat* play a crucial intermediary role in Islam, assisting the believer in finding his or her way to approach the divine. They reduce the distance between the individual and the stern God of Islam and embody a response to the almost universal wish to venerate. Most people know their own frailties and admire those who may be able to protect them. Christianity focuses on the martyr, drawing a parallel with his or her suffering and that of Christ on the cross. Islam elevates those who appear to have come close to a relationship with the Creator and who gain a certain charisma as a result. Both religions believe in the possibility of transmission of virtue, the Christian through the apostolic and papal successions, indeed through baptism itself, and the Muslim through the *silsile* of authority, an unbroken chain of virtue ideally tracing back to the Prophet.[15]

The *tarikat* draw on this transmission of virtue. In the first stage of their development, the embryonic community would feature a small retreat hosting a holy man who would attract devotees through his teaching or the miracles attributed to him. In a second stage, such a retreat would develop into a shrine and centre of congregation and pilgrimage, with the master's disciples spreading out and disseminating his insights. Slowly, links would formalize and, in a third stage, gain the structure and formality of an order, united in reverence of the figure inspiring the *tarikat*, committed to broadening the spread of his way to approaching the divine, and bound by the newly developed hierarchy and disciplinary precepts that the order had developed.[16]

For the early Muslim orders, in Anatolia the second stage coincided with the apogee in the thirteenth century of the Seljuk Turks' Sultanate of Rum, and the third stage with the long foundation of the Ottoman

Empire. What few, if any, could have imagined is the fourth stage evident in contemporary Turkey, where *tarikat* have become commercial enterprises, acting on a national and sometimes international scale, and penetrating, and in one case suborning, institutions of the state like schools, security services, and the judiciary, and becoming an inherent part of the support system of twenty-first-century government.

In the first of these stages, there is no mention of a sheikh or master, nor attribution of any authority to him. The saint is a guide, not an autocrat. His followers may constitute a community, but, as long as he was alive, there was no order, and, in this sense, no master ever founded the order that would grow and adopt his name. Integral to the credibility of these early circles were links to their spiritual master, who in his turn would be ennobled with links through the heirs of the Prophet to Mohammed himself. In some cases, the new masters would result from a linear, hereditary process; in others, they would be the designated *khalifa* (*halife* in Turkish, meaning deputy or successor) of the incumbent.

The earliest known dervish centres were in Baghdad and the Khorasan area of north-eastern Iran, and date to around the tenth century. Khorasan, the Land of the Sunrise, is as abstruse as it was once important. A seamless area ranging from Samarkand in the north to Baluchistan in the south, and west to the Caspian, it encompassed much of classical Transoxiana. Between 651 and the thirteenth century, the ruling dynasties in the region changed a dozen times, and the definitions of its borders also shifted accordingly. It was there that in 747, under a black flag, Abu Muslim started the rebellion that led to the Abbasids of Baghdad taking over Iraq, Syria, Egypt, and Arabia, and launching their long-lived caliphate.

Initially, the Arab influence was enormous, but almost as soon as the initial Arab conquerors had turned their horses for home, Khorasan attracted free thinkers. By the tenth century, the region had become the centre of Islamic thought, with its great scholars leaving behind the foremost collections of the Prophet's traditions. The Persians were usually more liberal than the Arabs in their interpretation of Islam and, understandably, insistent on equality between different races. For some Western commentators, these scholars detached Islam from a narrow Bedouin outlook and Bedouin mores, enabling it to become a universal religion and culture open to all people.[17]

Despite the protracted maelstrom as conquerors came and went, most of the great cities of Khorasan—Bukhara and Samarkand (now in Uzbekistan), Merv and Nisa (Turkmenistan), Mashhad and Nishapur (north-eastern Iran), and Balkh and Herat (north-eastern Afghanistan)—continued to flourish. Indeed, turmoil seems to have stimulated rather than stifled the cultural development of the region. The Khorasan intellectuals of the Samanids and their successors were among the world's leaders in mathematics, astronomy, medicine, physics, geography, and geology. The region became the cradle of the main early Persian poets, including Celaleddin-i Rumi (1207–1273), who would settle in the Sultans of Rum's Konya and inspire the Mevlevi Sufi order.

Throughout this period, Islam remained the religion of the rulers, and all of these followed the Sunni persuasion. All too showed a sensitivity to the traditions of the region, whose population was largely Zoroastrian but also included Buddhists, Christians, Hindus, Jews, Manichaeists, Shamanists, and sun worshippers.

From this ferment emerged what is now called the School of Khorasan, a flock of believers known for their emphasis upon poverty and indifference towards public opinion. Some of these were Melamiyye, named after the word *malama*, often translated as blame, but in essence indicating a state of humility. Others included ecstatic antinomians, the wandering ragged dervishes often known as Qalandariyya. It was a land whose product was saints.[18]

It was the rich and variegated Islam of this region, with its orders and eremites, that was to shape the religion of the Turkic peoples to its north and the Turcoman tribes and nomads who crossed it on their way west, not least to Anatolia and the Caucasus. As the Turkic tribes conquered Baghdad rapidly and Asia Minor slowly, so they brought these orders with them. Thus it was from these now barren lands, over 3,000 kilometres' ride from the rich pastures of Anatolia, that came the faith that would inspire the Ottomans as they expanded to conquer the Arab world.

The Turks' vanguards were bands of raiders, fast-moving mounted archers who outclassed their adversaries—Arab, Byzantine, Armenian, and Georgian. They were followed by groups of nomadic pastoralists, the men also warriors—there was no real division between military and civilian—but this time accompanied by their women, children, and livestock. Such was the pattern in the eleventh and twelfth centuries when the Seljuk Turks, now Sultans of the Abbasid Caliphate in Baghdad, defeated the Byzantines at Manzikert (Malazgirt) in 1071. At its apogee, the Great Seljuk Empire stretched from the steppes through Persia and Mesopotamia to the Gulf and Oman, with only the Fatimids in Cairo holding out against it. But by 1300, all that remained was the Sultanate of Rum in Anatolia. By then, the Mongols, also Ural-Altaic speakers, had erupted from the depths of the

Eurasian Steppe. Fleeing ahead of them, fresh waves of Turcoman families and their livestock found refuge in Anatolia.

Dervishes and the imperial enterprise

During the Ottoman centuries, dervish lodges marked the life of city and country alike. The early lodges were the soul of Islam in Asia Minor, concrete manifestations of the arrival and spread of the new faith, and embodiments of the trust and mutual support between the dervishes and the power of the rising state. The dervishes were not just contemplative or ecstatic observers, but an active part of the colonial process, installing themselves on populated land, applying themselves to agriculture or livestock, and controlling the rural economy of the lands they occupied.

In the Balkans, the Ottomans tasked these "colonizing dervishes" with the additional role of missionaries, as in Anatolia, giving the dervishes every encouragement as the Empire spread its domain north of the Danube. The dervishes soon began to enhance their prestige through stressing their links to earlier saints. The resulting orders spread widely, developing relations with the guild organizations that dominated the crafts in the towns. These guilds, like their later medieval European counterparts, upheld a set of values and ethics sanctioned by religion.

For almost a millennium, the orders were omnipresent, with the majority of the population affiliated to their ideas and activities by either formal, individual oath of allegiance or attendance of rituals. Their physical presence was "ubiquitously manifest in the brick and mortar of the built environment of every city in the form of the various centers of Sufi activity."[19]

There were between two and three thousand lodges in the Empire. Records for İstanbul are more complete than for the provinces and show that between 1820 and 1890 the number of *tekke* in the capital varied from 171 to 319.[20] Some fell into disrepair, later to be restored with funds from the imperial treasury. Some were converted to *medrese* (religious schools). Most of the İstanbul *tekke* were small: only five had over thirty permanent residents.

In the census carried out from 1882, the number of male *tekke* residents in the capital was 1,259 and of females 859. A further 5,560 males were resident in its *medrese*.[21] Estimates of non-resident disciples are at best indicative. A recent German historian quotes a "competent observer" that these totalled around 60,000 on the eve of World War I, more than one in five of the city's male Muslim inhabitants.[22] Earlier historians' estimates are even higher. An American missionary writing in the 1930s said that around the First World War "one of Turkey's greatest scholars" told him that "in Constantinople where presumably the proportion is less than in the rest of the country, probably sixty per cent of the people belonged directly or indirectly to dervish fraternities."[23]

The orders not only served as an intermediary for the believer in his relationship with the divine but also in dealing with more immediate challenges such as those posed by Ottoman officialdom. Leading sheikhs could exert strong influence even in the highest circles.[24]

From the beginning, the orders had a symbiotic relationship with the Sultan. His goodwill was essential for their charitable status and exemption from certain taxes, while their support for the ruler—like that of the *ulema*—confirmed the Sultan's conformity with the precepts of Islam and enhanced his legitimacy. Successive Sultans' associations with the dervishes ranged from intimate to distant. Several Sultans turned to the leader of a dervish order to invest them with the sword of office. Others appointed *şeyh* as their own or their children's tutors or as advisers on matters of state. The Sultan's sympathies were evident in the lodges that he or his family endowed, and the assignments he would give to individual preachers at the imperial mosques, as senior judges, or to senior religious posts, in particular that of *şeyhülislam*.

For their part, the dervishes gave their support to the imperial enterprise, not least the Bektaşis, who were allotted to the 99th Janissary company, their senior '*baba*' honoured as a colonel and their dervishes acting as regimental *imam*.[25] Akşemseddin, the Sufi mentor of Mehmed the Conqueror, was notable for his martial qualities during the siege of Constantinople—even if, as he candidly wrote to the Sultan as the struggle dragged on, "You know well that fewer than a few among [the besieging forces] are ready to sacrifice their lives for the sake of God, but as soon as they see booty they are ready to walk into fire for the sake of this world."[26]

Selected Sufi leaders were often part of the councils who advised the Sultan on whether to launch a military campaign. Particularly prominent in the golden age of the empire was Aziz Mahmud Hüdayi Efendi, who girded at least one Sultan with his sword of office, structured a peace treaty with Russia, urged the release of imprisoned religious judges, and recommended who should govern Egypt.[27]

Dervishes would accompany the army on their campaigns and pray for its success. They could also mobilize the rural population. This was evident in the Babai revolt in 1239 and the rebellions by *Şeyh* Bedreddin, a famed astronomer and commentator on Islam. The subsequent struggle between the Ottomans and their eastern neighbours, the Safavids, became fought along religious lines, with Shiite dervishes fomenting discontent among Turcoman tribes and dispossessed cavalry. The rebels were termed *kızılbaş*, the name reflecting the red headdress of the Shiite agitators. In one sixteenth-century revolt, a *Şeyh* Celal proclaimed himself the *Mehdi*, but from the 1650s the dervishes tended to align themselves with the Sublime Porte.[28]

In the end, the Bektaşis' relations with the Janissaries cost them dearly. After the Janissaries were suppressed in 1826, seven of their leaders were executed and many exiled, their books burnt, their land converted to tax farms, their convents less than sixty years old demolished, and their older convents converted to mosques or *medrese*, or handed over to other orders, in particular the Nakşibendi. But it was as allies of the Janissaries, who were being extirpated as enemies of reform, rather than as dervishes that the Bektaşis were persecuted. And even while Mahmud II was still on the throne, they began to rebuild their presence, in a world where all the orders were now on the defensive.[29]

The palace and the orders

The spiritual font of the dervishes traces back to the *Shari'a* (Turkish *Şeriat*), and so too do the legal principles that allowed the religious orders to establish *vakıf*, the foundations that underpinned the flourishing of their activities.

The *vakıf* are central to implementing the precepts of the *Shari'a*, with the support they gave to every activity—religious, educational, and charitable—responsible for making the Islamic world as it is. They provided, at no cost to the central government, a myriad of essential services such as health, education, and municipal management.[30] They carried out the tasks of banks, lending to the needy and supporting new enterprises. They were the venture capitalists of their times. They also worked to redistribute income in favour of those in need.

The concept of foundations, established to contribute for perpetuity to charitable purposes such as health and the welfare of the poor and travellers, pre-dates Islam, being evident in the Roman and Byzantine empires. Early Muslim jurists developed arguments convenient for the new Islamic rulers that also allowed the founder of a *vakıf* to be a beneficiary of that *vakıf*, an approach that has survived for over a millennium.

The Ottomans continued such practices. Initially, their new territories were largely Christian but the sixteenth century saw them conquer Muslim territories through the Levant, raising issues regarding the ultimate ownership of land taken from fellow believers. It fell to Ebüssuûd Efendi, the formidable *şeyhülislam* of Süleyman the Magnificent, to codify the situation, his precepts reinforcing the ruler's power, allowing the Sultan to alienate tributary lands and tax the *vakıf*.[31]

In general, the *tekke* in rural areas were self-sufficient, with the Bektaşis in particular being directly involved in the economy as estate managers, moneylenders, and landlords.[32] By contrast, the urban *tekke* depended mainly on their endowment fund, followed by direct or indirect allocations from the state treasury or the Sultan's privy purse.[33] Imperial munificence was common at the New Year, on the occasion of the birth or circumcision of a prince, or after meritorious events. In 1799, after Napoleon was forced to lift his siege of Acre, the Sultan rewarded seventy-seven *tekke* in İstanbul for the efficacy of their prayers.

Under the first Sultans, the economic role of the *vakıf* was limited, but it developed over time. By 1527/28, revenue collected from the *vakıf* and freehold properties accounted for 11 per cent of the revenue of the Empire, covering the expenses of 2,409 charitable foundations, one quarter of these being dervish lodges.[34]

The system was open to abuse, not least by high-ranking members of the Empire's ruling class who placed property in trust to create an inalienable resource for their descendants rather than for the charitable and religious purposes that had characterized earlier endowments. All this led to a progressive weakening of central control over the resources of the Empire. By the early nineteenth century, one historian writes, "some foreign observers believed that a half to two-thirds of Ottoman land was held as family mortmain (*vakıf*) outside state control, though this is open to question."[35] One scholar argues that by this time as much as 80 per cent of urban land was in trust,[36] as, another claims, was much of the best arable land.[37] In the eighteenth century, the revenue potential from the foundations accounted for between one quarter and one half of the state budget.[38] A century later, they accounted for about one sixth of economic activity.[39]

To regain control, in 1826 Mahmud II set up a new ministry, *Evkaf-ı Hümayun Nezareti*. Soon, all foundations had to be registered with the central government and, with the enthronement of each new Sultan, have their registration confirmed or cancelled. The establishment of the *Evkaf* had in part been intended to tackle the shambolic state of the lodges' finances, but it achieved the opposite. Before long, foundations lost control of their revenues, which were transferred to the state treasury, to the grasping officials of the *Evkaf* and tax farmers. Only whatever remained after tithes was paid in kind to the dervishes.[40]

The foundations' protection for perpetuity and immunities from taxation had been swept away. Thousands of foundations were devastated, unable to meet their current expenses and having to halt their charitable activities. A mid-century writer lamented that:

> a considerable number of these works (i.e. mosques, bridges, fountains, inns, tekkes and the like) which are destroyed and useless now, were in a tolerable good state of repair no farther back than the year 1820. But the reformers, who are uprooting religion and a respect for it in every direction, have utterly destroyed the security which the mosque, and the mosque alone, could give to any landed property; they have destroyed the independence of the Turkish Church—if I may so call it; they have laid their greedy hands on nearly all the vakoufs of the empire... Hence, with very few exceptions, we see the heads of the mosques and the medressehs in abject poverty, the rabble of (religious) students in rags, the most beautiful of the temples and the minarets shamefully neglected and hurrying into decay.[41]

By mid-century, however well-endowed the lodges had once been, subsidies from the state had become a general pre-condition for their survival, while the *Evkaf*—underfunded in large part because of peculation by its officials—was unable to help.

All this coincided with increasingly vociferous pressures from the Ottomans' new creditors, particularly the British and the French, to gain access to the revenue flow from *vakıf*. Leading in the same direction were demands that foreign citizens should have the same rights to property as Ottomans and that the *vakıf* system should be abolished. As foreigners took over management of the Ottoman debt, their interest in the revenue potential of the *vakıf* increased.[42]

In parallel with the state seeking to gain more control over the foundations, particular measures had begun to be applied against the *tarikat*. An imperial decree of 1812 subjected all lodges to the control of the order's main lodge in İstanbul. Before long, appointment of new lodge heads had to be confirmed by the *şeyhülislam*. A further step in centralizing control of the *tarikat* came with the formation of the *Meclis-i Meşayih* (Council of *Şeyh*). This started operating in 1866 and was soon chaired by a Mevlevi *şeyh* with other members from each of the Halvetiyye, Kadiriyye, Nakşibendiyye, Sa'diyye, and Sünbüliyye.[43] In 1874, a Rifai representative was added. The Council was under the control of the *şeyhülislam*, bringing the *tarikat* and their *tekke* under the Seraglio.

With Abdülhamid a committed defender of the *Shari'a*, most Islamic orders gave him their support, welcoming his slowing of the *Tanzimat* process and the elevation of non-believers to the same status as Muslims. The Nakşibendis found Abdülhamid to be a salutary change from his immediate predecessors, and most of the Kadiris applauded his work.[44]

In the capital itself, Abdülhamid made little use of the lodges' leaders, perhaps because doing so would injure his dignity.[45] His preferred tool was the religious establishment, rewarding the loyal with patronage, and, with help from a pervasive network of informers, isolating the potentially turbulent. He expected full support from his *şeyhülislam*, removing three for political reasons and then settling on Cemaleddin Efendi (1848–1919), who spoke out against the foreign borrowings that were subverting state finances and whose religious writings had impressed him.[46]

The Sultan's assiduous approach to religion pervaded every aspect of life. He involved the *ulema* in controlling the curricula in the burgeoning state education system. He supported sending its members to proselytize against the influence of foreign missionaries. Yet, despite his commitment to protecting Islam, a number of the *ulema* gave their support to the opposition groups that had developed and, in turn, were approached by these groups for the legitimacy that the *ulema* could bestow.

When it came to individual orders, Abdülhamid generally worked by cooption, exercising his control over them through the Council of *Şeyh* and his management of their funding. In exchange, he expected them to submit reports from all corners of his far-flung domain.[47]

His approach to the different fraternities varied. In the case of the Sünbülis, he gave full support, inviting their leader to break the Ramadan fast with him. But to some, he was openly hostile, not least to the Mevlevis. His deposed—and long-surviving—half-brother had been close to this aristocratic order. Nor was he wrong to be concerned; the Mevlevis had at different points conspired to bring his half-brother back to the throne, supported the cause of the heir apparent, the future Mehmed V Reşad, and assisted opposition groups, including that which was eventually to cause his overthrow.[48] He also kept a close eye on the quietly reviving Bektaşis, initially because of their role in supporting the Albanian nationalist movement and later because of their support for his opponents.

In practice, all orders risked having their *şeyh* exiled. Those so affected included the Bedevis, Halvetis, and even the Sünbülis. By contrast, the Sultan appreciated the full-blooded support that various Nakşibendi *şeyh* gave to Ottoman armies, particularly in the Caucasus, "nimble and fiery heroes, their rifle at their shoulder, revolver at their side and dagger at their waist."[49] That three Nakşibendis, including *Şeyh* Muhammed Esad Erbili, were sent into exile reflected moves against individuals rather than the Nakşibendis as a whole.[50]

Through all this, the students of religion, themselves as coloured by the *tarikat* as the entire Muslim community, tended to give their full support to the palace.

Growth of political opposition

Defeat abroad and the arrival of wave after wave of refugees intensified the debate on how to save the Empire, but, the rare extremists aside, most of the Sultan's early opponents were in awe of his spiritual role. Such was the case of the Young Ottomans, a group of ruling-class intellectuals who believed in the enduring role of the Sultan and in recourse to the sense of brotherhood inherent in Islam. Their movement, which dated back to the 1860s, pressed for an amalgam of constitutional reform and religious nationalism.

The need for more fundamental reforms was to colour liberal criticism during the first decade of Abdülhamid's rule. The most durable of the protest groups were established by military medical students in İstanbul from the late 1880s, most notably the Society of the Ottoman Union (*Osmanlı İttihat ve Terakki Cemiyeti*), which envisaged a broad-based movement for reform. Its followers took the Meiji Restoration in Japan as an example of how a traditional state could modernize without losing its identity. It worked mainly among military students, organizing cells along lines similar to the Italian Carbonari and Russian nihilists. Its calls for reform and democratization won considerable support, not least among junior officers. It also began trying to recruit followers from the *ulema.*

The Society developed a following in military centres from Macedonia to Damascus. A premature putsch in December 1895 led its activists to flee İstanbul for the garrison towns, where they advocated that Abdülhamid should be replaced by one of his half-brothers.

These opponents began to develop contacts with critics of the Sultan in Paris. Abdülhamid lured several of the rebels back from abroad, promising them the chance to put their ideas to work in government, but was soon at odds with what is now remembered as the Committee of Union and Progress (*İttihat ve Terakki Cemiyeti,* CUP). In 1897, he exiled seventy-seven of its members to Tripolitania and the Fezzan.

However, the new schools, military and civilian, were producing a fresh and impatient generation of officers, administrators, and intellectuals. Also disaffected were the officers involved in years of fruitless struggles against Macedonian terrorists and Bulgarian *komitadjis*. Reflecting this discontent, a group of young officers in Damascus set up the Fatherland and Liberty Association (*Vatan ve Hürriyet Cemiyeti*). In early 1906, one of these officers, Mustafa Kemal, who was later to play a pivotal role in Turkey's history, travelled clandestinely to Salonika (now Thessaloniki) to promote this entity. Its manifesto called for the Sultan to observe the mothballed 1876 constitution and establish a government responsive to the needs of the army and other state bodies. It drew on the ideas that Mustafa Kemal had developed in İstanbul. His activism had already led to his detention in the Red Dungeon of the Beyazıt barracks; his appointment to the Levant was a mark of disfavour.

After setting up a branch of this association in Salonika, he returned to Damascus. In 1907, he arranged to be posted to Salonika, arriving to find the leadership of the association had amalgamated with the Young Turks in Paris. It was this organization, soon calling itself the Committee of Union and Progress (CUP), that would rule during the disastrous closing years of the Empire.[51]

In May 1908, the CUP demanded reinstatement of the Ottoman Chamber of Deputies. Abdülhamid sent inspectors to identify the authors of these seditious words and then troops to crush the rebels. A Sultan's aide was assassinated, and the troops, instead of fighting the rebels, joined them. Various mass meetings followed, expressing support for the constitution. With the Third Army now threatening to march on the capital, Abdülhamid announced he would recall the Chamber of Deputies and reintroduce the constitution. Reportedly, the only adviser who had dared to counsel this step was his dervish astrologer, Ebü'l-Hüda, ill at the time and carried into the Sultan's Council on his sick bed.[52] The Sultan had managed to outflank his opponents for thirty-two years, but, for all intents and purposes, he had finally surrendered.

2

THE YOUNG TURKS AND THE YEARS OF SIEGE

> *The German alliance was a gamble and the outcome of the war proved that they had backed the wrong horse. But events had shown that they had no other horse to back.*
>
> Feroz Ahmad, "Great Britain's Relations with the Young Turks, 1908–1914"[1]

Counter-revolution and the religious backlash

The Sultan's reintroduction of the constitution caused crowds to gather in all the main cities, members of the different *millet* (religious communities of the Empire) mingling in celebration. Armenians, Greeks, and Jews believed they would have the equality guaranteed in the constitution; Catholics and other Christians, in practice long protected by European ambassadors, looked to better governance; and many Ottoman citizens believed that the doors to modernization were now open. The acute observer, Halidé Edib Adıvar, remembers the scene on Galata Bridge:

> There was a sea of men and women all cockaded in red and white, flowing like a vast human tide from one side to the other. The tradition of centuries seemed to have lost its effect. There was no such thing as sex or personal feeling. Men and women in a common wave of enthusiasm moved on, radiating something extraordinary, laughing, weeping in such

> intense emotion that human deficiency and ugliness were for the time completely forgotten.[2]

A decision by the Council of Ministers abolished the budget allocations for the multitude of informers feeding the Sultan with their intrusive reports. The newspaper owners threw the government censors out of their offices.

The British, allied with Russia the previous year and less concerned about democracy than their own interests, were far from overjoyed. On 31 July, Sir Edward Grey, the British Foreign Secretary, wrote: "If, when there is a Turkish Constitution in good working order and things are going well in Turkey, we are engaged in suppressing by force and shooting a rising in Egypt of people who demand a Constitution too, the position will be very awkward." A few days later, he warned, "we must be careful not to give Russia the impression that we are reverting to the old policy of supporting Turkey as a barrier against her and should continue to show willingness to work with Russia when possible."[3]

A short period of liberalization followed, but before long there was a crackdown on the press and political dissent, while a series of reverses abroad eroded support for the new regime: Austria formally annexed Bosnia and Herzegovina, Cretan deputies declared union with Greece, and Bulgaria declared its independence.

Formal government was in the hands of a former grand vizier, Kamil Paşa, but the reins of power were in the hands of a committee sent by the CUP from Macedonia that remained in the shadows. Elections in December saw the CUP emerge as the dominant force in a new Chamber of Deputies, but it was unclear who was in charge. Muslims who had believed that a constitutional Ottoman Empire would have the support of Europe began to turn to the old Sultan. Nationalists from the minorities saw that their chances of autonomy were evanescent. Most of the population lost faith in the hope that the peoples of the Empire might work together for its preservation. The appearance of unveiled women and the new equality for non-Muslims shocked religious conservatives, who began to campaign against the constitution, reviving the centuries-old arguments that the Empire's decline was caused by departure from the true principles of Islam and that Islam could be adapted to meet the demands of the time.

The coalition that had come together against the Sultan also split. The main opposition to the CUP came from the Liberals, named after their Liberal Union Party (*Osmanlı Ahrar Fırkası*), but they were liberal in neither the political nor the economic sense. Their leaders belonged to the upper classes of Ottoman society. They supported a constitutional monarchy implemented by their peers among the high bureaucrats. They looked to Britain, whose model they appreciated, to support them with funding and experience and to help them implement the limited social and economic reforms they envisaged—and British officials, in İstanbul more actively than in London, sympathized with them.[4]

Other supporters of the beleaguered Sultan included the many families linked to the palace by interest or employment, the majority of the *ulema*, the graduates of the *medrese*, and the 20,000–25,000 students in the city's long-neglected *medrese* now threatened with the draft. These groups soon gained the support of the small shopkeepers and traders. Also aggrieved were the rankers in the army, treated with disdain by the graduates of military academies, and quickly understanding that the CUP had little to offer them. Leavening the mix were several thousand convicts freed from the Sultan's jails by the CUP in the clumsy implementation of an amnesty for political prisoners.

These groups were ready fodder for Islamic propaganda, and fanning their discontent were Derviş Vahdeti, a Cypriot of Nakşibendi training and spirit, and the newspaper *Volkan* (Volcano) that he launched in December 1908.[5] His invocations mustered the motley crowd that surrounded the Chamber of Deputies in late February demanding introduction of the *Shari'a*. In April, he launched the Society of Muhammed (sometimes termed the Society for Islamic Unity). This had its first public meeting on 3 April, staged at the premier mosque of Ayasofya and timed to coincide with the Prophet's birthday.[6] The already charismatic Said Nursi—later to feature in the religious history of the Republic—gathered his 'students,' leading them to the meeting and speaking for two hours from the mosque's minbar.[7] Up to 100,000 people participated, while there were parallel gatherings in other cities where the Society was developing a regional network in competition with the CUP.[8] That day, the Society's followers dispersed peacefully, but a few days later the murder of a prominent anti-CUP newspaper editor changed the mood.[9]

On 13 April, soldiers from the First Army in İstanbul mutinied and were joined by several groups, the most significant being thousands of teachers and students of religion, and lower-ranking clerics. The rebels invaded the Chamber of Deputies, killed the Minister of Justice and a deputy, and demanded the restoration of the *Shari'a*, resignation of the government, and reinstatement of unjustly dismissed ranker officers. The soldiers' first targets were officers, thirty-six of whom were executed, one in Yıldız Palace in front of an apparently condoning Sultan.[10]

In an initial day of terror, the mutineers ran wild. An estimated 1.5 million bullets were fired. There were attacks on the houses of CUP supporters and the offices of *Tanin* (Ringing), a newspaper close to the committee. Edib, told her name was on a blacklist, took a boat to Üsküdar to seek refuge in a dervish convent. Near the landing, a "human hurricane" separated her from her two sons: "It was soldiers from the Selimiye barracks who, after killing their officers, were rushing down to take the boat and join the counter-revolution."[11]

The main thrust of the rebellion had come from the ranker soldiers and officers. As for who was responsible, one historian who has focused on the event concludes: "neither the Palace, nor the Porte, nor the Liberals initiated the anti-CUP outburst. Contrary to received wisdom, even Derviş Vahdeti and his top aides do not seem to have had any role in instigating it, and from all indications they too were taken by surprise."[12] Contemporary observers, however, insist on the role of "Hamidian gold" in financing the mutineers, citing not least confessions by the second eunuch, Nadir Ağa.[13]

Popular opinion continues to insist the British were involved. As Edib wrote in 1926, Vahdeti "was thought to be a paid emissary of the British Embassy, a tool of Mr. Fitzmaurice."[14] Gerald Fitzmaurice, red-haired and ubiquitous, was the dragoman (chief interpreter) of Sir Gerard Lowther, the British Ambassador at the time. He had encouraged a press campaign against the Young Turks, galvanizing British consuls in this task.[15] Even the Foreign Office felt compelled to tell Lowther to rein in this "impressionable Irishman."[16]

The counter-revolution used the language of religion, but had been less supported by the established religious authorities than by the *sans culottes* of the religious world. Some of the religious orders may have discreetly encouraged the unrest, including perhaps the Nakşibendis, but not the Mevlevis or the Bektaşis. In one view, "the dervishes seem to have allowed themselves to be used as a tool in a political game which they did not understand."[17] Their limited role did not protect them from later perceptions of fuller involvement, a judgement that would cost them dearly.

Turkey's Cromwell, a death foretold, and the CUP at war

Turkish troops in Macedonia moved quickly to crush the uprising. After securing the capital, their commander, Mahmud Şevket Paşa, had 196 participants in the counter-revolution hanged and some 10,000 soldiers punished. He also purged the *medrese*, reducing enrolment to 5–6,000 before ordering them closed for holidays.[18]

Abdülhamid had become a clear symbol to the CUP's opponents, and the army had him replaced by his half-brother, Mehmed V Reşad. The latter did not impress all observers:

> Our new Sultan produced a most painful impression on me and my colleagues. He has all the appearance of being half witted and as he has been growing a beard since his accession he looked frightful. He has very short legs and a fat stomach and has not the vaguest idea what to say. No doubt precisely the individual that the ultra Young Turks want.[19]

The deposition of Abdülhamid found the CUP in control of the Chamber of Deputies, but with its leadership scattered and recalcitrant—it did not move its central committee to İstanbul until 1912—it initially decided to stay outside government. Real power, in any case, had moved to the army for the first time in a century and would remain there through the conflagration that was to end the Empire.

The year 1911 saw rebellions in Yemen and Albania and the loss of Tripolitania and the Dodecanese islands in the Aegean to Italy. The next year, early battles of the First Balkan War stripped the Ottomans of all their remaining territories in Europe apart from four besieged cities.

Concerns that the beleaguered government of Kamil Paşa, back as Grand Vizier for the fourth time, would sign away Edirne, hallowed as the Empire's capital before İstanbul, caused a group of CUP officers to burst into the Sublime Porte. A first shot was fired by a rebel officer "well oiled with cognac," and the Minister of the Navy and four officials were killed.[20] Enver and Talat, the leaders of the coup, told the Sultan that they wanted a government representing all parties to save Thrace. The Sultan called on Mahmud Şevket to form this government. The general did so on 23 January 1913, the eleventh cabinet formed in the five and a half years since the restoration of the constitution. The general included only three of the CUP's leaders among his ministers.

Further battlefield setbacks and Bulgarian massacres of Muslim peasants forced the Ottomans back to the negotiating table. In May, the government agreed to cede Thrace and Edirne to the Bulgarians and surrender all rights to Crete and the Aegean Islands. Seven weeks later, the Ottoman army was able to recapture Edirne and all of eastern Thrace—the Bulgarians were caught up in the Second Balkan War, a six-week summer squabble between the victors of the First Balkan War. But the general was not around to see this. On 11 June, he was assassinated by a motley bunch of CUP opponents, several of whom had already served time for murder. As a British diplomat in İstanbul wrote at the time: "… he was the Cromwell of the Revolution here and the effect of his murder is as though Roberts, Kitchener and Asquith were murdered on the same day."[21]

Mahmud Şevket's meticulous diaries end with a 1,600-word entry on 10 June, describing retiring early, being woken to deal with two telegrams from Berlin, and sending an offer to the Greeks to form a defensive alliance.[22] The next day, as he was being driven from the Ministry of War to the Sublime Porte, he was assassinated.

The security services had known a plot was afoot but took no precautions. Only chance led to the assassins being rounded up. A fortnight later, twelve men were hanging from gallows in Beyazıt Square, near the scene of their infamy. They had been financed by Kurdish Şerif Paşa in Paris and Damad Salih Paşa, a son-in-law of the Sultan, both supporters of the Liberal Party.[23]

It was a sore blow, depriving the Empire of a great statesman when it was most in need. This time, accusations of British involvement were not confined to the press. At the beginning of 1914, Cemal Paşa asked Lowther's successor as ambassador to remove Fitzmaurice and Major Gerald Tyrrell, the British military attaché, from İstanbul, accusing them of prompting the murder. For Cemal, Fitzmaurice was "a diabolic man who was the true instigator of the assassination."[24]

Now that the CUP was acting as a political party, it appointed one of its members, Prince Said Halim Paşa, a grandson of Mehmet Ali of Egypt, as Grand Vizier and took four other key cabinet posts. The CUP's leading figures were now clear: Talat, a former post office official; Enver, a dashing officer who, with Mustafa Kemal, had been sent to try to save Tripolitania; and Cemal, a staff major. The first was cool-headed, modest, "gave the impression of a *grand seigneur*," and was "a statesman… in the truest sense of the word"; the second a "*beau sabreur*," "short of stature and slender of waist, with widest fiery eyes, and an up-pointed well-groomed moustache;" and the third trim, short, and assertive.[25]

The new government was soon caught up in the diplomatic tussles that ushered in the First World War. The intrusions of the Great Powers into the

Empire had long been tempered by policies limiting the spread of Tsarist Russia. But the Anglo-Russian Entente of 1907 ended Britain's balancing act. Thenceforth, Britain and Russia, immediately joined by France, prepared to carve up the Ottoman lands still stretching 4,000 kilometres from the banks of the Danube to the shores of the Arabian Sea.[26] The CUP could thus look for no comfort from the Triple Entente powers, their offers of alliance to Russia and France killed by opposition from Grey in London.

By autumn 1914, with Britain refusing to deliver ships paid for by the Ottomans, Russia laying 1,200 mines at the Black Sea entrance to the Bosphorus, and Germany saying it would only finance the cash-strapped Ottomans if they entered the war, the opponents of an alliance with Germany had few arguments left. At the end of October, Enver sent ships to bombard Russian ports, triggering Tsar Nicholas's declaration of war. On 11 January 1915, an initial treaty with Berlin was upgraded to a renewable German-Ottoman defensive alliance.

The Kaiser contended that the Sultan-Caliph could incite uprisings in French and British colonies in North Africa and India, as well as among the Turkic peoples (almost all Muslims) under Tsarist yoke. Mehmed V Reşad, encouraged by the Kaiser, used the resonance of religious office to declare their alliance a Holy War. That said, few Germans saw it as a partnership. As the German Ambassador in İstanbul in 1918 would write: "Being allies to the Turks, it is not easy for us to tell them that we consider them politically inferior and unworthy of any acquisitions of territory... my idea was to transform Turkey into a German Egypt."[27]

Whatever the case, the Ottomans joining the war served Berlin well. The Empire's entry drew Russian troops south; in September 1916, one fifth of Russia's 3.7 million troops were fighting in Anatolia and the Caucasus. It also added massively to British costs, with 2.5 million British and British Empire troops, about one third of the war's total, deployed against the Ottomans.[28]

The CUP's reforms and the religious orders

From the assassination of Mahmud Şevket Paşa until the Ottoman defeat, the powers of the CUP were unconstrained. Despite the carnage of the time—some, like the massacres of Armenians, often classed outside Turkey as a genocide, of its own creation—the CUP launched a series of reforms which had eluded earlier modernizers, and were to shape the future Turkish Republic. These began with the apparatus of government itself. Ministries were reorganized for the first time since the early years of the *Tanzimat*. Administration of İstanbul and the provinces was streamlined. The police were restructured and brought under civilian control, and tax farms abolished.

Where religion was concerned, state control was established over the *ulema* and religious courts. This included the complete secularization of religious courts, schools, and foundations, as well as limitation of the role of the *şeyhülislam*. Control of the dervish lodges also shifted to local councils.

A similarly radical approach was taken to family law. The state took over the power to enforce the basic regulations of the *Shari'a* and Jewish and Christian law, and marriage contracts were classed as secular contracts. Women could now obtain divorce if their husbands committed adultery, wished to take extra wives without the first wife's consent, violated the marriage contract, or had "been seized after marriage with mental alienation, leprosy, elephantiasis, and certain other maladies."[29] By this time, elementary and middle education for girls had been expanded and women admitted to higher schools. Vocational education for women was also introduced, and a Commission for the Employment of Ottoman Muslim Women and a Battalion of Workers for women established.[30]

All these reforms came despite the support that in earlier years the orders had given to the CUP.[31] Abdülhamid's fostering of the Rifaiyye in Arab lands engendered sympathy for the CUP among the other *tarikat*. The Kadiriyye in Damascus joined the CUP in an abortive coup attempt in 1897.

The CUP long instructed members to carry out propaganda activities in the *tekke*.[32] Its interest in the brotherhoods continued after the revolution of 1908, but as the CUP developed, its relationship with Islamic groups became increasingly ambiguous. Many of its luminaries saw religion as an obstacle to social progress. But, just as the regime of Abdülhamid legitimized itself through Islam, so the CUP would seek religious dicta from the *ulema* to refute the Sultan's criticism.[33]

Some members of the *ulema* had supported the CUP when it was still in opposition, being exiled to the corners of the Empire—and ensuring the spread of their sedition. The *şeyhülislam*—of whom six were appointed between February 1909 and July 1912 alone—stayed aligned with the fast-moving politics of the time. Indeed, in 1911, the *şeyhülislam*, Musa Kazım, disturbed by the hostility to the CUP which had emerged during the counter-revolution, launched the Sufi Association (*Cem'iyyet-i*

Sufiyye). The association's founding articles committed its members to eschew politics.

Closest to the CUP were the Bektaşis. Some two decades later, one CUP leader wrote that some viziers, one field-marshal, an ambassador, many judges, writers and at least two *şeyhülislam* had been Bektaşis.[34] He recorded that Musa Kazim, "was like me and Talat Paşa a Bektashi and a master mason at the same time… nearly all the bektashis helped the committee to succeed in its aims."[35]

Other orders too, their *şeyh* freed from exile, welcomed the restoration of the constitution, as did the Melamis, a secretive and often persecuted order that was experiencing a revival in the Balkans and had a close relationship with officers in the Macedonian army.

Particularly significant were the links of the courtly Mevlevis with the CUP. During the attempted coup d'état in 1895, the Mevlevi *tekke* at Galata acted as an intermediary between the Young Turks and the Sultan's heir apparent, Reşad, a devoted Mevlevi. A second *tekke* in İstanbul at Yenikapı distributed CUP material published in Paris. Two other Mevlevi *şeyh* were arrested for sedition and exiled. "The CUP had several branches in İstanbul and one was ours," a Mevlevi leader later declared.[36]

In 1909, the Mevlevis' head, Abdülhalim Çelebi, was summoned to İstanbul to invest Reşad as Sultan—though the next year the CUP had the *Çelebi* replaced by his more reliable cousin, Veled Çelebi İzbudak.[37] The Bektaşis and Mevlevis both sent companies of dervishes to support Ottoman troops in the First World War, with the Mevlevis taking part in the Ottomans' first attack on the Suez Canal. However, the Committee's secularizing measures meant that, by the time it fell, its support among the *tarikat* was much reduced except among the Bektaşis.

The CUP and Turkish nationalism

The CUP's initial members included many from the various minorities of the Empire. Most subscribed to the CUP's promises of equal treatment of all these communities, whatever their religion. However, this Ottoman approach to minorities was progressively pushed to the margins. Before long, it was the concept of Turkishness which dominated, making the name Young Turks increasingly appropriate. With this seeding the nationalism which in recent years has become so important, it is worth examining its roots.

The turn of the century had seen a rise in concern about the Turkic peoples living in Tsarist Russia. These Turks outside the Sultan's domains were commensurate with those inside them. Tatars of Crimea and the Volga, Azeris, Kazakhs, Kirghiz, Turkmens, and Uzbeks—most of them were Muslim, and all were subject to Russia's policies of assimilation. Honed in resistance to an intrusive state, a number of their leading writers and thinkers sought refuge in İstanbul, being welcomed by the CUP and its supporters.

Initially, the discourse was mainly Pan-Turkist, calling for the union of all Turks and drawing on the atavistic vision of Turan. The reference is to an undefined Shangri-La in the steppes of Central Asia, which is variously identified with the ancient Greeks' Transoxiana and the Tsars' Turkestan.[38] Various magazines invoking this mystic name were established, not least in Salonika, a hub of intellectual dissidence. Those influenced included Ziya Gökalp (1876–1924), a dominating figure who had "almost the vision and role of a Biblical prophet in the Young Turk revolution."[39] As he wrote in 1911:

> The Fatherland for the Turks is neither Turkey, nor Turkestan
> The Fatherland is a large and eternal country—Turan.

That same year, Halidé Edib published the novel, *Yeni Turan* (New Turan).

A number of these Turkic exiles established the Turkish Association (*Turk Derneği*) at the end of 1908 and launched a journal in early 1911. Other initiatives included the founding of the Turkish Hearth (*Türk Ocağı*), and the launch of the Turkish Homeland Association (*Türk Yurdu Cemiyeti*) and its influential magazine.

For many, there was little difference between Turanism and Pan-Turkism, with their irredentist sub-tones, and the more narrowly nationalist Turkism. But before long, Gökalp, despite his poem cited above, was guiding the CUP to the more innately instinctual clarion calls of Turkishness.[40] His creed was: "Our national ideal will be Turkishness, our international ideal will be Islam. We also favour the ideal of Ottoman unity of the [religious] communities and the ideal of humanity among the great religions, to the extent that we see the same applied to us."[41]

For Gökalp, nationalism had to be based on the historical continuity of the people's Turkish and Islamic traditions. He urged Turks to look for the sources of their literature in stone engravings, deer skins, folk poems, and epics. "We must discard foreign rules from our grammar, foreign metre from our poetry, foreign symbolism from our literature... we must discover Turkish music as well as Turkish poetry in the oral traditions of the folk," he proclaimed.[42] He would have the complex Ottoman language, with its drawings from Arabic and Persian, replaced by demotic Turkish. His successors were to extend this idea into the purification of the Turkish language launched under the Republic.[43]

Gökalp maintained that nations developed through stages in which they change their civilization but, at the risk of losing their identity, maintain their culture. According to him,

> The Turks have adopted three distinct and dissimilar civilizations during the course of their social evolution. When they were in the stage of ethnic-state organization, they belonged to the civilization of the Far East. When they passed to the stage of the sultanistic state, they entered into the area of Eastern civilization. And today, in their transition to the stage of nation-state, we see the rise among them of a strong movement which is determined to accept Western civilization.[44]

His analysis insisted on the compatibility of Turkification, Islamicization, and modernization.[45] He explained:

> For us today modernization [being contemporary with modern civilization] means to make and use the battleship, cars and aeroplanes that the Europeans are making and using... When we see ourselves no longer in need of importing manufactured goods and buying knowledge from Europe, then we can speak of being contemporary with it.[46]

He believed in a nationalist education but rejected unthinking attachment to a misunderstood past. Knowledge of their history, traditions, and Islamic background could provide the Turks with a stable base for participation in contemporary Western civilization. In his view, religious culture and Western culture were inimical, but Turkism resolved this clash by making conscious the unconscious ideals of the people.[47]

He had a detailed knowledge of Islam and a profound respect for it as the most important factor in the creation of a national consciousness. He considered a limited number of men of piety as indispensable, and welcomed both the prayers of the individual and the inspiration unleashed by collective worship.[48] "The Turkish hymns and mystic poems sung in mystic convents during the rite of *zikir* have also been a great source of ecstasy," he declared.[49]

He considered Islam the most modern of the great religions, being born among free citizens, not among the slaves of a great empire with no hopes of political independence. To ensure religion played its true role as a source of ethics, he argued that Islamic rituals should be fully comprehensible to the believer and that all judicial activities and courts should be brought under the government. Through upgrading education and better administration of mosques, *medrese*, and dervish lodges, a revitalized *şeyhülislam* should counter "the utter incompetence of the teachers of religion" and the decline in mosque attendance; the new office should also work "to make the *tarikat* a social institution in accordance with their original aims and to transfer the convents into genuine educational institutions."[50] Trusted preachers should be sent all over the Islamic world for the purpose of the furtherance of piety, but the interests of the Turkish nation had to be prioritized.[51]

Gökalp's celebration of the origins of the Turk (however imaginative some of his history), his determinedly rationalist and positivist approach, and his clear separation of state and religion—all these were to survive him. In his own time, he articulated reforms in terms that dramatically broadened their appeal. As one sociologist concluded when Turkey still seemed on a path to secularism: "... he paved the way to a view of Turkey as a nation, as a national state, and ultimately as a democracy. By differentiating Turkey from a theocratic conception of the *ümmet* (Islamic community) he prepared the Turks for a secular view of religion, culture and civilization."[52]

İstanbul in torment—occupation and liberation

From early on, the Great War proved to be a catastrophe for the Empire. In January 1915, the Ottoman Third Army was destroyed in the snow-bound mountains north-east of Erzurum. That same month, a force of 80,000 Ottoman troops was driven back from the Suez Canal. A year later came a rare victory with the expulsion of British-led forces from Gallipoli, but celebrations of that were overshadowed by a series of further devastating defeats in the Caucasus and eastern Turkey.

Concerns over the Armenian population's support for Russian troops caused Talat Paşa to order the removal of Armenians from the areas of combat. In the massacres that followed, some 1 million Armenians died.[53]

The Ottomans were only able to regain the eastern areas now within the borders of Turkey after post-revolutionary Russia ceded Tsarist gains in the Treaty of Brest-Litovsk in March 1918. For a short period, they were again in control of much of Azerbaijan.

They had no such success in the territories that they had ruled for four centuries to their south. Adept British diplomacy triggered what became the Arab Revolt. By late 1918, the last Ottoman defences had fallen in Syria, the Dardanelles were blockaded, the capital was overrun with starving refugees and running out of food, the Allies were invading Thrace, more than a million deserters were wreaking social havoc,[54] and only 72,000 of the Ottomans' 1.5 million soldiers had rifles.[55]

On 30 October, the Ottomans signed the Armistice of Mudros that ended hostilities and stripped them of their lands in the Levant and Middle East. The British took over Mesopotamia and Iraq; the French gained Syria and extensive regions around today's Adana; and the Italians were confirmed in Libya.

The troops of Britain, Italy, and France landed in İstanbul in November 1918. Initially, the occupiers' powers were restricted to police matters, but in March 1920 British troops took control of the city, killing at least a dozen protesters, parliament was dissolved, and a docile government was imposed.[56]

The five-year Allied occupation of İstanbul was fractious from the start, the disputes symbolized by the call to convert Ayasofya, a mosque for 465 years, back into a church. For British philhellenes, and they were many, returning this to the Ecumenical Patriarch of Constantinople was a chance to cement the strategic alliance with Greece. But when a group of Greeks tried to install a cathedral bell, Ottoman soldiers drove them away by threatening to blow up the entire structure.[57] The Greek landings at İzmir had made the issue too sensitive to be resolved.

These landings started in May 1919 after British, French, and American warships cleared the way for a Greek division, the first forces in what would become a 215,000-strong occupation army. The day after the Greek landings, Mustafa Kemal sailed out of İstanbul, appointed by the Sultan to control all Ottoman forces and civil servants in east and north-central Anatolia. Before long, he had launched the nationalist movement. The next spring, the British took full military control of İstanbul and authorized Greek troops to break out from the area to which they had been contained around İzmir. The Greeks took this as the green light to launch a full invasion.

By this time, Britain, France, and Italy had obliged the Sultan to accept the provisions later incorporated into the Treaty of Sèvres, dismembering what remained of the Empire.[58] His acquiescence to this death knell for the Empire completed the break between his government in İstanbul and the troops and civil leaders of Anatolia. Mustafa Kemal eventually brought together the disparate forces available to him into a coherent movement that two years later routed the Greek invasion forces. It was a time of atrocities and, as the Greeks retreated, scorched earth. The debacle brought down the governments responsible in London (where Lloyd George had encouraged the Greeks) and Athens. Vahdeddin himself abdicated in November 1922, being exfiltrated by a British battleship.

It took another eight months before the Treaty of Lausanne settled the borders of Turkey, which returned to the defensible heartlands of Eastern Thrace and Anatolia, and stand virtually unchanged a century later. The Treaty also triggered the population exchange of over 1,200,000 Greek Orthodox Christians and 400,000 Muslims. On 2 October 1923, British troops evacuated İstanbul, the Coldstream Guards band on the quayside playing the Turkish march "Long live Mustafa Kemal Paşa."

PART TWO

INCUBATION

No heathen's hand shall ever touch the bosom of my sacred Temples.
The call to prayer and martyr's testimony are the foundations of my religion,
And may their noble sound thunder across my eternal homeland.

...

For freedom is the absolute right of my ever-free flag;
For independence is the absolute right of my God-worshipping nation!

From *The Independence March*, national anthem of the Republic,
Mehmed Akif Ersoy, 1921

To rebuild a wounded nation, the founders of the Republic sought to leap past recent history back to the heroism of the Turks of Central Asia, founders of dynasties that dominated the Arabian and Persian worlds. The next half century was to show that Islam would survive repression and that culture could not be separated from Islam.

3

FAITH AND SECULARISM IN THE NEW REPUBLIC

Our Prophet became a servant and a messenger of God in order to convey the realities of religion to mankind. We all know that the fundamentals of his Law are the verses of the most glorious Kur'an. Our religion, which gives enlightening spirit to mankind, is the final religion. It is the most wonderful religion. This is so because our religion is in agreement and in accord with the intellect, logic, and the truth. If it had not harmonised with the intellect, logic, and the truth, a contradiction between our religion and the other divine natural laws would necessarily have existed. This is so because it is God who makes the laws [that govern] all creation.

Mustafa Kemal, Sermon at Zağnos Paşa Mosque,
Balıkesir, 7 February 1923

Dislodging the Caliphate

Mustafa Kemal drew his initial authority from the Sultan, buttressed it with the military forces in Anatolia, and extended it through a flood of telegrams to potential allies and public meetings, in particular the congresses held in Erzurum and Sivas.

In December 1919, a new Chamber of Deputies was elected in İstanbul, with Mustafa Kemal chosen to represent Erzurum, though never taking his seat. The new chamber rejected the occupation of İstanbul, triggering the occupying allies to take military control of the city and later oblige the pliant Sultan to close the turbulent body. By this time, they faced a hostile clone in Ankara, built up by Mustafa Kemal from deputies throughout the country.

The rebel parliament, which opened its proceedings on 23 April 1920, elected him as its president. Its composition reflected the alliances that Mustafa Kemal needed to consolidate his control over the nationalist movement. Its 400-some members included local notables, lawyers and officials, soldiers and doctors. They also included the heads of thirty of the tribes—many of them Kurdish—which dominated eastern and south-eastern Anatolia. One in six were men of religion.[1] Among these were the leaders of the Bektaşis and Mevlevis, and eight other *şeyh*, at least two of whom were Nakşibendis and one probably Sünbüli. Mustafa Kemal had the two *tarikat* leaders appointed as Deputy Speakers.

Seeking to counter critics for being 'Godless Unionists,' he sent out a circular describing the ceremonies which would precede the opening of the Assembly. Selections from the *Kur'an* and the traditions of the Prophet would be recited; sheep would be sacrificed; a hair from the Prophet's beard and His reputed standard would be borne in procession; and prayers would be offered for the safety of the Sultan and Caliph and his people. The opening date chosen was a Friday, and deputies met for prayers at the Haci Bayram mosque. The following day, Mustafa Kemal declared: "We, your deputies, swear in the name of God and the Prophet... that the claim we are rebels against the Sultan and the Caliph is a lie. All we want is to save our country from sharing the fate of India and Egypt."[2]

The nationalists had to fight on many fronts—against two short-lived forces sent by the Sultan, a British contingent east of İstanbul, some thirty uprisings, Greece's invasionary armies, and French and Italian regiments. By autumn 1923, they had overcome these challenges. They had also taken full control of what was left of the Empire, stripping Vahdeddin of his title as Sultan, transferring authority from the Sublime Porte to Ankara, and appointing Abdülmecid, a cousin of the last four Sultans, to take over as Caliph.[3]

The latter was of a different hue from his predecessors. He was widely read, loved his books and his garden, and was a fine painter. As a frequent visitor wrote: "This man was a living protest against the corrupt environment into which he was born. He led a monogamous family life and disdained the endless possibilities of physical luxuries and excesses to which birth and old palace traditions entitled him."[4] He was also virtually the only member of the Ottoman dynasty who criticized the concessions made with the Treaty of Sèvres.

Even many from Ankara wished him well. The nationalists' representative in İstanbul, Refet Paşa, a battled-hardened general, presented him with a stallion named Konya, writing: "I kiss the hands of His Majesty with feelings of humble and sincere loyalty."[5] Gökalp believed that ridding the Caliph's office of temporal responsibilities would mean "our religious life which has been for many centuries in a state of lethargic slumber will re-awaken, and, in accordance with the promise of our Prophet, the splendor of Islam will shine much as it shone in its Golden Age;" he described the house of Osman as having "served and elevated the Turkish nation for a thousand years and both Islam and the Turkish nation for six centuries."[6]

For all his qualities, Abdülmecid's honeymoon with the new rulers in Ankara did not last long. The newly appointed Caliph became a symbol for critics of the increasingly authoritarian Mustafa Kemal. The latter watched askance at Abdülmecid's "tours in great pomp; his private life in the Palace where he goes even so far as to receive dismissed officers to whose complaints he is listening, mixing his own tears with theirs."[7]

A year before, the first Grand National Assembly had argued painfully over abolishing the Sultanate and transferring the right to appoint the Caliph to the Assembly. Its successor, operating since August 1923, was a more malleable body. Belaurelled with success in the War of Independence and at Lausanne, Mustafa Kemal had culled the men of religion from its members. The new body was dominated by soldiers and allies, and excluded critics of his growing autocracy. It was less impressed by Islamic tradition.

Nevertheless, Mustafa Kemal appreciated the resistance he might face in eliminating the Caliphate. In November 1923, he sought to mollify such anxieties by incorporating the following clause in the new constitution: "The religion of the Turkish state is Islam." Next, he launched a public relations campaign, in a series of secret meetings in İzmir in January 1924 winning to his cause the top military personnel, the president and deans of İstanbul University, and seven newspaper editors.

The Turkish newspapers duly started contending that the continuation of the Caliphate endangered the unity and stability of the country. The Caliph's office wrote to Ankara expressing disturbance and requesting an increased allowance. This led to the tart rebuke from Mustafa Kemal that the Caliph and his office "have in reality neither a religious nor a political meaning or any right to exist;" it was "impudence" for Abdülmecid's secretary even to approach the government.[8]

The Caliph continued to inspire Muslim opposition to British rule in India—and this became one of the pretexts for its downfall. Muslim princes in India had long looked to the office to sanction their rule and had been among the main contributors to the nationalists in Turkey's War of Independence. In November 1923, the Aga Khan III and Syed Ameer Ali of the London Muslim League wrote to İsmet İnönü, the general who had become prime minister, arguing the importance of the Caliphate for India's Muslims. Their timing was poor, their intervention being used by Mustafa Kemal and İnönü to assert that Britain was interfering in Turkish politics.[9] On 3 March 1924, Abdülmecid was removed from office and his post, transferred to the Grand National Assembly, de facto abolished.

India—the Muslim rebellion that never happened

In 1919, a series of factors came together belatedly to inflame Muslim opposition to the British Raj, the unrest that the Germans and the Empire's Pan-Islamists had sought to provoke five years earlier. Poor harvests, famine, wartime suffering and profiteering, the Amritsar massacre of that April, horror at British policies towards the Ottoman Empire and its Caliph, and the compelling personality of Muhammad Ali Jinnah—all these strengthened the All-Indian Muslim League, which invited Mahatma Gandhi to chair the Khilafat conference that November. The next year saw publication of the Khilafat Manifesto, which called upon the British to protect the Caliphate and for Indian Muslims to hold the British accountable. The Khilafat leaders allied with the Indian National Congress, the largest political party in India, and became a major part of the non-cooperation movement—a nationwide campaign of peaceful civil disobedience.

This was the first time Hindus and Muslims had come together since the 1857 Indian Mutiny, and for a brief period they seemed to be a major threat to the Raj. But in 1922, Gandhi withdrew after the killing of police officers who had fired on demonstrators that February. At this point, the feelings of Indian Muslims "were turned to perplexity and gloom as [Mustafa Kemal] in turn dethroned the Sultan and then abolished the caliphate altogether. The effect was to make them feel more alone in the world than before... By 1924, communal riots had replaced the Congress-League alliance."[10]

"By 4 March 1924, every Turk was asking himself, 'How was it that I did not discover for myself sooner that these theocratic institutions had become obsolete, and totally lacking in vitality? How could I mistake those gilded clouds for real convictions rooted in the minds of the people,'" wrote Ahmed Emin Yalman, one of the participants in Mustafa Kemal's İzmir meetings.[11]

The Caliphate after the Ottomans

For the Caliph of the Messenger of God, exile was soon to be followed by a cloak of oblivion. Hussein, the Sharif of Mecca, asserted his own Caliphate, but could not win public support before he was driven out of Arabia by Ibn Saud.

Conferences on the issue in Mecca and Cairo in 1926 were marked by an audacious claim to the title by King Fuad of Egypt, but led to no result. A further conference in 1931 in Jerusalem also ended in disarray. King Faruq, who succeeded his father in Egypt, then staked his claim to the post. Abdülmecid, who had attended the Jerusalem conference, died unfeted in Paris in August 1944, just as the city was being liberated from German occupation.

The Ahmadiyya, a community of 10–20 million believers originally in India but recently led from London, have claimed the Caliphate for over a century.[12] The Sultans of Yogyakarta on the south coast of Java long used Khalifatullah as one of their titles, though in 2015 Sultan Hamengkubuwono X, to facilitate his daughter's inheritance of the throne, renounced any claim to the title.

One supporter of the Muslim Brotherhood has called for the restoration of the Caliphate of the "United States of the Arabs" with Jerusalem as its capital.[13] The *Hizb ut-Tahrir* (Party of Liberation) also calls for re-establishment of the Caliphate; founded in Jerusalem, the party is banned in most Arab countries. In June 2014, the Islamic State of Iraq and the Levant (ISIS, also known as ISIL), proclaimed itself a worldwide caliphate. The territorial gains that prompted this hubris proved evanescent, resonant today only in sub-Saharan Africa. Today, despite desuetude and abuse, the title remains, waiting for shoulders broad enough to carry it.

But many did not share this roseate approach. For them, the personality of this figure was not the point. Rather, the mere existence of a Caliph with a moral claim to leadership of the world's Muslims conveyed the reassurance of that individual as a living confirmation of the divine and the existence of a supra-national community of believers. This was especially the case in eastern Turkey, where the resurgent and secular Turkish nationalism was viewed with instinctual distaste by the Kurds, most of whose leaders were Sunni *Şeyh*.

Şeyh Said—Nakşibendis and Kurdish nationalism

Mustafa Kemal's approach to the Caliphate had shown his determination to prevent exploitation of religion from undermining his political agenda. This resolve was to be tested by the first major rebellion of his years in office, when Kurdish tribes combined religion with nationalism to demand autonomy.

Many of the Kurdish tribal leaders were also religious leaders. In September 1919, Mustafa Kemal had promised them, "Turks and Kurds will continue to live together as brothers around the institution of the Caliphate."[14] At that time he needed their support. But, as time passed, his tone changed, the promise on the Caliphate was voided, and, from October 1923, the president rarely if ever used the word 'Kurd.' Fewer tribal leaders were appointed to the new Assembly, and in 1924 use of Kurdish language in public places was banned.[15] Tax inspectors became the new face of the Republic. The mood among the Kurds shifted.

Abdülhamid had sought to bind the Kurds to the Ottoman state by establishing cavalry regiments headed by Kurdish notables who were brought to İstanbul for training. But these notables' loyalties were torn, an example being Colonel Halit, leader of the Cibran tribe who ruled the mountains north-west of Lake Van. During the battles against the Russians in the First World War, this valiant, still in his thirties, was in overall command of four of the Sultan's Hamidiye regiments. What his troops did during the deportation of the Armenians in 1915 is shrouded in silence, but, once the Russians had been driven back in 1918, he understood the Kurds' enemy had changed: "Brooding in his tent after the fray, Halit was asked by a comrade why he was not celebrating like everyone else. 'We have whetted,' he replied, 'the sword that will cut our own throats.'"[16]

In 1923, Halit and Koçzade Yusuf Ziya, deputy for Bitlis, established the Kurdish Independence Committee (*Kürt İstiklâl Komitesi*) and its underground organization, Freedom (*Azadi*). Halit proposed to the Alevis that they should join him to end six centuries of subjugation by the Turks. His offer was rejected but became known to Turkish officers. The next year saw a planned mutiny by *Azadi* officers in Erzurum—learnt of just before Mustafa Kemal arrived at the garrison town. During dinner with the president, the local army commander asked if he was preparing to betray his homeland:

> Halit replied bitterly: 'Does someone living on land that has been thickened by the blood of his forefathers, of his entire family—does such a man commit treason against his own land?' He glanced in Mustafa Kemal's direction: 'And then someone from goodness knows where has the nerve to come and play the patriot.'[17]

Four months later in February 1925, the fire that Halit had been stoking burst into flames in the form of a widespread rebellion of Kurdish tribes, 7,000 to 10,000 of whose members marched on the strategic city of Diyarbakır. They expected to be joined by other tribes, but were left to fight alone. After three weeks, strafing by Turkish planes and news of the impending arrival of a Turkish army division caused the rebels to retreat. They were encircled by a steadily narrowing force of Turkish soldiers. As they scattered, their leader, *Şeyh* Said, was betrayed and captured. The uprising had lasted eight weeks.

Halit was shot and Yusuf Ziya hanged, as were *Şeyh* Said and forty-six of his accomplices, fourteen of whom were also Nakşibendi *şeyh*. Thousands of less influential Kurds were slaughtered without a trial. The populations of entire districts were transferred to the west.[18]

Unlike the Senusis in Libya, the Nakşibendis are a diffuse, decentralized family of parallel sub-orders, each paying obeisance to a *şeyh*, but with no generally recognized supreme head. But certain *şeyh* gain acceptance for their spiritual qualities, ability to resolve disputes, or wealth. *Şeyh* Said had all three of these attributes, as well as being a committed nationalist. He had had a distinguished career in İstanbul, being exiled by Abdülhamid before throwing in his lot with the Young Turks and occupying senior religious posts. He was a vigorous man of 59–60 years, with a full white beard and piercing eyes, and was married to Halit's elder sister.

It seems that Halit always planned to exploit *Şeyh* Said's charisma in order to mobilize the mass following that his political organization lacked. But it was only in part a religious movement; its main aim was the establishment of an independent Kurdistan, with both the planners and leaders of the revolt appreciating that the motivating power of Islam would gain wider support than nationalist propaganda alone. But once the leading *şeyh* had been killed or dispersed, little remained of the once messianic image of the rebellion.[19]

The revolt had dramatic consequences. The government launched what Kurdish nationalists call a policy of denial, rejecting the existence of a separate Kurdish people and aiming for assimilation. Policies such as resettling over 500 tribal leaders and *şeyh* in western Turkey did little to quell unrest. All but one of the Turkish military's seventeen further engagements during Mustafa Kemal's lifetime would be in the Kurdish areas. The rift continues as Turkey's most important domestic problem, but the *Şeyh* Said rebellion was arguably the last one in which religion was so much at the fore.

In Ankara itself, the *Şeyh* Said rebellion accelerated the nationalists' shift from a revolution aiming for popular support to a dictatorship by fist and fiat. In March 1925, Mustafa Kemal replaced the hesitant Fethi Okyar as prime minister, bringing in the steelier İnönü. Martial law was introduced in eastern Turkey; the draconian Revolutionary Courts of the East (*Şark İstiklal Mahkemeleri*) started their work; the stifling Law on the Maintenance of Order was promulgated; and critical press was silenced. Over half the daily newspapers in İstanbul were closed, and relatively independent journalists such as Yalman were forced to apologize to the Diyarbakır court for having fostered rebellion.

That summer a failed plot against Mustafa Kemal in İzmir ushered in a fresh wave of repression. By the end of the year, the opposition party that Mustafa Kemal had once condoned, the Progressive Republican Party, was banned, attacked for encouraging Islamists. In parallel, Mustafa Kemal launched a frontal assault on political use of religion. In February 1925, those who set up associations with this purpose became liable to the death penalty. The *tarikat* were identified as conspirators, the prosecutor of *Şeyh* Said alleging that they served as centres of secret political plotting. The president increasingly criticized their lodges as dens of idleness and superstition, identifying them with political resistance to reform.

But even then, Mustafa Kemal did not deny the role of Islam as a legitimizing force; the 500-Turkish-lira banknote printed that year showed two minarets beside the president's portrait.

Closure of the tekke

Some lodges had supported the nationalists against the allied occupation. One was the Özbekler *tekke* of the Nakşibendis, which acted as a signals link between nationalist officers in İstanbul and their colleagues in Anatolia; it was there that Edib had sought refuge during the counter-revolution of

1909. Another, the Hatuniye *tekke* in Eyüp, led by *Şeyh* Sadeddin Ceylan Efendi of the Nakşibendi and Kadiri traditions, housed an organization transferring Ottoman army weapons to the rebels. The Bektaşis sent a regiment to the Caucasus. A *şeyh* of Nakşibendi background, Said Kurdi (later known as Said Nursi), raised and led a company to fight the Russians.[20] The Mevlevis also contributed, sending a regiment to Damascus and supplying grain to the nationalist armies.[21] However, many of the orders and *tekke* had contributed far less. They had also become the butt of *bien-pensant* criticism.

In 1922, the most talked-of movie in İstanbul was *Bosphorus Mystery*, an adaptation of the novel *Nur Baba* by Yakup Kadri Karaosmanoğlu. The story is set in a Bektaşi lodge in Çamlıca, İstanbul, and describes the wiles of the *şeyh* of the lodge, Nur Baba, to win, take their property, and later destroy a series of female devotees, most notably Nigar, the wife of an Ottoman ambassador. First published in serial form, the story also appeared as a book. Karaosmanoğlu's insights—he had been initiated at the Bektaşi lodge—proved grist to the mill of those claiming the lodges were degenerate pillars of resistance to modernity. With cinema houses having developed into major magnets of social activity, the critique resonated far and wide.

Mustafa Kemal had the writer summon the *şeyh* of the lodge, Ali Nutki Baba, to his presence. Finding that Ali Nutki, though fine looking and apparently having a penchant for ladies, could scarcely read or write let alone sing, he exclaimed: "Yakup Kadri, this man has no resemblance to the *baba* whom you described;" the writer replied: "My Paşa, he is the raw material."[22]

Mustafa Kemal was increasingly concerned about the role that religious conservatives could play in blocking the changes that he believed were necessary. He thus set out to remove religion from the social realm and "to confine it to the conscience of people," making it a set of beliefs that would remain relegated to the private sphere; "the purpose in this period was to secularize not only the state and the 'political', but also society and the 'social.'"[23] In his view, the Islam that he professed contained nothing contrary to reason and progress, but the nation had a second religion, a mass of irrational superstitions and prejudices—and the lodges fostered these.[24] Before long, newspapers close to the regime started denouncing the *tekke* as centres of sloth and the fallacies he abhorred. "Idle infidels are called monks, idle Muslims are called dervishes," spread as a local saying.

In August 1925 came his oft-quoted: "Know this well: The Turkish Republic cannot be the country of *şeyh*, dervishes, religious disciples and fanatics. The truest, the most genuine path is the path of civilization;" building on this, he continued: "The heads of the *tarikat,* accepting this manifest reality, should close their *tekke* voluntarily and immediately... The aim of the *tekke* is to put to sleep and stupefy the people."[25]

The court in Diyarbakır condemning *Şeyh* Said and his accomplices also ordered the closure of all dervish lodges in south-eastern Anatolia. Three months later, the Council of Ministers extended the court's order to the whole country, shuttering all lodges, Sufi centres and tombs, banning the religious orders and use of the titles of *şeyh,* dervish and disciple, and closing saints' tombs to visitation. On 30 November, the Grand National Assembly incorporated these provisions into Law 677 on "the Closure of Dervish Monasteries and Tombs, the Abolition of the Office of Keeper of Tombs and the Abolition and Prohibition of Certain Titles."[26]

The new provisions threw the residents of the lodges into the streets. Only incumbent heads of lodges (*postnişin*) and their families could stay on, as simple citizens rather than religious figures. Most *tekke* decayed into ruins, with repairs not gaining ground until the present century. Today, a mere handful are inhabited by descendants of Ottoman worthies. One example is the Kadirhane in Tophane, İstanbul, where the great-grandson of the *postnişin* of 1925 continues the ceremonies of the Kadiris today. Another is the lodge of Kenan Rifai in Fatih, where his grandson, Professor Kenan Gürsoy, runs a cultural centre honoring the Rifai tradition.

Those buildings that could be used as mosques would be thus employed. Others were transferred to the state. A century earlier, the suppression of the Bektaşi order had seen treasures bequeathed by the faithful sacked by the hands of local looters.[27] This time, the pillaging was by the state rather than the opportunistic citizen. It was a massive transfer of property, with some buildings becoming schools, others appropriated by local government, and the rest—the majority—transferred to the *Vakıflar İdaresi* (Foundations Administration). This was the successor to the Sultans' *Evkaf-ı Hümayun Nezareti*, and proved just as skilled in letting buildings crumble away. Books were sent to the national library in Ankara, and furniture, artefacts, and robes to the museum of the *Vakıflar*.[28] But the latter was unprepared, and the Ethnography Museum designated to shoulder the task only completed its own buildings in 1928. Countless treasures disappeared.

The cultural trauma has been at least as durable as these material losses. Long ignored, it is now the focus of many Turkish sociologists.

Mustafa Kemal's association with the *tarikat*

In recent years, historians have begun to draw together the scattered material on Mustafa Kemal's links with the religious orders that he so famously banned, honing in on his relations with three orders in particular: the courtly Mevlevi, the convivial Bektaşis, and the often-proscribed anti-establishment Melamis.

His father's ancestors had headed the Mevlevi lodge in Salonika, one of the richest convents in the Balkans. The aunt who arranged his parents' marriage was the daughter-in-law of the *şeyh* of this convent. While a soldier, with a *tarikat* background typical of many Ottomans, he would visit the Mevlevihane during his visits to Salonika. As one letter explains,

> When Mustafa Kemal returned to his home in Salonika during his vacations [from Manastır], he used to go to the *tekke* of [the father of] my father-in-law during the *ayin* (religious ceremonies), taking his place in the dervish circle and repeating Hû Hû [the 'Beloved,' God], he would go on whirling until he was dripping with sweat.[29]

The Mevlevis in the Balkans had close links with the Bektaşis. Many of the Young Turks were Bektaşis, and that Mustafa Kemal was acquainted with both Mevlevis and Bektaşis would not be unusual. Most historians doubt whether he ever became a Bektaşi, though one Bektaşi insists Mustafa Kemal submitted himself to Tayyar Baba of the Abdullah Baba Tekkesi in Katerini.[30] Certainly he was to show sympathy to the Bektaşis, exempting their leaders from the original draft of Law 677 banning the *tarikat*, and turning a blind eye when Salih Noyan Dedebaba, head of the Bektaşis' elected line, opened a conventicle in Ulus, heart of the capital, in 1926.[31]

In this period, a former Mevlevi, Abdülbaki Gölpınarlı, was commissioned to write the textbook to be used in compulsory religious education, and there is a description of Mustafa Kemal being moved by a performance of Mevlevi dervishes in 1931.

The Alevis in general and the Bektaşis in particular supported the independence movement. In December 1919, Mustafa Kemal, keen to cement this support, visited Hacibektaş, spending a day or so with Salih Noyan and Cemaleddin Çelebi, head of the hereditary branch of the Bektaşis.

In 1911, he had become close to Abdülkerim Paşa, his commanding officer, carrying out a correspondence with him couched in Sufi phraseology. Abdülkerim later turned out to be a *şeyh* of the Melami order.[32] The Melamis traced their origins back to the Melamis of ninth-century Khorasan and in the nineteenth century had a revival in the Balkans. In 1931, the state printing press published Gölpınarlı's *Melâmîlik ve Melâmîler*, a rare study of an apparently proscribed tradition.

Turkish historians tend to conclude there is no evidence of Mustafa Kemal's continuing submission to any master. But some suggest that, had he not studied with the Sufis, he would not have been able to sustain his arguments on matters of religious jurisprudence with his almost universally Muslim colleagues. Indeed, it was his deep grounding in Islam that assisted him in countering the arguments of religious conservatives in the Grand National Assembly and forcing through the dismissal of the Caliph and the laws reducing the formal role of Islam.

The generation of secularism

Abolition of the Caliphate had been combined with a series of further changes. Prime among these were the termination of the historical post of *şeyhülislam*; the closure of the *Evkaf* Administration and confiscation of the assets of the country's centuries-old foundations; and the unification of all educational institutions and religious schools (subsequently slashed in number) under the Ministry of Education.[33] These were momentous changes, so much so that, for some reason, the three laws concerned—numbers 429, 430, and 431—were published twice in the *Official Gazette*.[34]

These decrees were followed by closure of the Muslim courts that applied religious law on matters of personal status such as marriage, divorce, and inheritance. The oft-ignored ban on alcohol was also formally lifted. There was then a pause until the *Şeyh* Said rebellion refocused attention on the dervishes.

Five days before the orders were closed and their lodges shuttered, the Assembly had voted to ban the traditional fez, requiring citizens to replace turbans and fezzes distinguishing rank and religion with the hat, decreed to be "the common headgear of the Turkish people."[35] By contrast, Mustafa Kemal condemned the fez "as a sign of ignorance, of fanaticism, of hatred to progress and civilization."[36] There were more demonstrations against this change than against the closure of the lodges. The response was unsparing. Of the 138 death sentences handed down by the Independence Tribunals between March 1925 and March 1926, at least twenty can be attributed directly to the hat demonstrations.[37] A number of these—in Kayseri, Erzurum, and Giresun, for instance—were Nakşibendi *şeyh*.

Later came the excision from the constitution of the clause "The religion of the Turkish state is Islam." This amendment was made in April 1928. By then, secularism was on the march, and in 1931 its Turkish implementation, laicism—the subordination of religion to state (as in France and, in fact, the Ottoman Empire)—was adopted as one of the "six arrows" of Mustafa Kemal's governing Republican People's Party; in 1937, laicism and the other five principles—republicanism, nationalism, populism, revolutionism, and étatism—were enshrined in the constitution.[38]

The legal framework for 'the Turkish model' of secularism was thus complete. It was complemented by a massive exercise in social engineering. In the 1920s, apart from the change of headdress, citizens were required to obey new European-based civil, penal, and commercial codes (1926); to adopt the Gregorian calendar instead of the Islamic one; to replace the Muslim day beginning at sunset with the Western 24-hour clock (both from 1926); and to change their numbers and written language, adopting a modified Latin alphabet in place of the Turkish form of the Arabic script (1928).

In the early 1930s, adoption of the metric system (1931) followed, as did the start of removal of Arabic and Persian loanwords from the language (1932); the launching of an initially outlandish rewriting of Turkish history (1932); the introduction of hereditary surnames (1934); the abolition of titles and appellations such as *Efendi*, *Bey*, or *Paşa* (1934); the banning of public wearing of the religious dress of all faiths except during religious ceremonies (1934); and the changing of the weekly holiday from Friday to Sunday (1935). This period included advances in the rights and status of women.

Many of these initiatives encountered resistance, but Mustafa Kemal did not brook dissent. As he had told Edib in her farmhouse in Ankara one evening in autumn 1920: "I don't want any consideration, criticism or advice. I will have only my own way. All shall do as I command."[39]

The subsequent decade demonstrated his success in this endeavour. He proved adept in sidelining potential military rivals and marginalizing political opponents. The Progressive Republican Party lasted six months before it was closed down, being presented as somehow connected with the previous year's İzmir plot on the president's life.[40]

Three years later, confident that fresh rebellions around Mount Ararat by the Cibrans and other Kurds would be crushed and that his regime was now secure in Ankara, he decided the time had come to resurrect the idea of a loyal opposition. He chose a name for this, the Free Republican Party, decided on its leaders, and vetted its programme. The party was officially constituted on 12 August 1930, but, far from proving a reassuring partner to Mustafa Kemal, it revealed the tides of disaffection beneath the well-policed surface. Over 100,000 people turned up to an opposition meeting, the offices of Mustafa Kemal's own party were stoned, and photographs of his prime minister were torn up.

The new party was allowed to contest the local elections that October. It won about 40 of the 502 contests, but a month later, its leaders, faced with obstruction and fraud, decided to close it down.

The Menemen incident—making the Nakşibendis pay

Just as Mustafa Kemal was coming to terms with the limits of his popularity, an incident erupted that seemed to justify his worst fears. On 23 December 1930, the seventeen-year-old Derviş Giritli Mehmed took to the streets of Menemen, a traditional Aegean market town, proclaimed himself the *Mehdi*, shot and decapitated a young reserve officer, Mustafa Fehmi Kubilay, and paraded the latter's sawn-off head on the green banner of a nearby mosque. Reinforcements were brought in. Derviş Mehmed and two of his five disciples were killed.

The episode lasted only a few hours, led to the death of only three security personnel, and was instigated by Derviş Mehmed without any collaboration with wider Sufi networks. The incident was clearly the work of an isolated individual, but Mustafa Kemal was outraged by the adulation that Derviş Mehmed had whipped up during his brief hours of zealotry.

The political elite was quick to turn it into a national issue, and the net was cast wide. The state prosecutor ordered the investigation of Sufi activities throughout the country. Around 2,200 people were taken into custody and 600 brought to trial. Those arraigned included the venerable 83-year-old Nakşibendi *Şeyh* Esad Erbili and his eldest son, Mehmed Ali. They were brought from their home in the small village of Erenköy in Anatolian İstanbul, and on no convincing evidence were convicted of being the leaders of the rebellion. Mehmed Ali and twenty-seven others were hanged. *Şeyh* Esad died in prison, the result, according to the poet Necip Fazıl Kısakürek, of the use of poisoned food and a syringe.

The *şeyh* was well known in nationalist circles. Fevzi Çakmak, the general leading the independence armies, had sought his blessing, presenting himself as: "Your slave, Fevzi."[41] However, Esad had long been in the government's sights. On 18 July 1930, the pro-government paper, *Vakit*, had published an extensive attack on the secret rituals he practised in his secluded white villa behind the pines in Erenköy.

Mustafa Kemal was joined by other ministers in fulminating against the dangers of reaction, demonizing the religious orders, and calling for the crushing of the Nakşibendi. As Joseph Grew, the American ambassador at the time, was to write, the Menemen incident was a "golden opportunity for the regime to reassert its prestige."[42]

The state victims—Kubilay and the two village guards who died with him—are commemorated in a large hilltop mausoleum, the only one erected in the Republic before that for Atatürk. Kubilay was long a symbol, but in today's Turkey it is *Şeyh* Esad who resonates more, the disciples of this ill-fated recluse constituting one of the most powerful Islamic movements in Turkey and being active in seventy countries abroad.

Religious education in the early Republic

Mustafa Kemal was a lifelong opponent of superstition. His commitment to education is one of his key legacies. It did not include training *imam*.

The Republic inherited three channels of education. The first and most widespread was that devoted to the teaching, based on Arabic, and learning by heart of the *Kur'an*; the second were the schools set up in the *Tanzimat* period and having some discourse with modernization; and the third were the schools of the minorities. As one study describes: "In these three channels were three separate philosophies, three separate styles of life, indeed they were creating people for three different epochs. Their bookshops were different. The manuscript sellers of Beyazıt served the first, the bookshops of Cağaloğlu the second, and those of Beyoğlu the third."[43] These last two channels were particularly well represented in İstanbul; the first was active throughout the country. Most of the 70,000 charitable foundations in operation at the time of the declaration of the Republic had been set up for educative purposes. Many of the schools were under the control of the *tarikat* and their numerous *tekke*.

For the founders of the Republic—and for subsequent secular commentators—this was an unacceptable situation. The March 1924 subjection of all education, religious teaching included, to the unified control of the Ministry of Education had led to the closure of 479 *medrese* with 16,000 students. In their place were opened a mere twenty-nine *mektep—imam* and *hatip* lower secondary schools (*ortaokul*) promoting the ideals of the state—and a theological faculty at İstanbul University.

In their first year, the religious *mektep* attracted around 2,000 students. Five years later, enrolment was down to 100, and all but two of the *mektep* had closed. The following year, these two also closed. The state institutions providing religious training for *imam* and preachers had scant support from the authorities and could only offer an uncertain future to their graduates, not least as these were denied the status and protection of being classed as civil servants.

In 1927, religious lessons were stopped at lower secondary level and the next year were dropped from general primary schools too. In 1933, the theology faculty was also closed. By then, the Religious Affairs Directorate began developing the *Kur'an* courses, but their teaching was weak and registrations were few, reaching a mere 409 in 1936–1937. A vacuum had been created. It was only a generation later that it became clear that the religious orders, banned but not destroyed, were filling it.

Mustafa Kemal and the Turkish variant of secularism

Writing in the early 1960s, the sociologist Niyazi Berkes concluded that Mustafa Kemal believed the abolition of the Caliphate had been necessary if, for the first time in an Islamic country, popular sovereignty was to be established: "The struggle was not over the question of separating the spiritual and temporal, but over the difference between democracy and theocracy."[44] In Berkes's view, for all the contradictions in his lifestyle, Mustafa Kemal combined a belief in the reasonableness of Islam with a deistic conviction. As an officer, he had seen the value of Islam in motivating fighting troops. When establishing local defence societies throughout Anatolia, he included local religious officials in over 90 per cent of them. During the months before abolition of the Caliphate, he visited mosques, joining the prayers, mounting the minbar to deliver the impromptu sermon in Balıkesir cited above, entering into debates on Islam with local religious leaders, and discussing nuances of the *Kur'an* and *hadis* with deputies in the Grand National Assembly.

Later, his practices differed from those of the more puritan Muslims.

> There is no evidence that, when he was out of the public eye, he ever prayed, visited a mosque, or fasted during the Islamic holy month of Ramadan. He was also a notoriously heavy drinker, particularly of the aniseed-flavored spirit *rakı*; to the extent that the primary cause of his premature death in 1938 was cirrhosis of the liver.[45]

However, an officer from his private guard at Çankaya remembers riding out with him early one morning to Gölbaşı:

> When we arrived at the lake, we saw a peasant performing his morning pre-prayer ablutions with sand from the shore. Atatürk [as he was named in 1934] was furious. He dismounted, told the peasant that sand was only used when water was not available, carried out his ablutions using water from the lake, and started praying. The peasant, terrified as he had recognized his exemplar, struggled to follow.[46]

The contrasts in his approach were evident in his call to his companions at a dinner in Çankaya in August 1933:

> Let us drink a toast together! ... Let me inform you: I will not become Luther! ... Not a bit like Shah Akbar! Because Luther and Shah Akbar painted Europe and India with blood. I am [simply] carrying out what our religion says... My religion is Islam! I am looking at whatever the *Kur'an* says.[47]

It was to counter faith being built on ignorance that he believed worship should be in the demotic language of the people. With the *Kur'an* being dictated by the Prophet, its language, Arabic, is an inherent constituent of its integrity, and for the faithful the same applies to the call to prayer, the *adhan* (Turkish *ezan*). With the rise of the CUP, the argument that Turkish should be the language of worship of the Turks had gained ground. Gökalp called for the *Kur'an* and prayers to be in Turkish so that the nation could understand the true essence of its religion and obtain greater spiritual relief. As he wrote:

> A country in whose mosques the call to prayer is read in Turkish,
> The peasant understands the meaning of the prayers in his worship.
> A country in whose schools the *Kur'an* is read in Turkish.
> Young, old, everyone knows the commands of God.
> Oh son of the Turk, there, that is your homeland![48]

Mustafa Kemal shared such views and, after abolishing the Caliphate, devoted considerable efforts to making religion intelligible to the everyman. For him, "The drive for a rational understanding of the *Kur'an*, the determination to make it available to people in their vernacular, was a logical outcome of the conviction that Islam was rational and natural."[49] Central to this endeavour was providing the people with a Turkish translation of the *Kur'an*. Seven such translations were published in the 1920s, but none could win the approval of the government-appointed—but continuingly conservative—Directorate of Religious Affairs, the *Diyanet*.

Where the use of Turkish during rituals was concerned, the *Diyanet* accepted it was permissible to read one or two *Kur'an*ic verses in Turkish during a sermon, but not to translate ritual prayers. Mustafa Kemal ordered recitals from a translation of the *Kur'an*, first at Yerebatan Mosque, then at Sultan Ahmet Mosque, and then on 3 February 1932 at Ayasofya itself. The last reading was during *Kadir Gecesi*, the night in Ramadan commemorating when the *Kur'an* began to be revealed. Twenty-five *hafiz* (one who has learnt the *Kur'an* by heart) took turns to recite parts of the new translation, with their readings broadcast by radio, as was the *mevlid*, a fourteenth-century Turkish poem on the birth and life of the Prophet. A crowd of 70,000 assembled for the event, according to *Cumhuriyet* (Republic) newspaper, a dutiful supporter of the regime.

By any measure, it was an impressive turnout and an apparent vindication of Mustafa Kemal's convictions. And yet, after a flurry of further readings, the recitals soon stopped. One *hafiz* who had taken part in preparatory meetings with Mustafa Kemal speculated that the latter had not found the readings appropriate. Others suggest that the *Diyanet* may have intervened, either because of concerns over the translation or because of the difficulty of supervision.[50] A 1934 report for the Ministry of Education cited Abu Hanifa, founder of the Hanafi school of jurisprudence followed by the Ottomans and most Turks, who argued that the meaning of the *Kur'an* was essential rather than its wording, hence it could be expressed in any language. The government never sought to exploit this theological justification.[51]

A similar but earlier dispute was over the use of Turkish in the Friday sermon (*hutbe*). This sermon is an inherent feature of the Friday noon service, the attending of which is integral to the sense of community of the Islamic *ümmet*.

In November 1922, a deputy marked the initiation of Abdülmecid as Caliph with a sermon in Turkish at the revered Fatih Mosque in İstanbul. Earlier during the Independence War, the introduction of Turkish into the *hutbe* had been practised, being used to mobilize popular support for the nationalist government. This had been done by dividing the *hutbe* in two. The first part, exalting the Prophet, His companions, and the Caliph, continued to be in Arabic. The second admonitory part, which covered daily activities and praised the new government, the Grand National Assembly, and national sovereignty, was in Turkish.

Again, this reflected the belief of Mustafa Kemal that mosques should be centres of spiritual nourishment with sermons understood by the people. He underlined this in his speech opening the Grand National Assembly on 1 March 1922, and in February 1923, in his sermon delivered in Balıkesir, proclaimed:

> Sermons are meant to enlighten and guide the people, and nothing else. To recite sermons of a hundred, two hundred or even one thousand years ago is to leave the people in a state of ignorance and negligence... Therefore, sermons should and will be totally in Turkish and suitable to the requirements of the day.[52]

When the *Diyanet* published its *Turkish Sermons* (*Türkçe Hutbe*) in 1927, a book distributed to all *müftü* in Turkey, the preface reiterated the position that only the admonition could be in Turkish. It did not include prayers in Turkish. Infringements of its ruling were rare. On 5 February 1932, the *hutbe* in its entirety was read in Turkish at Süleymaniye Mosque, but this too was little repeated.

Slightly more durable was a third change introduced at this time: the use of Turkish rather than Arabic for the *ezan,* the call to prayer. This innovation was again the result of the direct involvement of Mustafa Kemal. In January 1932, he had summoned eight *hafiz* to Dolmabahçe Palace to discuss this change.

The result was first chanted from a minaret of the grand Fatih Mosque on 30 January 1932 and six months later was made mandatory. Music was commissioned, with a separate accompaniment for each of the five ritual prayers. Soon, a gramophone recording of the results was distributed to *müezzin* throughout the country. The requirement to use Turkish was extended to the *salatüselam*, the prayer announcing a funeral, and to the *tekbir*, the affirmation of Allah, when expressed after funeral prayers. In February 1933, a warning was circulated to *müezzin* that they would be liable to penalties if they failed to use the Turkish *ezan,* though it was only in 1941 that specific penalties of up to three months in prison or a small fine were introduced.

The government justified this amendment to the Penal Code as being "to rescue the people from the influence of the Arabic language attaching them to old mentalities and old traditions."[53] For İnönü, who took over as president upon the death of Atatürk in 1938, the use of Turkish was a nationalist and modernist necessity.

The ambiguities of Turkish secularism

For the new Republic, its reactions to the *Şeyh* Said rebellion of 1925, the Menemen incident of 1930, and the Alevi uprising in Dersim of 1937–1938 were exercises in *realpolitik,* where demonizing one's opponents as religious reactionaries was a necessary mobilizing call, even if it was only a partial explanation of the underlying events, for the Republic itself had been born in a struggle which was religious as well as nationalist.

That struggle was, in the view of the theologian İsmail Kara, a *cihad* (*jihad*). He and others have pointed out that, when the disparate group of *ulema, şeyh*, nationalists, and socialists met in 1921 and chose a national anthem, they united round the Islamist-inspired poem cited at the beginning of this chapter. As Kara asks: "Why didn't the administration and ideology of the Republic choose a path that separates matters of religion from matters of state and politics instead of adopting a style where religion and state co-exist while suppressing and controlling religion?"[54] Another influential modern sociologist has pointed out that, in many ways, the relationship between Islam and secularism was to be one of accommodation, rather than simply conflict and confrontation.[55]

Secularism is a term and concept fraught with interpretive difficulties. Max Weber was the first to develop the view that whatever secularism is, it still represents a religious history. He saw the increased rationalism of the modern Anglo-European world not as the triumph of a new, anti-religious authority, but as a byproduct of Protestant influence. For more modern writers, secularism is marked not by the repression of religion, but by the relative invisibility of religion and creation of a context that actively oppresses visible—that is non-Protestant—religions and peoples.[56]

For their part, the Republic's founding fathers eschewed the definition of secularism as separation of state and religion, instead creating a Turkish version in which religion was not disengaged from the state but designated as yet another area to be controlled by the nascent and perennially insecure authorities of the Republic.

This ambiguity is reflected in works of scholarship, such as Berkes's *The Development of Secularism*, which finely detail the past but, as Mardin wrote in 2005, leave out many elements that could explain the loosening of Islamic bonds that came with Turkish modernization and, despite years of secularizing state policy, the revitalization of Islam in contemporary Turkish society.

Kara and Mardin both look to the essence of Turkish culture to explain this. For them, the Turks have no history in Anatolia that is not inextricably linked to Islam.

Mustafa Kemal sought to separate nationalism from religion, but could only suppress rather than destroy the link between them. A generation later, this link was revived, since underpinning the rise of the nationalism which colours the political mainstream in Turkey today.

4

POST-WAR
THE REVIVAL OF THE PAST

If you want, you can bring back the Caliphate.

Adnan Menderes in election speeches in 1950 and when trying to calm rebellious deputies on 29 November 1954

Menderes opens the doors

Turkey emerged unscathed from the Second World War, but achingly poor. The country had avoided the battles of the war, staying neutral until after the Yalta Conference of February 1945. But it had not been spared the costs of keeping 900,000 men under arms—one in five of the adult male population—and of maintaining defences against the Axis powers and the Soviet Union. Public debt had doubled, inflation was raging, and profiteers were rampant, while the villages, untouched by electricity or metalled roads, continued to cleave to the traditions of centuries.

The war years had stressed the early Republic's alliance between the military elite, the landlords, and the bourgeoisie. The private sector had grown considerably and was chafing at state controls. The divisions were played out within the ruling Republican People's Party (*Cumhuriyet Halk Partisi*, CHP), and came to a head in mid-1945 when İnönü attempted to improve the peasants' situation by a land reform. His aim was to break up traditional feudal structures and develop a nation of independent peasant proprietors. His measures achieved little, affecting only one twelfth of cultivated land. However, the altercations over the reform triggered a split in his party.

Tensions were high, not least as Stalin had refused to extend a non-aggression pact and was demanding chunks of eastern Anatolia and joint control of the Turkish Straits. Fanning anti-communism was easy, with the pro-government *Tanin* exhorting its readers to the streets. On 4 December 1945, students gathered at İstanbul University, developing into a mob that ravaged the premises of the newspaper *Tan* (Dawn) and two other publications advocating good relations with Moscow. A number of people were injured and the presses ruined. Among the aggressors was at least one future president of Turkey, Süleyman Demirel.[1]

It was in these fraught times that dissident notables in the CHP set up the Democrat Party under the leadership of Adnan Menderes, an eloquent lawyer and scion of a Crimean Tatar family owning large estates south of İzmir. With only six months to organize before the elections of July 1945 and a hostile voting environment, the new party gathered a mere one seventh of the seats in the Assembly. However, the elections revealed a state of simmering discontent. Four years later, the Democrats swept to power, winning a crushing six sevenths of the Assembly.

The introduction of a multi-party system had coincided with a rising sense of self-awareness of the long-forgotten periphery. Three quarters of the population lived in rural areas, and lacked not just basic services but teachers and *imam*. Schooling was limited, in practice tending to be for three years rather than the prescribed five. Finding teachers was a challenge.

Prompting special concerns were the problems caused by the lack of religious education. The schools to train *imam*, reopened in 1932, only graduated around 100 people a year, a paltry few for a nation of some 18 million. Particularly acute were the challenges of arranging burial. Islam ordains that, after a corpse has been washed and wrapped by the deceased's family and those close to them, an *imam* lead the prayers protecting and guiding the soul of the departed. However, with so few *imam* available, corpses could wait for a week or more before interment. As trained *imam* retired or died, the dearth intensified.

The failures of the state increased the space for alternative voices. In 1950, the head of the *Diyanet* warned the prime minister:

> ... some profane creeds and false *tarikat* are insidiously but systematically spreading and breeding in almost every corner of the country. In order to counter the effects of these vicious elements... we desperately need

> powerful religious figures, who have received a fundamental religious education and knowledge and are equipped with positive sciences, and educated preachers.[2]

Between 1945 and 1949, at least seven political parties sympathetic to Islam were launched. Accepting that, in the new multi-party world, religion had begun to serve as a means of political mobilization, the CHP sought to regain the initiative. The party amended its programme to include a clause expressing respect for religion, and undertook to protect worshippers from political interference. It had a theologian, Şemsettin Günaltay, appointed as prime minister. Its government started allocating foreign exchange for pilgrims to Mecca; introduced elective religious instruction for primary school students; launched three-year *imam-hatip* courses; reattributed the management of mosques and religious personnel to a long-emasculated *Diyanet*; and opened a Faculty of Theology at Ankara University. It also opened to visitors some twenty tombs of Ottoman Sultans and other religious and political heroes.

These measures were welcomed by the more pious, but to the many critics of the CHP's long suppression of religion, they were too little too late.

Unrest was thus beginning to be articulated on religious issues. Polarizing the debate were the activities of the Ticaniyye, a Sufi order of North African origin, headed in Turkey by Kemal Pilavoğlu. This preacher had a following in Ankara. In February 1949, two of his disciples disrupted the Grand National Assembly, reciting the *ezan* in Arabic from the public gallery.[3]

The call to return the *ezan* to its original tongue had been endorsed by the Democrat Party, becoming a central tenet of the party's platform. Menderes argued that insisting on a Turkish *ezan* would be "fanaticism against the freedom of conscience… damaging the principle of secularism."[4] Indeed, after the Democrats came to power, the first law they passed allowed the *ezan* to be recited in Arabic. The CHP deputies gave the measure their unanimous support.

The new rulers had also promised to introduce religious lessons in public schools and to develop training of religious personnel. *İmam-hatip ortaokul* (lower secondary schools) were duly opened, followed by *imam-hatip lise* (high schools). By the end of the decade, there were thirty-five such schools with over 4,000 students. High Islamic Institutes (*Yüksek İslam Enstitüleri*) had also been added, with some of these developing into full theology faculties.

Menderes and his party argued that religious education was useful to fight the poison of communism and, in general, cast their approach as restoring the rights of the individual rather than endorsing fundamentalist Islam. Their government programme of May 1950 proclaimed: "While never permitting any reactionary provocation, we will respect the necessities of freedom of religion and of conscience. ... we understand that true secularism requires the lack of any relation between religion and state politics and the absence of influence of any religious idea on legal arrangements and practices."[5]

This was the first time since the launch of the Republic that secularism had been redefined by conservative nationalists, and this redefinition was, by and large, adopted by the conservative parties which ruled Turkey for much of the next half century.

For the republican establishment, ever-anxious about religious revival and fixated on the need for central control, not least of Islam, the government's programme was deeply disturbing, particularly after the disruption caused by the Ticaniyye and the cries of *Allahu akbar* at the funeral of the revered Marshal Çakmak in April 1950.

Enhancing the tension was the Malatya Incident of 22 November 1952, a failed attack on the prominent liberal journalist, Ahmed Emin Yalman. The would-be assassin, Hüseyin Üzmez, was shown to have links with Islamist publications.

For the Kemalists, this was *irtica* (political reaction) at work and proof of the need for doubling down on secularism. It led to Menderes briefly dissociating his party from association with such forces. As he said two weeks after the Malatya event, "This country has no tolerance to the abuse of a sacred concept like religion by certain social debris and self-seeking politicians."[6]

He launched an intra-party purge of extreme Islamists, denounced Islamic publications that were abusing the freedoms created by his party, and heightened penalties for the abuse of religion for political benefit. He also personally blocked Ahmed Sırrı Baba, leading the global Bektaşi community from Cairo, from settling in the lodge of Hacı Bektaş Veli.

The presence in the Democrat hierarchy of Celal Bayar, a long-term colleague of Atatürk, served to legitimize the party's moves, with Bayar acting to restrain steps against secularism. But the DP's caution concerning religion was to wane. In October 1956, Menderes declared: "On the issue of freedom of conscience, the Turkish nation is Muslim, and will remain Muslim. The inculcation of religion first in itself and in future generations and the instruction of the principles and rules of religion are indispensable conditions for it to remain forever Muslim."[7] He was speaking in Konya, a centre of traditional Islam, and began to make increasing use of religious symbols, idioms, and practices. The state radio initiated programmes on the *Kur'an*.

This debate on secularism became more acute. Those classing themselves as Kemalist urged control by the state of religious practices for the sake of modernization and nationalism. For this group, the threat from reaction was ever present. Cartoons in the Kemalist press depicted dark-faced, bearded men with prayer beads and women in baggy outer clothing arriving in the cities: the images reflected the urban elite's trauma at the increasing visibility of rural Islam in cities now hosting numerous migrants, who, uprooted, brought with them what they could from their village culture.[8]

The opposition CHP made this duality a central theme of its campaigning in the 1957 elections, and ratcheted up the discourse in the following years. Grist to its mill was that, after surviving an aircraft crash in February 1959 near Gatwick Airport, Menderes's first act upon return was to offer prayers at the historic mosque of Eyüp.

Particularly condemned by the CHP was the Democrats' condoning a revival of the *tarikat*, evidenced by the burgeoning following of Bediüzzaman Said Nursi, an Islamic theologian of Kurdish origin. Prosecutors alleged that he had 600,000 disciples, and his followers claimed there were 600,000 copies of his writings. A second grouping causing concern was the community of Süleyman Hilmi Tunahan, a leading teacher of the *Kur'an*.

These two men are among the most prominent of those who survived the leaden years for Islam in Turkey. During the years of persecution, many holy men turned inwards. A number, flouting official opprobrium, refocused their lives to keep the Islamic flame alight. Nursi and Tunahan are examples of these. Both spent months in prison—as Nursi already had in the gaols of both the Sultan and the Tsar. Both had their burials marred by controversy. And both became hailed as saints.

There is no spiritual authority to confer the status of sainthood in Islam. Rather, it is the fellowship of believers who coalesce around the certitude that a particular teacher has a wisdom akin to a form of divine inspiration. As one leading Turkish sociologist described it: "In Islam, sainthood is an attribute of the religious prestige which persons build up in their community during their lifetime."[9] Another scholar prefers the phrase 'friend of God' and argues this should be restricted to those classed as *veli* or *evliya* by their peers. In Ottoman times, the community of a holy person was almost always co-extensive with the *tarikat* within which he had developed. Republican repression reduced the number of followers of *tarikat* who could contribute to defining succession to such figures.

Where Nursi and Tunahan stand out is that neither was shaped by nor could draw on the support of an existing, even if suppressed, order. By contrast, it was the personal qualities of both which caused them to develop followings which were only limited by the boundaries of the country. Both came to inspire orders which have attracted millions.

Both were to die just as the Democrats were about to lose office. Tracked by the police, arrested, tortured or subject to internal exile, and harassed by continuing lawsuits, their experiences show an atmosphere of manipulated—and not always erroneous—suspicion.

Both were the sons of religious teachers—one a Kurd from east of the Tigris, the other from south of the Danube, and their legacy marks the area between these two rivers, influencing the Turkey of the latter half of the last century, and living on in Erdoğan's Republic today.

Six months before his death in March 1960, the long-frail Nursi was taken ill. A disciple arrived from İstanbul telling him of Tunahan's death. "When did my brother die?" Nursi asked, and was told that it was at the moment that he himself had fallen sick.[10]

In the case of Nursi, it was only when he was nearly fifty years old that he began to develop a significant following. Exile to a small settlement beside a remote lake in Central Anatolia only added to his mystique. Tunahan also suffered from intrusive policemen and physical abuse by the judicial system. For him too such incidents served to elevate his status among the thousands who sat at his feet and then spread talk of his lustre.

The influences of these two men are very different. Nursi devoted the second half of his life to writing. His *magnum opus*, the fourteen volumes known as the *Risale-i Nur Külliyatı* (The Epistle of Light Collection), totals over 5,000 pages, largely addressing the layered meanings of the *Kur'an*. Handwritten copies of this were distributed by devoted 'students,' with official permission for printing only granted four years before his death. The work has been of major impact on Islamic discourse in Turkey, and is now supplemented by memoirs repeating tales not as miraculous as those of medieval saints but still wondrous. It was not until 1979 that scholarly appraisals began to appear, seeking to explain the nature of his appeal and his contributions to the debate on how Islam should handle science and modernity.[11]

Tunahan left few documents. The best known of these is a "brand new approach" to learning the *Kur'an*, a work of a mere seven pages. Around two million copies of this have been printed, as have a similar number of copies of Nursi's main work.

Close to Tunahan and promoting Nursi was the nationalist polemicist and poet, Necip Fazıl Kısakürek, a man under Nakşibendi influence and whose writings on the glories of Ottoman Islam gained pace in the 1940s and 1950s, taking advantage of the mass media to build a large following.

The lives of these three figures help understand the varieties and vigour of Islam flourishing in Turkey today.

Said Nursi—rising in exile

The three Saids—the Old, the New, and the Third

The final meeting between Nursi and Mustafa Kemal took place one evening in spring 1923 on a platform at the Ankara railway station, then the eastern terminal of the Anatolian railway. Nursi had spent five months in the nationalists' capital. He had been honoured in the new Grand National Assembly, blessing the nationalist army, and denouncing the British as "the enemy of the Turks and of Islam." The Greeks had been expelled and the Sultan displaced. But, disturbed at the neglect of religious practices in the Assembly, he decided to return to his roots in south-east Turkey and to solitude.

Learning of Nursi's travel plans, Mustafa Kemal left his temporary quarters in the stationmaster's house, approached Nursi, and asked for his views on statues. Nursi, unawed by the leader whom he had recently admonished for failing to pray, told him: "Our *Kur'an* condemns statues. The statues of Muslims should be hospitals, schools, dormitories for orphans, shrines, and roads leading to our monuments."[12]

Relations between the leaders of the Republic and the dervishes were more complex than the secular narrative records. Nursi had been invited to Ankara by Fevzi Çakmak, the nationalists' prime minister and military leader—indeed, when the latter died, he insisted on being buried beside a Nakşibendi *şeyh*. General Rauf Orbay, Çakmak's successor as prime minister, had expressed his admiration for the Caliph. General Kazım Karabekir, hero of the east, was to write in the newspaper that later published Nursi's *Risale-i Nur*. But, after the *Şeyh* Said rebellion of 1925 and the Menemen incident of 1930, the Nakşibendis became the chief bogey of the new rulers, and the now recluse Nursi came to personify much of what they most feared.

Nursi was born in the remote Kurdish village of Nurs, south of Lake Van. He was a brilliant but headstrong youth, reading extensively from an early age, and refusing to accept the authority of most of his teachers. He displayed a prodigious memory, causing one teacher to bestow on him the sobriquet by which he is often known, Bediüzzaman (the Wonder of the Age).[13] He was brought up in an area dotted with Nakşibendi schools but was also influenced by the teachings of the Kadiri *tarikat*. It was a largely Kurdish area and he was to be proud of his Kurdish heritage. In 1909 he called on the "Kurdish lions" to wake up from their "five-hundred-year slumber" but he never advocated separatism from their Turkish brothers.

A year earlier, he had petitioned Abdülhamid to modernize the education system and establish an Islamic University of the East in Van, planned as a sister institution of the venerable Al-Azhar University of Cairo. His unfawning presentation to the Sultan and criticism of the ruler's passivity as Caliph led to his being committed to a mental asylum for *lèse majesté*. A doctor inspected him, but concluded: "If there is a trace of madness in him, there is no sane person in the world."[14] He was transferred to prison. His devotees report that the Minister of Justice, Şefik Paşa, visited him there, offering him a salary, to be increased after he returned to the east. Nursi refused the inducement but was released.

For a brief period, he gave his support to the Young Turks, but during the turmoil of April 1909, he preached in Ayasofya, "with that famous Kurdish dress and heroic manner of his, as always with a dagger at his waist."[15] He was briefly arrested, accused of being part of the counter-revolution. He then left İstanbul for Van where, for a short period, the Porte sent him funds for his cherished university.

After Abdülhamid's deposition, he re-presented his petition for the university to Mehmed V Reşad. The new Sultan invited Nursi to the opening of a university in Kosovo, placing the young Kurd beside him on a receiving balcony. Nursi returned to Van, and, again supported by the Porte, laid the foundation stone for his university.

The Russian invasion of 1914 saw Nursi at the head of a Kurdish militia, on horseback, a gun in hand. He would later paint himself as a compelling leader who assured his troops: "Advance. A heathen shot cannot kill us. We will not stoop to retreat."[16]

In February 1916, he was taken prisoner, being held for two years in the Volga town of Kostroma. At one point, Nicholas Nikolaevich, the

Tsar's uncle, passed in front of him. Nursi remained seated, not rising. The Grand Duke, insulted, asked Nursi to explain himself. Nursi replied: "I am a Moslem scholar. I have faith in my heart. A man with faith is superior to one without. If I were to pay respect to you, I would be dishonouring my faith."[17]

The Grand Duke ordered his arraignment. Nursi refused to apologize and was sentenced to death. He asked for fifteen minutes to say his prayers. During this time, the Grand Duke returned and, according to the approved history, said that he accepted that Nursi had acted because of his religion, and asked for forgiveness.[18]

In the confusion following the October Revolution, Nursi escaped. News of his return to İstanbul was on the front page of the pro-government *Tanin*, and he was received by Enver Paşa. Police reports of the time describe him as being of medium height, with hazel eyes, a complexion the colour of wheat, and no distinguishing characteristics. Photographs reflect an almost swashbuckling character. He was a public figure and in March 1920 became one of the founders of what became the Green Crescent, a charity to protect people from drugs, alcohol, tobacco, and gambling.

Five months after his return, İstanbul came under Allied occupation. Nursi's writings of that time include a poem thanking the monkey whose bite had killed the Greek King Alexander I, a placeman of the British, and an anonymous tract supporting the nationalists. The British commander wanted him executed, but, warned of the outrage this would cause, was dissuaded.

Leaving Ankara in spring 1923, on the long journey to Van, Nursi left behind what he called the Old Said, and committed himself to eschewing political activism, arguing that individual piety could be cultivated under any political system. For the New Said, such piety should be combined with "positive action" (*müspet hareket*). "Nursi considered that a grass-roots social and religious transformation of the individual was required first, and that broader social transformation would follow when the time and circumstances were right."[19]

He spent the next two years by the shores of Lake Van and in a ruined monastery. In the fevered days at the end of the *Şeyh* Said rebellion, he was arrested, mounted on a horse, accompanied over the snow-covered mountain passes to Trabzon, embarking to İstanbul. He was able to show that he had given short shrift to offers of gold to join the rebellion. He said he had told the *Şeyh*'s representative:

> The Kurds and the Turks are one. They are brothers. The Turkish nation has carried the flag for Islam for a thousand years and given millions of martyrs on behalf of religion. For this reason, no sword should be drawn against the grandsons of the heroic and self-sacrificing defenders of Islam, and I will not do so.[20]

All the same, he was exiled, first to Burdur then Isparta in southern Anatolia, both market towns of 40,000 people. He was soon attracting so many visitors that he was sailed to the remote village of Barla. In all, he was to spend twenty-five years in internal exile.

The New Said eschewed politics, concentrating on teaching a few disciples and writing, but, amid the paranoia of the time, those were dangerous activities. In July 1932, he was detained for making the call to prayer in Arabic—a breach of government rules, but not an imprisonable offence until later. Further arrests started in 1935 and continued through the İnönü period. The usual charge was infringing Article 163 of the Penal Code forbidding exploitation of religion for political purposes. The first of these cases saw him and 120 of his disciples tried in Eskişehir.[21] He received a prison sentence of twelve months, while fifteen of his followers were given sentences of six months. On release, he was sent to Kastamonu, being kept there under enforced residence for seven years.[22]

A similar case was opened in 1944 in Denizli. This time, after eight months in prison, Nursi and seventy-three of his alleged students were found innocent; a committee of law professors opined that *Risale-i Nur* was a purely religious work.[23] A third case led to his spending much of 1948 and 1949 in prison in Afyon. Alleged disciples from elsewhere were rounded up. A number of the students were bastinadoed, one young teacher who had been seen talking with Nursi being beaten until he passed out. In December 1948, he was given a twenty-month sentence, and twenty-one others received terms up to eighteen months. An appeal court acquitted them. The court in Afyon was incensed and held the prisoners for a further nine months.

With the election of the Democrats to power, religious themes began to re-emerge in public discourse. Nursi, sensing the change, moved on to what he would call his Third Said stage, one where he favoured accommodation with political power in order to further the cause of religion. He was quick to congratulate Celal Bayar on his election as president and to commend the government for sending troops to Korea. He visited İstanbul for the 500th anniversary of its conquest by Mehmed the Conqueror. He sent a copy of his major work to Pope Pius XII; called on the Ecumenical

Patriarch, Athenagoras I; and welcomed Turkey's accession to the Baghdad Pact linking Turkey, Iran, and Pakistan with the U.K. and the U.S. (a non-signatory).

His staunch anti-communism aligned well with the Cold War mood of the Turkish establishment, and conditions improved for him. The Minister of Education, Tevfik İleri, asked him to host a deputy minister from Pakistan. Nevertheless, in 1952 he still faced two further court appearances. On both occasions, thousands of students turned out to support the beturbaned Nursi. His followers too continued to be prosecuted. During the ten-year rule of the DP, thirty-seven cases were brought against the readers of his works, each of which ended in acquittal.

In this last decade of his life, he showed slightly more political involvement than he had in the New Said phase. He argued that the rule of law provided the best environment for the rejuvenation of Islam. However, he discouraged the establishment of pro-Islamic parties in the polarized conditions of the time, fearing such parties might seek to exploit Islam for opportunistic goals. He continued to maintain that, if the majority of the population began to consciously identify with Islam, the anti-religious policies of the Kemalist Republic would wither away. He asked the state to publish his works so as to combat atheism and nihilism.

Nursi had produced his work by dictating in the Turkish of the day to a disciple who wrote it out in Ottoman script.[24] Numerous copyists would then set to work, with a veritable cottage industry developing in towns close to Nursi's place of exile in Barla and in the villages around Kastamonu. An English devotee of Nursi who has written his biography records:

> ... there were eventually thousands of Nur students, men and women, young and old, who devoted themselves to writing out copies of [the *Risale-i Nur*]. Of these, some did not emerge from their houses for seven or eight years. Even in the village of Sav [near Isparta], which came to be known as the Nur School, the treatises of the *Risale-i Nur* were duplicated by literally a thousand pens.[25]

This steady trickle of clandestine texts became a stream in the 1940s when the hidden fellowship got its first duplicating machine. Come 1956 and the courts finally accepted the legality of his *Risale-i Nur*, opening the way for it being printed in the Turkish alphabet. Paper, a scarce state-controlled commodity, was made available. Turkey's largest exercise in *samizdat* (self-publishing) was over, ending before this practice had even begun in the

Soviet Union. Nursi exclaimed, "My duty is finished. This is the time I have long awaited. Now I can go."[26]

In December 1959, Nursi became anxious that the Democrats would be ousted by İnönü's CHP, Islam would suffer, and Turkey would be subject to invasion by communists. He urged the Democrats to convert Ayasofya back into a mosque. His visits to Ankara, Konya, and İstanbul—in a 1953 Chevrolet contributed by his supporters—caused thousands to flock to him, and the CHP to react with alarm. Journalists dogged his steps and, while Menderes defended Nursi's freedom of travel, in January 1960, the police prevented him from re-entering Ankara.

Two months later, suffering from pneumonia, he arrived in Urfa. Learning that hundreds of visitors were flocking to his hotel, the Minister of Interior, Namık Gedik, ordered his deportation back to Isparta. A crowd of 5,000 people, a local doctor, and the chairman of the local branch of the Democrat Party blocked this. Nursi died forty hours after his arrival in the city and was buried at the Halîlürrahman Külliyesi, a grand local mosque complex. The local governor, deputies from the Democrat Party, and followers from all over Turkey attended the funeral.

That May, the military seized power and exhumed him in July. They changed the original wooden coffin for a smaller galvanized one, flew it to Isparta, and buried it in an unmarked grave. Nursi might have appreciated this; he did not wish for his tomb to become a shrine. It did not stay unknown long. In 1969, villagers digging a fresh grave in the cemetery of Sav, a town east of Isparta, came across a galvanized coffin. One of them claimed to recognize the hennaed hair and features of Bediüzzaman. Until at least 2015, the grave remained unmarked.

Almost his last recorded words were: "They never understood me. They always wanted to mix me up with politics."

Epistle and legacy

Nursi had not supported calls for the restoration of the Caliphate as a central Muslim institution. His emphasis was on the individual believer and the latter's interactions with his fellow believers. He resisted calls for establishment of an order on the lines of a *tarikat*, as he believed not in leaders of Islam but in the body of the faithful. The recurrent theme in his works is the need to mobilize Muslims as individuals and as members of the community, but not as subjects of a political order. This support for social mobilization perhaps explains the apprehension towards him from the rulers of the Republic.

In an introduction written to one of his early works in the late 1950s, he describes the stages of his sloughing off the intellectual and philosophical sciences in which he was steeped. He writes that "the wound of philosophical discourse" prevented him from finding the ultimate truth in the *tarikat* and that the Indian mystic, Ahmed-i Sirhindi (Ahmad as-Sirhindi, 1564–1624) sent him a hidden message to find a single master. "This came to the deeply wounded heart of the Old Said as: 'The true master is the *Kur'an*. Finding a single master will be with that one.'"

Half a millennium before Sirhindi, the impressive Persian polymath, Abu Hamid al-Ghazali (1058–1111), argued that God is the source of all essence, and nature a marvel of creation. No one who had studied anatomy, he argued, could fail to recognize in the perfection of human and animal organs evidence of the Creator's master hand. In his view, seeking to defend Islam by going against mathematical or logical truth was committing a grievous crime against religion.[27] His *Ihya Ulum al-Din* (The Revival of Religious Sciences), with its emphasis on the importance of correct ritual, is a favoured text in modern times.

Nursi drew on these ideas as well as the constructs of the Andalusian theosophist, Muhyi al-Din Ibn al-Arabi (1165–1240). Ibn Arabi affirmed that the goal of each seeker of divine knowledge should be to explore every known path of knowledge in order to experience the infinity of the divine in one's self.[28] From Ibn Arabi, Nursi derived the notion of subject and object merged in a unity of being (*vahdet-i vücûd*). Man is the microcosmic being through which God contemplates himself on earth. "God, then, is the mirror in which those seest thyself as thou art, His mirror in which He contemplates His names."[29]

Nursi himself showed some influence of European Enlightenment ideals when he wrote that mankind "will obtain all its strength from science. Power and rule will pass to the hands of science."[30] More than fifty of the 724 pages of the Vahide translation of Nursi's *The Words* have favourable references to science.

In Europe, thinkers such as Leibniz had kept a bridge between religion and science, but in the Ottoman Empire and early Republic there was no precursor, and Nursi had to develop his thesis that there was no clash between the *Kur'an* and modern science. He did so by limiting his use of an inevitably elitist mysticism, instead drawing from the findings and metaphors of biology, knowledge of which was relatively advanced in the Empire, combining this with a folk imagery familiar to his main audience, the everyday inhabitants of Anatolia.

In Nursi's time, this region was a periphery in flux, its people, rooted in the mosque, *tekke*, and *tarikat*, shaken by the rhetoric and practices of the Republic, which was linking their past to Central Asia and offering them a future modelled on Europe. Nursi understood the needs of those left out of the modern stream, the "traditionals on the move," as Mardin called the broad stratum from which Nursi drew his followers.[31] They were looking for a new expansion of human horizons, for which religion fuelled the discourse. Nursi enriched this discourse, while also appealing to the pride of those resenting "becoming beggars of Europe for science and enlightenment," as one retired officer put it.[32] In Nursi's view, it was the *Kur'an* that could be used to raise his tormented compatriots' vision.[33] Nursi considered that the *Kur'an* had a face that looks to every age, and set out to explain that face which looked to his time. The *Risale-i Nur* is a commentary on themes and truths set out in the *Kur'an* rather than on its texts. [34]

Nursi's impact in Turkey has been of a scale to cause Islamic historians to suggest that he is one of the renewers of Islam whom God will provide. For Nursi himself—and most Nakşibendis—the most recent renewer was Halid el-Bağdadi, one of whose cloaks was presented to an appreciative Nursi in around 1940. The classic definition of a fresh *müceddid* (*mujaddid*), as such a renewer of the faith is termed, is one who has a "palpable and broad influence attested by one's contemporaries." For one Islamic scholar, Nursi met this definition.[35]

Nursi ascribed a divine contribution to his teaching.

> As for the *Risale-i Nur* and its spokesman [or interpreter: *tercüman*, i.e. Bediüzzaman itself], this exalted work contains a sublime effusion [*feyz*] and infinite perfection that have never been encountered in any similar book. It is manifest that it has inherited, in a fashion unattained by any other work, the effusions [*füyüzat*] of the *Qu'ran*, which is a divine lamp, the sun of guidance and the star of felicity. It is therefore a truth as bright as the sun that the foundation of the *Risale-i Nur* is the unmixed light of the *Qur'an*...[36]

Many Muslims look askance at all this. Causing particular objections are Nursi's claims that thirty-three verses of the *Kur'an* foreshadow the *Risale-i Nur* and the Nurcus' identifying Islam with one man, Said Nursi, and so focusing on his writings.

Such concerns have limited his influence on mainstream Islamic theology, but where he has won broad respect is in inspiring a movement that revived the reach of Islam in the face of the Kemalists' secularist attacks and made a conscious effort to grapple with the problems of reconciling Islamic beliefs with scientific discovery.[37] The spread of this influence is the more remarkable given the punitive conditions of the times and the long censorship of his works.

With the free publication of *Risale-i Nur*, the study centres (*dershane*) which were to become such a feature of the Nurcu movement—and of Fethullah Gülen—began to be opened throughout the country.

Süleyman Tunahan—keeping the flame alight

The year 1959 saw a seemingly abstruse quarrel in Ankara, when the pugnacious Gedik, overruling his fellow ministers, forbade a preacher to be buried in the hallowed grounds of the mosque of Mehmed the Conqueror in İstanbul. Süleyman Hilmi Tunahan had served as a teacher at the imperial mosque, but, with four arrests and copious police files built up during three decades of harassment, he was too well known to the authorities and, in particular, to the vengeful Gedik for them to respect his dying wishes. Instead, as a crowd of mourners waited in the mosque, the police forced his family to a graveyard on the other side of the Bosphorus.

Today, the grave of Gedik is unfeted; he was arrested by the military in May 1960, committing suicide three days later by jumping from a window at the Ankara War College, or so his captors claimed. By contrast, the last resting place of Tunahan is visited by thousands each month.

His elegant mausoleum, with its seven columns representing the seven levels of Sufi enlightenment, is located under the tranquil conifers of Karacaahmet graveyard. His venerants included Erdoğan's late mother, who asked to be buried beside him. Her wishes led to the area being brusquely cleared of a dozen Ottoman tombs for her and her husband (previously entombed elsewhere)—with four plots left beside them under a gilt inscription from the *Kur'an* in Arabic and the words "the Erdoğan family" in Ottoman Turkish. Many believe that the president too wishes to be laid here.

Kısakürek, who met Tunahan in 1946, described him as "a person with a rosy complexion, a light brown beard tinged with grey, an aquiline nose, smiling inside his chestnut-colored eyes, and worthy of his beautiful expression."[38]

Few photographs survive of this man who continues to inspire millions of his countrymen. There is one of him in his thirties, large black eyes blazing above a cropped black beard. The pose is that of a man in front of a police camera. The more familiar image is from the decade before his death, of a slight, trim, avuncular, warm, and humorous figure, wearing a turban in the white-and-black colours of the Nakşibendi. It is a more appropriate representation of this *şeyh* who claimed a line of initiation reaching back to the Prophet, and it is this image which is in the heart of his followers throughout Turkey and the Turkish diaspora, and which they are asked to recall in all their prayers.

Tunahan was born into a mid-ranking Ottoman family in a small town south of the Danube. His father, Osman Efendi, was a well-known Islamic scholar following the Nakşibendi tradition. While studying in Silistre, Tunahan dreamt that he entered the company of Bahaeddin Nakşibend who, seeing the young man, told him an empty seat was for him and that a teacher would find him. Just after this, Tunahan came to İstanbul and, still only a nineteen-year-old student, met the Nakşibendi *Şeyh* Selahaddin Sakıb. Selahaddin reportedly asked the young Tunahan if he had had a dream where he was told to fill an empty seat. Answered in the affirmative, Selahaddin told Tunahan he had come from Turkestan to be his teacher and, after a month's instruction, appointed Tunahan to be his precocious successor.

This unlikely tale is found in all the admiring histories of Tunahan, and allows him to claim a *silsile* to the Prophet, even if it requires the suspension of judgement that is sometimes necessary with such claims. Whatever the case, Tunahan proved a capable student at the three main schools of the Empire. He graduated in 1923, his studies having included logic and astronomy, and started teaching at the main *medrese* of the capital.

In March 1924, the new Republic subjected all education to the Ministry of Education. The various changes left many Islamic teachers without a job. Tunahan, who had become president of the association of *medrese* teachers in İstanbul, gathered around 520 of them and, proclaiming he wished to ensure the survival of Islam, urged them to carry on their teaching on an unpaid basis. A few agreed, together with him telegraphing Ankara with their offer. They were told they would be breaking the law.

With official teaching blocked, Tunahan continued as a preacher in several of the most prominent mosques of İstanbul. He also continued giving lessons, delivering underground *Kur'an* courses in the basement of his home in old İstanbul and in private houses.

In 1930, Tunahan, his teaching restricted by recurrent intimidation, left İstanbul for Thrace, rented a farm, and became a distributor of kerosene. He leased an oak forest and started producing charcoal. He would gather those working there and instruct them in the *Kur'an*. Interference by the local police caused him to move to the mountains south-east of Konya where he started rearing dairy buffalo. At one point, he bought a tile factory in Adapazarı.

The biography on his supporters' website emphasizes his commitment to instruction, whether in forest or farm, mosque or basement: "He also taught on intercity trains. At times when he failed to find any students, he taught his two daughters at home."[39] One follower recounts how, sent as an officer to trace Tunahan, he noted two passenger cars idle in a siding at Erzurum station. The station manager confided that they housed Tunahan and a group of students. The follower covered for them.

In November 1937, the *Diyanet* formally accepted him as an *imam*, and he moved back to İstanbul, preaching in small mosques before leading prayers in various imperial mosques. As his prestige grew, so did the numbers of disciples who came to his clandestine Islamic lessons—and so did police interest. It was a period of ordeal, with numerous police raids on his house. On two occasions, he was held in the coffin cells of the İstanbul Security Police, being tortured there, according to the *Diyanet*'s *İslam Ansiklopedisi,* in 1939 and 1944.

In 1943, his preaching authority was cancelled by the Ministry of Interior. However, he was paid a monthly wage until February 1950—and payments resumed a year later when the Democrats appointed a new head to the *Diyanet* and his permit was restored.[40]

That year, he started his first *Kur'an* course with boarding facilities, taking in twenty-five students at a borrowed house in Çamlıca. Uncritical biographies of him recount that he insisted that no money should be taken from the students. By 1955, he was sacrificing a lamb a week for his students.[41] In parallel, he started courses for *imam*. These continued despite an interrogation by the police for castigating Turkish support for France in Algeria. He reminded his questioners of the help the Muslims of Algeria had given the Turkish army during the War of Independence.

In this case, the questioning was less hostile than in 1939 and 1944 and than it would be in 1957, when he was detained for a further fifty-nine days, again being maltreated. The last arrest followed a call to rebellion by a self-proclaimed messianic redeemer in Bursa, and electoral politics played a role. His son-in-law, Kemal Kacar, was standing against the Democrat Party, and it suited the Democrats to hobble the latter's election campaign. Tunahan was insulted and beaten unconscious. Kacar was arrested at the same time and treated similarly. They were released at the first hearing and later acquitted. The prosecutor had asked for a death sentence.

Tunahan died from diabetes in 1959 and was succeeded by Kacar, a student of his since 1936 and husband of his elder daughter, Hatice Bedia, since 1944. The two men were close, sharing a sense of mission and ordeals with authority. Kacar, though happy for adulation, never formally advanced himself as the spiritual heir of Tunahan, whose declared chain to the Prophet ended with his death. The followers of Tunahan are now known as Süleymancıs. It was Kacar who developed them into the international body they have become.

Necip Fazıl Kısakürek—nurturing the Ottoman dream

In 1946, Kacar had introduced Tunahan to the nationalist poet, Necip Fazıl Kısakürek, starting a friendship that, with reservations caused by Kısakürek's gambling and wayward behaviour, would continue through Tunahan's life. The latter had understood the importance of print media in propagating the faith, and this allied him to Kısakürek, whose reach spread through the country's urban communities.

Kısakürek was a poet, author, journalist, and polemicist. He grew up in the mansion of his grandfather in the Çemberlitaş area of old İstanbul. His grandfather had been president of the Criminal Court of Appeals and prided himself on descending from notables in south-east Turkey. The young scion was encouraged to read translations of French romantics, but his early grounding in French culture left him in a state of disorientation. Writing of this when in his seventies, he emphasized the gulf between the culture of this household and that of the Empire:

> At the time when women's hair descended to their ankles, my grandmother with her clipped hair reminiscent of women's fashions of today, with her grand demeanour and jewels which were the envy of İstanbul, the parties she gave, her mechanical piano and her baskets full of novels mostly translated from the West, with her interior decoration that was a mix of every possible style, exhibited the model of the refined lady of İstanbul; a style passed on to the Young Turks by the preceding Hamidian era, a taste made of Eastern and Western condiments in equal proportions, a residue of the *Tanzimat* reforms, racked by neurotic fears, a person displaced from her axis who had found none to replace it.[42]

His early years were dominated by this angst over cultural identity. He spent a year at the Sorbonne in Paris on a government scholarship, his interest in literature helping him develop a capital that he was to use throughout his writing career. It proved a bohemian phase distinguished by two enduring elements of his character: an addiction to gambling and periodic dissolution followed by bouts of contrition worthy of Dostoyevsky. His memoirs and autobiography emphasize that Paris, for all its "designs of miraculous refinement," disguised "ruin and darkness; a civilization that was condemned to hit its head against one wall after another and play hide and seek from one crisis after another."[43] This consuming doubt about the fundamental values of the West and its spiritual crisis was to colour his later discourse.

Aged around 29, he met Abdülhakim Arvasi, *şeyh* of the Kaşgari Murtaza Efendi Mosque in Eyüp and a prominent Nakşibendi. Arvasi was a product of the network that el-Bağdadi had established in the Ottoman Empire. A sense of unity with the history and culture stretching through these lands was to inspire Kısakürek.

A regular contributor to the press, in 1936 he launched his own magazine, *Ağaç* (Tree), which followed a spiritualist and idealist line contrary to the materialist ideas of *Kadro* (Cadre), a magazine which had flourished in the early 1930s, advocating development that would be neither capitalist nor socialist but Turkish. *Ağaç* attracted some of the most talented writers of the time, not least the great Ahmet Hamdi Tanpınar. But, short of readers, it closed after seventeen issues.

At this point, Kısakürek wrote the play *Bir Adam Yaratmak* (Creating a Man), a resonant tale of spiritual angst, suicide, and murder, which ran in state theatres for four years. He then won a prize for rewriting the national anthem. The prize had been offered by *Ulus* (Nation), the newspaper of the ruling CHP, and led to his *Büyük Doğu* (Great East), an eighteen-line paean that opens "Oh, liberated land, chosen by Allah" and concludes "Let the Great East be born, born from me! The mirror of my horizon a flag of fire! My father's ashes, you, black earth!"

The project to change the national anthem was apparently quashed by Atatürk, but Kısakürek had declared his colours. Five years later, under the name *Büyük Doğu*, he launched a periodical evoking a heritage of which every Turk could be proud and which made no bows to any cultural superiority of Europe. Despite his good terms with at least part of the establishment in Ankara, after thirty issues, *Büyük Doğu* was closed down. His followers allege that the British considered the weekly as supporting the Axis, and lent on the wartime government. It was not to reopen until the war was over.

This was only the first of numerous interruptions that *Büyük Doğu* was to suffer during its thirty-five years and 521 issues. A number of the breaks were because Kısakürek was under arrest. He spent nineteen months in prison after the 1960 coup. More time in jail followed. Only his death in 1983 saved him from serving an eighteen-month sentence for criticizing Atatürk.

From late 1939, *Büyük Doğu* adopted a clearly pro-Islamic tinge, publishing extracts from the teachings of Arvasi and from Nursi's *Risale-i Nur*. By this time, Kısakürek had set out his stall as a polemicist, attacking secularism and promoting religion, denouncing communism, freemasonry, and the Jewish influence on Turkey and the world.

Antisemitism was rife in the young Republic. It was evident in the state apparatus, which tolerated a pogrom in Thrace in 1934 and bought 40,000 copies of Cevat Rıfat Atılhan's inflammatory *Suzy Liberman, Jewish Spy* for army officers.[44] It was also a rallying cause for conservative opponents of the secular regime. Contributing to this was Hitler's *Mein Kampf*, published in Turkey soon after it appeared in Germany in 1925, with a fresh print run every year until 1945.[45]

To some of this generation of traditionalists, the Young Turks were a Jewish conspiracy, backed by the British to weaken the Empire. Central to their assertions was that the Young Turks came from the largely Jewish city of Salonika and included among their leaders various *dönme*. The Turkish word for a convert, this term is used to refer to the descendants of Jews who converted to Islam at the end of the seventeenth century along with their messiah, Shabbatai Tsevi.

Kısakürek chose as his focus for abuse the journalist and newspaper owner, Ahmed Emin Yalman. His writings seem to have encouraged the attempt on Yalman's life by the nineteen-year-old Hüseyin Üzmez in Malatya in November 1952. Kısakürek was arraigned for this—and, finding it a convenient pretext to cast their net widely, the prosecutors also named Nursi as a conspirator. Both were acquitted.[46] The lawsuits against Kısakürek continued. But the Democrats found other ways to support him, paying him from the prime minister's secret budget during at least six of their ten years in office.[47]

A term in prison is no handicap in Turkey. Before Kısakürek died, he was to be termed "The Sultan of Poetry" by the Turkish Literary Foundation and "The Intellectual and Artist of the Year" by the Turkish Writers' Association. But one Turkish critic from the Second New literary school was less appreciative, writing that Kısakürek had gone to Paris as a Turk without a personality and returned as a Westerner without a personality.

As a French historian had written a century earlier, "in the absence of institutions, literature becomes one," and Kısakürek's influence during Turkey's troubled 1960s and 1970s was pervasive.[48] In the provinces, his network of *Büyük Doğu Fikir Ocakları* (Great East Thinkers' Hearths) provided a forum for intellectual debate. In the major cities, he became a mentor for youth seeking to counter the influence of the rising wave of radical leftism. He was particularly appreciated by the MTTB (*Milli Türk Talebe Birliği*, National Turkish Students Association), the rightist student movement. They cheered his 1965 call to reopen Ayasofya to prayer, and it was at their National Youth Night in 1975 that he first read his stirring "Oh youth, Oh youth, Oh youth," a clarion call to take inspiration from seven centuries of bloodshed for nation and religion.[49]

The young Erdoğan was almost certainly there that night. A year earlier, today's president had won a prize for his recital of a poem by Kısakürek about a wrongly imprisoned father writing to his son. "I write the poems, you declaim them," Kısakürek told him.[50] A year after the MTTB night, Erdoğan became the MTTB's director of cultural affairs.[51]

Many of the MTTB's members, Erdoğan included, supported the pro-Islamic National Salvation Party (*Milli Selamet Partisi*, MSP). Erdoğan himself—in contested elections—had become head of the party's youth wing.[52] When the MSP cast off its Akıncılar youth movement as too violent, Erdoğan turned to Kısakürek for the inspiration of the party's new youth movement, with the latter describing this as a burning light bulb.[53]

Erdoğan has shown his enduring respect for the poet, attending the funeral of his son, Ömer, in 2005, tweeting a poem by Kısakürek on the 35th anniversary of the intemperate sage's death, and citing him when reopening Ayasofya for prayer. Nor is Erdoğan alone among those influenced by the crusty writer. There is a photograph of Turgut Özal at Kısakürek's funeral in 1983. Just before this, Özal had sought the poet-polemicist's advice on his new party, being told: "Turgut Bey, you must be like the tracks on a tank. You must travel fast and adapt to the terrain."

Kısakürek promoted the centrality of Islam in Turkish culture, countering the accusation of Turkish secular thinkers that Islamic thought is intrinsically primitive through his literary works and their characteristic modern discourse. Completing this atavistic offer was his recourse to selected nationalist themes of Ottoman glory, which blended seamlessly with Islam in a way that the secular Republic's recourse to the legends of the Turks in Central Asia never could. He reached those affected by social disruption far more effectively than the secularists did. As Mardin concluded, social scientists have too often failed to see the function of culture in binding people: "Paradoxically, in Turkey the growth of modern media *reinforced* rather than weakened the Islamic cultural thrust."[54]

5

THE NAKŞIBENDIS
ON THE PATH OF THE MASTERS

Trafficking with kings and conquering their souls to protect the Muslims from the evil of oppressors.

A description of his policies by Ubeydullah Ahrar, a fifteenth-century Nakşibendi *şeyh*, possibly the richest man in Transoxiana[1]

The world of the Nakşibendis

Of the 306 dervish lodges in late-Ottoman İstanbul, 62, a mere one fifth, belonged to the Nakşibendis. So recorded a survey on behalf of Abdülhamid's prying bureaucracy, and this overstated their presence: up to 20 of the lodges attributed to them belonged to the Bektaşis but still could not be admitted as such.[2]

Six generations later, the Nakşibendis' competitors have fallen by the wayside. Today, all the religious orders and communities shaping Turkey's politics are hued by this one fraternity, which gives honoured place to a fourteenth-century mystic with blood on his hands, and reflects the teaching developed as its masters tried to counter the British blighting of Muslim power in India. They are, in effect, the only show in town.

The Nakşibendis are one of the great Sufi orders, challenged only by the Kadiris (Qadiris) and Wahhabis in their spread, and competing with the latter in political impact. From Chechnya to eastern China, they are at the forefront of Muslim resistance to external domination. They are prominent from Pakistan to Indonesia, being sparse only in the Maghreb, sub-Saharan Africa, and the Arabian Peninsula.

Various explanations have been put forward for their rise. It is a phenomenon lived to the full in Turkey but evident across the world. Some have sought to link their vitality to the order's doctrines, the inherent simplicity of their focus on the primacy of the *Kur'an*, the mobilizing force of their polemical opposition to the Shia and the Wahhabis, and their visceral distrust of a colonizing Europe. Others suggest that it is because the privacy of their forms of celebration has enabled them better to weather oppression. A few point to their decentralized, non-hierarchical structure and the paucity of the hereditary practices that weakened other orders. Others argue that from early on, they believed in working with the realities of the time. They are, of all the Sufis, the consummate politicians.

The order was born in Khorasan, was re-established in Mughal India on an anti-colonial basis that the Khorasanis never dreamed of, and flourished in the Ottoman Empire. Its trajectory colours its activities in Turkey today. Khorasan is the heartland of Sufi mysticism, with the dervishes proselytizing among the shamanistic Turkic tribes and being left largely alone by the Islamic judges, preachers, and teachers in the region's storied cities. In Mughal India, the order faced the problem of how to respond to a largely Hindu society with its own religion and intellectuals who were in no manner inferior to those of Islam.[3] Later, they were prominent in Muslim reaction to the inroads of avaricious powers as Britain and France challenged Muslim authority in India, threatened the Ottoman Caliph's position in the Arab world, and competed with Russia for control of İstanbul and the Bosphorus. They thus more clearly focused on the West as the 'other' rather than on backsliders who had forgotten the orthodox Islamic emphasis on the unicity of God.[4] Indeed, for the Ottomans, they also formed a natural part of a polity pervaded by Sufi orders but anxious for allies against the heterodoxy which had come with the Turkic tribes.

Like other orders, over the centuries, their original fount of mystical spirituality has split into a hundred or more rivulets, some lost in the sands of time, others growing in strength across time. Each of these links to a *silsile* tracing back to the Prophet, enhancing the prestige of the order's members and helping bind them to one another.

The uncertain quality of these links does not diminish the nature of the great institutions that many of these rivulets became, with foundations and lodges (not always in good repair), arcane and extensive hierarchies, lifelong career patterns, and prestige. Instead, the links reveal the characteristics that later members of the chain thought meritorious. But, as such historical details tend to distract attention from the mysticism at the heart of Sufism, it is worth remembering the place of Sufi devotions in a Muslim's rightful worship:

> ... the punctilious observance of the forms of worship prescribed as obligatory for all Muslims (canonical prayer, fasting, pilgrimage) has primacy over all else; simply to enumerate the methods of *dhikr* [Turkish *zikir*, remembrance] practised by the order would be deceptive. Contrary to much common belief, the ritual acts prescribed by the *Shari'a* are neither inherently defective practises that the distinctive rites of Sufism must supplement nor mere prerequisites or points of departure for the practice of the path. These acts, if performed with devotion and regularity, create in those predisposed to receive it a fund of constantly renewed spiritual energy.[5]

The God of Islam is loving but stern, and the Sufi orders make the divine more accessible. For the Muslim, binding him or her to the *ümmet* are the communal rituals of Friday prayers and the *hajj*, the pilgrimage to Mecca during the holy month. To its practitioners, Sufism is a natural expression of personal religion, an assertion of a person's right to pursue a life of contemplation seeking contact with the source of being. For such believers, *zikir*, the act of union with—or at least of remembrance of—God, is a link to the spirit of Koranic piety which had flowed into the lives and modes of expression of the early devotees and ascetics.[6] And for the orders, the *zikir* is central to their identity and a centripetal force for their disciples, involving a collective recollection of the disciple's unity with God at a ceremony of joint remembrance, performed at a gathering with fellow believers, under the guidance of the head of the order, the *şeyh*, or his nominee.

This ceremony helps bring the individual close to his creator, in its ultimate extension leading to a form of ecstasy, which varies from states induced by the self-piercing of the Rifai, through those resulting from the haunting rituals of the courtly Mevlevi, to the private experience of the individual.

For almost all *tarikat*, the celebration of the *zikir* is the pivot of his (less often, her) membership of the *tarikat* and the framework uniting the *tarikat* itself. *Zikir* takes three forms: daily (*dhikr al-awkat*, the prescribed five prayers), personal (*dhikr al-khafi* and *bi'l-jalala*), and communal (*dhikr al-hadra*). It is the last of these, with rituals involving music and dancing, which inspires orders such as the Cerrahiyye and the Mevleviyye, as well as the Rifaiyye, some of whose adepts' frenzies made them a visitor's attraction in nineteenth-century İstanbul.

The communal *zikir* takes place in the *tarikat*'s lodge one evening a week, normally Thursday or Friday, as well as on religious occasions and the anniversaries of deaths of important *şeyh*. The rite usually starts and ends with a repetition of the divine names as in the first verse of the *Kur'an*, *Al-Fatihah* (The Opening). This is often through the *tahlil* (rejoicing) formulation *la ilaha illa Allah* (There is no god but Allah), accompanied by controlled breathing. The use of breath control, important to other religious disciplines and yoga, may limit the supply of oxygen to the brain, inducing an unusual psychic state. Other rituals follow that may enhance this, including the head jerking of the Kubrawiyye-Nuriyye (a Central Asian order), the gentle turning from right to left of the Kadiriyye, and the spinning of the Mevleviyye.[7]

Sufi rites generally fall into three categories: sitting (*kuudi/qu'udi*), standing (*kıyamı/qıyami*) and step by step or grouped in turning circles (*devrani/dawrani*).

In the first, the *şeyh* sits on a sheepskin, generally red, the colour of manifestation, though other colours are also used, and the Celvetiyye prefer a prayer rug to a hide. The participants sit in circles around him, their places predetermined by rank and seniority. After recital of *Al-Fatihah* comes commemoration of the Prophet and reaffirmation that the Prophet has a higher claim on the believers than they have on their own selves (the sixth verse of the *Al-Ahzab sura*). This is followed by recitation or incantation of selections from the *Kur'an*, each order having its own selections. Next comes recitation of the *Kelime-i Tevhid*, the declaration of the unity of God. Further verses from the *Kur'an* are read, and after a prayer and repetition of the name of God, the ceremony draws to a conclusion.

Standing rites are performed by the Kadiri and Rifai and a few other orders. Worshippers generally start in the sitting position, and then rise and start swaying or dancing. As for the *devran* rituals (when dervishes circle step by step or dance, often with their arms on each other's shoulders) these are characteristic of orders developing in Turkish lands, not least the Mevlevi and Halveti.[8]

Where the turning is concerned, the eleventh-century Sufi master, al-Ghazali, writes:

> The dancing is a reference to the circling of the spirit round the cycle of existing things on account of receiving the effects of the unveilings and revelations; and this is the state of the gnostic. The whirling is a reference to the spirit's standing with Allah in its inner nature and being, the circling of its look and thought, and its penetrating the ranks of existing things.[9]

The use of music as an aid to Sufi devotion and ecstasy is evident from early days, with some Sufis describing it as one of the most effective ways of showing love. What form this music took is not described in the subsequent attacks on, and defence of, its use. While the Christian is stimulated by the pomp of organ (and choir), the Sufi makes use of simpler classical instruments. Use of the *ney* (a reed flute) is common in Mevlevi rituals. Only rarely is the more complex *kanun*, a zither probably dating back to Minoan times, to be found. The voice, always male, is used in incantation of a sacred prescription, never in aria or oratorio.

In Ottoman times, two orders were particularly known for their music. The first was the Mevleviyye with their stylized music used to accompany spiritual texts, often those of Mevlana himself. The second was the Bektaşiyye whose music generally draws on folk traditions.

A prominent recent commentator writes: "All communal *dhikrs*, though differing in form and style, seek to achieve a submergence of the individual into the communal identity and, by means of such temporary loss of ego-consciousness, a sense of the 'unity of the beyond and the within.'" The *zikir* is thus a manifestation of the quest for human brotherhood and physical solidarity inherent in the *hajj* and the ritual discipline of congregational prayer.[10] It is also performed individually by men and women following the ritual prayer or separately, in mosques or at home.

The *zikir* has survived through the centuries. Ibn Ata Allah wrote a treatise on it in the thirteenth century and by that time it had become one of the seven chief features of the life of all *tarikat* inspired by the "paragon of the sober Sufis," Junaid of Baghdad (Cüneyd-i Bağdadi, 822–909). A century before this treatise, in the view of J. Spencer Trimingham, the Yorkshire missionary who delineated the Sufi orders, the "mechanization (if one may so put it)" of the orders had occurred, and the dervishes acquired a complete technique:

> They employed all sorts of methods to condition the person, open up his consciousness to the attractions of the supra-sensible world: sacred numbers and symbols; colours and smells, perfumes and incense; ritual actions and purifications; words of power, charm-like prayers and incantations, with music and chant; invocations of angels and other spirit beings; even the use of alcohol and drugs.[11]

Each order has its own time-honoured rituals. The different branches of the Halvetiyye, for instance, follow the structure of *zikir* developed half a millennium ago by Yahya Şirvani (d. 1464). Known as *Vird-i Settar*, their ceremony starts with the opening verse from the *Kur'an* and, after five other verses, leads into a series of prayers. The community sits on the ground in front of its *şeyh*, with the rhythms and head-swinging gathering in intensity as the *şeyh*'s invocations become accompanied with a simple cymbal. The *Vird-i Settar* has changed little since it was first written down, and, with few variants, is common to all followers of the Halveti tradition from Indonesia and Chechnya to Anatolia and the Balkans.

Attracting particular attention have been the extravagant *zikir* of the Rifaiyye. These date back to Ahmad ibn Ali ar-Rifai (1106–1182), who lived almost all his life in the marshlands between Basra and Baghdad. A thirteenth-century chronicler records him as a holy man whose "followers experience extraordinary states during which they eat living snakes and enter ovens blazing with fires which are thereupon extinguished. It is said that in their country [the marshlands] they ride on lions and perform similar feats."[12]

Travellers' accounts of such feats continue through the centuries. In the 1860s, the dragoman of the U.S. Legation in Constantinople used to schedule tours to Rifai ceremonies. Some Kadiri lodges shared these rituals. The Dutch anthropologist, Martin Van Bruinessen, describes watching dervishes at a Kadiri *khanaqah* (cloister) of Tabriz in 1973:

> Suddenly one jumped up, grabbed a skewer (some 40 cm long, 5 mm in diameter, with a wooden head to which short metal chains were attached) and, shouting loudly, carried it around the *khanaqah*, holding it up, so as to draw everybody's attention to it. Though he seemed to be in a state of trance he made sure the *khalifa* [the *şeyh*'s deputy] and I, the foreign visitor, took good notice. He then knelt down in front of me and, opening his

> mouth widely and pulling his head far backward, put the skewer with its sharp point on the back of his tongue. Pressing strongly he pushed the skewer through his lower jaw, so that its point came out under his chin. He got up and walked round the *khanaqah*. After some five minutes he pulled the skewer out again, and pressed the wound closed with his thumb. There was not more than just one drop of blood. A few minutes later we shared a cup of tea.[13]

That this was a Kadiri rather than a Rifai *khanaqah* confirms the close relations between the two orders.

In 2019 in the Rifais' Şeyh Mehmet Efendi lodge in Skopje, a Turkish professor calmly explained the use of two instruments on display, the *tığ* and *şiş*, thin and thicker skewers, which would be heated and lain on a dervish's tongue or used to pierce his cheeks or flesh. The professor's audience included the grandson of a Rifai *şeyh* and the *şeyh* of a branch of the Halvetiyye. To them, such harrowing mortifications were marginal to the order's activities. But to many, they were central.

Public worship, mostly less antinomian than that of the Rifais, is practised by all the *tarikat* whose *silsile* trace back through the formalistic Cüneyd-i Bağdadi to the Imam Ali. A second tendency, perhaps more rapturous, looks to the teachings of Abu Yazid al-Bistami (Bâyezîd-i Bistâmî, d. 848 or 875), prioritising personal *zikir* and denouncing exhibitionism. Examples of this heritage in Turkey are the Nakşibendis and Melamis, and abroad the Wahhabis. These believe that the *zikir* should be internal, silent, even occult. They disagree with the concept of public performance of personal rituals—apart from the communal ones of Friday prayer and *hajj*. They reject the use of music.

Shaping the rituals of the Nakşibendis in Turkey are the "renewers of the faith," Ahmed-i Sirhindi of Delhi and the later Halid el-Bağdadi from Kurdish Iraq. The Halidis proclaim that their path rests on four principles. The first is *sohbet* (*suhba*), fellowship with one's *şeyh* and fellow disciples. Next comes *rabıta*, maintaining a constant integral awareness of el-Bağdadi or his hallowed successors. Third is the silent *zikir*. And finally, there is *murakaba* (*muraqaba*), contemplating the divine presence as a bridge to effacement of self and permanence in God.

Shared with other orders is the requirement that, as a channel of divine grace, the *şeyh* should himself be perfect. Nineteenth-century Halidi handbooks stipulate that the *şeyh* should live and think in conformity with the *Shari'a*; be free of desire for fame; acquire and maintain true humility;

be unostentatious in his display of knowledge; and never use his disciples' property for worldly purposes.[14] Twenty-first-century practice often dispenses with this last injunction.

The obligations on the Halidi disciple are many—belief that only his *şeyh* can help him on the path, implying avoidance of other *şeyh*; supplanting his own likes and dislikes with those of his *şeyh*; and respect for his fellow disciples, eating with them whenever possible and never borrowing even a needle or thread.

While such norms are shared with other orders, the Halidis' emphasis on *rabıta*, their second principle, underpins their crystallization as an autonomous Nakşibendi suborder. *Rabıta* is held to open up a channel from the heart of the *şeyh* to that of the disciple, along which passes the divine effulgence that is stored in the *şeyh*'s heart. The beneficial acts of the Sufi masters are believed to continue after their death. Those who wish to so benefit should visit the grave of the dead *şeyh*, stand at its foot on the right side, and call up the spiritual being of the *şeyh* in the form of a column of pure light. Novel in the Halidis' teaching was that el-Bağdadi himself should form the object of *rabıta*, a requirement that has been maintained by some *şeyh*, but has largely been eclipsed in the Halidi communities dominant in Turkey today who propound *rabıta* to their *tarikat*'s more recent saints.

The form of the disciple's silent *zikir* is determined by his *şeyh*. As for the last Halidi principle, *murakaba*, practising this and achieving the direct confrontation of the heart with the reality of the divine essence requires a certain advancement along the Sufi path.

Particular to the Halidis is the *hatm-i hacegan* (*khatm-i khwajagan*), a litany recited in a closed, often darkened room by disciples linked by arms on each other's shoulders. This comprises pleas for God's forgiveness recited silently; verses from the *Kur'an* and calls for blessings on the Prophet; and a spoken prayer (often that composed for this purpose by el-Bağdadi).

The Nakşibendis' "solitude (with God) in the midst of the crowd" makes them far less dependent on the communal meeting place than the "musical" orders who gathered in lodges. Faced with oppression, whether in Tsarist and Soviet Russia or in the early Turkish Republic, the Nakşibendis have not just survived but emerged with an enhanced predominance among the faithful, underlining the abiding appeal of their message of how to manage a challenging world.

Joining an order

In Ottoman days, the faithful would attend the local mosque, participating in the prayers and rituals led by the mosque's *imam*. But for their spiritual solace, many sought the comfort and sense of community created by the *tarikat*. The ceremonies of *zikir* offered a route to greater and eased communion with the divine than did the more limited prayers in the mosque.

A believer would thus draw on both for his/her religious practices, while, as was often the case, concentrating on what the *tarikat* offered in form of esoteric and sometimes ecstatic ritual. Participation in the rituals of a lodge required submission to the *şeyh* running each lodge. Fathers would induct their sons. Membership would thus have an element of tradition and respect to family.

The various orders lived in parallel universes. Some orders were close to each other; others were divided by practices such as the use of music or lack thereof. But the underlying principle was one of respect to those who shared the reverence of the faith. Joining a different *tarikat* did not always require leaving the original one. While a serious step, it was not disrespected.

The early years in Khorasan and Delhi

The saint whose name is carried by the far-flung stalwarts of the Nakşibendi order was born in a small village east of Bukhara, now in Uzbekistan. A feted *şeyh*, Muhammed Baba Semmâsî, used to remark when passing that he could smell the scent of spirituality rising from the local soil. When Bahâeddin Nakşibend (Baha ad-Din Naqshband, 1318–1389) was born there, the *şeyh* declared that he understood the scent, and adopted the infant as his spiritual progeny. Later, he assigned the training of Bahâeddin to Emir Kulal. The latter is said to have been one of the Sufis consulted by Tamerlane, the last of the mighty conquerors from Central Asia. The name Nakşibend derives from the Persian word for the crafts of adorning and embroidering.

So runs one version of how Bahâeddin became a follower of Kulal. A second account tells of how Bahâeddin was an executioner in the services of a certain ruler, Qazan. This must have been a demanding role as a contemporary chronicler records Qazan as "voraciously inclined to the uprooting of ancient families and great amirs."[15] In this role, Bahâeddin was called on to behead a follower of Kulal, but as the condemned man thrice invoked his master's name, thrice did the sword rebound from his neck. In amazement and penitence, Bahâeddin approached Kulal and became his disciple. Later, following the precepts received from a Sufi elder in a vision, he adopted the silent *zikir*, separating himself from the circle of Kulal whenever they engaged in vocal worship.

Bahâeddin left court in 1347, returning to his village of birth and resuming his interrupted spiritual career. His reputation prospered, and half a century after his death, a local ruler built a grand mausoleum over his tomb and convent. This soon became one of the most important places of pilgrimage in Central Asia.[16]

His shrine was in a state of neglect when Turgut Özal, then president of Turkey, visited it in April 1993. Nihat Gökyiğit, one of the businessmen accompanying Özal, was disturbed at what he saw. He wrote on his visiting card a promise of 10,000 USD for repairing the complex. Others in the group followed. The resulting 40,000 USD has since been well augmented, with the shrine, adopted by the post-communist government, now in prime condition, surrounded by peach orchards, with a fish-filled pond, and reverently visited.

Much of what we know of the Nakşibendis comes from the flowing work of an English Shiite. The writer, Hamid Algar, influenced by Ayatollah Khomeini, converted to Islam in the 1960s. Self-described as an erudite recluse and remembered by one student in Berkeley, California as a pious fanatic, he has written extensively on the Shiites' main foes, the Nakşibendis and the Wahhabis. He shares the contrast between the "laconic and elliptic nature" of the sources on the personality of Bahâeddin and the saint's central role in the history of the fraternities perpetuating his name.[17]

Most orders' *silsile* trace back to the Prophet through his son-in-law, the Imam Ali. At times of political ferment, this link with the man who inspires Shiites and Alevis occasionally eroded the standing of these orders in Sunni polities. The Nakşibendis have no such crypto-baggage. Their Golden Chain reaches the Prophet through the revered Abu Bakr, companion and father-in-law of Muhammad, financier of his rise, and first of his successors. It was Abu Bakr who, in a brief twenty-seven months, consolidated Muslim rule over the Arabian Peninsula and launched Muslims against the Sasanian and Byzantine empires.

For Nakşibendis, Abu Bakr is not only a paragon of a ruler but also "a figure of unparalleled spiritual status—the best of all men after the prophets." It was to him that Muhammad bestowed the title of *sıddik* (eminently truthful, *siddiq* in transliterated Arabic) because of his unquestioning acceptance of the Prophet's description of his bodily ascent to heaven. Today, it is "held that the distinctive sobriety of the Naqshbandiya, its strict adherence to the *Shari'a* and shunning of outward display, is a characteristic ultimately inherited from the *siddiq* who is the fountainhead of Naqshbandi tradition."[18]

The early saints in the Nakşibendi *silsile* form part of the common patrimony of Sufism. With the ninth of these, the great Sunni theosopher Yusuf el-Hemedani (Yusuf al-Hamadani), the Nakşibendis became known as "the path of the masters." It was Hemedani who encouraged Abdülkadir-i Geylani (Abd al-Qadir Jilani) to follow the path of Sufism. It was a serendipitous event. Geylani inspired the Kadiri order, and this and the Nakşibendis are now two of the greatest universal orders, with a generally close relationship that has stood the test of centuries. Nor did Hemedani's influence stop there. Of the four successors he named, one, Ahmed Yesevi (Yasawi), inspired the rise of Islam among the Turkic tribes of Central Asia, and a second, Abdülhaliḳ Gucdüvani (Abd al-Khaliq Ghijduvani), bequeathed the Nakşibendis the basic principles they still apply.

Yesevi impressed the fearsome Tamerlane more than any other figure in the spiritual heritage of the lands he conquered, with the Emperor commissioning and helping to design a huge mausoleum in the saint's honour. This is a soaring structure of fired brick, with a dome of turquoise tiles, a rotunda of delicate mosaics and Kufic verses from the *Kur'an*, its features influencing the Taj Mahal in Agra, the tomb of Humayun in Mughal Delhi, and the glories of Samarkand. Commissioned between 1389 and 1398, it was still unfinished when the Emperor died of a winter illness in 1405. That the conqueror stooped to its construction is an indication of the lustre that this mystic had for Muslims in Khorasan.

This appeal continued through the centuries with Yesevi a star in the firmament of Turkish historians as they sought to link the fledgling Republic with the glories of the Seljuks and the early Turkic empires of Khorasan. The historian Mehmed Fuad Köprülü devotes half his *magnum opus*, *Early Mystics in Turkish Literature*, to the saint, seeing him as inspiring the dervishes who would influence Anatolia.[19] More recent scholars suggest that it was impossible to determine the affiliation of each mystic who came with the Turkic tribes and their flocks.[20]

Gucdüvani, the second notable successor of Hemedani, made the silent *zikir* a central characteristic of the order's practice, differentiating it from the vocal *zikir* of Yesevi and his followers. Gucdüvani's other bequest to the *silsile* to which Bahâeddin would be joined was the eight-fold set of principles, which, with three added by Bahâeddin, have served to inspire Nakşibendis for over half a millennium.

The original eight principles included: remembrance; restraint from straying thoughts; concentration on the imminence of the divine; an interior journey from blameworthy to praiseworthy qualities; watching one's steps to avoid losing direction; and solitude (with God) in the midst of the crowd. To these, Bahâeddin, six links down the *silsile*, added: keeping account of how rightly one passes one's time; performing the necessary number of undistracted remembrances of God; and forming a mental picture of one's heart with the name of God engraved thereon.[21]

There are another thirteen links in the *silsile* before we come to the early nineteenth century and el-Bağdadi, the Nakşibendi *şeyh* whose presence is most strongly felt in today's Turkey. In the intervening period, two figures deserve particular note. One is Ubeydullah Ahrar (d. 1490), the chief *şeyh* in Taşkent, who helped the Timurid prince, Abu Said Mirza, seize power in Transoxiana.

Ahrar committed himself "to convince kings not to transgress against God's law or to torment the people."[22] His defining legacy to the Nakşibendis was that they should work with rulers to advance the cause of the faith and, by corollary, with their opponents if they do not. Such dissent has been evident in the Caucasus and Central Asia against the Russians, in eastern Turkestan, against China, in parts of the Indonesian archipelago against the Dutch, and in Turkey for more than a century. That this approach should have spread so widely is again in part because of Ahrar, whose dispatch of disciples made the Nakşibendis a common element in the shared culture of the Ottoman lands, Central Asia, and India.[23]

The second outstanding Nakşibendi of this period is Ahmed-i Sirhindi, known in Turkey as İmam-ı Rabbani, the Divine Imam. Sirhindi was born when the Mughal Empire was flourishing under Akbar the Great. Such has been his impact that he is often termed a *müceddid* or renewer of the faith.

Ahrar's message had come to India with Babur, who, while marching his troops to conquer the Indo-Gangetic Plain, had distracted himself by translating a treatise of Ahrar from Persian prose into Çağatay Turkish verse.[24] Akbar, his grandson, had sidelined this message. Faced with the problems of ruling a multi-communal empire, he had developed an ambitious creed of unity, combining principles that Islam, Christianity, Zoroastrianism, Hinduism, and Buddhism considered of merit. The resulting *Din-i ilahi* (Divine Religion) incorporated generosity and tolerance. It elevated the Hindus to a status comparable with the Muslims.

This and development of a cult centred on Akbar led to resistance from Islamic teachers, not least from Sirhindi. The latter had been initiated into the Nakşibendi order around 1600 and developed a large following, including inside the Mughal court. Sirhindi was arrested by Jahangir, who succeeded Akbar, on the pretext of having boasted that he exceeded the first three Rightly Guided Caliphs. A year later, he was released and returned to court to hold spiritual dialogues with his former captor. He now described himself as a valueless soldier in the "prayer army" of the ruler.[25]

He is remembered—his tomb is a much-visited shrine on the road from Delhi to Lahore—not for his politics but his epistles which blend the need to obey the accepted customs of the Prophet, the *sünnet* (*sunnah*), with obedience to the *Shari'a*, which he considered the prime method of spiritual advancement. As he wrote:

> The *sharia* consists of three parts: knowledge (*ilm*), deed (*amal*) and sincerity (*ikhlas*). Unless all three are present and realized, the *sharia* cannot be said to have been fulfilled... The *sharia* is the guarantor of all happiness, both in this world and the hereafter... The *tariqa*... is the servant of the *sharia* and has the function of perfecting its third component, sincerity. The purpose of the attainment of the *tariqa* is merely the perfection of the *sharia*, not the creation of something additional to the *sharia*.[26]

This rejection of mystical ecstasy as a goal in itself reinforced the Nakşibendis' message of sobriety.

For Sirhindi, all being was a reflection, not an emanation, of divine reality, and the unity was one of witness not of being, *vahdet-i şühûd* not *vahdet-i vücûd*. He posited an absolute and unbridgeable distinction between the Creator and his creations. Mystics and orders should be subordinate to the *Shari'a*, and the *ulema* be supreme. Islam was rigidly opposed to Hinduism; by keeping company with infidels, the believer dishonoured his own religion. The implications of this are fateful, with Sirhindi's rejection of communalism sowing the seeds for the Hindu-Muslim tensions which have splattered through the centuries as well as underpinned recent movements like the Taliban.[27] A further legacy of Sirhindi was hostility to the Shiite state of the Safavids.

One of Sirhindi's successors and his sons set out to harmonize the differences between the four schools of Sunni jurisprudence and took the radical step of translating the *Kur'an* into Persian and Urdu, the demotic language of Indian's Muslims. These Nakşibendis issued *fetva* criticizing the British, though stopped short of calling for revolt or objecting to Muslims holding positions under the British or learning their language. From their circle emerged Ahmad Barelvi, a man who launched a *jihad* against the Sikhs, anticipating the end of communal co-existence in India. Barelvi was to inspire development of the Darul Uloom Deoband seminary north of post-Mutiny Delhi and its offshoots in what are now Bangladesh and Pakistan. The Darul Uloom Deoband became the second largest focal point of Islamic teaching after the Al-Azhar University, Cairo, and a centre of Muslim opposition to British rule.[28]

Long before this, followers of Muhammad Masum, the third son of Sirhindi, had carried the Nakşibendis' teachings to Kabul and Transoxiana, from where they spread into the Caucasus and Central Asia, creating the future backbone of Muslim resistance to Russian expansion. Another of the many disciples of this saint, Muhammad Murad Buhari, launched the *Müceddidi* branch of the Nakşibendis in Ottoman lands.

Growth in Ottoman lands

Disciples of Bahâeddin are first recorded in the empire at the time of Mehmed the Conqueror when two initiates of Ahrar arrived carrying their saint's teaching. One was Abdullah-ı İlâhî, a native of Simav in western Anatolia, who returned from studying under Ahrar and a year's retreat at the tomb of Bahâeddin. Abdullah's message, brought to the ears of the Sultan, led to a summons to the Ottomans' new capital. Abdullah settled in a *medrese* in Zeyrek beside the Golden Horn but, disturbed by a surfeit of admiring visitors, moved to Giannitsa, west of Salonika, where he died a year later. He left behind him an impressive corpus of writing, disseminating the ideas which Ibn Arabi had brought two centuries earlier to Konya, Erzincan, and Malatya on the oneness or unity of being.

The second carrier of Ahrar's teaching was Emir Ahmed-i Buhari, who had met and befriended Abdullah in Samarkand. Emir Ahmed established the first Nakşibendi *tekke* in the Ottoman capital. A further Nakşibendi *tekke* was set up in Sarajevo, endowed by the frontier province's governor, Mihaloğlu İskender Paşa, scion of a Byzantine general who in earlier, more religiously fluid days had converted to Islam.

İskender Paşa had previously favoured the Mevlevis, endowing their still evocative lodge in the Galata district of İstanbul. That his later *tekke* in Sarajevo was on behalf of the Nakşibendis reflects the success of Abdullah and Emir Ahmed in court. Indeed, before long, the order came to be seen in the Seraglio as a steadying hand. Its respect for the state and the *sünnet* meant that Nakşibendi *şeyh* seeking refuge from the persecutions of the Safavids were welcomed by Ottoman rulers keen to buttress their population against challenges to Sunni orthodoxy.[29] Helping the order's spread was its direct communication with believers daunted by the Persian-based works of many Sufi orders: the Nakşibendi made use of works in Turkish and Arabic.

In the early eighteenth century, the Empire saw the rise of the second wing of the Nakşibendis, the *Müceddidi*, which had risen to dominance in India and was active throughout Central Asia and Anatolia. With Ottoman lands under increasing threat from abroad, Sirhindi's polemical anti-Shiism resonated well. Murad Buhari influenced the then *şeyhülislam*, and survived being shipped to Alanya by an irritated Grand Vizier and left on a deserted shore. As the *Müceddidi* message spread, so too did the order's lodges, with the eighteeenth century seeing these in regions as far apart as Bosnia and Tokat. Two Sultans were close to them: Abdülhamid I and Mustafa IV.

The *Müceddidi* strand was to gain fresh impetus with the activities of the saint now often classed as the Second *Müceddid*, Halid el-Bağdadi.[30] El-Bağdadi was born in 1779 in south-east Kurdistan, and studied and taught in Sulaymaniyah. In 1805/6, while on the pilgrimage to Mecca, a dervish told him that his preceptor was waiting for him in India. El-Bağdadi resumed his teaching and three years later met a disciple of Gulamu Ali (also known as Abdullah ed-Dihlevî). The disciple invited him to Gulamu Ali's teaching hospice in Delhi. After a year at that sage's side, el-Bağdadi returned to Sulaymaniyah in 1811 as the latter's designated *halife*. From Gulamu Ali's death in 1824 until his own in 1827, el-Bağdadi was the thirtieth link in what is now one of the main branches in the Nakşibendi chain, with his name being given to a sub-order of the *tarikat* in his honour.

Two centuries earlier, at the time of Sirhindi, the main threat to the Mughal Empire came from the Shiite Safavids. By the time el-Bağdadi arrived in Delhi in 1810, it was the British East India Company whose 200,000 troops—twice as many as those of the British army on the eve of the Napoleonic Wars—ranged the subcontinent.

Gulamu Ali was hostile to the British and critical of a *fetva* authorizing Muslims to serve under them. Like him, el-Bağdadi was disturbed by the decline of Mughal authority, concluding that the main threat to Muslims came from the empire-building of the Europeans and that only the Ottomans were capable of giving a focus to Muslim cohesion.

Back in Sulaymaniyah, he fell out with the ruling Baban emir and the local Kadiri *şeyh* who found him to be a threat to their interests. After a period in Baghdad, he moved to Damascus in 1823, living there until his death from the plague four years later. One hagiographer records that the plague stopped the day after his death and that more than 300,000 people prayed behind his coffin.[31]

The city was an important staging post on the pilgrim route to Mecca, enabling el-Bağdadi to meet and influence men from much of the Muslim world. He sent out at least seventy disciples (one account says 116), each with a defined region of responsibility. The letters he left behind focus on organizational matters and issues of the *Shari'a* and religious law, not on mysticism; the books in his personal library were similar. He instructed his followers to "pray for the survival of the exalted Ottoman state which is the pivot of Islam and for its victories over the enemies of religion, the cursed Christians and the despicable Persians;" this last letter was written at the height of the Greek rebellion—no other Islamic order issued such a rallying call.[32]

He imposed an unprecedented degree of central control on his disciples, requiring their devotion via the practice of *rabıta:* "He defined it in novel fashion as 'an imaginary fixing of the form of the shaykh between the eyes of the *murid*', and proclaimed that *rabıta* was to be practised exclusively with him, even after his death."[33]

His disciples appear to have been well chosen, and to have brought a message that bolstered a series of beleaguered Islamic communities, not least in the Caucasus. There they led resistance against Moscow and inspired Sheikh Mansur of Chechnya, Imam Shamil of Dagestan, the Caucasus uprising of 1877, and the founders of the White Russian North Caucasian Republic. Their influence lingers on, the Halidiyye sharing with the Kadiriyye the devotions and insurgency of Islamist Chechens. They are also active among the Tatars and Bashkirs in Russia, constitute a leading presence among the Uyghurs of western China, and feature in south-east Asia. They are to be found in Libya and Syria, long opposing the Assads. By contrast, they are scarce in Egypt and sub-Saharan Africa and absent from Saudi Arabia, but not from Yemen in the skirts of the Arabian Peninsula.

Inside the Ottoman realm, el-Bağdadi's disciples were quick to dominate the Nakşibendi lodges from the Balkans to the Caucasus. They were particularly effective in the Kurdish areas, inducing important Kadiri families to change over to the Nakşibendiyye, with considerable effect upon the subsequent history of Kurdish nationalism.

In İstanbul itself, his disciples ran into initial problems. In 1819, Mahmud dismissed the *şeyhülislam*, Mekkizade Mustafa Âsım, a dedicated Halidi sympathizer. However, Asim soon returned to office, and in 1826 the Halidis helped mobilize the city's population against the Janissaries. The Halidis fell briefly out of favour again, but from 1833 the pendulum swung their way. Mekkizade was reappointed as *şeyhülislam*, settling down to become the second-longest-serving occupant of this post in the 19th century. Exiled Halidis, re-appreciated for their commitment to the Empire, were summoned back to the capital. It was largely to them that Bektaşi lodges, closed for their links with the Janissaries, were transferred. Mahmud's successor, Abdülmecid, ordered a mausoleum and hospice to be built by el-Bağdadi's tomb.

During the three decades of the *Tanzimat* reforms, *Müceddidi* calls for conservative purity were out of tune with the authorities, but, as this period gave way to Hamidian absolutism, the order regained its influence. The mid-century *şeyhülislam*, Mehmed Refik Efendi, was a Halidi and ensured Nakşibendi representation in the Council of *Şeyh*. Their Özbekler lodge, which was later to shelter Edib, collected information from Central Asian Muslims for the benefit of the Porte.[34]

Of the many missionaries appointed by el-Bağdadi himself, four stand out: one, Ali es-Sebti, as the grandfather of the rebellious *Şeyh* Said, and three because they inspire four of the six *tarikat* dominant in Turkey today. The first of the three was Tâhâ-yı Hekkârî, whose disciples established both the patrician Erenköy *tarikat* in İstanbul and the populist Menzil movements. Taha's disciple, Abdülhakim Arvasi, inspired the poet Necip Fazıl Kısakürek and Hüseyin Hilmi Işık, after whom the briefly flourishing Işıkçı community is named.

The second, Abdullah Mekki Erzincani, figures in the line leading to the venerable Mahmut Ustaosmanoğlu, founder of today's influential İsmailağa *tarikat*.

The third disciple of el-Bağdadi in this short list of merit is Ahmed el-Ervadi, who was sent to İstanbul. He identified the young Ahmed Ziyaeddin Gümüşhanevi, who was soon bringing the *Müceddidi* message to the various Sultans for whom he acted as spiritual adviser. Ahmed Ziyaeddin trained disciples who were active from Crimea to China. Abdülhamid's appreciation of him was such that he was buried next to Süleyman the Magnificent. Almost a century later, the generals running Turkey allowed Mehmet Zahit Kotku, continuer of Ahmed Ziyaeddin's tradition, to be laid there too. The generals' decision reflected the way Kotku had become one of the most influential powerbrokers in Turkey. Presidents Turgut Özal,

Abdullah Gül, and Erdoğan, and Prime Minister Necmettin Erbakan all trace their rise to the support of Kotku and his İskenderpaşa *tarikat*. Halid el-Bağdadi chose his emissaries well.

Of the main Islamic currents active in Turkish society and politics today, two others derive from saints of Nakşibendi formation. These are the two figures profiled above, Said Nursi and Süleyman Hilmi Tunahan.

Before exploring how these Halidis have shaped today's Turkey, it is worth remembering what divides them from the Wahhabis of the Arabian Peninsula.

Reaction in the Arabian Peninsula

The two orders differ fundamentally in their interpretation of traditional Islamic doctrine. Like the Nakşibendis, the Wahhabis call for a return to the teachings of the *Kur'an*, but they also reject many of the sacred traditions, the *hadis*. The difference is especially seen in the two groups' approaches to the core idea of the unity of worship, *tevhid ibadeti* (*tawhid al-'ibada*), the doctrine that all worship should be directed to God alone. The Wahhabis abjure the concept of a religious order as a privileged catalyst for spiritual transmission and execrate all ideas of tomb worship. They go a step further in arguing that those who disagree with this doctrine should be excluded from the Muslim community. And, in ways which many Muslim scholars and teachers consider aberrant, if not abhorrent, they sanction the killing of all, Muslims and others, who dispute their teachings.

This last point is readily espoused in our times by al-Qaeda and ISIS. It echoes a debate dating to the prolific Hanbali jurist, Taqī ad-Dīn Aḥmad ibn Taymiyya. A political activist, he stayed in Damascus when many others fled the Mongol Ilkhanids, and then, while visiting Ghazan Khan to ask for clemency for the city, upbraided the sovereign for breaking his promises. Legend has it that 200,000 men and around 15,000 women attended his funeral.

A pugnacious iconoclast, he claimed to base his teachings exclusively on the truths of the Prophet and his immediate successors, the pious predecessors (*al-salaf al-ṣāliḥ*), often equated with the first three generations of Muslims. It is in honour of these that Wahhabis and many Islamists prefer the more broadly encompassing name Salafist. He restored the *Kur'an* and the *Sünnet* to their place of honour, rejecting use of later consensus or reason. Often cited by those in authority are his words:

> God has imposed the duty of enjoining the good and forbidding the evil, and that is possible only with the authority of a chief… It is thus that people say 'the Sultan is the Shadow of God on earth' and 'Sixty years with an unjust *imam* is better than one night of anarchy.'[35]

On some subjects including Sufism, Ibn Taymiyya's writings are more nuanced than is generally presented. Some Western commentators argue that he did not denounce mysticism in itself or Sufism or Sufis as a group, but only excesses which he saw as inconsistent with the *Kur'an* and *hadis*.[36] He was particularly critical of Shiites, and on the issue of *jihad* he foreshadowed much of what the Wahhabis proclaim today. His definition of when *jihad* is obligatory was broad, requiring action against Muslims as well as non-Muslims who failed to observe "unambiguous and generally recognized obligations and prohibitions." For those who become martyrs, eternal rewards and blessings were assured. He left an extensive corpus, and the eighteenth-century Muhammad ibn Abd al-Wahhab adds little to this, though goes beyond it in certain areas, not least in a more complete rejection of Sufi practices.

It was not the finer points of doctrine which caused this message to appeal to the ambitious Muhammad ibn Saud, emir of a then obscure oasis on the outskirts of today's Riyadh. Rather, al-Wahhab's promotion of the ruler's role was used by Ibn Saud and his successors to justify raids on other tribes, to sanction payment of tribute as a religious duty, to condone the sacking of the Shiite shrines at Kerbala in 1802, and to promote rebellion against the Ottomans. The rebels could only be put down by recourse to the presumptuous Muhammad Ali, originally sent to Cairo to ensure Ottoman rule.

Abdullah ibn Saud was brought to İstanbul in 1818, and beheaded on the shore below Topkapı Palace. Before executing him, the Ottomans entertained him with a lute, goading him over his interpretation of Islam which forbade music. As for the rebels' religious leaders, some of them were bundled into the muzzles of cannons and mortars and blown to pieces.

Defeat of their ruler did not mean defeat of the Wahhabis, who through the nineteenth century suppressed all *tarikat* in Arabia. Family quarrels divided the Saudis until Abdulaziz ibn Saud (1876–1953) took control of Nejd in 1902. Tolerated by the Ottomans, he broke from them in 1915, joining the Arab Revolt.

In those acrimonious times, few Ottomans sought to understand Wahhabism, the rare exceptions including Eyüp Sabri Paşa, an Ottoman naval officer who in 1879 published a history of the Wahhabis, and Ahmed b. Zeynî Dahlan, a *müftü* of Mecca, who published a work on them a decade later. These works describe Wahhabi torturing of Muslims and the barbarous killing of women and children "if one can bear to read them."[37]

With the Wahhabis widely considered to have betrayed the Ottomans at an hour of need, their creed has found little following in republican Turkey. Hüseyin Kazım Kadri, a politician and lexicographer, published his *Epistle of Wahhabism* (*Vehhabilik Risalesi*) in 1929.[38]

As we will see below, active Saudi proselytizing in Turkey did not begin until oil revenues began to soar in the 1970s and 1980s. Two generations on, it is the Kingdom's businessmen, not its clerics, who have made a mark in the country that ruled its ancestors for four full centuries.

PART THREE

FLOWERING

In those years in İstanbul, there was a saying: "On Sundays, for the morning prayer you go to the mosque in Çarşamba and listen to Mahmut Efendi. For the noon prayer, you go to Zihni Paşa Mosque in Erenköy to listen to Sami Efendi. And for the afternoon prayer, you come to İskenderpaşa Mosque and listen to Mehmet Zahit Kotku."

An immigrant from Konya in the late 1960s[1]

Turkey's emergence as a modern economy led the pious to seek ways of bridging faith and commerce. A state machinery concerned with combatting leftist currents tolerated the emergence of groups founding again, and on a more materialistic basis, the religious orders that had long served the Ottoman faithful. Some of these orders targeted the businessman and trader, others the small tradesman and craft worker, and others the mass of rural migrants to the cities. This section describes the key communities that developed, the quest for Mammon of several, and the long march of the egregious Gülen movement, demonstrating their links to the fractured politics of the last half century.

6

INDUSTRIALIZING TURKEY AND THE EROSION OF SECULARISM

Tarikat and cemaat, like associations and trades unions, are a reality of this country. Both tarikat and cemaat visit our politicians and learn their opinions. Our Prime Minister's talks should not be considered strange. These are normal activities in a democracy. But, in my opinion, there is a little unnecessary sensitivity here.

President Süleyman Demirel, asked about Prime Minister Tansu Çiller's receiving Fethullah Gülen, *Hürriyet*, 29 January 1995

From coup to coup

The rolling out of electricity, water, and roads from the 1950s changed the face of rural Turkey. Both Süleyman Demirel and Turgut Özal cut their teeth enabling this change. Demirel graduated from İstanbul Technical University a year before Özal, three years his junior. He was from provincial Turkey, growing up in Isparta, centre of the country's production of rose attar. He had helped his father as a shepherd and then come to İstanbul. He was a withdrawn and solitary student, according to Necmettin Erbakan, the third future political leader at the university. Like others, he was swept up in the political turmoil of the time, being part of the mob which ransacked *Tan* newspaper—a lonely advocate of good relations with Moscow—in December 1945.[1]

He started his career working on the electrification of the country. An Eisenhower Fellowship and studies in the U.S. followed. After that, he moved on to dam construction, becoming head of the infant State Hydraulic Works (*Devlet Su İşleri*, DSİ). With the 1960 coup, he was drafted for military service. That completed, he became representative of the ubiquitous American company, Morrison-Knudsen, whose projects ranged from Minuteman missile silos to the tiger cages in South Vietnam. He then plunged into politics. By October 1965, "Morrison Süleyman" was prime minister. He was forty years old. In the twenty-eight years before he became president, he was to head six further governments, acting as prime minister for almost half this period.

Demirel was a classic economic liberal, believing that economic progress would bring social advance. For him, Turkey was "a giant in pygmy's clothing," constrained by the lack of the normal amenities of a modern nation. His regular press conferences, punctuated by a plethora of data on roads, hospitals, factories, and jobs, were like company reports. He was responsible for the first Bosphorus Bridge, for foundation of the Ereğli Iron and Steel Works, and for the massive Keban Dam on the Euphrates. His opponents accused him of being a freemason, and all the evidence is that so he was. He was tolerant to his political opponents and to criticism. He welcomed what he called "a talking, discussing Turkey." He combined energy with an unerring personal touch. He travelled the country endlessly, his trademark hat in hand, always asking those he met again about their children or family—and punctiliously taking their telephone calls to his ground-floor office in leafy Güniz Street, Ankara. He was never seen to get people's details wrong.

Those years seem to belong to a now alien world. Ankara was a garden city, the evening resonating with the mournful mooing of trains shunting around its station yard. Turkey was a closed country. High customs tariffs and limited import licences kept foreign goods at bay. Could Turkey make men's suits? Could it start exporting fruit and vegetables? Could it fabricate petrochemicals? The country is now carrying out an annual 600 billion USD of foreign trade, but the answers to those questions were not so obvious then. To address them, Demirel made Özal head of the State Planning Organization.

The two men had been friends since university. They shared offices in 1950 and again after the 1960 coup. They lived in neighbouring homes. Özal deferred to Demirel as '*abi*', a term meaning elder brother and indicating esteem. Like Demirel, he had spent part of the 1950s at an

American university, in his case what is now Texas Tech University. Together they changed not only the economic base of the country, but its social one as well. But Özal represented a different face of Turkey's conservatism, a more radical one, his aim being a free-market country reintegrated with its Ottoman heritage.

When the military pushed Demirel aside in 1971, Özal first worked with the World Bank in Washington, then with some major companies in İstanbul. In 1977, he ran against his old friend's Justice Party (*Adalet Partisi*, AP), standing for Erbakan's MSP. He was not elected, but in late 1979, Demirel invited Özal to become undersecretary to the prime minister. Two months later saw the celebrated measures of 24 January 1980. These involved removing capital controls, opening most sectors to foreign investment, freeing foreign trade, replacing import substitution with an export drive, setting out to reduce the share of the state in the economy, and devaluing the Turkish lira by 30 per cent. It was the start of Turkey's participation in a globalizing world.

While Demirel took political responsibility for the measures, Özal had been their architect. When the generals seized power eight months later—their third intervention in twenty years—they asked Özal to continue their implementation and to help them through a debt crisis. He telephoned Demirel, under arrest in a coastal military base: "They have offered me a post. What should I do?" "You should accept," Demirel replied.

Özal became deputy prime minister, the start of his political rise. Demirel was less fortunate. The generals had him banned from politics until 1992, as were Erbakan, Bülent Ecevit, the head of the CHP, and 239 other former party officials.[2] The two friends had now split, and it was against Özal's acrid opposition that Demirel and the other banned politicians regained their political rights in a referendum in 1987.

Demirel's original political vehicle, the Justice Party, had been set up seven months after the earlier coup of May 1960. The party's initial symbol—an open book on a lectern—had a clear religious connotation, and the party continued the Democrat Party's approbation of religion. In October 1965, Demirel won it 52.9 per cent of the vote, a figure never since surpassed by any single party.

Demirel's nuanced approach to religion was popular among the supporters of the former Democrat Party and ensured the support of the main religious communities of the time—the followers of Süleyman Tunahan and Said Nursi. Kemalists were aghast at these linkages.

Demirel, the *Diyanet* and political recourse to religion

Four months before Demirel first took office, the Religious Affairs Directorate (*Diyanet İşleri Başkanlığı*) was given the statutory obligation "to carry out works related to the beliefs, worship and moral principles of the religion of Islam, to enlighten society about religion, and to manage places of worship." This was a major upgrading for a body which had long been a poor relative of government. With Demirel in office, the directorate's share of the general state budget recovered. It also started staffing the *imam-hatip* schools, whose students more than trebled during Demirel's first five years. Officials at the *Diyanet* and preachers were required to be graduates of these schools or higher-education institutes.

The governments following the military ultimatum of March 1971 cut these numbers, but transferred to the *Diyanet* authority over *Kur'an* courses and the assets of the Süleymancıs.

The young Republic had subjected the *Diyanet* to the control of the prime minister, stripping its head of the prestige that had surrounded the Ottomans' *şeyhülislam*, and tasking it with controlling religion on behalf of a suspicious state. In 1931, it lost responsibility for mosques and its budget was slashed. That said, even in those fervently laicist days, religion was seen to have an important legitimizing role, and the *Diyanet*'s opinion was sought—and largely followed—on matters such as the use of Turkish in Friday prayers. It was not until 1949 that it was given back control of mosques and their personnel, but not their sermons.

Law 633 of 1965, adding moral principles and religious enlightenment to its remit, indicated "that the state preferred to use the organization as an ideological tool in a manner different from the original intention of the founding elite."[3] *Diyanet* began to take control of sermons in mosques, and after the 1980 coup, the generals invigorated it with a new proselytizing mission, charging it with "aiming at national solidarity and integrity."

To social scientists who have specialized on the role of religion in Turkish politics, the 1965 law marked the first transformation of the *Diyanet*. Some argue that a second transformation has taken place since Erdoğan's AK Party won power in 2002, with the *Diyanet* central to AKP's policies of social engineering. The *Diyanet* has since been charged with broadening its reach at home, for instance taking in prisons and hospitals and in 2012 launching Diyanet TV. It has also been deprived of autonomy so that "the institution has been turned into an extension of the Party." Abroad, it has started staking a claim to being the representative of European Islam and, with activities in thirty-six countries as of 2018, begun to play a leading role among other Muslim umbrella organizations.[4]

For his part, Özal was long committed to the İskenderpaşa *tarikat*. His links to this fraternity track those of his younger brother, Korkut, who submitted himself to Mehmet Zahit Kotku, head of the order, in January 1960. Those dealing with the State Planning Organization in the late 1960s were told of prayer sessions in its offices. By the end of the decade, Turgut Özal was taking its members to listen to the talks that Kotku, revered as *Hocaefendi* (respected religious teacher), gave when he visited Ankara. As one manager at the SPO wrote:

> Towards midnight... we found ourselves kneeling in front of *Hocaefendi*. He took our hands one by one into his. He asked us to repent for the sins of our past and all the mistakes that, intended or unintended, we had made... We promised that we would not deviate from the path of the *Kur'an* and the practices of the Prophet, and that we would live in accord with the morality of the Prophet and the peace of living those moral values... Then we all put our hands on our knees and closed our eyes. *Hocaefendi* said '*Allah*' three times and we opened our eyes. And all together we raised our hands in prayer. *Hocaefendi* prayed for us. He told us: 'Perform your prayers without interruption, do not lag in remembering *Allah*, and come back in six months.' And we left the house feeling as light as a bird.[5]

At this stage, the chief beneficiary of Kotku's political support was Özal's fellow student, Erbakan, a figure already prominent in the academic and business worlds in İstanbul. Erbakan, the son of a judge, had shone at university. He obtained his doctorate at RWTH Aachen and then worked in Germany on the firing system of Leopard tanks, returning to become a professor at his former university.

Erbakan had been one of the early disciples of Kotku. The engine plant that he established in 1956 was named Gümüş Motor in honour of the name of Kotku's order, Gümüşhanevi, before it became known as İskenderpaşa after the mosque where Kotku later officiated.

By this time, Erbakan's route had separated from that of Demirel. In 1969, responding to İstanbul industrialists' concerns, the Justice Party blocked Erbakan from becoming Chairman of the Union of Chambers of

Commerce and Industry of Turkey, a body influential through its allocation of much-valued import licences. It then rebuffed him when, following Kotku's advice, he decided to stand in the coming general elections. Running as an independent, and with Kotku helping him mobilize the *esnaf* (the small tradesmen and practitioners), he was elected as a deputy from Konya, a conservative constituency.

He was quick to form the National Order Party (*Milli Nizam Partisi,* MNP). The party's symbol, a raised forefinger, proclaimed its determination to make a mark, but its programme was circumspect. It pledged to unleash the high morality and merit of the nation, bringing order, peace, and social justice to the community and prosperity and salvation to the citizen. It promised the development of true science, freed from positivism and imitative methods. And, echoing the ideas of Kotku, it talked of adding modern sciences to the duties of the *Diyanet* so as "to accelerate the technical development of the country, to increase the initiative, ability and power of the people, and to add dynamism to their souls."[6] It reassured the army that it would develop a national defence industry. Its programme made no reference to Allah.

The nascent party survived a year before being closed two months after the military ultimatum of March 1971. The generals themselves were divided, with some advocating the need for religious education to counter an increase in left-wing activities.[7] But the Constitutional Court ruled that the party aimed to institute an Islamic order.

Seventeen months later, Erbakan helped launch the National Salvation Party. This, the second of the five parties he was to sponsor, won 11.8 per cent of the vote in the 1973 elections. The fragmentation of Turkey's political parties made his party key to formation of a government, and by January 1974 he was deputy prime minister. His first term in office was in coalition with Ecevit, a coupling dubbed by its opponents as a watermelon, green (religious) on the outside and red (socialist) on the inside. When this fell, he served two further terms as deputy prime minister in the Nationalist Front coalitions led by Demirel.

By this time, the original message of the MNP had been developed into the broader manifesto of the National Outlook (*Milli Görüş*), a label that has been applied to the successive pro-Islamic parties that succeeded it. All these avatars took their names from the various benefits that the MNP had promised the electorate in 1970.[8]

As set out by Erbakan, the National Outlook stood on four pillars: industrialization, culture, education, and social justice. He argued that Turkey's failure to develop, despite its glorious past as a world power, derived from its warped understanding of modernity. Turkey had chosen to imitate Western culture but not its manufacturing industry. His party's slogan was "A Great Turkey Once Again," and this would be achieved by a renaissance of Turkish Islamic civilization and industrialization.

For Erbakan, Europe was the enemy, and, in 1974 when Greece applied to join the European Economic Community, he vetoed Turkey's following suit. His priority was building Turkey's relationship with the Islamic world. He advocated creation of a United Nations of Muslim countries, formation of an Islamic economic market, adoption of a Pan-Islamic currency, and development of an Islamic passenger car.

It was from this *école* that Erdoğan's AKP (*Adalet ve Kalkınma Partisi*, Justice and Development Party) would develop.

The National Outlook movement and Turkish society

Just as the Democrat Party had stepped in to meet expectations that the Republican People's Party had been unable to satisfy, so the successive National Outlook parties responded to the unmet needs of the emerging group of small merchants, craftsmen, and farmers.

The customary analysis is that imposition of Kemalism on a reluctant and suspicious countryside led to religion becoming part of the counterhegemonic identity of the broad periphery.[9] But a more recent view is that it represented a marriage of anti-communists seeking to strengthen nationalist and conservative values and Islamists happy to forge an alliance with the establishment.

> In short, contrary to popular belief, Islamism in Turkey during the Cold War era was never a movement representing a periphery oppressed and victimized by the political center. Rather, it had the full blessing of the center, which had seen it as an antidote to the post-1960s ascendancy of the Left. Consequently, the Turkish establishment was unperturbed by the fact that the Islamists began to form parties and take part in coalition governments from the 1970s onward or, during the same decade, to run critical ministries.[10]

The Democrat and Justice parties were associated with the larger groups which had allied themselves to the state. The National Outlook parties catered to the interests of those outside such circles. Erbakan was instrumental in creating the networks that facilitated the growth of what he later called the "Anatolian tigers," corporations often headed by pious, conservative businessmen from the heartland that became the financial and industrial backbone of his movement.[11]

His own list of the MSP's achievements during the 1970s included the seizure of northern Cyprus; taking Turkey into the Islamic Conference and the Islamic Development Bank; turning Turkey from an importer of wheat to an exporter; building eight fertilizer factories; developing heavy industry and the country's defence industries; and launching the country's motorway programme. He gave particular importance to the 350 *imam-hatip* schools, ten higher Islamic institutes, and 3,000 *Kur'an* courses that opened in those years. By 1994, when he set out this record, 1.3 million young people had graduated from the *imam-hatip* schools, "a new generation of believers." His list also included stopping prosecutions for religious activism, easing use of the headscarf for women, and removing limitations on Turks travelling for the *hajj*.

Kotku seems to have been less impressed by all this than concerned about the radical political activism of the party's youth movement, the Akıncılar. "Necmi should withdraw from the leadership of the party," he told Erbakan's brother-in-law in the late 1970s.[12]

The generals embrace Islam

The year 1980 was a bitter one for Turkey. The economy was in a continuing crisis and the streets divided by civil strife. Over fifty people died in the Çorum incidents when Sunni militants attacked Alevi neighbourhoods. Few days passed without fatal clashes between left and right. In this already tense atmosphere, Erbakan called a mass rally to energize his followers. Ostensibly to protest the Israeli Knesset's designating Jerusalem as the "eternal capital" of Israel, the meeting took place in Konya on 6 September. It was a national sensation. There were calls to turn Turkey into an Islamic state. Some of the demonstrators sat down when the national anthem was played. A number of participants wore turbans and fezzes, and carried placards inscribed "*Şeriat* or death." Erbakan himself proclaimed: "May you, the new army of Sultan Fatih Mehmed, be victorious and your holy struggle be blessed. Be prepared, we shall sharpen our swords."[13] The television channels were quick to foster establishment outrage.

Six days later, Turkey awoke to find the military had ousted the politicians. The Konya meeting had proved a useful pretext for the coup that the generals had been preparing for at least six months.[14] A National Security Council headed by General Kenan Evren, the Chief of Staff, took power—like coup leaders the world over dignifying its pronouncements with broadcasts of Beethoven's Fifth Symphony and its resonant fate motif.

Turkey's new rulers were soon to show that they believed in the value of religion in combatting the socialist and communist ideas adopted by some of the new immigrants to the city fringes. An early indication of this came with the opening of the imperial graveyard at Süleymaniye for Kotku to be buried beside earlier leaders of his *tarikat*. They soon set out to strengthen state control of religion and to determine which forms of religion were legitimate.[15]

The generals are often presented as seizing on religion because of their lack of ideology, but this is to belittle the debate that had been taking place within the military. The head of the coup was a leader in this debate:

> [Evren] used religious arguments for raising national consciousness, social responsibility, and health concerns, promoting birth control and social cohesion of the Turkish society to overcome its ethnic and ideological divisions. He underlined the rational nature of Islam to promote modernity and stressed religion's role as a unifying agent or social cement. His goal was to free Islam from backward interpretations and political influence.[16]

Much of this could be said about Atatürk too.

This warrior scholar—as some academics do not flinch from presenting him—was the son of an *imam* who had come to Turkey as a refugee from the Balkans. After serving with the Turkish brigade in Korea, he rose through a series of posts, becoming head of the army and then of the General Staff.[17] In his personal notes, he used the Ottoman script, not the modified Latin alphabet prescribed in 1928.

He had been in charge of the Land Forces' training schools, and supported the role of religion as the cement of society, the source of morality, and an intellectual force to arm ordinary Muslims against the communist threat. He had a course on Islam introduced in all military academies, using a textbook stressing the necessity of Islam for the development of a moral society. The book has little to say on Alevi interpretations of Islam.

Giving an aura of legitimacy to this symbiosis of Islam and Kemalism was the three-volume *Atatürkçülük* (*Atatürkism*). Printed by the armed forces in 1981–1982, it concludes with thirty-six statements on religion extracted from speeches by the great man, underlining his role as a pious leader who saw Islam as "compatible with reason and logic" and fitting with the nation's interests, a figure who implemented reforms to create a religion free from reactionary forces. The unnamed authors, who repeat but rarely analyze the leader's statements, note that in Atatürkism, "The aim of religion is to make the individual moral as a person and useful to his family and country."[18]

In their own policies, the generals tasked the *Diyanet* with furthering national solidarity while also requiring it to act "in accordance with the principles of secularism, removed from all political views and ideas." They mandated compulsory religious education in primary and secondary schools.

It had taken six decades to go from the banning of religious education to its affirmation as a central value of Turkish society. This change was combined with an unapologetic revival of nationalism in what has become known as the Turkish-Islamic synthesis (see Chapter 8). For Turgut Özal, the generals had been useful allies.

The 1980s and Özal

Ozal established the Motherland Party (*Anavatan Partisi*, ANAP) in May 1983 and won the elections held six months later. Advancing Islam was to prove central to his efforts as prime minister. His Minister of Education, Vehbi Dinçerler, issued instructions banning the teaching of evolution. He also revised the curriculum in *imam-hatip* schools to teach that Turks had been the "leaders in the rise and dissemination of Islam throughout the world" and that "amongst the fundamentals of the Turkish way of life is the need for the Islamic religion."[19]

Özal gave a renewed boost to the *imam-hatip* schools, their students increasing by one quarter during his six years of premiership. He encouraged a boost in mosque-building, ensuring completion of the prime mosque for Ankara, the retro-styled Kocatepe Mosque. He had TRT, the state broadcaster, raise the profile of religious programmes. He freed private broadcasting, fuelling an explosion of overtly religious radio and television channels, and eased controls on publishing, leaving in place restrictions only on offending public decency or exploiting sexual desire. By contrast, he increased penalties for those who prevented or abused ceremonies of the "heavenly" religions, destroyed tombs, or insulted the remains of the dead.

Prosecutions for abuse of religion fell to a trickle, inevitably leading to acquittals. One ANAP deputy, Eyüp Aşık, openly declared he was a Nakşibendi, and was left uncharged. The religious orders gained increasing de facto legitimacy. By 1991, when Özal had the provisions used to prosecute their members abolished, these provisions had become largely irrelevant.[20] Particularly striking was his decision to perform the pilgrimage to Mecca, the first serving prime minister of Turkey to do so. In July 1988, he led a full pilgrimage that included several hundred members of parliament and senior civil servants. He made sure that photographers accompanied him, returning to opposition accusations that he had exploited religion for political gain. Some newspapers printed photographs contrasting him in his white *ihram* towels and his wife in a cocktail dress in Turkey, drawing on one of her trademark cigars. Critics also reminded readers of the trading and financial interests in Saudi Arabia of his brother, Korkut. Indeed, one of the first decisions of Özal's government had been to open the way for Islamic banking, a move from which Saudi investors were swift to profit.

In this ever more open world, the generals' bans on many of the country's political leaders came to seem increasingly anachronistic. The year 1987 saw the bans put to a referendum. Özal ran a slick and vicious campaign calling for his former patron and other political leaders to remain banned until 1992. He lost. The Turks do not like leaders who interfere with their choices. However, it was a close run. Only 50.16 per cent voted for rehabilitating the politicians.

Özal called elections before the newly legal leaders could build up their following, stayed on as prime minister for twenty-two months, and then had the Grand National Assembly elect him president. The 1991 elections brought Demirel to power, and he was quick to box his former protégé into a largely ceremonial role. When Özal died in April 1993, Demirel succeeded him as head of state.

The 1990s and Erbakan

The 1980s were largely a lost decade for the National Outlook and the movement that took its name. The MSP had been closed by the generals, with Erbakan among the party leaders banned from politics. His followers set up the Welfare Party (*Refah Partisi*, RP) in 1983, but were prevented from running in that year's elections.

The hajj

In the Erbakan-influenced 1970s, Turkey suddenly emerged as the country sending more pilgrims on the *hajj* than any other in the world. In Ottoman times, Sultans had taken their role as Guardians of the Holy Cities seriously, each year dispatching large caravans with sumptuous gifts. Such relations with the holy cities came to an abrupt end with the Arab Revolt and the launching of the Turkish Republic.

Making the pilgrimage to Mecca at least once during his or her lifetime is one of the five duties of the Muslim, one of the five pillars of Islam, but was banned by the Republic until 1947. Menderes took some early steps to revive the practice, but came under pressure not to release Turkey's scarce foreign exchange to pilgrims. Those years, Turks who wanted to make the pilgrimage usually had to make their arrangements in Beirut or elsewhere abroad. It was only in 1963 that the annual number began to pick up, doubling during Demirel's first government to 55,000 in 1969. The figure fell again during the military-backed cabinets of 1971–1973, but soared to over 136,000 in 1977 and 1978.

The mass pilgrimages of the mid-1970s made Turkey the world's undisputed leader in Muslim pilgrimage, accounting for 14 per cent of all overseas hajjis, according to one study.[21] As pilgrimage boomed, the *Diyanet*, long excluded from *hajj* issues, emerged to manage every aspect of the *hajj* business.

The year Turgut Özal made the *hajj*, over 90,000 other Turks did so too. Özal had good relations with the Saudi royal family and in 1990 thought these relations allowed him to ignore the quota of 55,000 pilgrims set for Turkey. The *Diyanet*, apparently on the instructions of Özal, registered 120,000 would-be pilgrims. The Saudi foreign minister, Prince Faysal, flew to Ankara to inform Özal that the Saudis could make no special arrangements for violating their quota.

"The government had created a disaster. It was forced to cancel bookings for all overland travel to Mecca and managed to reroute only 15,000 people by air. Enraged applicants marched on the offices of the governing ANAP and the Directorate of Religious Affairs across the country."[22] The state had to refund 30 million USD to nearly 100,000 would-be pilgrims. Demirel, then the opposition leader, called for Özal to step down.

Four years later, after the ban on the former politicians was ended, the RP failed to cross the 10 per cent threshold for seats in the Grand National Assembly.

Undaunted, Erbakan soldiered on. He mobilized a veritable army of committed volunteers at the local level:

> Covered women (i.e. those wearing the Islamic headscarf), who had hitherto had no experience in politics or public campaigns, were now knocking on doors, explaining the party's program, distributing food, and recruiting other women to the movement... Those working for the party would also deliver food and coal, find hospital beds for the sick, go to funerals, attend weddings (bringing a gift), find jobs for the unemployed, provide scholarships to students, and organise summer camps.[23]

For Erbakan, the fall of the Berlin Wall was proof of the failure of communism to deliver benefits to the citizen, while, for its part, capitalism crushed people. The solution lay in the "Just Order" (*Adil Düzen*), the slogan he had developed to encapsulate the National Outlook's tenets. The five components of this "Just Order" were peace and calm; freedom; an equitable state ensuring justice; welfare and inner peace for the individual; and the individual controlling his future. He castigated the enslavement caused by "imperialism, Zionism and modern colonialism."[24]

At the heart of the "Just Order" was the imaginative proposal that taxes would be collected in kind and kept in government depots before being sold to consumers; the setting up of neighbourhood committees to distribute business permits on the basis of "honesty;" and the purchase by the government of all future production at current prices to be sold immediately to consumers, with goods to be delivered after production. This model would dispense with bank interest, inflation, and middlemen. Party brochures depicted chains of middlemen living off trading in goods produced by struggling farmers, and remitting funds to New York, for transfer to help Israel achieve its alleged expansionary aims.[25]

This iconoclastic platform led to his vote in the October 1991 elections increasing to 16.9 per cent. His star continued to rise.

In the municipal elections of March 1994, the social democrats were hit by a corruption scandal. Demirel's True Path Party (*Doğru Yol Partisi*, DYP), headed by Tansu Çiller after Demirel had become president, had its own corruption issues. And the economy was in free fall. Erbakan ran a relentless campaign promising that the "Just Order" would replace the current "Interest Order." In İstanbul, with Recep Tayyip Erdoğan, his mayoral candidate, beside him, he proclaimed: "We will meet in Ayasofya. May God be with you." When the results in İstanbul were counted, the Welfare Party had won a mere quarter of the vote but, with the opposition divided, Erdoğan was the new mayor. The party also took control of Ankara and four more of Turkey's top fifteen cities.

The economic collapse continued through 1995. This time, it was the late Özal's ANAP that was tainted by a corruption scandal. Sectarian tensions mounted following egregious police brutality against Alevis in İstanbul. The Kurdish insurgency dominated the headlines, with Çiller seen to do little to prevent a wave of counter-terror, torture, and abductions; between March 1994 and March 1995, 385 people disappeared after arrest, according to the sister of one of those who was never seen again.[26] Negotiating the Customs Union with the European Union—and a hollow promise from Greece that Cyprus would not enter the EU until the intercommunal problem was resolved—did little to lift the mood. In the ensuing general elections, Çiller's party's vote fell by almost a third to 19.2 per cent while that of the Welfare Party, with its deftly produced "Guarantee for Turkey" of "A New World" and the "Just Order," rose to 21.4 per cent.

Welfare now had the largest number of deputies in the Assembly. To head off a parliamentary investigation into her wealth, Çiller agreed to a coalition with the Welfare Party. Her party was outraged.

On 28 June 1996, Erbakan became prime minister. He proved faithful to his promises, not least in foreign policy. His first trip abroad was to Tehran, where, shrugging off U.S. attempts to embargo Iran, he signed a 25-year natural gas deal. He then went to Libya, where he was humiliated by President Muammar Gaddafi. Apparently unperturbed, he launched the D-8 Organization for Economic Cooperation, also known as the Developing-8, to counter the West's G7. The D-8 groups over 1.2 billion Muslims.

At home, his influence was not only felt in party politics, but in dress—he removed the ban on female civil servants wearing the headscarf. In education, his term was too short make an immediate impact, though he increased the number of *imam-hatip* schools.

All this deeply disturbed the country's Kemalists. The armed forces had set up what it called the Western Working Group and launched a public relations blitz that combined supplying trusted journalists with black propaganda and leaking a series of cassettes showing lesser members of Erbakan's party calling for the introduction of the *Shari'a*. Widely distributed images of outlandish behavior by the cassocked and antinomian Aczmendi dervishes served to confirm the secularists' worst fears (see Chapter 11).

Erbakan did little to calm matters down; on the contrary, he invited fifty-one venerable preachers and religious figures to break the Ramadan fast with him at a traditional *iftar* meal on 11 January 1997. The opposition watched with outrage as state television showed one limousine after another sweeping into the prime minister's residence in the hills above Ankara, bringing the long-bearded and cassocked Islamic leaders of the country to the inner sanctum of secularism.

His guests provide a valuable snapshot of the state of Islam in Turkey at the time. The *tarikat* had been banned since 1925, but those celebrating with him included the leaders of a number of Nakşibendi orders—in total, half the guests were of Nakşibendi persuasion—as well as heads of the Cerrahi, Halveti, and Kadiri fraternities, and various Nurcu communities. Fethullah Gülen, inspirer of 2016's failed coup attempt, was on the guest list, though did not attend. Only one Alevi leader was invited; the Alevis account for an estimated one sixth of the population.[27] Many of the long-bearded *şeyh* were wearing turbans, as proscribed by 1925 law as the *tarikat* themselves.

Erbakan was later to claim that he wanted to tell the *şeyh* that they should make peace with the state. He also pointed out that Demirel was concurrently hosting the heads of religious bodies in Islamic countries—but the symbolism of his evening stoked the relentless campaign that the General Staff had been running against his government.

In this fevered atmosphere, the mayor of Sincan, a town just west of Ankara, organized an evening in support of the Palestinian *intifada* against Israel. Portraits of the leaders of Hamas and Hezbollah hung from the walls as the Iranian ambassador added fuel to the flames by calling on Turks to obey the precepts of Islam. Thirty hours later, the military sent tanks to Sincan "to fine-tune democracy," and had the government arrest the mayor and expel the ambassador.[28]

The generals kept up their pressure. On 4 February, Demirel relayed their concerns to Erbakan who, Pollyannaish, continued to insist that he had no problems. However, at the meeting of the National Security Council on 28 February, the armed forces launched their "soft coup." The generals presented the prime minister with eighteen directives. Ten of these concerned application of laws to promote secularism, not least the law forbidding use of religious attire; three aimed at controlling religious education, in particular by religious orders; and two called for the ending of activities of these orders. Erbakan eventually signed the directives, but military pressure continued to mount.

In April, the military declared reactionary Islam as more dangerous to the state than Kurdish separatism or interstate war. It classed nineteen newspapers, twenty television stations, fifty-one radio stations, 110 magazines, and 1,200 student hostels as constituting the "reactionary sector." It was alleged to be behind a denigration campaign against 100 companies owned by conservative Muslims. In all this, it had the continuing support of a number of media groups, not least the Doğan Group, publisher of *Hürriyet* and *Milliyet*.

On 11 May, some 300,000 pro-Islamic demonstrators took to the streets to protest against closure of *imam-hatip* schools. The army announced its readiness to use force against Islamic groups. Erbakan, who had agreed with Çiller that they would serve rotating one-year terms, resigned. However, to form the next government, Demirel turned to Mesut Yılmaz, head of ANAP; following defections from Çiller's party, Yılmaz had the second largest number of seats in the Grand National Assembly. Yılmaz established a coalition with the Democratic Left Party (DSP) of Bülent Ecevit and with a breakaway group from Çiller's party. This coalition lasted eighteen months until falling in 1999, brought down by a fresh scandal.

As for Erbakan, after his overthrow, he was feted by international Muslim leaders. In April 1998, King Fahd of Saudi Arabia invited him to Mecca for the *hajj*—Erbakan's twenty-sixth pilgrimage; he would do four more before ill health restricted him. However, within the movement that he had built up, he faced increasing opposition from "reformists" who decided that his approach was condemned to permanent defeat and that a new approach was required.

In May 2001, the reformists ran a challenger to Recai Kutan, Erbakan's candidate for head of his new vehicle, the Virtue Party; the Welfare Party had been closed by the Constitutional Court in 1998 and Erbakan banned from politics for five years. The reformists gained an impressive 521 votes against the 633 of Kutan. When the Virtue Party in its turn was closed in June 2001, the reformists decided they needed a complete break with the National Outlook. Erdoğan's four months in prison for reciting a poem had turned him into a national figure, and his colleagues backed him to head the new AKP.

This had the fortune to emerge just after a fresh economic crisis had stripped the traditional parties of their little remaining credibility. A period of tutelage to reforms backed by the International Monetary Fund and spearheaded by Kemal Derviş, previously a vice president at the World Bank, opened the way to this new party. The elections of November 2002 rewarded it with a crushing 363 seats in the 550-seat Grand National Assembly. Four months later, Erdoğan, excluded as a candidate from those elections, took his own seat in the Assembly. His first cabinet drew two thirds of its ministers from the İskenderpaşa *tarikat*, which thirty-four years earlier had sent Erbakan to Ankara.

The legacy of Erbakan

Rebuffed by the electorate, Erbakan continued to face the courts. In 1998, the Treasury demanded that the Welfare Party return the 1 trillion Turkish liras (3 million USD) it had received as advances for its expenses. Convicted in 2002 for providing forged documents, Erbakan was sentenced to twenty-eight months' imprisonment, the penalty repeatedly deferred on health grounds and cancelled by a presidential pardon in 2008. His funeral three years later drew up to 2 million Turks and Islamic leaders from around sixty countries, including the chief figures of the global Muslim brotherhood.

The obituary that appeared in *Altınoluk* (Golden Channel), the monthly published by the Erenköy brotherhood, summed up the views of many. Pointing out that the country in which Erbakan had carried out politics was "no rose bed, no rose garden," it emphasized how the National Outlook and Just Order were not only imbued with moral values for society, but fulfilled a mission of reform.

> In one sense, the political journey of Erbakan *Hoca* aimed at creating a new consciousness in society. While building this consciousness, his movement at the same time took on the character of a school. Many young were brought up in this political school. If we look at the cadre managing Turkey today, the President and Prime Minister included, they were long kneaded in that school and the term *Hoca* is clearly not limited to the time Erbakan spent as a professor of engineering... Yes, if you sow a seed in history, when the time comes it will sprout. Erbakan *Hoca* sowed numerous seeds in this geography. The time for their fruit will come.[29]

The then Chief of Staff of Turkey hailed his "great services to our country as a valued man of science and politics"—a sign of the newly cowed state of the military that had so long sought to thwart him. *The Economist* noted his disavowal of violence and opined that he had been a moderating force on Turkey's Islamists.[30] His tomb lies on a rise in the cemetery of Merkez Efendi mosque, formerly a leading Sünbüli dervish lodge, overlooking the Byzantine walls of the city which he, in his own way, had conquered, and, through his obduracy, lost.

7

İSKENDERPAŞA AND THE RISE OF POLITICAL ISLAM

... people who are not distracted by trade or commerce from the remembrance of God and the observance of prayer and the payment of the zakat...

From verse 37 of Al-Nur (*Light*),
the 24th Chapter of the *Kur'an*[1]

Kotku and the creation of Turkey's Islamist parties

In the 1960s and 1970s, many of the great and the good of İstanbul would quietly congregate around the *imam* of the homely İskenderpaşa Mosque 300 yards south of the imperial complex of Mehmed the Conqueror—governors, rectors, professors, doctors, businessmen, and even generals—the range was broad, according to the *müezzin* of the time.[2] They were coming to listen to a preacher whose style of address "was awesome. He raised his voice considerably and talked extemporaneously to the audience, assuming the conciseness of an army commander addressing his troops."[3] So reminisced Korkut Özal, a man who went on to prosper in trade and finance with Saudi Arabia and become Minister of Agriculture and Internal Affairs. He was just one of those marked by "The Unseen University," as one biographer of Mehmet Zahit Kotku (1897–1980) referred to these sessions.[4] That *imam*'s calls for action have changed the political face of Turkey, inspiring those who have steered the nation's government for two thirds of the years since the generals gave way in 1983—Turgut Özal, eldest brother of Korkut; Necmettin Erbakan, the father of political Islam in recent Turkey; and Recep Tayyip Erdoğan, the current master of the country.

The mosque where this worthy served from 1958 to his death in 1980 is a gem from the early sixteenth century, endowed for the Nakşibendi by İskender Paşa, a trusted commander and Balkan governor of Mehmed the Conqueror and his successor. It is the name of his mosque that is usually attached to the religious order that continues the line of the *imam*.

The figure who so impressed Korkut Özal was a man,

> of above medium height and weight. His appearance was both imposing and inspiring. His skin was white and his cheeks were rosy. He had a rather large head with a wide and alabaster forehead. His eyebrows were widely spaced. At first glance, his eyes appeared chestnut in colour, but in reality his eyes were so profound in essence and so mysterious in appearance that a close look was almost impossible.[5]

Korkut Özal had met Kotku on New Year's Day in 1960. During a visit to the U.S., Özal had been impressed by how deeply rooted religion was in American society, not least where he and his wife had been staying among the Mormons of Spanish Fork in Utah:

> The more we learned about the importance and comprehensive place religion had in both their private and communal life and conduct, the wider and deeper was the change in our original concept of the role of religion in human life. The more details we accumulated, the more we came to the conclusion that the proposition that religion and progress were incompatible was founded on false premises.[6]

The Mormons thus set Özal on a quest to emulate them in Turkey. With Kotku, he found the teacher he sought. Before long, his mother, Hafize, and brothers, Turgut and Yusuf Bozkurt, had joined him as the pupils of *Hocaefendi*, as he subsequently referred to Kotku.

Kotku's father had been a refugee from nineteenth-century Tsarist oppression in the Caucasus, serving as *imam* in several towns around Bursa. Kotku himself, after fighting on the Syrian front in the First World War, returned to İstanbul, succeeded his father as village *imam*, and then moved to a mosque in central Bursa. By this time, he had made his mark with the masters running the Gümüşhanevi order of the nineteenth-century Halidi master, Ahmed Ziyaeddin. In 1952, he succeeded Abdülaziz Bekkine as head of the order and as *imam* at the Ümmü Gülsüm Mescidi in the Zeyrek district of İstanbul. He moved to İskenderpaşa Mosque in 1958.

He was a convinced believer in the classical Halidi precept of worldly action "for the sake of religion and its perfection." His originality was in combining Islam as the answer to the lack of ethics and self-discipline of the individual with advocacy of the skills and knowledge necessary to build a functioning and modern economy. He believed that Islam provided the shared ethical and spiritual language necessary for a harmonious community; that such mores had to be internalized by the individual for communal justice and tranquility to exist; and that Sufism had a crucial role in assisting this internalization and inner transformation.

For him, economic progress and industrialization were the best ways to develop society and ease the rigid grip of Kemalism. Drawing on two of his sermons, one sociologist reconstituted his themes as including:

1. Muslims do not practise their religion in private: Islam means being part of the Islamic community; where the Islamic community disappears, so does Islam.
2. To be religious is to be ready to engage in combat. Factories are not purveyors of consumer goods but places where this combat is to be elaborated. This combat demands that one get to know the worldly sciences, arts and commerce...
6. We think that by imitating the West we too can go to the moon, but we have lost our most precious characteristic: through imitation we have conceded the core of our identity. As a consequence, our country is ruled by the miniskirt, prostitution, drunkenness, bribery, adultery, gambling and the cinema...
7. ... We must deliver ourselves from economic slavery to foreigners...
10. Muslims should try to capture the higher summits of social and political institutions in their country and establish control over the society.[7]

This was the perfect creed for the post-war generation determined to lift Turkey from its long economic miasma. And Kotku proved a master at using the tools of his time—sermons, discussion groups, and books. His Friday sermons addressed the country's economic, political, cultural, and social problems, and were influential on adults and university students alike. Each Sunday, after the afternoon prayer, he taught the comments by Ahmed Ziyaeddin on the *hadis* or took up the issues of the day. His mentor had sought to inspire the Ottomans against the European financiers of the late nineteenth century, and that was a message which, updated, resonated with the dawning economic forces of Kotku's time.

He inherited the wide circle of notables and students built up by his predecessor. He also attracted the children of parents brought up elsewhere in the country in the Nakşibendi tradition and sent to İstanbul to complete their education. The authorities turned a blind eye to his activities, perhaps as he never came out against the state. For his part, in recommending that most of his disciples concentrate on trade rather than the civil service, he assured them that success would free them from dependence on the authorities. He warned against premature attempts to establish an Islamic state in Turkey, and stated a preference for the moral and cultural reorientation of Turkish society.[8] Unlike Said Nursi, he believed action on the political level was essential.

Having lost faith in the existing political parties, he encouraged the creation of an alternative. As he told a group he had invited to his house: "The core identity and character of this wounded nation is Islam. Your main heritage is Islam and as Muslims you can heal this wound by listening to what our Turkish Muslim people want. What they want is an Islamic sense of justice and the restoration of their Ottoman-Islamic identity."[9] He chose his listeners well. Many of the young businessmen went on to build companies that would drive Turkey's economic revival. The budding politicians he encouraged, particularly Erbakan and Turgut Özal, were to lead the renaissance of political Islam in Turkey.

The İskenderpaşa community under Esat Coşan

Kotku died two months after the generals seized power in September 1980. His funeral attracted thousands, turning into one of the first large assemblies of people after the coup. He was the first person to be buried in the prestigious Süleymaniye for over half a century—a confirmation of the influence that Turgut Özal, now deputy prime minister, was exercising in military circles.

Kotku did not nominate a successor (*halife*) to carry on his chain to the Prophet, but left behind four deputies (*vekil*). These were his son-in-law, Mahmud Esat Coşan (1938–2001), a deputy professor at the Sakarya State Architecture and Engineering Academy; Cevat Akşit, a former *müezzin* with Kotku who had embarked on an academic career; Ahmet Akın Çığman, a scholar; and Ömer Faruk Göze, *imam* at the Yahya Efendi Mosque in Beşiktaş.[10] The community settled on the first of these as a figure imbued with the teaching of Kotku himself and respected in religious circles.

Coşan, who two years later became a professor of theology, had already taken over the failing Kotku's Sunday talks, travelling to İstanbul each weekend to give them, and delivering similar talks and lessons in Ankara during the week. He was part of the commission preparing a report on Turkey's spiritual development for the State Planning Organization.[11]

Coşan set out to transform İskenderpaşa into an intellectual centre where urban and educated individuals would be socialized as contributors to Turkish society.[12] After his father-in-law's death, he continued the Friday sermons and Sunday teachings of Kotku's "Unseen University." Attendees included Erdoğan who, as mayor of İstanbul, would often meet up with political allies at Coşan's homilies. Echoing Kotku, Coşan would say: "As far as I am concerned, those who not have trade experience do not turn out to be good humans. The most pragmatic and realistic people are businessmen and merchants. If a businessman is also a Muslim, he is the most in tune with his religious station in life."[13]

Where his underlying beliefs are concerned, Coşan followed Kotku—and al-Ghazali a millennium earlier—in presenting God as the agent of every motion and event. He added a new element: that Islamic laws are able to affect events in nature. In his view, Muslims' failure to live a religious life could have material effects in nature, while abiding by Islamic laws initiates God's direct intervention in favor of people. He considered human reason as needing the guidance of superior religious knowledge. Accordingly, reason is able to recognize only the principles and truths defined by God.[14]

Never shy of action, Coşan launched a foundation to support education, the Hakyol Foundation for Aiding Education and Friendship (*Hakyol Eğitim Yardımlaşma ve Dostluk Vakfı*). It started activities in 1980, and in the early 1990s, Coşan opened further foundations and some women's associations, though little was to be heard of these.[15]

Convinced that preaching alone was no longer sufficient, he projected the order into the world of mass communications. He proved a prolific writer and commentator, his followers' website listing thirty-eight books by him. He added magazines to the lodge's activities—*İslam Dergisi* (The Magazine of Islam, from 1983) and then periodicals on female and family issues and science and art—and a daily newpaper, *Sağduyu Gazetesi* (Common Sense Newspaper). As with Kotku, his teaching was followed by part of the intellectual elite, in this sense mirroring a number of contemporaneous Islamic movements. A survey of readers of *İslam Dergisi* in 1987 showed that 76 per cent were graduates of universities or high schools, 95 per cent were men, and 80 per cent were under thirty years old. Only 19 per cent lived in villages.

In his second editorial in *İslam Dergisi*, writing under the pen name Halil Necatioğlu, Coşan addressed "*Jihad* on the Path of Allah." Defining *jihad* as endeavour, work, effort, and patience, he describes the enemy as the unbeliever, that disbelief is one nation, and, working both externally and internally, "has its eyes on our land;" in his view, "the first [of the enemies] to come to mind are the Greeks." [16]

His message of a bipolar world of Muslims under threat from infidels continued through the sixteen years that *İslam* appeared. No distinction was made between the Soviet Union which invaded Afghanistan, Israel which killed Palestinians, or the U.S. which bombed Libya. In his view, Islamic countries should unite to resist the profiteers and former colonists worried about losing their privileges.[17] The magazine often sided with radical Islamic movements against Arab kingdoms and sultanates whom it termed the "gendarmerie of the U.S." All this extended his message to new audiences but also changed the nature of dialogue between the leader of a *tarikat* and his followers, reducing the traditional figure of mystical inspiration to that of an editor.

In the years when Erbakan's political activities were restricted, Coşan had a relatively clear field. His sermons and teaching at İskenderpaşa Mosque drew hundreds, and the report—never substantiated—spread that sales of his monthly *İslam Dergisi* exceeded 100,000. His Hakyol Foundation acted to mobilize youth for the fledgling Welfare Party. Erbakan's withdrawal of this mandate irked Coşan, and tension between the two grew.[18]

While Erbakan venerated Kotku, he never felt the same for Coşan, a man eleven years younger than him. In May 1990, Erbakan insisted that the leader of a *tarikat* was just a soldier in the army. For him and the *Milli Görüş* movement, it was the politicians who would usher in the Islamic state for which it was the duty of every Muslim to fight. But that is not how Coşan saw it. He believed that the politicians owed him fealty. Politics should be the servant of religion. He and his followers started a fight within the Welfare Party, and lost. At the party congress that October, Erbakan won 551 of the 552 votes cast.[19]

Marginalized in politics, Coşan proved to be far from the otherworldly saints of the past. He was one of the first to take a religious order into the world of commerce. In 1987, he added the education company, ASFA, to the publishing companies set up to print his magazines. He started a general trading company, Vera. Come the 1990s and he expanded into food (Sima Ağ and Süfür Gıda) and television film production. A radio (AK Radio) and (short-lived) television station (AK TV) followed. His company, Haksağ Sağlık Hizmetleri, was behind the foundation of the Private Nisa Hospital in the Bahçeşehir district of İstanbul, and he added two further health companies.[20] In 1995, the companies were grouped under Server Holding.

Following the soft coup of February 1997, Coşan left for Australia, ceasing publication of *İslam* and his other publications, and devoting his energies to opening mosques and Islamic cultural centres there. In 2000, Erdoğan travelled to Australia, ostensibly to visit the small Nakşibendi community there, but possibly to obtain Coşan's blessing for launching a new political party.[21] The following February, Coşan was killed in a car crash in New South Wales. His wish to be buried beside Kotku in the hallowed graveyard of Süleymaniye was refused by the president, Ahmet Necdet Sezer. Princess Neslişah Sultan, a member of the Ottoman dynasty, thanked Sezer "for bringing calm to the souls of our ancestors in their eternal sleep."[22] But the ancestors would soon have other souls close to Erdoğan with whom to make peace.

Two subfusc decades with Nureddin Coşan

Coşan had not nominated a successor and, when his only child, Muharrem Nureddin (sometimes Nurettin, b. 1963), claimed leadership, the İskenderpaşa movement was torn. The spiritual successor of Coşan, or rather of Kotku, was Cevat Akşit (b. 1938), who had served as *müezzin* for Kotku in the latter's first mosque in İstanbul and moved with him to İskenderpaşa Mosque in 1958. At the time, Akşit was closer to the National Outlook tradition, while Korkut Özal favoured Nureddin as successor, partly because the latter supported the new AKP and partly because, under the laws of inheritance, Nureddin was the beneficiary of a strong position in the İskenderpaşa community's foundations and commercial enterprises.

Nureddin, who had been working at the family's Server Holding since 1996, duly prevailed. Early on, he told friends that he had no interest in religious affairs, and this trait has been apparent during his quarter century running İskenderpaşa. In this period, the community has virtually abandoned any public attempt to guide its followers in Turkey on faith, instead concentrating on its commercial interests and—briefly—on the governance of the country.

Nureddin was a graduate of the Ankara *İmam-Hatip Lisesi* and studied at the Theological Faculty of Ankara University. After this, he went to the language institute of King Fahd University of Petroleum and Minerals in Dhahran and to New York for an MBA.

Under his guidance, Server Holding and its commercial enterprises appear to be lasting the course. The holding now vouchsafes little about its activities, but in 2020 its website listed activity in food, education, energy, media, construction, technology, and "other." Nureddin is registered as owning 100 per cent of its shares.[23] The holding company used to list its brands—AKRA (AK Radio), ASFA (education), Halas Teknoloji (web services), Necat Yapı (construction), Server İletişim (communications), and Yemekshah (catering).

These are not passive companies, while health has become a particular focus. In the mid-2000s, Haksağ and its Private Nisa Hospital activities were subsumed into the community's health foundation, TESA. In 2009, the latter set up the Medipol University in İstanbul on properties leased on favourable terms from the state. Medipol now runs a university with a 220,000-square-metre campus in the Kavacık area of İstanbul, sixteen schools and seventy-five departments, and the Nisa Hospital. In 2018, a second foundation, TEBA (*Türkiye Eğitim Sağlık Bilim ve Araştırma Vakfı*) set up the Ankara Medipol Üniversitesi. TEBA's website provides four reference links, all to TESA activities. The founding chairman of TESA was Fahrettin Koca, family doctor of Erdoğan and from July 2018 to July 2024 Minister of Health.[24]

Nureddin Coşan's most grandiose recent project has been a building now looming over İskenderpaşa Mosque and housing a massive kindergarten whose offer to 3–6-year-olds includes religious education.

The İskenderpaşa foundations were active in the 1998–1999 Kosovo war and the 1999 Marmara earthquake, arranging tents and support for those rendered homeless, and, later, repair of the damage suffered by the İskenderpaşa Mosque. They claim to have assisted 200,000 people afflicted by the Indonesian tsunami of 2004 and to have supported refugees from Syria and "East Turkestan," as they refer to Central Asia. The work in Indonesia was supported by the MEC (Mahmud Es'ad Cosan) Foundation, set up in Queensland, Australia in 2002. In 2021, MEC wrote that since 2006, it had supplied sacrificial lamb to 821,379 families in Indonesia.[25]

In Turkey, İskenderpaşa's foundations have been maintaining the gravestones of the *tarikat*'s members in the graveyard of Süleymaniye mosque and restoring the *tekke* in Eyüp of Murad Buhari, bringer of the message of renewal of Sirhindi. But, where Islamic learning is concerned, Nureddin Coşan has been conspicuous in his absence. His ventures on YouTube have mainly been to assert the legitimacy of his succession to his father. Apart from some brief comments on life-planning, he is virtually absent on issues of Islamic behavior, his few broadcasts rarely attracting over 10,000 views. His most viewed spiritual message is one of a mere 2 minutes and 25 seconds on how to add value to life, released by a follower in January 2014 and viewed by less than 20,000 people.[26] By contrast, Esat Coşan was a prolific and inspiring speaker and writer. YouTube hosts a large number of his talks and *sohbet*—as today's communities now call discussions—one of which gained 499,000 views in the first five years after its release.[27]

In all this, Nureddin Coşan appears to be acting as the leader of the material heritage of İskenderpaşa. How this community continues its spiritual legacy and the chain of *rabıta* to its saint is more shadowy.

İskenderpaşa started on close terms with the AKP. In December 2002, fresh from his party's election victory, Erdoğan celebrated a Friday prayer at the newly opened Mehmet Zahit Kotku mosque in Ankara. Fourteen of the twenty-three ministers of his first cabinet had links with the order.[28]

Initially, Nureddin Coşan kept some distance from the AKP, indeed creating his own Common Sense Party (*Sağduyu Partisi*) in 2002. It has never presented candidates during elections. Just before the June 2011 general elections, he suddenly declaimed: "our spiritual garden is now haunted by herds of pigs, hyenas, treacherous dogs, cunning foxes, carrion crows, leeches, and suckers." He (vainly) called on his followers to vote for the nationalist MHP. Three years later, his message was back in tune, urging support for Erdoğan in the August 2014 presidential elections and the June 2015 general elections.

However, a bridge had obviously been built before those elections. In 2013, the Ministry of National Education commissioned the Server Foundation to support a national competition on ethics. This has since become an annual event, with 3.4 million children participating in the first eight years of the competition. The holding's publication company often provides the books. In 2020, its *Edeb Mektebi* (School of Manners) told readers: "music is *haram* (forbidden by religion) and films that bring women to the fore are objectionable."

The İskenderpaşa community has had its gains during the past two decades, but the real beneficiary of its activities has been Erdoğan himself. Just as it served him by delivering loyal lieutenants to his early cabinets, so it has acted as an employment agency for his party, delivering respectful staff to help him build up the presence of his fledgling movement in the machinery of state.

Initially, this role was shared with the avid Gülenists. But, as the split between Erdoğan and Gülen developed (see Chapter 13), so Erdoğan's need grew for safe pairs of hands, figures who would obey rather than seek to usurp. The Hakyolcu—as they would term themselves after Esat Coşan's foundation—had always sought a presence in the police and judiciary. Since the execration of Gülen, they have become ubiquitous. Seasoned followers of the courts have been impressed by how many accused would seek to deflect charges by opening their defence with the words: "*Ben Hakyolcuyum*" (I am a Hakyolcu).[29]

In the weeks before the 2023 elections, a rapporteur warned the CHP that, if it came to power, its main challenge in the capital could be the Hakyolcu and its "little princes." In some institutions, their name stalks like a spectre, warns one theologian. But the spiritual heart of the community has withered:

> Today, that *cemaat* has a name, but it does not exist. The winds are blowing around the mosque in the district of İskenderpaşa right now. But most of its old names have gone to Paradise... if you seek the background and infrastructure of today's political power, yes, it is based on İskenderpaşa. But a lot of water has flowed under that İskenderpaşa. For better or worse, those people have become unrecognizable.[30]

A split in the chain

The death of Esat Coşan had left a spiritual void. Some of those unimpressed by the master's son turned to the Cerrahi, a traditional non-Nakşibendi sect long appealing to intellectuals. Others joined discussion groups (*sohbet*) seeking to recreate the spirit of the *Milli Görüş*. A number looked to Cevat Akşit, the close disciple of Kotku, for spiritual leadership and guidance. Indeed, it was he who stood between Erdoğan and his son-in-law, Dr Berat Albayrak, when they were paying their last respects to Kemal Unakıtan, one of the key figures in the closely associated *İlim Yayma* community.

Akşit's following is solid. He has a firm grasp of religious law and scholastic theology, applying this to the daily problems of life as he seeks to assist the individual to be a good Muslim. He is an active contributor to YouTube, with one s*ohbet* on sexual etiquette and Islam delivered in September 2011 since viewed over 3 million times.

Born in Yatağan in 1938, Akşit went to the *imam-hatip* school in Isparta, one of the early intakes of these schools. He met Kotku when appointed as his *müezzin* in Zeyrek. Akşit remembers spending every evening with him before starting out on his own career. In one of his *sohbet*, he recounts how he was asked by Demirel (also from Isparta) to become head of the *Diyanet*, but preferred to continue a teaching career. He alleges that at separate times both the Süleymancıs and the Gülenists wanted to kill him.[31]

Twice passed over as head of the Gümüşhanevi community, he proselytizes tirelessly. Best known in pre-COVID-19 days were his weekly talks on Sunday when, installed in an armchair in the *mihrab* of the Süleymaniye mosque, he would take over this grand imperial monument for the two hours between the afternoon and evening prayers. One such event in November 2019 attracted about 150 men and, gathered under a nearby column, 40 women. It seemed a modest group, but mixed in among the small traders and municipal workers were academics and successful businessmen, his aide told me a week later. The aide did not comment on suggestions that Akşit is almost a personal pastor for Erdoğan.

Nonetheless, his relationship with Erdoğan is not that of earlier leaders of İskenderpaşa. In the photograph of the prayers for the second anniversary of the 2016 coup attempt, Erdoğan and Ali Erbaş, the Director of Religious Affairs, are upright while Akşit is bent and crumpled. As one author of books on the *tarikat* commented: "*Şeyh* Kotku would never, never have accepted such a situation."[32] It is a moot question whether he still cherishes leadership of the community. As he and Nureddin both know, in most ways that matter, Erdoğan has usurped that role for himself.

8

THE TURKISH-ISLAMIC SYNTHESIS AND THE PATRICIAN ERENKÖY COMMUNITY

Forgetting, and I would even say historical error, are an essential factor in the creation of a nation... Of all cults, that of the ancestors is the most legitimate, for the ancestors have made us what we are...

Ernest Renan, *Qu'est-ce qu'une Nation?* A lecture delivered at the Sorbonne, Ancienne Maison Michel Lévy Frères, 1882 (translation by the author)

Adding nationalism to the blend

With Kotku, faith had been integrated with commerce. Developing this into a movement of mass appeal required leavening the blend with nationalism, and here it was academics who led the way. Their efforts took shape in the late 1960s when a group of conservatives espoused the Turkish-Islamic synthesis developed by the disputatious Seljuk historian, İbrahim Kafesoğlu. Within scarcely a decade, this concept was adopted by the generals who seized power in 1980. It is now fundamental to the nation-building inherent in Erdoğan's New Turkey and its successor, the Century of Türkiye.

Kafesoğlu and his colleagues argued that the story of the Turks had to be rewritten in the light of the cultural elements that were specific to the Turkic peoples as they emerged in Central Asia, founded several states, converted to Islam, and successfully merged their Turkish cultural heritage with that of their new religion. The conservatives gained the support of businessmen supporting religious education who saw the need for a public platform to promote conservative values. And they combined with nationalists seeking an alternative to the left-wing currents of the time. The result was formation of one of Turkey's more effective ginger groups, the Intellectuals' Hearth (*Aydınlar Ocağı*).[1]

With the synthesis becoming so influential, it is worth setting out what it comprised. The starting point was the premise that the pre-Islamic structure of the Turks was based on a society where the family and the military were the two most important institutions, with a cultural outlook emphasizing specific moral principles around which individual behaviour was oriented:

> This morality, on the one hand, taught the value of virtue, trust and justice in social relations. On the other hand, it led to the emergence of a unique political philosophy, the pillars of which rested on love of country, fear of God, sanctity of custom, and obedience to state authority. As part of this political outlook, the Turks also learned, from very early times, the importance of preserving their racial purity and political independence, both of which depended on keeping foreign cultural influences at a minimum.
>
> This cultural heritage later met with Islam and from the synthesis of two civilizations a 'national culture' emerged upon which, according to Kafesoğlu, two great empires were built, the [Seljuk] and the Ottoman. However, despite a thousand years of history behind it, the Turkish-Islamic cultural synthesis collapsed as a result of a disease which inflicted [sic] Turkish intellectuals, namely, imitation of the west. The disastrous effect of such imitation was the disturbance of the balance that the 'national culture' had achieved between the family, the mosque, and the barracks which, for centuries, had inculcated in the Turkish collective consciousness respect for elders, discipline, and the sacredness of duty.[2]

The Hearth positioned itself "not as influenced by masonic circles as is the Justice Party (AP) nor by religious circles as is the National Salvation Party (MSP), nor by nationalist circles as is the Nationalist Action Party (MHP)—close to all but representing none."[3]

In 1973, the Hearth's leaders sought to impress on Erbakan's MSP that the latter's natural partnership was with the other two main nationalist-conservative parties of the right. These efforts culminated in an open letter published in November 1974 calling for the formation of a "nationalist front" coalition of the three. This duly happened four months later, and the Hearth has since claimed responsibility for catalyzing the creation of this right-wing coalition and of two short-lived successors before the military coup of September 1980.

The Hearth's creed was resolutely anti-communist and its early years coincided with the time when the U.S. was instigating the concept of Islam as an ally against Moscow. This idea, notably advocated by the Russian-French scholar, Alexandre Bennigsen, gained full traction under his student, Zbigniew Brzezinski, close adviser to presidents Lyndon B. Johnson and Jimmy Carter, and imbued with a true Polish hostility towards the Soviet Union.

Bennigsen argued that

> The fact that all of the nations between Greece and China were Muslim gave rise to the notion that Islam itself might reinforce that Maginot Line-style strategy. Gradually, the idea of a green belt along the arc of Islam took form. The idea was not just defensive. Adventurous policy makers imagined that restive Muslims inside the Soviet Union's own Central Asian republics might be the undoing of the USSR itself—and they took steps to encourage them.[4]

In 1978, Brzezinski set up the Nationalities Working Group to foster Muslim unrest in the southern Soviet republics. The first head of this group was Paul B. Henze, just returned from Turkey where he had been CIA station chief.

Turgut Özal had been a regular attendee at the meetings of the Hearth, sharing their views on how education and the media could be used to enhance a sound national identity. These ideas are evident in the SPO report that he commissioned, *National Culture*. This argues that positivism is a force for evil, resulting in a materialist view of life that has led to spiritual decadence in both the West and Turkey. Specific mention, and criticism, is made of Marxism, Darwinism, Freudism, pragmatism, and humanism.[5] "Science without religion is a source of disaster," the report writes, blaming the lack of religious teaching in the education system for having sapped students' morality.[6]

The Hearth's ideas were brought together in its working document *National Accords* (*Milli Mutabakatlar*), circulating in the early 1980s.[7] "Whereas communism has stood as political threat to Turkish independence, humanism has become the tool for Western cultural imperialism" is how one political scientist describes their concerns.[8]

When Özal decided to set up his own party, he drew on the Hearth for his cadre, giving its members posts in the government, education, and broadcasting after being elected prime minister in November 1983. He attended the Hearth's dinner to celebrate the fourth anniversary of the coup. Its influence continued during his decade as prime minister and president.

The Hearth may also have had some mark on the generals' constitution of 1982. Two members of the Hearth had been in the committee drawing up this constitution. The Turkish-Islamic synthesis had now become part of the standard discourse of the country. At this point, it did not displace Atatürkism—this was impossible in a nation accustomed to identifying with the legacy of Mustafa Kemal—but arguably joined it as the operating ideology of the Republic.[9]

İlim Yayma—"the story of Turkey"

A number of the businessmen supporting the Intellectuals' Hearth also belonged to a body set up to promote Islam. This was the Association for Spreading Knowledge (*İlim Yayma Cemiyeti*). Relations between this and the Hearth have always been close, and they long operated from the same building. "While the basis of the Hearth was nationalism, the basis of *İlim Yayma* was religion."[10]

İlim Yayma started as a group of sixty-eight "fine people who gave leaf to a plane tree under whose shade would benefit all mankind."[11] It opened its first *imam-hatip* school in October 1951 at Samatya on the Marmara slopes of İstanbul. The director of the school was Celal Hoca (Mahmut Celalettin Ökten), whose teachers had included Mehmed Akif Ersoy, writer of the poem used as the Turkish national anthem. The students were all male. Photographs show them wearing the long-banned fez.

Arguing not a day was to be lost to develop an enlightened generation to secure the future of the country, the association started more schools, with Menderes trowelling cement into at least one foundation. It also developed dormitories for mid-school students. It emphasized that it was "kneading the young with civilization" in order to train the architects of an inspired future. Science and education were necessary for the development of the country. Serving science was a form of worship.

Takeoff was slow but steady. After a decade, the number of *imam-hatip* middle schools (*ortaokul*) was 19, that of high schools (*lise*) 17, and the student body totalled a mere 4,500. Another decade later, and students had risen ten-fold, the association being the force behind this growth. In these twenty years, private individuals contributed six times more than the state to the building of the physical plant for religious instruction.[12]

By 1955, *İlim Yayma* had secured reserve officer status for graduates of *imam-hatip* schools during military service and eligibility for these students to enter university entrance exams. The mainstream Kemalist paper, *Cumhuriyet*, reported on the annual meeting of the association but was not perturbed: "Religious people with a suitable reform mentality will be trained," ran its soothing headline.[13] But other parts of the secular establishment were less sanguine. In October 1953, the CIA, presumably briefed by its Turkish counterparts, published a report entitled "Moslem Brotherhood in Turkey." It described *İlim Yayma* as "the cover name of an Arab secret organization which has as its purpose the establishment of secret schools to train Imams and preachers in all countries where the teaching of Arabic speech and writing is not allowed, and the support of these schools with funds."[14] At this point, the CIA had still to develop the concept of using Islam to counter communism.

İlim Yayma continued to grow. It faced a temporary setback in 1960 when the generals took over its management, but the advent to power of Demirel changed this, and it was soon freed to resume its work. At this point, Kemalists' concerns that political leaders were again condoning reaction led to earlier accusations against *İlim Yayma* being dusted off and updated. This time, it was the left-wing İstanbul weekly *ANT* which became the channel for highlighting the links between *İlim Yayma* and the Saudis, who at that time were hosting Muslim Brothers from Nasser's Egypt and had allowed them to take over religious education in the Kingdom.[15] "The Muslim World League, that is the Moslem Brotherhood, manages its reactionary activities in Turkey via the *İlim Yayma* Association," wrote *ANT*.[16] Saudi support to the association was condoned by King Faisal who contributed to a new *İlim Yayma* dormitory, having a rosette pinned to his robes at its opening.[17]

ANT's article described the associations and newspapers supporting links with Saudi Arabia and the figures behind them. Not least of these was Muammer Topbaş, a member of a major business family and a founder of the Turkey-Saudi Arabia Friendship Association. He and six other members of his family were soon to be involved in the *İlim Yayma* Foundation, set up in 1973 to take over the assets of the association. That year, Korkut Özal served as director of the association, while he and his brother, Turgut, were among the 101 subscribers to the new foundation.

The original group from 1951 had now broadened. Apart from the seven members of the Topbaş family, benefactors included two members of the growing Ülker group of companies, and leading figures in the city. The mayor of İstanbul was listed *ex officio* as a member of the foundation, as was the governor "as the biggest landowner in the city." The foundation's first two presidents were Sabri Ülker, head of the Ülker group, and Eymen Topbaş, later to become İstanbul head of Turgut Özal's ANAP.

In the 1980s, Saudi interests in religious education in Turkey again became news headlines. The government of Turgut Özal had been lifting restrictions on Islam, and this time it was *Cumhuriyet* that led the attack. "Saudi capital is coming," proclaimed the newspaper on 13 March 1987 during a series of articles triggered by the Saudis funding the wages of Turkish preachers in Germany. "The *İlim Yayma* Association and Intellectuals Hearth, hand in hand with their Saudi partners, constitute a financial empire that is growing day by day."[18]

The last point was no fantasy. Saudi Arabia (and Bahrain) had taken advantage of Özal's decree allowing Islamic banking—signed a mere three days after he took office—and the Topbaş and Ülker families and Özal's brother, Korkut, had been quick to join them as shareholders. The Muslim World League sent 25 million USD to help finance mosques, notably the Kocatepe mosque in Ankara's centre and mosques at the Grand National Assembly and Middle East Technical University. The Saudi-American Bank started operations in Turkey, as did the Saudi Fund and a Saudi-Turkish investment fund.

İlim Yayma's role as the first charitable body to promote religious education in the Republic has led to some ambitious claims. In 2006, Professor Sabahattin Zaim, one of the movement's leading figures, exulted that *İlim Yayma* had given material or moral support to all the *imam-hatip* schools established in the country.[19] More realistic—and still impressive—may be its statement that by 2020 it had founded over 100 *imam-hatip* lycées, 184 dormitories, and over 80 education facilities. It has also established a university, named in honour of the late Zaim, and a range of schools and dormitories and cramming colleges, with some 10,000 students in 2019–2020.

İlim Yayma's style has been to stay close to politicians. It smoothly navigated the shift from Özal, through Erbakan to Erdoğan. In 1994, as mayor of İstanbul, Erdoğan attended the celebrations of the 43rd anniversary of the founding of the association, saying: "The story of the *İlim Yayma*

Association is the story of Turkey." He insisted on being accepted as a full founder of *İlim Yayma*, not *ex officio*.

His first Minister of Finance was Kemal Unakıtan, earlier director of the association. In 2016, Erdoğan repeated this message on *İlim Yayma* and its role in the history of Turkey at its 65th anniversary. A year later, now president of Turkey, he attended the Annual General Meeting of the foundation, congratulating it for its support of the Republic in its most sombre days and describing it as the "memory of Turkey." In March 2024, he and his second son, Necmeddin Bilal, were listed among the 123 living founder members of the foundation. Bilal has been serving as Chairman of its (all-male) Board of Trustees.

Such relations have helped *İlim Yayma* take over at least eighteen state properties since the AKP came to power. Two of these are prime Ottoman monuments. The first is the imposing Ottoman Veterinary School at Halkalı and its 357,000 square metres of land, rented in 2010 to *İlim Yayma*'s İstanbul Sabahattin Zaim University. In 2020, the rent was a mere 7,000 USD a month. The site had previously been designated as a campus for Marmara University. The second is the even more resonant Akdeniz Sahn-ı Semân *medrese* of the imperial mosque of Mehmed the Conqueror, once the peak of religious training in the Ottoman Empire. *İlim Yayma* has restored these graceful buildings, with around 127 cells and a library, to much of their original charm and is using them as its education and research centre.

İlim Yayma has good relations with the Ministry of Education, in 2017 signing a protocol under which the ministry would fund distance courses offered by the association on "social, cultural, professional and technical issues." Its public style has been low-key, stressing its role in helping the young. It publishes a monthly bulletin now called *Vefa Dergi-Bülten* and an academic publication, which is now continued by its related university.

It has never actively proselytized or opened a television channel, but politics has its risks. In June 2019, when Ekrem İmamoğlu of the CHP ended the AKP's long hold on the Municipality of Greater İstanbul, he froze the funds that the municipality had munificently doled out to charities favoured by Erdoğan. *İlim Yayma* had received over 2 million USD of such funds. İmamoğlu also started battling to take back possession of a fine Ottoman building in Eyüp that *İlim Yayma* Foundation had used as its headquarters. Visited shortly after this freeze, an officer of the foundation emphasized the foundation's services to under-funded students: "I was one of those who benefitted when, after my father's death, I came from Erzurum to İstanbul. I will never forget."[20]

The Erenköy community—classical Islamism for the elite

There had been one member of the Topbaş family among the founders of the Hearth, two members of the family among the founders of the *İlim Yayma* Association, and six members among the founders of the *İlim Yayma* Foundation. Forty years on, the family contributed a dozen of the 123 members of the foundation, and two of the fourteen trustees of the foundation's university.

The nineteenth-century patriarch of this pervasive family, Ahmed Kudsi Efendi, was a *şeyh* of a Halidi branch of the Nakşibendi *tarikat* in Kadınhanı, Konya. His grandson, Ahmet Hamdi, came to İstanbul in 1917, working in the Laleli district of old İstanbul, then moving to Erenköy on the Asian flanks of the Marmara. He was a friend of the last but one *şeyhülislam* of the Ottomans, Mustafa Sabri, no admirer of the new Republic.

His descendants have left their mark. Their main business has been in textiles, including three major combines: Bahariye, Kader, and Hisar. Come the 1980s and family members were partners in the first Islamic banking operation in Turkey, Al-Baraka. They next expanded into retail and food. They were linked to Turgut Özal, who in 1983 turned to Eymen, a grandson of Ahmet Hamdi, to head his new party's İstanbul organization. Since the 2000s, another grandson, Mustafa Latif, has been known for his closeness to Erdoğan. Ranked in 2017 as the 27th richest Turk by *Forbes*, he claims the idea of the lightbulb as the emblem for Erdoğan's party. He was sufficiently close to Erdoğan to have been briefly arrested and have his bank accounts frozen during the short-lived investigation into alleged corruption at the heart of Erdoğan's government in December 2013.

The commitment of the family to supporting the spread of Islam has continued for almost a century, and the link with Erenköy has coloured its members' vision of Islam. For it was in that small village a short walk north of the Marmara that lived the two Nakşibendi *şeyh* who inspired succeeding generations of the Topbaş family and the religious community they have developed.

The first of these *şeyh* was the ill-fated Esad Erbili. Head of a *tarikat* tracing back to Halid el-Bağdadi, he had been brought up in the Nakşibendi tradition, later aligning himself with the Kadiris. He was a respected member of the Ottoman *ulema* and served as head of the Council of

Şeyh, the Ottoman body controlling the dervishes. His writings angered Abdülhamid, and he was exiled to Erbil, now capital of the Kurdish Region of Iraq, organizing local networks against increasing British influence in the region. With the advent of the Young Turks, he returned to İstanbul, again being appointed head of the Council of *Şeyh*. He resigned to continue his publishing and teaching. With the closure of the *tekke*, he secluded himself in a grand wooden house sheltered by pines in Erenköy.[21] He remained in the sights of the ever-suspicious security police and in December 1930 was one of the victims of the crackdown on religion following the Menemen incident, dying in prison ten weeks later.

Esad had named a young accountant, Mahmut Sami Ramazanoğlu (1892–1984), as one of his successors. Following the closure of the *tekke*, Ramazanoğlu went to Adana, working as an accountant in a timber company and clandestinely teaching Islam from his house. He was one of the first Turks to make the pilgrimage to Mecca after Ankara lifted its ban on the *hajj*. On his return, now known as Sami Efendi, he started proselytizing in Anatolia, eventually establishing himself in Erenköy. Once there, while again working as an accountant, he started giving sermons at the Zihni Paşa Cami, spending the rest of his time teaching. He was obviously an inspiring figure. As a *müftü* of İstanbul in this period said: "It is more difficult to get rich people on their knees for hours than to moor a Bosphorus steamer at Sarayburnu. We cannot do it. Only Sami Efendi can."[22]

He had a following among the anti-communist youth. In the early 1970s, one president of the MTTB had sought Ramazanoğlu's blessing, and his two successors continued their veneration for the saint.[23] In 1977, Ramazanoğlu agreed to support Necmettin Erbakan, then leader of the National Salvation Party, in exchange for Erbakan nominating as candidates two figures selected by Ramazanoğlu. He spent his last years in Medina, dying there in 1984. He left behind fifteen books on religious interpretation and history, a six-part work on accountancy, and a number of anointed successors.

The two of these to make the most mark were Tahir Büyükkörükçü of Konya, and Musa Topbaş of Erenköy. Büyükkörükçü's career is similar to that of many Islamic personalities in Turkey in that it includes both public office and prison. He rose in the official hierarchy to become *müftü* for his city, served as deputy for Erbakan's MSP from 1977, preached to Turkish workers abroad, spent eleven months in detention after the 1980 coup, and died widely respected locally, with hundreds of thousands at his funeral, including three of Erdoğan's ministers. He was a friend of men who would lead three of the six most active Nakşibendi *tarikat* as well as of the ubiquitous Kısakürek. While visiting Konya in 2005, Erdoğan called on his house and in April 2017 attended Friday prayers in the mosque named in the late worthy's honour.

Like the other successors of Ramazanoğlu, Büyükkörükçü was a believer in an evolutionary rather than a revolutionary approach to restoring the role of Islam in society: "... we will have generations trained in belief and faith. Factors such as drinking, gambling, prostitution, adultery and use of interest which destroy society will be eliminated and, with the resulting political mindset, we will assure the cleanliness of the pool."[24]

While Büyükkörükçü continued to retain a following in Anatolia—and on YouTube where a talk he gave in February 2012 has attracted 2 million views—in İstanbul itself, Ramazanoğlu's heritage was continued by the second and most influential of his named successors, Musa Topbaş.

Musa Topbaş had early developed a strong interest in Islam, marrying the daughter of a Nakşibendi trader, and providing Said Nursi with a car when the latter came to İstanbul. He submitted himself to Ramazanoğlu in 1956, and, after taking on the latter's mantle, proved a charismatic figure among the businessmen and tradesmen who were benefitting from Turkey's economic takeoff during the Özal period.

When he died, he was succeeded by his son, Osman Nuri Topbaş, a fatherly figure who has been preaching, writing, and publishing extensively since 1990. The Erenköy community long insisted that Osman Nuri was the organizational successor rather than religious heir of his father—perhaps to deflect categorization as a formally banned *tarikat*—but recent years have seen that distinction being blurred.

Osman Nuri had been one of the early students at the *İlim Yayma*'s *imam-hatip* school in Samatya. He combined work in the family textile trading companies with helping *İlim Yayma*. He was a financial supporter of Necip Fazıl Kısakürek and the latter's *Büyük Doğu* magazine.[25]

In his writings, Osman Nuri sets out a simple message: God governs the universe. Natural events are the results of God's unceasing intervention. He is an integral part of every person's daily life, and, in this world of direct divine governance, Muslims should organize their lives in accordance with the reality of a divine causation rather than natural law, for natural laws are uncertain, while the divine rules and God's management are constant. For him, free will is non-existent and in any case lies beyond human comprehension. He is thus extremely sceptical of human reasoning.[26]

In spring 2024, Osman Nuri's website described him as having written 100 works published in 51 languages to a total of over 600 editions. The languages included Chinese, Uyghur, Mongolian, and Tatar from Asia, and Amharic (Ethiopia), Luganda (Uganda), Swahili (sub-Saharan Africa), Tigrinya (Eritrea/Ethiopia), Twi (Ghana), Wolof (West Africa), and Zarma (Niger) from Africa.

As the preface to his work, *Muhammad, The Prophet of Mercy, Scenes from His Life,* writes of the author: "One recurring subject in his writing bears on demonstrating the importance of mercy, of love and of care in our social relations as the very fabric of an authentic Islamic way of life."[27] He gives weekly talks on religious themes, always dressed in white and with a white prayer cap. His websites allow access to fifteen years of these talks and also link to the weekly *sohbet* he gives on the movement's Erkam TV and other talks subtitled in Arabic, English, and Japanese.[28] YouTube records that thirteen of these have been seen by over 100,000 people. He has over 400,000 followers on X, a similar number on a Turkish-language YouTube account, and 265,000 more on an English-subtitled YouTube account.[29]

Ramazanoğlu had developed his message to enable Muslims to operate during the secular decades of the 1930s and 1940s and to adapt to the opening commercial world. Musa Topbaş and his son Osman Nuri have built on this approach—advocating Islam as ever more relevant to handle the challenges faced by the believer as society changes around him, and promoting the role of the believer as the catalyst for change.

For the movement today, as for Ramazanoğlu, the *Kur'an* is, of course, the most important point of reference. While also accepting *fıkıh*, the prescripts of religious law, Osman Nuri gives weight to *hadis* and *tefsir*, the traditions of the Prophet and commentaries on them. This approach reflects the broad education of Ramazanoğlu's *şeyh*, Esad, and includes some elements found in the looser Kadiri tradition. Its tone is that of the classical Ottoman approach to religion, tending to a mild version of Sunnism, with the Erenköy community clearly differentiated from the more demonstratively puritan precepts of, say, the İsmailağa community.

Members of the Erenköy *cemaat* are largely from the business and academic world, and the community is frequently termed elitist. In 2003, the community was described as "the currently most powerful" of the Nakşibendi branches, and in 2022 an official at MİT, the country's national intelligence agency, assured the writer this was still the case.[30] Like other Nakşibendi communities, it opposed Turkey giving support to the U.S. invasion of Iraq in 2003, but it has generally maintained a low political profile, keeping its distance from the liberal wing of the AKP. Its followers are characterized by humility and modesty. In all this, it is closer to the classical *tarikat* structures of the past than the other religious orders.

Osman Nuri suggests his followers call him *hoca*, but his adepts refer to him in terms ranging from *Şeyh* to *Sultan Baba*. The figures responsible for different regions are known as *halife*. As with the Gülen movement, *sohbet* (discussion groups)—those for women held in the daytime and those for men after the evening prayer—are an integral part of the community's activities, with the *sohbetçi* or *grup başı* (group head) a recognized part of the hierarchy. The followers of the community are known as *mürid*, the traditional Sufi word for disciple, and refer to each other as *ihvan*, the Sufi equivalent of comrade.[31]

The community carries out most of its material activities through the Aziz Mahmud Hüdayi Foundation. This was set up by twenty notables including Osman Nuri Topbaş, his cousin Ahmet Hamdi Topbaş, his son-in-law Fahrettin Tivnikli, the latter's younger brother, Abdullah, and the ubiquitous Korkut Özal. Active since 1986, the foundation has become the umbrella for a wide range of education, cultural, and religious activities and is almost a role model for other religious communities in Turkey. Its education activities now spread from *Kur'an* courses and *imam-hatip* schools through to supporting graduates, postgraduates, and teachers. It has a research centre, *İlmi Araştırmalar Merkezi* (İLAM), and has started personality and leadership courses in deftly negotiated historical buildings. Its aid activities include soup kitchens, *iftar* dinners, cash and provisions, and disaster relief. In 2013, it organized a three-day symposium on the Nakşibendi renewer, Sirhindi, and one on Nakşibendism in 2016. Both attracted high-profile attendance.[32]

A foundation brochure distributed in 2019 mentions its activities in Turkey but emphasizes its work abroad. It gives considerable importance to education and claims to have built up nearly 200 schools in over thirty countries and to serve around 45,000 students per year. Among its facilities outside Turkey are one higher education facility, twenty-two *imam-hatip* schools, sixteen *Kur'an* courses, fifty-six student dormitories, and ten crèches.[33] Examples of its activities are humanitarian aid in Syria, food and *kurban* (sacrifice contributions) in Somalia, Ramadan *iftar* dinners in Tanzania, and drinking water supplies in Uganda. Two other foundations work abroad under the Erenköy umbrella: Rahmet Eli (Hand of Mercy), which in 2019 stated it distributed food to 1,200 families per month and supported 350 students, and the Sami Efendi Foundation, working in Ankara, Gaza, and Nigeria. All these activities have fitted well alongside the soft power projection of Turkish diplomacy under the AKP and have become an integral part of this.[34]

In August 2019, the new mayor of İstanbul listed the Aziz Mahmud Hüdayi Foundation among the bodies that the municipality would no longer fund. The municipality said that up to 2018 the foundation had received TL 10.5 million (about 3 million USD). The foundation was aggrieved. It claimed that its founders paid 80 per cent of its expenses, that the rest came from donations, and that it had not received any municipal funds.

The Erenköy community is indeed different from other Nakşibendi movements in Turkey in that it has not set up companies seeking to benefit from the lustre of faith among its adherents. In this, it comes closer to the philanthropists of Victorian Britain than the evangelists of modern America. The community spirit is one where virtue is its own reward, with its members often well heeled and patrician.

Here, it can look not only to textile and food magnates but also to the most successful of all the Green Capitalists of Turkey, Sabri Ülker and his son, Murat. Sabri, a Tatar immigrant from Crimea, progressed from selling biscuits off the back of a lorry with his brother to running a nationwide company. He went on to build his share of the business into a group which, under his son, Murat, has continued to grow, comprising forty-six manufacturing plants in twelve countries, and in 2020 employing 60,000 people with sales over 10 billion USD.[35]

The "Biscuit King's" alliances were fortuitous. In 2003, the brother of his son-in-law established a company with Erdoğan, who by then had become prime minister. A few years later, Sabri Ülker's grandson, Ali, married the daughter of Mustafa Latif Topbaş, Fatma Zehra. In this continual intermeshing of faith, business, and family, it is no surprise to find two representatives of the Ülker family sitting beside three representatives of the Topbaş family on the fourteen-person Board of Trustees of the *İlim Yayma*'s university—nor to find the rector of Erdoğan's cherished Ibn Haldun University on the academic council of another foundation with which the Aziz Mahmud Hüdayi Foundation cooperates. This is İSAR, the İstanbul Research and Education Foundation (*İstanbul Araştırma ve Eğitim Vakfı*), which was originally set up by another Green Capital family, that of the Tivniklis, into which Osman Nuri's eldest daughter, Zeynep, married.[36] The Tivniklis (whose members had been among the founders of the Aziz Mahmud Hüdayi Foundation) handsomely endowed İSAR, and political links then enabled it to occupy the Özbekler lodge which had helped nationalists evade British patrols a century ago.

The lodge had passed to the Ertegün family whose last scion, Ahmet, co-founder of Atlantic Records, restored it, inviting Henry Kissinger to its opening. Ahmet Ertegün bequeathed the lodge, its 17,000-square-metre garden, and funds to the Turkish state on the condition the lodge stayed a museum. İSAR managed to circumvent such obligations. In AKP Turkey, dying wishes count for less than the clout of the new Green Capital.

To the Erenköy movement's many supporters, such links are confirmation of the value and merit of the community with which they have chosen to identify.

Erenköy is unflagging in its use of social and mass media, running a television station, Erkam TV, and a radio station, Erkam Radyo, whose 10-minute promotional video on the radio's cultural and family values in June 2020 was noteworthy for not showing a single woman. In 2016, Erkam bought most of the Moral FM network of the Nurcu *Yeni Nesil* group. (See Chapter 11.) Erenköy publishes monthly magazines aimed at families and the young and on cultural matters, but its flagship magazine has long been the monthly *Altınoluk*.[37] Publication of this started in March 1986, with its articles generally homilies on living a correct life. Its political forays are rare and muted. Instead, it has tended to act as a platform for news and discussion between members of the community.

From 1988 to 2014, the editor of the magazine was Ahmet Taşgetiren, an unflappable and measured journalist whose recent career has been indicative of the relations between Erdoğan and the Erenköy community. Taşgetiren served as chairman of the Central Anatolian section of the government-sponsored Wise People's Commission (*Akil İnsanlar Heyeti*), a grouping of sixty-three coopted intellectuals designed to show that Erdoğan was listening to the people after the Gezi incidents of summer 2013.

In September 2017, after attack by supporters of the AKP, he stopped writing for the pro-government *Star* after it refused to publish his response. The next year, the Hüdayi foundation asked him to suspend his daily programme on Erkam Radyo and to stop writing in *Altınoluk*. Taşgetiren had just appeared on TV5, the television station operated by the heirs of the Erbakan tradition, saying: "I wrote during the periods of March 12th, September 12th and February 28th [the military interventions of 1971, 1980 and 1997]. I did not feel myself as restricted as I feel these days."

By March 2021, his departure from the magazine where he had worked from its first day was complete.

Erenköy has been fully supportive of the AKP, but the president did not afford Taşgetiren's employers any more leeway than he gave to other media owners. Even Mustafa Latif Topbaş has been humbled by today's state machinery. In October 2021, the Competition Authority announced fines for price gouging on six supermarket chains, with the most penalized being Mustafa Latif's BİM, which had to pay over 50 million USD. In late 2022, Erdoğan stayed on the sidelines as Bahçeli accused BİM of links to the proscribed followers of Fethullah Gülen.

As one of their students wrote thirty years ago, Erenköy's strength is mainly a reflection of the wealth of its followers. But then, as now, it remains closer to the classical *tarikat* structures of the past than the other religious orders, jostling for space on what has become an increasingly crowded stage.[38] In 2018, Erenköy's Hüdayi foundation had been among the first to announce its support for Erdoğan's bid for the presidency. In 2023, it kept its silence.

9

THE RISE OF THE PURISTS
THE SÜLEYMANCI AND İSMAİLAĞA COMMUNITIES

> *The influence of the West and the modernity which underpins it have led to the appearance of multiple centres of resistance in the contemporary Islamic world. One reaction is a regression towards original mythology, in the hope that it will resolve in miraculous fashion all the moral sufferings and social inequalities that afflict these societies; another is a* fuite en avant *into increasingly perilous adventures; yet another, a categorical refusal to accept the challenges posed by the new age.*
>
> Daryush Shayegan, *Cultural Schizophrenia: Islamic Societies Confronting the West*, tr. John Howe, Saqi Books, 1992, p. 3[1]

Two Turkish orders in particular have sought refuge in the "original mythology" of Islam, seeing this as an answer to the challenges of Westernization that have perturbed Islamic thinkers in Turkey for nearly two centuries. These are the Süleymancı and İsmailağa communities.[2] Both have returned to the pristine truths of the early faith, the first to the *Kur'an* and the initial traditions of the Prophet, the second to a more legalistic approach based on the *Kur'an* and *fıkıh,* Islamic religious texts. Both provide a rigid and conservative education and are social purists. Their leaders are revered by hundreds of thousands, perhaps millions, and both have made their mark abroad, with the Turkish diaspora in Europe, and among other Muslims from the west coast of Africa to Indonesia.

The Süleymancıs, acting largely sub rosa, have set out to respond to the unmet spiritual needs of Turkey's rural dwellers, until recently more numerous than those in the country's burgeoning cities, and of Turks abroad afflicted by a sense of distance from their homeland. İsmailağa—or, as its devotees prefer, the followers of Mahmut Efendi—reaches out to the new migrants to the cities, to the urban dispossessed, and to the small traders.

Both have suffered from internal divisions and have responded differently as Erdoğan's state has started supplying many of the religious services that had previously been the orders' *raison d'être*. The Süleymancıs have made political choices that have kept them estranged from this state, but not diminished their covert following. By contrast, İsmailağa, long distanced from party politics, has shown signs of fracture as it now seems to embrace Erdoğan's party. The history of the two shows the risks when purity of teaching comes face to face with daily political reality.

The Süleymancıs and their lurking legions

Providing a service in villages and exile

The politicians' exhortations long resonated fitfully in rural Turkey. The plains and mountains of Anatolia and Thrace were no mere appendage to the cities, but the home of most of the population, the fief of tax farmers, the source of cannon fodder at time of war, and an area where religion had more legitimacy than the state. During the Ottoman centuries, the countryside accounted for three quarters of the Empire's subjects, and under the Republic this ratio would not begin to drop until after the Second World War—to one half in 1980 and under one quarter today. The incorporation of this traditionally ignored world into the political process is one of the feats of modern Turkey. However, party promises weighed, and weigh, little in the villages, where roads and electricity have opened access, but standards of behavior and expectation draw largely on religion. For over four fifths of their inhabitants, the religion is Sunni Islam.[3]

Until the late 1990s, compulsory education was for five years, but was not fully on offer and the requirement was only partially enforced. Village parents who wanted their child to advance, whether by attending an *imam-hatip* school with the job security this implied, or starting mid-school, high school, or university education, needed either to relocate to a city or send their child away. Offering families a secure route for the latter was the contribution that the Süleymancıs made, establishing a network of dormitories with the discipline and environment that reassured parents that their child would not be led astray. These dormitories allowed children to attend *imam-hatip* schools and the cramming courses essential if the child wished to succeed in the annual exams that decide students' high schools and universities and what they will study. The classes were affordable, and they became highly frequented. *Kur'an* courses were an inherent component of the offer.

An *imam*'s brother in an Aegean mountain village told a visiting American scholar in 1996: "... from this small village of three hundred people, there are thirty five studying with the [Süleymancıs], ten of whom are girls. He added that students do not have to pay to study, an obvious incentive for poor village families."[4] Some of these became official *imam*, as had the informant's brother. The schooling benefitted girls interested in religious education. The gender segregation of the Süleymancı community "provides women with more opportunities to study and lead within the group than they would experience if they followed the *Diyanet*'s version of Sunni Islam."[5] This segregation creates the need for female teachers who can teach the *Kur'an*, deliver sermons, and lead *Kur'anic* readings to groups of women. The official system allows women to rise to become public school religion teachers or preachers (*vaiz*) but the lower role of *imam* is not available to them.

This remarkable penetration of a religious community into the daily life of a single village was widely replicated as parents throughout Anatolia endorsed the strict regime in the Süleymancıs' dormitories, teaching facilities, and *Kur'an* courses. As Hart comments, these dormitories involve eating, praying, worshipping, and studying together: "The prevailing ethos is that of the group and those who wish to succeed within the group need to devote themselves to it. Lessons in reading the *Kur'an* are integral to the group's activities and it is doubtful whether such lessons are registered and controlled, as required."[6] The regime is not only strict but bonding.

Stimulating the fraternity's momentum was the installation of the Süleymancıs among the communities of Turkish emigrants proliferating in Europe from 1961. The Süleymancıs were quick to minister to these souls, uprooted from their traditions, largely excluded from local society, and united in *gurbet*, homesickness for their country. By 1979, the Süleymancıs had 150 *imam* in Germany, a similar number to Erbakan's *Milli Görüş*. Just as workers' remittances were important to the Turkish balance of payments, so the Süleymancıs' contributions bolstered their community in Turkey and stimulated the continuing expansion of its network.

Hart, who in the 1990s spent time with a Süleymancı community in Bamberg, Bavaria, underlines the parallels between these communities in Europe and their rural cousins in Turkey:

> Those who are nostalgically searching for the coherence of a pious community in a contemporary form find social and moral sustenance in the neo-*tarikat* or other religious associations or foundations. The broad appeal of these groups is not that they target those who suffer from alienation but that they appeal to devout people generally, regardless of where they live and what form of modernity they have experienced.[7]

It was partially to counter such influences that, after the ousting of Erbakan as prime minister, his immediate successors deftly blended the extension of compulsory education from five to eight years with the closure of the *imam-hatip* secondary schools served by the Süleymancıs. Between 1996 and 2001, enrolment at *imam-hatip* schools fell from a peak of over 500,000 to one seventh of that. The number of registered *Kur'an* courses run by associations also fell, by over one quarter.

But the sense of community could not be legislated away. As of May 2002, the Süleymancıs had 800 associations in Turkey supporting 1,200 dormitories and schools and helping around 100,000 students. It also had some 400 clubs in Europe.[8] One study dating to this time concluded: "As of 2003, they run the most powerful dormitory networks in Turkey and the second-largest mosque network in Germany. Their dormitories are cleaner and more highly disciplined than those of the state and are equipped with up-to-date technology to meet the needs of the university students."[9]

The AKP's years in government have seen a surge in such activity. Students at *imam-hatip* middle and high schools have risen from 100,000 to 1.3 million (See illustration 28) while in the pre-COVID 2017/2018 academic year attendees at registered *Kur'an* courses exceeded 1 million, with the number of these courses having quintupled. The Süleymancıs have of course benefitted but face increasing competition from the state and from other orders. Their share of this crowded landscape is hard to judge, but one ex-member claims they run about 2,000 dormitories in Turkey and have 250–300 branches in Germany.[10]

The material aspects of the schools are good, but mental conditions are usually Spartan, with ball games, backgammon, and chess forbidden, and the administrators sometimes incompetent.

Reports on these facilities are rare, usually appearing after accidents. There were reports of a suicide, a suspicious death, and violence towards students in the 1980s. In 2008, an LPG explosion in a dormitory at Taşkent, Konya, killed seventeen female students. In 2015, a twelve-year-old boy lost his forearm in a meat mincer in a Süleymancı dormitory. In 2016, a fire killed twelve people, ten of them students, in a girls' dormitory at Aladağ, Adana, and in 2017, there were reports of sexual harassment of Süleymancı students at Dikili (İzmir) and Besni (Adıyaman).

In the Christian world, the Jesuits' schools are often held to inculcate lifelong loyalty to its founding society. At least as ardent devotion characterizes the products of Süleymancı education. The *cemaat*'s sense of community is intense, being policed by rigid excommunication of apostates. A survey carried out in 2011 found that it and the Menzil community (see next chapter) came second only to the Gülenists (see Chapters 12–13) in their following. Their share of the sample was 1 per cent each, indicating that each have 600,000 members.[11] Others cite a following as large as 4 million.[12] Numbers of this scale, combined with its formidable discipline, make it a hidden army. But, unlike Fethullah Gülen who always aimed to infiltrate the institutions of power, the Süleymancıs focus on advancing the penetration of Islam in society.

As one former branch leader says: "Our goal is to struggle until everyone in Turkey becomes Süleymancı. We are now in the period of *jihad*. Until this goal is reached, even lying and the practice of interest are permissible. Every way is fair. After reaching our goal, we will enforce the rules of Islam."[13]

Teaching—a return to the past

Teaching in the Süleymancı schools is traditional. Tunahan followed Sirhindi, who called for a return to the textual sources of Islam. Worried that the lack of scholars meant that Muslims "were flowing into hell like debris in a flood," he sought to assist students to complete their courses more quickly than required for the full syllabus of Islamic sciences in the Ottoman *medrese*. His courses started with the *Kur'an*, continued with religious law, and moved on to a series of fundamental texts covering grammar, law, logic, and doctrine. He taught the traditions of the Prophet "whenever he could."[14] His official website continues: "Apart from Islamic Sciences, he would inform his students about topics related to Astronomy and medicine, keeping them well informed about the progress of the time."

Such may have been the content of the classes that he would give in mosques, disciples' houses and, on one occasion, in a passenger wagon in a railway siding. However, the sole text he left behind is his short *Kur'an Harf ve Harekeleri* (The Letters and Vowel Points of the Kur'an).

The contrast between the paucity of his literary heritage and his adulators' claims that he was a fresh renewer of Islam is striking. His critics also point to his sparse interactions with the learned masters of his time and the lack of religious education of his leading followers, including Kacar. As for his teaching being "brand-new," it is questionable what he added to the procedures of recital named after the sixteenth-century Ottoman saint, Abdurrahman Karabaş.[15]

Around 2 million copies of his text have been printed, yet to many more formally trained Muslims, its contribution to Islamic literature is zero. Indeed, the education of members of the community is relatively limited. The İstanbul courses of religious training for future preachers in Germany last only eight months.[16] The focus of his followers is often restricted to teaching the recital of the *Kur'an*, emphasizing traditional learning by rote, and discouraging innovation.

In general, the Süleymancıs eschew the exegesis which Tunahan himself practised, instead emphasizing links to their saint, "with a strict order of members, leaders and teachers who are connected to a spiritual chain of commanders with Tunahan at its origin."[17] As one anthropologist comments: "They believe in an inner meaning (*batini*) of the *Quran*, which is attained only by those who have spiritual access. Reason does not play a role in finding Islamic truth and knowledge. Instead, it is submission to a spiritual master that opens the path."[18]

Where the practical world was concerned, Tunahan encouraged his followers to read Kısakürek's *Büyük Doğu*. This publication called for an end to secularism, praised the Ottoman Sultans, and contrasted the moral decay of the West with the cultural superiority of the East. He commended his students to spread throughout the country, and to sit the state examinations for official posts as *imam*, preachers, and teachers. During his lifetime, as until a few years ago, the community advocated passive civil resistance to the state, underlining the need for education to be inspired by the Islamic community as a whole and not by official bodies.

The community discourages women from working outside the home, arguing that doing so distracts them from their primary tasks of educating children and taking care of the house. Female students were long impeded from going on to non-religious high schools or universities, though practice here has slightly eased in the past decade.

Kacar makes it a family business

The most famous of the students to be influenced by the Süleymancıs is Recep Tayyip Erdoğan himself. His parents, Ahmet, a Golden Horn boatman, and Tenzile, sent him first to a primary school in Kasımpaşa and then to the İstanbul *İmam-Hatip* school in Fatih. While in Kasımpaşa, he attended the Süleymancıs' Büyükpiyale *Kur'an* course. His mother appears to have been particularly impressed by the community; before she died in 2011, she asked to be buried close to the domed mausoleum of Tunahan. Creating space for her and her family required the destruction of tombs dating back to Ottoman times, a desecration and disturbance of graveyard calm that deeply disturbed Tunahan's disciples.

The Süleymancıs were already vexed with Erdoğan. Four years earlier, he had not helped prevent destruction of the building where the Piyalepaşa courses were held.[19] Some members of the community also remembered that, when Kacar had died in 2000, Erdoğan had failed to attend the funeral. But in the 1980s and at least the early 1990s, Erdoğan had venerated Kacar, serving as his assistant in internal prayer meetings of the Süleymancıs and welcoming the elder politician to the İstanbul Municipality when he turned up to review the new mayor's progress.

The Süleymancıs have long had a tortured relationship with the successive political rulers of the country. Tunahan initially welcomed the Democrat Party, but fell out when the party subordinated the *imam-hatip* schools to civil servants at the Ministry of Education and not to the more religiously qualified *Diyanet*. Up to this point, the *Diyanet* had been happy to turn to Tunahan for help in filling posts such as *müftü*, *imam*, and preacher. As the state began to build up its own *imam-hatip* schools, it was inevitable that the graduates from these schools would compete for preaching positions previously filled by those trained by Tunahan's *cemaat*. The Süleymancıs found themselves accused of being enemies of Atatürk.

By this time, Tunahan and Kacar were also at odds with the Democrat Party over Turkish support for French repression of Muslims in Algeria. In the 1957 elections, Kacar stood for the Republican National Party (*Cumhuriyetçi Millet Partisi*, CMP), starting the community's association with the political right, which has continued for much of the past six decades. His election campaign was unsuccessful, not being helped by his two-month detention (together with Tunahan) for criticizing government foreign policy. Tunahan died two years later. Kacar took over.

Educated at elite high schools in İstanbul, Kacar was firmly conservative. Kısakürek, who met him in a shared taxi going to their homes in Erenköy, remembered their first meeting well. He was struck by the radiant face of the twenty-nine-year-old Kacar:

> From our appreciation of Abdülhamid to our deepest outbreaks of love and friendship and the most miserable and terrible targets of our enmity, we were as one. From hatred of Jews and Free Masons to judgements on the revolutionary and rootless classes, I found all my arguments had made their nest in the soul of this young man. In particular drawing me completely to him was finding in this young man a love for the path of the *tarikat* and the value he gave to the Blessed İmam-ı Rabbani.[20]

In 1965, Kacar became a deputy for the right-wing Nation Party (*Millet Party*, MP). He then started a long association with Demirel's Justice Party, being elected twice as deputy for that party, and helping Demirel weather several challenges, not least the rising power of Erbakan.

Kacar never claimed his father-in-law's spiritual mantle, but his followers pressed that role upon him as he continued the movement's focus on education, building student dormitories throughout Turkey, and developing a vigorous presence among the growing Turkish diaspora in Europe. He had to see off rivalry from other students of Tunahan who were looking for a more collegiate leadership but, an imperious figure, soon became venerated in his own right. The dark blue prayer cap that he wore has been adopted de rigueur as a mark of adherence to the community.

The Süleymancıs faced a reverse with the 1965 law requiring most employees of the *Diyanet* to be graduates of *imam-hatip* schools or of university faculties of theology. This law also put the *Diyanet*, together with the Ministry of Education, in charge of all *Kur'an* courses.[21] To the Süleymancıs, the graduates of *imam-hatip* schools who had entered the *Diyanet* had no knowledge of Islam, were akin to the reviled Wahhabis, and should never be accepted to lead prayers. Six years later, the community received a further setback when the military-imposed government nationalized *Kur'an* courses and took over many of the Süleymancıs' schools. It also purged the *Diyanet* of those considered close to the Süleymancıs.

All this did not prevent the spread of their influence. There is a vivid description of Kacar entering the annual general meeting of the Süleymancıs' associations in May 1979. The salon of the İstanbul Sport and Exhibition Palace was filled with over 2,000 well-dressed individuals, all the men wearing ties, none with beards and none smoking. They greeted their leader by rising to their feet and prolonged applause. He then raised his hand, and the applause stopped as if a button had been pressed.[22] The discipline was meticulous. A description of the movement by Ruşen Çakır in the late 1980s emphasizes the veneration that the Süleymancıs felt for Kacar. In Çakır's view, the discipline within the community was appropriate to that in a fascist movement. He cites one of the internal rivals of Kacar: "The Süleymancıs contend that Kacar is the Prophet Jesus, expected to descend from heaven before the coming of the *Mehdi* (Messiah)."[23]

The generals' coup of September 1980 saw renewed problems for the Süleymancıs. The leader of the coup, General Kenan Evren, made them an immediate target, setting out to take over their schools and course facilities. In the end, the pursuit led nowhere. The Süleymancıs claim this was because of the exemplary operations of the schools, but there are questions over whether a bargain was made, with the Süleymancıs keeping their property in exchange for supporting the generals in the constitutional referendum of November 1982. There is no doubt that Kacar came under pressure. He was arrested and taken to Antalya where he was held for eight months. He and 115 others were sentenced to two years in prison for exploiting religion, with his sentence reduced to three months as he was over 65 years old. The conviction was overthrown on appeal.

Evren denies that any bargain was made, but an army officer who was a member of the *cemaat* claims that Kacar confided that he had indeed been presented with the choice of confiscation of all the *cemaat*'s assets or submission.[24] Internal critics of Kacar alleged that he subsequently aligned too closely with the state, rowing back on the Süleymancıs' traditional criticism of authority and ensuring his movement's premises hung photographs of Atatürk and even of Evren himself. Public figures with a liberal image were invited to openings of new dormitories.[25]

With Demirel banned from politics, Kacar supported Özal's ANAP in the 1983 and 1987 elections. After Demirel returned to the fray, he backed the latter's new DYP. He then had the *cemaat* follow Erbakan's Refah Party. He was one of the fifty-one religious leaders invited to the fateful *iftar* hosted by Erbakan on 11 January 1997.

When Kacar died in 2000, a crowd of some 20,000 people attended his burial beside Tunahan's tomb in Karacaahmet graveyard. The mourners included the leaders of two political parties, the İstanbul head of a third, and the mayors of İstanbul and Ankara, but, for whatever reason, not the community's one-time student, Erdoğan.

Feuding with Erdoğan

After his death, the *cemaat* split. Kacar had been married to the elder daughter of Süleyman Tunahan, and leadership now passed to the children of the younger daughter, Feriha Ferhan, and her husband, Hüseyin Kamil Denizolgun, a modest trader and dealer in real estate in the Çamlıca area on the Anatolian slopes of the Bosphorus. A part of the community followed their elder son, Mehmet Beyazıt Denizolgun, who had linked his fate to that of Erdoğan's AKP, being a founder member and then a deputy from İstanbul. Today, Mehmet Beyazıt lives on, paralyzed after a stroke. His son, Fatih Süleyman, long active in the AKP's youth movement, was elected on that party's ticket for İstanbul in 2018 but was placed too low on its list for election in 2023.

The main movement backed the younger son, Arif Ahmet Denizolgun. Arif Ahmet had kept his distance from the activities of Erbakan, being elected as a deputy for ANAP from Antalya after the 1995 elections and serving for five months as Minister of Communications in 1998. He had few of the qualifications normally associated with leader of a religious order, lacking formal religious education and pursuing horse breeding and golf. Where the community was concerned, he maintained a low, almost invisible profile. But, robust and calm according to family friends, he helped weather the quarrels that had broken out over inheritance of the family home and the movement's assets.

He adopted a less confrontational policy towards state-directed political Islam, and this in turn led to a more tolerant approach by the state. The detente is reflected in the measured tones of the profile of Tunahan published in the *Diyanet*'s *İslam Ansiklopedisi* in 2012, which describes the contribution of the *cemaat* in providing high school and university students in provincial centres, districts, and villages with computer-equipped education facilities and dormitories as well as *Kur'an* courses linked to the *Diyanet*. It notes that past tensions between the *cemaat* and *imam-hatip* schools have been "significantly removed thanks to the development of a culture of reconciliation among the religious groups, as well as the more conciliatory contributions of the new cadres in the Süleyman Efendi community."[26]

When Arif Ahmet died of a brain haemorrhage in September 2016, Erdoğan did not attend his funeral, perhaps kept away by the stresses of dealing with the aftermath of the July coup attempt, or perhaps because the president had clearly sided with Arif Ahmet's elder brother. Possibly clouding his relations with the community were the vituperative attacks on him by blogs purportedly close to Arif Ahmet.[27]

Leadership passed to Arif Ahmet's nephew, Alihan Kuriş, the younger son of the Denizolgun brothers' sister, Ayşe Gülderen. Kuriş, an architect, has faced criticisms from within the movement for a lack of religious training. His selection was followed by some image polishing, including one bemusing claim by a follower that he should be seen as a heavenly messenger. Chided on this by Mehmet Görmez, president of the *Diyanet* from 2010 to 2017, Kuriş commented: "I am an engineer. The *hoca* say this."[28] Some '*hoca*' even attribute to him the august title of Commander of the Faithful.[29]

As of mid-2024, he had made few pronouncements on religious issues. Indeed, his public persona is impressively minimal. There is a locked account in his name on *X*. He has made no use of YouTube. One of the few records citing his name is a 2014 entry of the Turkish Jockey Club noting his ownership of a racehorse called Ascot. To his followers, such activities are irrelevant.[30] For many, the role of Kuriş is to administer the material legacy of Tunahan and direct the 'İstanbul Secretariat,' the anonymous cabal which has long run the fraternity. For these, the latter's spiritual legacy is continued—as to some extent it had been under his two predecessors—by the movement's mystical leaders, men connected through inspiration, often in dreams, to Tunahan and thus ensuring the integrity of the chain of *rabıta* to their saint.

In 2017, the Süleymancıs signed a protocol with the Ministry of Education to provide values training throughout the country.[31] Kuriş himself had started by supporting the MHP rather than the AKP. When these two parties became allies in 2018, he initially gave public support to the AKP but then, against some internal resistance, urged his followers to back opponents of Erdoğan, in particular the *İYİ Parti* breakaway from the MHP.

In the elections that June, the community encouraged its voters to support whomever would be the strongest local candidate against the AKP and its allies. A year later, it supported the CHP's Ekrem İmamoğlu against the AKP's Binali Yıldırım in the İstanbul Municipality election and its runoff. It said it would deliver 300,000 votes in that contest.[32] This was no idle promise. A national poll carried out in 2011 found that 60 per cent of respondents had a positive view of the Süleymancıs, far more than of any other community.[33] In the 2023 elections, Kuriş advised Muslims to beware of hypocrites; he did not name Erdoğan, but made clear that the president should be avoided. A similar stance was evident in the March 2024 local elections.

A global mission

Tunahan's spiritual legacy is preserved and continued through his most knowledgeable students and those taught by them. These wise figures are revered as maintaining the link to the esoteric mystery of their master and have a clear hierarchy. A document in the 1970s instructed followers: "The sainted master did not die. He has risen to the surface, and from there he directs us with his guidance. The orders of our elder brother Kemal [Kacar] and our brother Hüseyin [Kaplan] are his orders."

Half a century on, Hüseyin Kaplan had broken with the main body of Süleymancıs but another figure, Mustafa Özaltın of Zeytinburnu, now known as '*Müftü* Abi,' continued to inspire and was one of the "distinguished group that can establish a connection with the spirit of Süleyman Efendi. Only these people who are called 'people of the *rabıta*' can know the true meanings of the sacred verses and *hadis*."[34]

The order does not brook challenges to its hierarchy. Its discipline is as formidable today as when Kacar silenced the crowd by raising his hand. Its members must be clean-shaven. Only those over sixty years old may, subject to special permission, grow beards, according to one former regional organizer. Girls are discouraged from attending normal high schools and university. Even the colour and types of cars that Süleymancıs may buy are prescribed, with black, white, and blue vehicles being acceptable and all BMW models eschewed. Rebellion is punished with excommunication. One friend told me that, when he decided to leave the community, his father stopped talking to him, and his mother only continued to do so covertly. "Wherever I go, I face this anathema." [35] He is one of the very few who have decided to seek a life elsewise. The great bulk are cohesive, and the fraternity all the more formidable for this.

Managing the order's material legacy is the task of Kuriş, and is a full-time job. Core to this is ensuring the revenue stream of donations from disciples. Fundraising activities include contributions for mosque-building, for Ramadan sacrifices, for *zakat*, the charitable alms prescribed in the *Kur'an*, and for *ıskat*, the alms given on behalf of the dead as compensation for their neglected religious duties.[36] One branch director in Ingolstadt, Bavaria, remembers a visitor from Turkey who chided them: "You in this region have not accustomed people to giving money... In the eyes of our superiors, you are not worth a gram."[37]

Like Nureddin Coşan of the İskenderpaşa brotherhood, Kuriş also has to deal with a sizeable commercial operation. There is a retail chain, Arden Süpermarketleri, with nine markets in İstanbul as of March 2024 and an online operation. This works closely with the community's Akdeniz Toros Et, a *helal* meat wholesaler. There is the Hisar Intercontinental Hospital, operating in the Ümraniye district of İstanbul from 2005. And there is Hisar Turizm, a travel agency supporting pilgrims that claims branches in thirty provinces and "thousands of honorary representatives and tens of thousands of spiritual friends" for its work organizing *hajj* and *umre* travel.[38]

Unlike most other brotherhoods, the community does not have a television channel, but, like the others, it operates a number of publishing houses, the oldest, Fazilet Neşriyat, dating back to 1969. Its magazines a range of family and children's titles. It also publishes educational books. Most of its companies are registered at its large Hisar Plaza in Güneşli on the western fringes of İstanbul. It is also associated with the İsabet chain of over forty schools, one of these being in London, and with TÜZDER, an association to help gifted children.

All these are run in parallel with the Süleymancıs' focus on spreading Islam in Turkey and its policy of global Süleymancı-ism. Proselytization in Europe continues, with the Süleymancıs' showpiece in Germany set to become their 70-million-euro Union of Centres of Islamic Culture (İKMB) in the western outskirts of Cologne. The mayor, perhaps unaware of their record of stealth in Turkey, has welcomed it: "The new headquarters of the İKMB—just like Cologne—represents transparency and respect."[39]

Interest in North America has been evident since 1980 when the community's United American Muslim Association opened its Fatih Mosque on 8th Avenue in Brooklyn. In 2021, as well as at least two mosques and eighty-seven masjid, the UAMA operated fifteen education centres in the U.S. and one in Mexico. Each evening during Ramadan, almost 100,000 people attended the *iftar* dinners it arranged. "They send American Muslims folks to Üsküdar to study for several years and become *imams* back in the U.S.," a friend who attended a masjid connected to Fatih Mosque told me in 2023.

A military report of 2002 listed *cemaat* activities from Finland to Brunei. These included proselytizing in Albania, Bosnia and Herzegovina, and Bulgaria, and launching activities in Ukraine and Georgia. One former regional organizer of the fraternity told me that in 2021 they had around 150 dormitories in the Balkans alone. Africa has been a particular focus for the group. There, its mix of activities is similar to that of the Erenköy community and its scale impressive. A *cemaat* video shows the activities of the Tunahan Boys' Medrese of the Universal Islamic & Cultural Trust in Johannesburg. In this, the trust is described as one of more than 7,000 international Islamic education and welfare organizations.[40] That was in 2002, and a video of six years later seeks to raise funds from Turks for religious sacrifices in Ghana, Kenya, Mali, Rwanda, and Senegal. Videos from around 2020 show the activities flourish.

The Süleymancıs have also built up their presence in Asia. They have over 6,000 dormitories in Indonesia, according to one former director of their foreign activities. For a long period, they survived in the febrile politics of Pakistan and Afghanistan. As of the end of 2020, they had over 200 dormitories in the former and a growing presence in the latter that was beginning to disturb the then president, Ashraf Ghani.[41]

In all cases, they have maintained the distance from the Turkish state that they also show within Turkey. Their contribution to the soft power advocated by AKP governments is thus coincidental, even involuntary, unlike that of Erenköy and İskenderpaşa.

In Turkey itself, the Süleymancıs are sometimes described as being far from the force they once were. Some argue that the historical mission on which they embarked has been achieved, others that their traditional disdain for other Islamic communities makes it impossible for them to forge alliances, and others point to the political choices they have made. To the followers of Tunahan, such characterizations miss the point. They do not need transitory figureheads to carry the spiritual torch of their inspirer but continue their *rabıta*—their links to their revered saint—through the *imam* and *hoca* who keep his spirit alive. "My aunt finds an ecstasy through this *rabıta* which strengthens her for daily life," one sociologist of Islam told me. Such experiences help the Süleymancıs to build a group where the experience gains approval and meaning, and where membership clearly has economic benefits too as members seek to support each other.

The cohesion of these covert cohorts remains as strong as their missionary zeal. As Erdoğan's mother showed with her choice of resting place, this furtive community remains so deeply rooted that its lack of public leadership is no measure of its chilling discipline and abiding appeal.

The İsmailağa tarikat—faith for Turkey's sans-culottes

Creating an Islamic ghetto

A second order which has focused on addressing unmet needs is that which has grown up around, and taken its name from, the İsmailağa mosque in the Çarşamba area of old İstanbul, ten minutes' walk north from the great mosque commemorating Mehmed the Conqueror.

There is nothing surreptitious about this community. On the contrary, its adherents pride themselves in dressing as similarly to the Prophet as they can, the men in cloaks, baggy trousers, and white turbans, and the women in black chadors known as *çarşaf.* Such attire was viewed askance in pre-Erdoğan Turkey, but is now an integral part of the neighbourhood's landscape.

This community too has focused on teaching the *Kur'an*, building up a series of dormitories of which the flagship is the İsmailağa *Kur'an* Course, a gargantuan six-storey edifice stretching 100 yards down the street beside the mosque, with a footprint half the area of a football field; it has a reported capacity for 1,330 students but in 2019 housed 450, according to three of its residents, interviewed as they set off for a Sunday stroll.

The İsmailağa order targets a more modest populace than that of Erenköy, reaching out to the urban demi-monde and the small traders such as the grocers and butchers. It differs from the Süleymancıs too in that its teaching concentrates on the *Kur'an* and *fıkıh*, religious law, rather than embracing the broader range of sources accepted by the Süleymancıs. And it is even more conservative than the Süleymancıs in its approach to family matters and the role of women.

The strength of the community comes from the saint who inspires it, Mahmut Ustaosmanoğlu. Devotees prefer to call themselves followers of His Excellency Mahmut Efendi rather than use the name of the mosque where Ustaosmanoğlu served as *imam* for over four decades.

Ustaosmanoğlu was a seemingly mild and fatherly figure whose advancing physical diminution did little to weaken his charisma. In the *Life Story of Hazrati Mahmud Effendi*, a 148-page book given to visitors to the complex where he lived his final years, there is a photograph of the Grand Mosque at Mecca showing much of the inner precinct, the Kaaba slightly off centre, surrounded by the disciples of the Turkish saint, the men ringed round the shrine robed in white with ladies in black encircling them. A second such photograph shows the sacred precinct filled by the saint's devoted followers. Both were taken during the *umre*, the Islamic pilgrimage at times other than the *hajj*. The first dates to June 2005 and the second to April 2011. In both cases, we are told there were 50,000 followers from Turkey present with Ustaosmanoğlu, and the photographs, if indeed of these two visits, show the claims to be credible.[42]

In May 2013, he drew a crowd of reportedly 60,000 for a ceremony held in a sports stadium in Silivri, west of İstanbul. He attracted a similar crowd in a meeting three months later in Bursa. And the faithful would regularly throng to the field under the balcony of his four-storey villa in the hills of Çavuşbaşı, east of İstanbul, until the field was dug out to make way for a new mosque.

This, a heavy-ribbed brown and ochre structure named after the master, was nearly completed when I visited his residence in September 2019, and sat in a well-tended garden, drinking tea with his aide, Mümin Günay, previously an exporter of morel mushrooms and importer of sheep. A gentle traffic of bearded clerics walked in and out of the high-walled garden. All except for a six-year-old boy, prayer hat on his head and skateboard under his arm, were dressed in the traditional garb of the disciples of Ustaosmanoğlu: a white turban, a loose grey shirt with four pockets, and grey *şalvar*, the baggy trousers familiar throughout the Middle East. It is a garb that shocks the secular but is central to the faith of these disciples. "It is our duty to imitate the Prophet as best we can, in clothes, behavior and thought," explained Günay. Ustaosmanoğlu expressed this thought more directly: "Allah the Exalted, gave you Islamic clothing and you still prefer to wear English-style clothes. How long will you go on playing with your honour?! When will you switch to your Islamic style?"[43]

In the years before his death in June 2022, Ustaosmanoğlu was progressively debilitated by failing eyesight, a series of strokes, and bouts of ill health. One of these bouts followed the murder of his son-in-law and heir presumptive, Hızır Ali Muradoğlu, in 1998. Another came in 2006 after the fatal stabbing of a retired *imam* and prominent intellectual in the community, Bayram Ali Öztürk. When Ustaosmanoğlu moved to his rustic villa in 2007, he had to be transferred in an ambulance. A hospital where he was later treated and his car were both subjected to a shooting attack.

A video released by the community in February 2018 shows him, the customary white *taç* (dervish hat) on his head, seated in a wheelchair, greeting a huge crowd from his balcony. The video includes recent visits by religious figures during which Ustaosmanoğlu showed little awareness of their kneeling reverence.[44]

The followers of this saint form one of most tenacious Islamic movements in Turkey. They reject the term sometimes used for them of Mahmutcu, the suffix denoting "those of Mahmut," saying that their leader has not established a new faith but helps people find the true path to God. They consider themselves a *tarikat*, a religious order whose head has a chain of succession tracing back to the Prophet. They are generally termed after the mosque where Mahmut Efendi served—and where the two murders mentioned above took place, as did the lynching of the man responsible for the second one.

The İsmailağa mosque is named after an eighteenth-century *şeyhülislam*. It is an elegant baroque construction damaged in a nineteenth-century earthquake and restored from the late 1940s to what is now a pristine state, housing a *medrese* where the murmur of *Kur'an* courses belies the violence it has witnessed. The repairs were managed by the Nakşibendi *şeyh*, Ahıskalı Ali Haydar Efendi (Gürbüzler), launched after his elder son dreamt of receiving instructions from an arm reaching out from the *şeyhülislam*'s tomb. Ali Haydar, whose spiritual line traced back to Halid el-Bağdadi, had been one of the outstanding *ulema* in the last years of the Ottoman Empire, heading the group which gave spiritual lessons to the Sultan during the holy month of Ramadan. Like Nursi and Tunahan, he spent time in the young Republic's prisons. He selected Ustaosmanoğlu, then carrying out his military service in the Marmara port of Bandırma, to be his spiritual successor, and, though himself denied a post as *imam*, seems to have ensured the appointment of Ustaosmanoğlu to İsmailağa mosque in 1954.

The hagiographical accounts of Ustaosmaoğlu describe him as having learnt the *Kur'an* by the age of six, and include the inevitable fateful vision. His mother "saw in her dream that the moon had come down from the sky, laid on her lap, and enlightened the world. A short time after this dream, Hazrati Mahmud Effendi [sic] was born."[45] His parents were farmers, living in the Of region of the Black Sea, an area from whose culturally confused heritage many of Turkey's prominent Islamic scholars have come. His father would walk every day from his distant farm to lead prayers at the local mosque, and his mother was fastidious in protecting the rights of her neighbours:

> She would cover the mouths of her cows while taking them to the meadow so that they couldn't graze on anybody's field. If one of her cows happened to [do so], she would immediately tell the owner of the property about

> what had happened and ask their consent of due rights and the milk she milked from that cow would be given to the owner of that field.[46]

Ustaosmanoğlu's teaching activities led to threats from the military. In 1982, he was detained and charged in connection with the murder of a *müftü*, eventually being exonerated. The arrest had little effect, and his fame and following began to grow. Each year, he would set off in a minibus with his closest disciples and proselytize in twenty or so cities in Anatolia. He long made a point of delivering an annual speech at the complex set up by his Bursa foundation five kilometres east of the city centre. His followers have set up similar foundations elsewhere.

Until weakening, he was a tireless teacher, each Sunday giving a talk after the dawn prayer that was so widely attended that it had to be moved into progressively larger mosques, for many years being in the imperial mosque of Yavuz Sultan Selim. In these talks, he would expound on couplets from a predecessor in Ustaosmanoğlu's Golden Chain of succession. These explanations have been published, but Ustaosmanoğlu was best known for his writings on the interpretation of the *Kur'an*. His *magnum opus* is the *Ruhu 'l-Furkan Tefsiri* (Commentary on the Kur'an), a detailed interpretation of the sacred book that aimed to distinguish truth from error. As of his death in June 2022, the scholars working on this had published nineteen of the planned fifty-seven volumes.

Characteristic of all his teaching is a devotion to the prescripts of the founder of Hanafism, Abu Hanifa, and of later jurists devoted to the latter's doctrine of religious law. He "approaches all the innovations of the modern world with great suspicion and rejects the majority of these, generally without even feeling the need to investigate them."[47]

The author Çakır noted that his disciples are preoccupied with the how of prayer rather than the why: "As in a number of orders, the emphasis placed on rank in the İsmailağa community leads to the emergence of rituals such as crawling into and out of their mentor's room on their knees."[48]

İsmailağa does not publish details on the scale of its activities, but proudly lists its activities abroad. The İsmailağa Association reports that its Federation of Associations for Empowering the Individual (İDDEF) has opened 63 *medrese* in 40 countries in four continents with 556 teachers giving Islamic education to over 12,000 students.[49] It has also built the Mosque of Abdülhamid II in Conakry.[50] The Federation claims that in 2019 it gave *iftar* meals to 450,000 people and sacrificed 56,265 animals to help feed 2.3 million people in Africa, Asia, and the Balkans.

1. Sultan Abdülhamid II in public procession to Friday prayers at Yıldız Mosque, around 1907.

2. Mahmud Şevket Paşa, dominant figure during the rise of the Young Turks from 1909, assassinated in 1912.

3. Mehmed Talat Paşa, assassinated in 1921.

4. Enver Paşa, killed in 1922.

5. Cemal Paşa, assassinated in 1922.

Die Hilfe kommt
von Gott und der
Sieg ist nah.
DER
FETWAH
Der Sultan verkündet den
DSCHIHÂD
den großen heiligen
Krieg gegen England,
Russland u. Frankreich.

6. 'The Fetva. Help comes from God and victory is near. The Sultan announces Jihad, the great holy war against England, Russia and France.' A German postcard from winter 1914–15 depicting Kaiser Wilhelm II, Franz Joseph I of Austria and Hungary, and Sultan Mehmed V Reşad.

7. Ziya Gökalp while exiled by the British to Malta, 1919.

8. Abdülmecid II, the last Caliph, in exile, about 1926.

9. Mustafa Kemal Paşa in robes given by *Şeyh* Senusi, leader of the Senusi order, with members of the National Assembly Sharia Committee in Ankara, 22 March 1921.

10. The legitimising role of religion in the new Republic: A 500 Turkish lira banknote printed in 1925, with the double-minareted Erzurum Mosque and Mustafa Kemal Paşa.

11. Nakşibendi *Şeyh* Esad Erbili, head of the Council of *Şeyh* from 1914–15, the Ottoman body controlling the dervishes.

12. Esad Erbili, prisoner of the Republic—condemned to death after the Menemen incident of 1930.

13. Said Nursi praying at the tomb of Mehmed the Conqueror, 1952.

14. Süleyman Hilmi Tunahan in the early 1950s.

15. The poet Necip Fazıl Kısakürek entering Ulucanlar Prison, Ankara, in 1953.

16. Adnan Menderes opening a school during his Aegean tour, July 1953.

17. Mehmet Zahit Kotku and Necmettin Erbakan in the 1970s.

18. Süleyman Demirel campaigning in Adapazarı to regain his political rights, 1987.

19. Turgut Özal leaving the Kaaba during his *hajj* in July 1988.

20. Turgut Özal (R) at the funeral of Necip Fazıl Kısakürek, 25 May 1983.

21. Recep Tayyip Erdoğan, carrying the coffin of Ömer, son of Necip Fazıl Kısakürek, 26 February 2005.

22. Recep Tayyip Erdoğan, then Mayor of İstanbul, and Fethullah Gülen in 1996.

23. President Erdoğan at the funeral of Mahmut Ustaosmanoğlu, head of the İsmailağa *tarikat*, 24 June 2022.

24. President Erdoğan at the funeral of Hasan Kılıç, successor of Mahmut Ustaosmanoğlu as head of the İsmailağa *tarikat*, 23 April 2024. Ahmed Fikri Doğan (bespectacled, front), successor of Kılıç, leads the prayers.

25. President Erdoğan after leading the prayers at the reopening of Ayasofya as a mosque.

26. The mausoleum of Süleyman Tunahan and the gilded Erdoğan family grave with four empty lots. The female pilgrims to Tunahan (left) remain behind a curtain of star jasmine. On visits, the President waters the grass on his parents' graves.

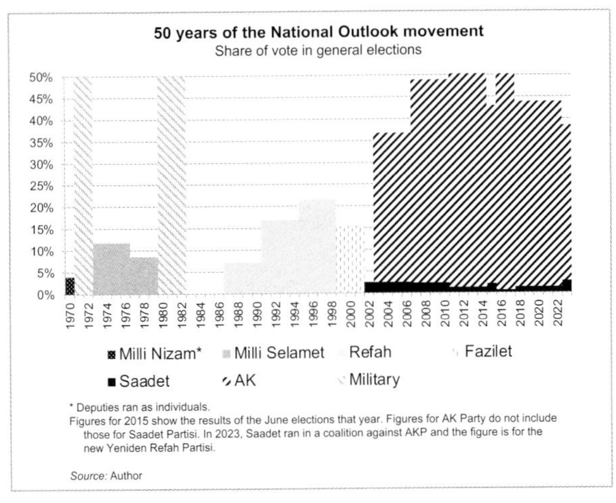

Share of vote in general elections

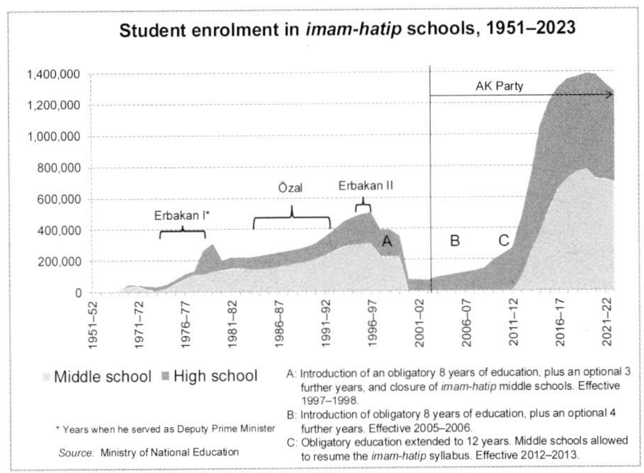

* Deputies ran as individuals.
Figures for 2015 show the results of the June elections that year. Figures for AK Party do not include those for Saadet Partisi. In 2023, Saadet ran in a coalition against AKP and the figure is for the new Yeniden Refah Partisi.
Source: Author

Student enrolment in imam-hatip schools, 1951–2023
Turks performing the hajj and umre, 1946–2023
AK Party
Erbakan I*
Özal
Erbakan II
A
B
C
Middle school
High school
* Years when he served as Deputy Prime Minister
Source: Ministry of National Education
A: Introduction of an obligatory 8 years of education, plus an optional 3 further years, and closure of imam-hatip middle schools. Effective 1997–1998.
B: Introduction of obligatory 8 years of education, plus an optional 4 further years. Effective 2005–2006.
C: Obligatory education extended to 12 years. Middle schools allowed to resume the imam-hatip syllabus. Effective 2012–2013.

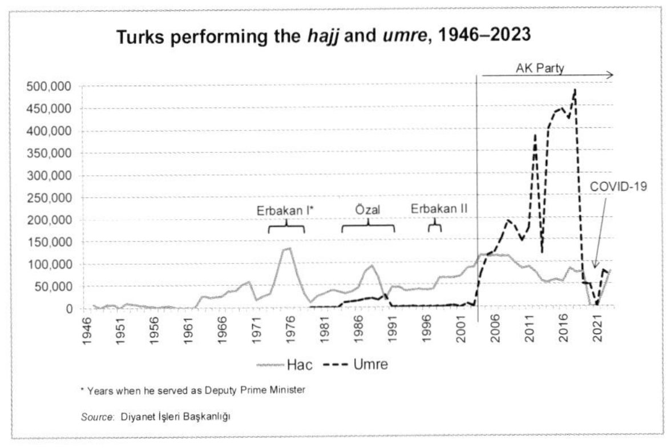

27–29. Graphs generated by the author.

30. A Bayraktar TB2 drone/UCAV, August 2019.

31. TCG *Anadolu*, an amphibious assault ship and the world's first drone aircraft carrier, in the Mediterranean, July 2023.

From its early days, the *tarikat* has appealed to migrants to İstanbul, with a particular presence among artisans and small-scale merchants of restricted education and income. To these "provincials in the metropolis," participation in the activities of the İsmailağa community offered an opportunity to raise their status within the religious-conservative stratum and locate themselves in the urban middle classes.[51]

Çakır emphasizes the moral support the community gives to the uprooted:

> ... the fact that the community's discourse is based entirely on radical opposition to the modern world causes it to resonate with people of provincial origin who are caught between their traditions and cosmopolitan culture in the largest metropolis of the country. In this ruthless modern jungle, individuals who are despised, oppressed, excluded from an economic, cultural, and even religious point of view, enjoy a collective revenge by causing uneasiness, anxiety and fear in the 'opposing ranks' even with their dress alone. But the main thing is not a desire for revenge. When they cling to traditions in the name of resisting modernization, they begin to live a meaningful, peaceful, safe life with the rituals that they never actually lived as a tradition, but which their *şeyh* has represented to them as the traditions of their ancestors.[52]

In this view, defining themselves as a force against the society in which they live naturally causes members of the community to define this society as hostile to their small community. Links within the congregation become closer, and the community isolates itself. "As a result, the foundations are being laid for a 'Muslim ghetto' in the heart of modern Turkey."[53]

Like a number of other Nakşibendi movements, the İsmailağa community draws strong support from women. In 1991, these women, considering Erdoğan's wife, Emine, did not dress in a sufficiently conservative manner, denied him their votes, delaying by a decade the young politician's taking a seat in the Grand National Assembly.[54] In 2022, a family friend in the Kurtuluş area of İstanbul explained her choosing to follow Mahmut Efendi as being because his teachings were stricter than those of the Süleymancıs.

Ustaosmanoğlu always preached the need for strict gender separation. For him, a married man should not let his brother see his wife. However, he also advocated women's education. He would tell questioners: "Build two *medrese* in each neighbourhood, one for boys and one for girls." Since in his view men could not teach women, he instructed his disciples to teach their wives to become teachers, encouraging women to become *hoca*.[55]

The community is notable for the limited scale of its commercial activities. It has no hospitals or trading companies. In 2010, Ustaosmanoğlu's nephew emphasized that this reflected the reservations that Ustaosmanoğlu had towards business:

> The wealth of the Muslim should be in his pocket. If it enters his heart, he will be miserable. A number of people in our community have made some mistakes... Compared to other communities, in the İsmailağa community such things are drops in the bucket. And they have nothing to do with His Sainted Excellency. Everyone knows how he looks at money. But things can get complicated as you go down a level or two.[56]

Ustaosmanoğlu had decided views on television:

> An intelligent man doesn't have a television at home. So far life without a TV was possible, why is it not possible now?! I am giving a *fatwa* right now that he who watches TV does not love his *din* [religion]. Better to sit with a snake than to sit with a TV. Television is *fitnavision* (viewing of discord and dissension).[57]

However, like all orders, the *tarikat* seeks to take advantage of traditional media and social networking. It has a range of publishing houses and magazines. Its views are also reflected on the Lalegül TV and radio channels.

"Which İsmailağa?"

When Ustaosmanoğlu moved to Beykoz in 2007, he left behind him a council of elders whom he had appointed and authorized to act on behalf of the community. Over the years, this became distanced from the family coterie living around the fading Ustaosmanoğlu.

The elders have acted under the name the İsmailağa Mosque Learning and Service Foundation. It is this body that has promoted the charitable and teaching works of the community in Turkey and abroad and is clearly its central institution. A monument to its aspiration is the imposing mosque complex named after Ustaosmanoğlu and located one street away from the İsmailağa mosque. Completed in 2020, this has the accoutrements of a classical Ottoman *külliye*, with a soup kitchen providing 10,000 meals per day, dormitories for 300, *medrese* for advanced and specialized Islamic studies, a 1,000-person conference salon, and ceremony rooms. There is also the twenty-first-century touch of a call centre able to handle 150,000 doctrinal enquiries per year.

It was the Ismailağa Mosque Foundation which announced that Hasan Kılıç would succeed Ustaosmanoğlu after the latter died in June 2022. And it is Kılıç whom Erdoğan visited after that death and in May 2023. When Kılıç died in April 2024, Erdoğan attended his funeral prayers in the great Fatih mosque.

The Beykoz coterie, which has had a number of spats with the mosque group, is usually referred to as the *Marifet* group, after the name of an association founded by Muhammed Keskin, the brother-in-law of Ustaosmanoğlu. *Marifet* means spiritual knowledge, and the group has emphasized its access to the fount of wisdom embodied by the order's leader. This group completed the large mosque next to Ustaosmanoğlu's residential complex in Çavuşbaşı. In November 2023, its magazine, *Yeni Furkan*, declaimed: "We have to do in Turkey what Hamas did in Palestine. There is no need for many men, the people here are enough… there is no reason why there will not be a revolution in Turkey."[58]

Faced with the foundation's announcement of Kılıç as Ustaosmanoğlu's successor, *Marifet* issued a statement neither accepting or denying this. Indeed, some contended that Kılıç was only the administrative heir of Ustaosmanoğlu, not his designated spiritual successor.[59] But when Kılıç died two years later, few challenged the announcement of Ahmed Fikri Doğan, a long-term İsmailağa insider, as the new leader of the community.

The community has also produced more militant figures attracted by its respect for the *Shari'a*, none more controversial than Salih Mirzabeyoğlu (Salih İzzet Erdiş), leader of the Islamic Raiders of the Great East-Front, İBDA-C. This was an anti-Shiite movement whose activities were mainly directed at low-risk, symbolic targets such as busts of Atatürk, empty churches, and synagogues.

İsmailağa has also supported a number of other initiatives, not least the Hiranur Foundation. In 2022 came the revelation that one of the senior members of this foundation had married off his daughter when she was only six years old. The daughter, then in her early twenties, sued her father, mother, and husband who in October 2023 were sentenced to 16–30 years in prison. İsmailağa has described her "gruesome humiliation" as "unacceptable in faith and conscience." Both Ustaosmanoğlu and *Cübbeli* Ahmet (See overleaf) attended the opening of one of Hiranur's schools.

Such controversy has long dogged İsmailağa. In 1997, two of the order's female students accused the order of abusing young female students from poor areas. A decade later, the chief prosecutor of Erzincan, İlhan

Cübbeli Ahmet—İsmailağa's enfant terrible

The last photograph in the authorized biography of Ustaosmanoğlu shows him kneeling with his 'precious student' *Cübbeli* Ahmet Hoca. But both the mosque group and *Marifet* have had their boundaries stretched by this once precocious and always presumptuous social media giant.

From the age of 12, this student of Ustaosmanoğlu has been attracting crowds to his sermons. His colourful imagery, folksy language, and statements such as those condemning chess players as liars have won him a huge following on television and the internet. As of spring 2024, his main account on *X* had 513,000 followers, and he had over 2.5 million followers on *Facebook*. He also had 1.6 million subscribers on YouTube where he had racked up some 500 million views for his broadcasts, some fifty of which had over 1 million views. His most popular video is "Information on the oral question. Is it forbidden by religion or just abominable?" In eight years, this six-minute item had attracted 7 million views, seemingly a record for any Turkish *şeyh*'s pronouncements.[60] That said, he makes no attempt to establish a *şeyh*-disciple relationship with his audience. He presents himself as a teacher not a guide.

Formally named Ahmet Mahmut Ünlü, the moniker *Cübbeli* reflects the cloaks in which he has long dressed. Photographs of this turbulent preacher on a jet ski in Malta in 2005 delighted his opponents but did little to diminish his following. He also survived distribution in 2010 of 400 copies of a CD purporting to show him involved in a sexual liaison, and a thirteen-month detention on accusations of trafficking women, charges of which he was eventually cleared.

Cübbeli Ahmet long broadcast on the pro-İsmailağa's *Lalegül* TV and *Lalegül* FM, but his relationship with the community has been intricate. At times, this errant preacher was forbidden access to the ailing Ustaosmanoğlu, but in January 2023, he and *Marifet*'s Muhammed Keskin together visited the Consul General of Uzbekistan to discuss how to protect Uzbek students from the "terrorist movements" of Salafism and Wahhabism. In autumn 2023, he was reported to have left İsmailağa, criticizing Hasan Kılıç's son, and to have transferred loyalty to a Kadiri *şeyh*, born in Syria and of Kurdish origin. In March 2024, Kılıç's group proscribed him.

Cihaner, opened a lawsuit against members of the order. Some received short, suspended sentences for operating illegal education facilities; others were cleared of the more serious charge of trying to overthrow the constitution. The judgement was symptomatic of the atmosphere of the times. Indeed, far from being rewarded, Cihaner, who had first made his mark in prosecuting members of JİTEM, the gendarmerie unit involved in assassinations, had by this time himself been arrested, with a prosecutor asking for a 26-year sentence.[61]

Disturbing though this is for many, it has not dimmed İsmailağa's attraction to a large sway of the population as a bedrock of moral stability.

Politics—a misleading aloofness

Ustaosmanoğlu used to be visited by Sami Ramazanoğlu of the Erenköy *tarikat*, and his relationship with İskenderpaşa's Kotku was such that he led the prayers at the latter's funeral.[62] But, unlike Kotku, Ustaosmanoğlu claimed to eschew political activism. His authorized biography cites him as saying:

> Leave me alone so that I may continue to talk about my Rabb's [God's] commands. I don't understand politics, but I will talk about *shariah*... We are not politicians... Our Creator didn't create us to seek positions of power. He created us for *ibadatullah* (servitude to Allah) and *marifetullah* (to know Allah).

That it has not always been easy to maintain this division is confirmed by these words being printed beside a photograph of Ustaosmanoğlu with former Prime Minister Erbakan.[63] He himself counselled the former presidents General Cevdet Sunay in 1973, Özal in 1992, and Abdullah Gül in 2015.

Politicians visiting him and his successor include prime ministers Erdoğan (August 2014 and, as president, January 2020 and May 2023), Ahmet Davutoğlu (June 2015), and Binali Yıldırım (May 2019), and the head of the Chechen Republic, Ramzan Akhmadovich Kadyrov (2018).

Erdoğan has long been diligent in his courtship of the community. He selected Hüsnü Kılıç, son of the eventual successor of Ustaosmanoğlu, as a parliamentary candidate in 2015. Two *imam* from the community helped lead the prayers for the reopening of Ayasofya to worship. And he attended the funeral prayers for Ustaosmanoğlu in 2022.

In the 2023 elections, the community declared "stability and experience will bring success." It was clearly calling on its members to support

Erdoğan—and Erdoğan made a visit to Hasan Kılıç the penultimate event of his campaign during the first round of the 2023 presidential election.

The relationship with the AKP has not always been easy. The *Marifet* group was angered with the party when police troops interrupted building work on their new mosque. But the major part of İsmailağa has long concluded its interests lie with Erdoğan's party. One study reports that it is rapidly organizing among the institutions under the Ministry of Family and Social Policies and becoming more influential in the Ministry of Education. Its main foundation was accepted as a public interest group at a time when the conflict between the AKP and the Gülen community was at its worst, and it has since stepped into the gap left by the latter's suppression. Like other orders, it has, a prominent theologian claims, "swooped around the power and engulfed it," particularly putting its weight on the *Diyanet*.[64]

Maintaining good relations with Erdoğan appears to be valued within the community. As one study concluded:

> No matter how much they are affected by the economic crisis, it is much more important for [members of İsmailağa] to continue the activities they have been carrying out below stairs for years with the knowledge of the President, and in case of the slightest problem to be able to reach Erdoğan by telephone.[65]

10

MENZIL AND THE IŞIKÇIS
THE LURE AND RISK OF MAMMON

Hold fast to the cord of God and let nothing divide you. Remember the blessings He has bestowed upon you; you were enemies and then He united your hearts and by His grace you became brothers; you were on the brink of an abyss of Fire, and He rescued you from it.

From verse 103 of Al-'Imran (The Family of 'Imran),
the 3rd chapter of the *Kur'an*[1]

Menzil and the weaponizing of repentance

Repentance without confession

The leaders of the Menzil order revel as fonts of faith. Penitents from all over Turkey have long travelled by the busload to kneel and repent before the heads of the two branches into which this order has long been split. The smaller branch is led by Fevzeddin Erol, a *şeyh* in his late 60s, from a domain in a fold of the Sakarya River south-west of Ankara. The other, a national force, was headed by his half-uncle, Abdülbaki Erol El-Hüseyni. He died in July 2023, with a quarter of a million devotees converging on the small eastern town of Menzil for his funeral. Abdülbaki had been "one of the spiritual guides of our country," Erdoğan said in a message to the grieving family. Leadership, since contested, passed to his son, Muhammed

Saki who, with his father increasingly restricted by health problems, had taken over management of the community.

For decades, the conscience-stricken have flocked to Menzil to be shriven, so numerous that in a single ritual, the *şeyh* passes forgiveness down thirty or more white cords to 100–200 faithful, each holding the cord in their hand above their right shoulder. "*Ya Rabbi* (Oh God)," they chanted in the mosque. "I regret all the sins I have made. I wish I had not. God willing, I will not err again. I accept *Şeyh* Abdülbaki as my teacher."

In this unusual form of mass communication, the personal hearing practised by Kotku in the 1960s and 1970s has been replaced by a wholesale ceremony, adapted to the needs of a more impatient age. But, if the form has changed, the content remains similar, with the Menzil community's Rules of Repentance for visitors setting out eight obligations: to wash while repentant; to perform a total ablution while repentant; to carry out the prescribed prayers while repentant; to express repentance thrice; to request the pardon of God twenty-five times with closed eyes; to repeat eight times the opening chapter of the *Kur'an*, *Al-Fatihah*; to accept one's mortality; and to submit oneself to the *şeyh*.[2]

The ceremony differs from Catholic practice in that the *şeyh* does not claim the right of absolution, a right most Muslims hold belongs only to God. But this repentance without confession has attracted millions. Menzil, now cleared of all rival landowners, has become a pilgrim town, the penitents usually arriving by bus for a stay of up to three days. At weekends, this remote town hosts up to 15,000 visitors. Many are those, often in state service, who choose to go there for their annual holidays, and work in the fields or as temporary shepherds. The supplicants come from all corners of Turkey.

Abdülbaki Erol, *şeyh* of what is often called the Adıyaman branch of this *tarikat*, claimed a chain of succession to the Prophet, passing through his father, Muhammed Raşid Erol and his grandfather, Gavs-ı Bilvanisi Abdülhakim el-Hüseyni.

Gavs-ı Bilvanisi studied in the Halidi tradition, spending his life preaching in the remote Kurdish villages south-west of Lake Van. He had twenty-eight children by three wives. Visiting Menzil in his later years, he laid stones beside the Şimdiki *türbe* in what was then a poor village in a dusty plain rising from the banks of the Euphrates, indicating that he should be buried there.

Muhammed Raşid Erol, his first son, became famed for his wisdom and reputed for saving people from alcohol, drugs, gambling, and other vices. It was in his time that the human stream to Menzil began. Visitors in the

1980s were struck by the way that his followers were attributing miracles to him, but not to his father. He was, it seems, a striking figure:

> He was tall... He had a long beard, neither goat-shaped nor round. His beard had turned white... He had a clean, 'spiritual' face. He was tubby, but handsome... He wore a skullcap of pure white silk wrapped carefully around his head... He wore a very long robe... of pure white silk and linen... His shirt was buttoned, with a black waistcoat on top. The waistcoat could be seen under a pale beige outer cloak. A gold chain dangled from the pocket of his waistcoat... He was spotlessly clean.[3]

An earlier visitor, less charitably, found him obese, and dressed as if on a Hollywood set for a film of the Arabian Nights.

Muhammed Raşid welcomed visitors with the lines often attributed to the mystic Rumi:

> Return (in repentance), return! Whatever you are, return!
> Be you an unbeliever, a worshipper of fire or a worshipper of idols, return!
> Our door is here. It is not a door of despair.
> Break your vows of repentance a hundred times, return![4]

His personality turned the small hamlet into a magnet for young members of the ultra-nationalist MHP. As they became increasingly attracted by Islam, they would travel to see him, venerating him, their *şeyh*, more than their party leader.

These were Turkey's dark years, when the flight from village to city had become a torrent, and the new arrivals in the city were torn by the collapse of the old certainties and the temptations on the fringes of urban life. For those dispirited by what they could find, Menzil offered a chance of salvation, and had the full support of families who had seen their young gone astray. Its adepts set up groups throughout the country, targeting their appeal directly to the individual and his/her desire to be at peace with their soul. Their approach gave no weight to learning or social status, and this inherent modesty made it accessible to many daunted by the traditions and writings of communities drawing directly on the *Kur'an* or their sages' writings. It combined a call to "authentic" moral values with a nationalism rooted in the warrior traditions of early Turkic empires and the grandeur of the Ottomans. It was this blend that drew its early supplicants from the nationalist political parties to its door, and it is this that it has continued to emphasize.

Busloads of youths, usually male, would make the long journey to Menzil. They would be rigidly policed from the moment of their arrival, forbidden from taking photographs, and expected to join in the community's rituals. These included experiences of communal living that not all appreciated. As one visitor in 1979 recorded:

> Waking at noon, the news came that we could have soup in the garden of the *tekke*. But, Ye Gods, what did that prove. Our eyes opened wide when we saw, as if intended to crush our souls, the wretched state of those attacking with wooden spoons which had earlier been used by several others the cauldron in which floated the occasional grain of wheat in a broth without oil or salt.[5]

Yasin, an *imam* in the Lonca district near the Theodosian walls of İstanbul, has described how he worked as a representative of the Menzil. It was a rough neighbourhood: "Twenty metres away they sell drugs. Here they buy ether. You can get shot in the leg. It's that type of area," said one aide at the association whose café acted as Yasin's base. The café was noteworthy as the young were allowed to smoke there, in contrast to the discipline imposed by the İsmailağa community to the area's south-east.

Yasin, a Kurd from Ağrı, explained:

> Before we came here, religion was very weak. ... Here we teach the minimum elements that a Moslem should know... In addition, we take people to Menzil. Every year, at least two busloads go. Some years four. Some of those who go are drug addicts, some wanting to quit. They go, they see and they return. The one factor saving them is the going to Menzil and back. They leave their old friends. They join in our activities. Lessons, discussions, service.

However, he noted, while the İsmailağa community could arrange jobs for its members, few of those who joined Menzil so benefitted.[6]

So effective was all this reputed to be that in 2008 ALMADER, an NGO combatting addiction, won the support of the Governor of İzmir for sending sufferers to express repentance—an alleged policy deplored by a local CHP deputy.

The large number of visitors received by Muhammed Raşid and his opposition to the generals' proposed constitution of 1982 led the junta to exile him to Gökçeada (Imbros), the island off Gallipoli. He was kept there for eighteen months and then brought to Ankara. He remained under restriction until 1986, an earlier request by then Prime Minister Turgut Özal for him to be reprieved rebuffed by President Evren as a "disgusting proposal." When Özal became president, he invited the *şeyh* to visit him.

Muhammed Raşid declined, saying: "If you come here the image of the state will be harmed, and if I come to you that of Islam will suffer."[7]

In 1991, while receiving followers beside his father's grave, he was attacked by a seventeen-year-old from Denizli with a syringe filled with pesticide, being poisoned but surviving. He was a devout advocate of education, saying "to educate one student is more blessed than to make seventy thousand people godly." His followers took this as a command to open their dormitories to girls as well as boys and his message appealed to women as much as to men. His funeral saw the small village of Menzil overflowing with visitors from every corner of the country.

From Adıyaman to fifty-five countries

Muhammed Raşid had nominated six successors. In the event, his half-brother, Abdülbaki Erol, seized the reins and long prospered, being endowed by his followers with the titles *Gavs-ı Sani Seyyid*—saintly creator and descendant of the Prophet. He continued the remarkable development of the once small village, devoid of water and vegetation, and hiding two or three houses in its bosom, according to Muhammed Raşid's granddaughter. His first challenge was to find water, and his reverential relative tells how, after walking a while, he struck the ground, telling his companions to dig there a month later. They duly did so, and an abundant spring came gushing forth.[8] Next, he started construction of a mosque.

For his part, Abdülbaki made sure that Menzil benefitted from munificent allocations of state funds for items such as a 20-bed hospital and a thermal bath. By 2020, the village housed 1,700 people and was dominated by the Seyyid Abdülhakim el-Hüseyni *Külliyesi*. The complex, built on a site which could house eight football fields, combines a *mescid* for 400 people, a conference room for 200 people, a salon which can host 2,100, a half-Olympic swimming pool, education facilities for 400 people, *Kur'an* course facilities for 200, a museum, and a library. Gaudily illuminated at night, it projects an aura of solid worth by day. A recent venture is the nearby development of 1,020 time-share apartments. With previous residents driven out, one family member says: "The village is completely ours... My grandfather had seven sons. None of them had less than five children... All the shops in the village belong to me and my relatives."[9]

The control extends to monitoring all visitors, with an extensive CCTV network and guards who monitor entrants to the order's ceremonies and prevent photography and note-taking. Its petrol stations are favoured: fuel bought there is reputed to last longer and to protect against accidents.

Equally striking is the presence that the Adıyaman branch of the Menzil movement has developed in Ankara. On the ring road north of the capital, the Semerkand Cultural Centre, with its Central Asian-inspired porticos, rises grandly on a 54,000-square-metre site. Beside it is the Biltek School, one of the four such schools set up by the community. Elsewhere in the city are five branches and ten representative offices of the Semerkand Foundation, two swimming pools, various conversation hearths, two communications centres, a bookshop, and a supermarket. There is also an office for its relief agency, the *Beşir Derneği* (Evangelist Association). Another twenty-eight listed representative offices exist in İstanbul alone. Visiting all this is time-consuming. Critics have distributed videos of the Menzil's leaders being wafted around in a Mercedes-Maybach S 600 salon, a car with a price tag of around 450,000 euros in Turkey.

The Semerkand Foundation is at the centre of the Adıyaman Menzil's operations, controlling their Semerkand Holding which groups over forty companies and foundations. Its commercial interests include the Emsey Hospital beside Sabiha Gökçen Airport, opened in 2012 at a reported cost of 100 million USD, bus companies, a travel agency, a furniture company, food distributors, and a producer of religiously modest clothing. The importance given to promotion is reflected in the range of Menzil's media operations. These include Semerkand TV, Semerkand Radyo, ten publishing houses, and four magazines.

The Adıyaman branch of Menzil has support groups throughout the country. It runs *Kur'an* courses through these and has a number of dormitories, in both cases less than the Süleymancıs in number but still influential. It particularly targets youth, running four confederations known for promoting nationalist moral values. The main one is GENÇKON (*Gençlik Eğitim ve Kültür Konfederasyonu*, Youth Education and Culture Confederation), a platform comprising 68 youth clubs, 35 primary schools, 23 *Kur'an* schools, and 14 student dormitories, according to a 2019 study. All run summer camps and training courses, and GENÇKON also provides religious education and support.[10] It sponsors the Association of All Industrialists and Businessmen (*Tüm Sanayici ve İş Adamları Derneği*, TÜMSİAD), known to have over 12,000 companies employing 650,000 people as members in 2018.

Like other Turkish faith organizations, it prides itself on its activities abroad. Its Beşir Association works with Muslims in fifty-five countries.[11] The association has supported tsunami victims in Indonesia, flood-stricken Pakistanis, and families afflicted by the fighting in Syria and Yemen. At the end of 2021, it was also running campaigns for Palestine, Somalia, and the Rohingya. In October 2023, it was quick to proclaim "Gaza is dying" to raise aid.

In 1995, one journalist wrote that Menzil had 2 million members.[12] Such claims are hard to prove and, if exaggerated then, may not be so today. A survey carried out in 2011 indicated it had 600,000 members.[13] Around 2020, Muhammed Saki claimed that he had trebled Menzil's membership since he took the helm from his father two decades earlier. It has also benefitted as Erdoğan has looked for fresh hands to replace the disgraced supporters of Fethullah Gülen.

A muscular message

The Adıyaman Menzil vision of Islam is deeply conservative, with its message not one of learning but of discipline regarding the community's rules and repetition of prescribed rituals. In common with a number of Nakşibendi orders, it practises strict separation of men and women. In the repentance ceremony in the women's mosque, female penitents do not see the *şeyh*, but only hear his voice. They are also subject to a stricter ceremony of repentance, being required to follow their vows with ablutions in cold water. If they approach the *şeyh*, it should be on their knees. Restaurants have separate entrances for women, and the order's buses allow for segregation of travellers, with women in the rear behind a curtain.[14] It is rare to see a woman among the ranks of white-turbaned, grey-bearded men present at its conferences.

Its books include *Aile Saadeti* (Family Happiness) published in 2006 by Muhammed Saki. This book attracted controversy for instructing husbands on the correct way to beat their wives.

> Beating is of two kinds. One is persecution, the other is necessary. The necessary beating is a medicine... Dangerous tools like clubs or iron rods should not be used. The beating should be hidden and in your own home. The woman should be beaten and not thrown out... Face, eyes, head, and abdomen should not be hit. Organs should not be injured and the hair not pulled out.

A number of members of the AKP apparently endorsed these views: the book was given out by some municipalities during weddings. Despite such views, the order has a devoted following among women who lead conversation groups and fairs to raise funds for the movement and mobilize fresh supporters.

It is often described as rural, but it also has followings in the largest cities of the west of the country, especially in areas of MHP strength such as the industrial hinterlands of the Aegean. And, while its conservative message was initially directed to the less privileged, it is now increasingly heard by professional classes, not least doctors.

The order holds regular seminars stressing the historical contribution of Abdülhamid II, and is more nuanced towards the Republic's hero, Atatürk. "Were mistakes not made? They were. Perhaps mine were more than his. Although mine should be fewer. Because he was a man representing the country. He should have made fewer." So Muhammad Saki, Abdülbaki's eldest son, said in 2019, particularly criticizing the Republic's change of script: "In my opinion, the alphabet reform was nonsense. I have been to Greece. They have Greek writing there and the Latin alphabet. That is excellent. If I knew Ottoman, would that be a bad thing? I wish I knew English or other languages. A language is a new world."[15]

Its nationalism is full blooded, and it gives vigorous support to the muscular foreign policy of President Erdoğan. Its main publication is the monthly *Semerkand*, which in 2018 wrote:

> As a state and a nation we are today fighting a national struggle more violent than that of 100 years ago. Yesterday's Euphrates Shield and today's Operation Olive Branch are the most important fronts in that struggle. And on that front, it is not with terror organizations but with the U.S. and other western states which are their cohorts that we are fighting.[16]

Its youth movement, GENÇKON, emphasizes the contribution of national and Islamic values in building Turkey's future and fighting 'the enemy West.' But youth should be trained with scientific knowledge generated in this West to "develop our own defence and space programs, aircrafts, ships, industry, and advanced technology."[17] The websites of Menzil's two science schools, the Cezeri Science and Technology Schools (*Cezeri Bilim ve Teknoloji Okulları*), are a paean to the technologies of tomorrow.[18]

Fevzeddin in Ankara and Sivrihisar

Further hundreds of thousands of penitents visit a second site of this community, the lodge run by Fevzeddin Erol from his 2,800,000-square-metre farm outside Sivrihisar. After his father's death, Fevzeddin committed himself to follow his half-uncle, who, in turn, appointed Fevzeddin as his representative in Ankara.

Born in 1957, he was the most learned of his brothers, and had been a frequent companion of his increasingly invalided father in the latter's later years. In their stays in Ankara, they would see Demirel every day, visiting him in his Güniz Street offices after a retired general had helped arrange his father's return from exile to the capital. "I remember there being ten ministers in the room," Fevzeddin says of this period. He and his father were living next to the then presidential palace at Çankaya, and he claimed later to meet President Turgut Özal every day. Erbakan asked him to stand as a parliamentary candidate while Çiller was another of those impressed, giving him a revolver when she was prime minister.

Fevzeddin moved to Pursaklar, midway to the city's airport, where he started building a religious centre. His relationship with his uncle began to weaken as he fell out with the increasingly commercial bent of the main community. In 2002, a local benefactor gave him the farm. Shortly afterwards, he switched his spiritual allegiance to the venerable Molla Abdülbaki, one of the nominated successors of Muhammed Raşid Erol.[19] The two lived together until Molla Abdülbaki passed away aged 105 in 2020.

Fevzeddin had the settlement next to the farm renamed Buhara, the rival city of Samarkand, after which the tradition's Menzil community name its foundations and schools.

When he moved there, a tractor was necessary to travel the last six kilometres. In 2011, the local headman, Mevlüt Altın, explained:

> It was a rubbish dump... Now we grow wheat, potatoes and onions in the fields. We irrigate by drawing water from the Sakarya River. We have planted thirty thousand fruit trees. As they grow, our village will become even more beautiful. We do not sell the products we grow. We stock them in our warehouse and use them to provide three meals a day for visitors.[20]

By 2023, the original settlement of three to five ramshackle homes had two mosques, one capable of holding 2,000 men, with a soaring Ottoman portico, two minarets, and a grand minbar, and a second for women, with no minarets, as well as small shops and restaurants with separate entrances for women and men.

The farm achieved notoriety when an air chief marshal was accused of drawing up plans to strafe the community. This was during the Balyoz case of 2010–2015 when several documents were leaked to the press. After Gülen and Erdoğan fell out, the prosecutor argued the digital evidence was faked, and the 365 accused were acquitted (see also Chapter 12).

As in Menzil, so in Sivrihisar, the visitors come from far and wide. An intelligence report used in the Balyoz case—and therefore possibly unreliable—noted that the number of daily visitors to the farm "has not fallen below 1,000-1,500, and this number increases to 10,000 at weekends and 15,000 during religious holidays. It is said that each year an average of 500,000 people come from every place in Turkey either as penitents or from curiosity."[21] Politicians who visited the farm included Muhsin Yazıcıoğlu, from 1992 to his death in 2009 head of the nationalist Great Unity Party (*Büyük Birlik Partisi*, BBP), and the social democrat leader, Murat Karayalçın.

Fevzeddin is treated with full reverence, referred to as *Seyda* (Holiness) or Sultan, with acolytes always on hand to lay a cloth under where he will pray and to take off and fold his socks. He insists that his followers focus on the heart while those of his Adıyaman confreres are interested in money.[22] His group has no radio or television stations and few commercial extensions. These include all the shops and restaurants in its area and, unexpectedly, a concrete plant in Ivory Coast.[23]

The two groups are similar in their welcome to busloads of penitents and their ceremonies of repentance. They are also similar in teaching and doctrine. On commerce, Muhammed Saki acidly notes that Fevzeddin cannot operate his farm without being involved in trade. They also differ in their attitudes towards politics. On this Fevzeddin says: "During my father's time and now mine, we absolutely never interfered in the affairs of the state. You talk of 'Today's Menzil'. That is a different thing."[24] But Fevzeddin does not want others to magnify this difference or exploit it. As he said in a homily posted in May 2014:

> As long as there is life in our souls, as long as there is spirit in our souls, we will be slaves to that family. We will put that family in the place of our heads. All the children of His Holiness Gavs are accepted by us... We and you for all our lives will be servants/slaves of the children of Gavs.[25]

Climbing the political tree

The family patriarch, Gavs-ı Bilvanisi, was Kurdish, as are his descendants, but the family has always identified with the Turkish state, even when it was being persecuted. "What need was there for all these expenses and so many soldiers! All those petrol costs to go from Menzil to Gökçeada. If a night watchman had come and shown me the order, I would have collected my family, got into my car and come," Fevzeddin records his father as saying.[26]

Their nationalism was evident from the 1970s, when followers of the Ülkücü youth group of the MHP started making pilgrimages to Menzil. These young bravadoes were no angels. A number of the earlier visitors were given death sentences for murdering leftists. Prominent disciples included those accused of triggering the 1978 Kahramanmaraş massacre of over 100 Alevis, and Muhsin Yazıcıoğlu, one of the leaders of the MHP's armed youth movements. Many of them were released in the amnesty of 1980.

The order has long put its weight behind conservative parties, first supporting Erbakan's MSP and Refah Party, then in the 1990s Yazıcıoğlu's BBP, before giving its support to Erdoğan's AKP. In the local elections of March 2019, the AKP received 1,035 of the 1,043 votes cast in Menzil, and in the general elections a year earlier 67 of the 68 votes cast in Buhara.

Prominent AKP figures associated with the sect include Professor Dr Recep Akdağ, who served as Minister of Health for eleven of the first fifteen years of AKP rule, and Taner Yılmaz, Minister of Energy and Natural Resources for six years from 2009. Fevzeddin says of the last two:

> They grew up in our house. They were with me every week. Now they do not greet me. They do not come to our community. But at the time of my father, they came all the time. ... We may not be powerful, but the Menzil group is powerful in every corner of Turkey. I don't know: they have their people in every part of the state. Why not?[27]

Adıyaman Menzil has identified sources of revenue unusual for a mystical order, especially in the health sector. During Akdağ's protracted years as Minister of Health, he filled the key posts in the Ministry and the Social Security Institution with fellow members of the Menzil community. It was in this period that many of the car plates and plane registrations of the ministry included the letters "GVS," in apparent deference to the title *Gavs-ı Sani* of Abdülbaki Erol. In 2012, Erdoğan attended the opening of its Emsey Hospital. In October 2015, his successor as prime minister, Ahmet Davutoğlu, visited Abdülbaki Erol in Menzil.

The nature of the penitents visiting the eastern town has changed. As the journalist Saygı Öztürk was told in 2019:

> In the old days, over seventy per cent of those who came here were uneducated. But in recent years, the majority of those who come are educated, with positions in state offices. Doctors, officers, teachers and members of other professional groups came. Some came to become members of the *tarikat* in a quest to worship better Allah. Others came to

> free themselves from alcohol, gambling and other bad habits. There was another group too, of those who came to advance their work. Some used here to rise in the bureaucracy, others to win work from the state.[28]

Öztürk cites the (unnamed) Ankara representative of Menzil, an employee of *Diyanet*, as telling him: "After [Akdağ] became minister, the number of visitors to Menzil trebled or quadrupled. To win favour from the Minister, everyone went to Menzil, everyone wore a skull cap, etc. When he left the Ministry, we saw nobody there."[29]

In Öztürk's telling, appointees would be required to vest a part of their income to the community and tenders would either be awarded to Menzil community companies, or their winners would be required to contribute to the community. He records one (also unnamed) high-level bureaucrat in the ministry as telling him:

> Contractors who won tenders from the Ministry of Health would be obliged to make a bequest of up to ten per cent of their earnings to Menzil associations or foundations. In some cases, they would deliver the money by hand, never through the banks. In other cases, they would use diplomatic channels to transfer the money from Turkey to Arab countries. From there, the money, whitewashed, would be transferred as if it were an investment.
>
> From the point of view of human resources, health was a gold mine. Hundreds of firms were involved. Companies providing services such as catering, cleaning, security, patient care, or medical secretaries both represented a source of recruits for the *tarikat* and offered opportunities for employment for its members.[30]

But the process seems to have been two-way. As one study concludes, after the break with Gülen, the AKP needed to expand the social base essential for its legitimacy, and Menzil helped it do so.[31] As for Menzil, it was among the first communities to declare its support for Erdoğan in both 2018 and 2023.

After Abdülbaki Erol

Apart from Muhammed Saki, Abdülbaki named two others of his sons as "eligible to accept repentance"—he seems to have avoided the word successor—namely Muhammed Mübarek and Muhammed Fettah.

Long managing the community, Muhammed Saki has a strong following, and in July 2023, ten days after the death of his father, he threw down a gauntlet, announcing that he no longer had any links with the Semerkand Foundation, the Beşir Association, Menzil's youth arm, GENÇKON, and its trade extension, TÜMSİAD. His new vehicle was the Serhendi Foundation, named after Ahmed-i Sirhindi, six saints earlier than Halid el-Bağdadi. He followed this up with instructions to those who follow him, which included:

> In the last 10 years we have become distanced from our main duty. Our main duty is guidance and we will now devote ourselves to this. Our main duty is providing services in the lodge and madrasah. In other words, our guidance is science and education.
>
> Collecting money in lodges is strictly prohibited. The custom of collecting money is not in line with the spirit of mysticism... Terms such as reading house or tea house will not be used for lodges...
>
> It is forbidden to talk about trade and politics in the lodges. The lodge is not the place for these, but a place of guidance.
>
> There is no acting harshly... to those who come. They are all our brothers. At every point, we will return to the ways of our elders. From now on, our works will be published by Dehlevi Publications.[32]

It was a radical shift, a de facto acceptance of the criticism levelled at the Menzil branch by its fellow fraternity in Sivrihisar. But it was a change that Muhammed Saki said he had been considering for a decade. His younger brother, Muhammed Yakup, will be in charge of the publishing house as well as the television station that this Serhendi wing is expected to found.

The subsequent months have shown no signs of any accommodation being reached with the two other brothers singled out by his father. Each had his own role: Muhammed Mübarek, who has focused on Menzil's commercial empire, and Muhammed Fettah, who has been active in promoting Menzil penetration of state bodies.

Erdoğan did not attend Abdülbaki's funeral, nor did any of his ministers. Menzil's succession problems mean that, like Erenköy and İskenderpaşa too, Menzil may be pressed to play as important a role as it did when Erdoğan was still consolidating his hold on the governance of the country.

Işıkçıs—commerce and its cost

It is not often that a religious order is named after a retired colonel with an expertise in chemical weapons, but Hüseyin Hilmi Işık (1911–2001) was *sui generis*. He was Turkey's first certified chemical engineer, publishing in Turkey and Germany on the synthesis of the ester phenyl-cyan-nitromethane. He became an expert on poisonous gases and an inspector at the gas-mask plant of the Turkish army. In this last role, he rejected as "disusable, good for nothing," a consignment of 100,000 gas masks the

British were trying to sell to Turkey after their original customer, the Polish army, had fallen to Hitler. He taught at a number of military schools, retired after the military coup of 1960, briefly operated a pharmacy, and then dedicated his final four decades to continuing the teaching of the Halidi masters with whom he had studied since his youth.

In the year he graduated from a military high school, Işık had met and taken lessons from Kısakürek's mentor, Arvasi. When Arvasi died, Işik continued his instruction with Arvasi's eldest son, Ahmet Mekki Üçışık. His official website contains a certificate apparently issued by Üçışık, naming Işık as his spiritual successor.[33]

Starting in the 1950s, Işık wrote some eighteen books calling for a Sunni revival against communism, positivism, and heretical interpretations of Islam like Wahhabism, Shiʿism, reformism, and Islamism. For him, revivalism meant to return to the authentic Sunni interpretation of Islam. From this perspective, new interpretations of Islam were unacceptable, the result being a staunch stance against any kind of innovation.[34] His most complete work is a catechism published in English under the title *Endless Bliss*. As each edition of it was printed, further pages were added, with the 120th edition of the work reaching 1,248 pages.

For him, the world of nature around us is the world as seen by al-Ghazali long ago—that is, the universe operates with dual causality, natural and divine, but the latter is superior. In his view, humans cannot possess or propose moral norms to understand God. Thus, the search for a logical explanation to God's custom on the basis of morality or rationality is not only meaningless but also heretical. Where the issue of free will is concerned, Işık saw God's sovereignty as the absolute agent of all human actions, an interpretation more conservative than that of el-Bağdadi. He also used the arguments of al-Ghazali to demonstrate the limits of human reason and sensation.[35]

He was a committed believer in the importance of the printed word, developing two printing houses, *Işık* and *Hakikat*, and in 1970 launching the paper also named *Hakikat* and two years later renamed *Türkiye*. Such was the thrust of his followers that through the 1990s this daily accounted for about 10 per cent of newspaper sales in the country.

Many of his followers became teachers, and one writer, Nazif Ay, has recorded how, as a poor student aged fifteen at the Eyüp *İmam-Hatip Lisesi*, he was targeted by these teachers and recruited to distribute their master's books and newspaper. He found it "rather comic" that the paper considered it necessary to use a primitive Photoshop-type programme to cover the legs of athletes on its sports pages; the main book they sold was Işık's catechism, which Ay found "boring" and "unnecessarily aggressive;" he also found curious the book's prescription: "Whether you are rich or poor, smoke a cigarette after every meal."[36]

Initially, Ay sold the books of Işık and el-Bağdadi in the streets of Fatih, at train stations, on trains, and on Bosphorus ferries. Shortly afterwards, the generals seized power, and he was struck how the martial law command permitted these sales to continue, even inside the Kuleli Military Academy. Ay icily records the development of the community's portfolio of companies, its sales of tawdry jewellery, the replacement of censored photographs with profiles of beshorted sportsmen, and the roping in of female pop stars to promote its products. It was, he thought, "resolutely developing a position where it could harm many." He notes how the Işıkçıs' representative for Central Asia helped Fethullah Gülen build up his network of schools there.

Like Kotku, Işık believed in the virtue of hard work and that believers "should utilize the latest scientific renovations and facilities. Earning through *halâl* ways is a great act of worship. Any way of earning that will not hinder the daily prayers and which will not cause one to commit sin is good and blessed."[37]

Decisive in the Işıkçıs' change from mysticism to Mammon was Işık's son-in-law, Enver Ören, who channelled the goodwill of the movement's followers into support for a range of trading ventures—distribution of home appliances, electronic goods, food, soft drinks, and automobiles; tourism; a hospital; and construction. In 1993, these were grouped together into İhlas Holding and joined by the television station, TGRT. In 1995, the group established İhlas Finance, a bank working on Islamic principles of profit sharing rather than interest and supporting the small and medium-sized entrepreneurs of Anatolia.

While dealing with politics, Işık sought to raise the religious values of society to counter the positivist orientations of the West advanced by the Kemalists. He cited with approval Arvasi's scathing: "The greatest enemy of Islam is the British. They tried to annihilate Islam with all their armies, fleets, and uncountable gold coins collected from their colonies, in short, with all their imperial powers."[38]

After supporting Demirel's Justice Party, he was an early proponent of the various parties launched by Erbakan, but then kept a distance as the latter's Islamist movements contested the boundaries of secularism. He positioned the Işıkçı community as an ally of the armed forces in their struggle with communism. Işık himself had served in the Turkish army in the early Cold War days, when U.S. advisers were stiffening the back of their NATO ally's forces. Ay describes the Işıkçıs under Enver Ören as having an "umbilical cord" to the U.S. In Ay's view, it was not they and other Islamists who were choosing America, but America who was choosing them.

It was a successful mix and from 1995 was underpinned by the increasingly active İhlas Finance. The group vaulted into the top ten Turkish groups ranked by turnover, but from 2001 it all fell apart. The financial crisis of the time—brought on by state banks defaulting on their obligations—forced İhlas Finance to close its doors. It owed nearly a billion USD to its 222,298 depositors. Two thirds of its creditors received some compensation, but in 2009, the then Minister of Industry told the Grand National Assembly that 68,000 people were still owned money. Ihlas Holding had to shrink. In 2006, it sold its main TGRT operations to Rupert Murdoch's News Corporation.

In December 1990, *Türkiye* recorded net sales of 1,361,553, still a record for a newspaper in Turkey (even if a number swollen by gift subscriptions). The financial collapse and subsequent illness and death of Ören sapped this once self-confident community, and yet a "human flood," according to *Sabah* newspaper, and 70–80,000 people, according to his followers, attended Ören's funeral in 2013. Erdoğan was among the politicians who carried the coffin on his shoulder; eight other members of his cabinet were present.

Ören's successor, his son, Ahmet Mücahid Ören, faced a hard task, not made easier by a conviction for conspiracy and fraud; he was chairman of İhlas Finance at the time it was taken over by the state. He was able to avoid prison by staying in the U.S., acting as Honorary Consul of Latvia in New York.

With the passing of the years, the family has been rehabilitated. In 2014, Mücahid Ören's wife came into the news for making a vanity payment of 50,000 USD to be photographed with Obama. In 2016, he was a panelist at the World Economic Forum in Davos and in 2017 signed an agreement with China Silk Road Group to develop Beijing's One Belt, One Road project. In 2019 and 2020, he was received by Erdoğan at the presidential palace.

In March 2024, *Türkiye*'s sales were 110,000, a fraction of its peak but still the second-highest-selling daily in the country. The Hakikat publishing house also continues on, with a catalogue of over 140 titles in over thirty languages. One of its bestselling works is *Confessions of a British Spy*, a work probably developed by wartime Germans to alienate the Wahhabis. An English version, published in 2021, was in its 20th edition.

Mücahid Ören has continued to uphold the works of his grandfather as the basis for the community he has sought to reconstitute. Meanwhile, the caravan of commerce rolls on. As the long-sceptical Ay comments: "The [traditional Sufi] philosophy of 'a cloak and a loaf' has become just a beautiful false slogan used in the hunt for disciples and a romantic religious phrase."

11

THE APOSTLES OF NURSI
A RAINBOW OF LIGHT

I seek refuge in Allah from Satan and politics.
Said Nursi, *Emirdağ Lâhikası*, Sözler Yayınevi, 1993, Vol 2, p. 460

The loyal, abiding, and divisive heirs

Through the 1960s, concerns about a revival of religious activism swelled with the rise of Demirel's Justice Party. In the last half of the decade, articles about *irtica* (political reaction) in *Cumhuriyet*, the pillar of the Kemalist establishment, were thrice as frequent as in the previous quarter century. The paper's particular bugbear were the Nurcus—the followers of Bediüzzaman Said Nursi—who were subject to an average of two attacks a month.[1] The number of cases against the Nurcu was extensive, even if they were usually fruitless. By 1971, over 700 trials had ended in acquittal, usually because studying a commentary on the *Kur'an* could not be classed as a crime.

For a short period after Nursi's death, those taking sustenance from his writings had accepted leadership by a consultation council comprising men who had been close to the dead figure. This collegiate approach soon broke down, not over interpretations of these writings, as would be normal in a text-based community, but over whether these sacred texts should be distributed in their original script, which was usually Ottoman, as the

Copyists (*Yazıcılar*, often translated as Writers or Scriptorialists) argued, or printed in the Republic's Turkish alphabet, and read and taught in groups or *dershane*, as the Readers (*Okuyucular*) advocated. A second issue of contention was whether to establish a political party.

The impact Nursi has had on religious discourse and practice is hard to quantify, but the few proxies for indicators confirm that within Turkey, he has reached the hearts of between 1 and 3 million citizens. Van Bruinessen has noted that in the 1977 elections, when the Nurcu had split with Erbakan's National Salvation Party, the latter's share of the vote fell by 3.2 per cent compared with the previous elections. In his view, the Nurcu movement was "by far the most important religious movement among the Kurds of Turkey;" M. Hakan Yavuz, writing at the turn of the current century, found the Nurcu groups "the most powerful and effective sociopolitical communities in contemporary Turkey;" and a 2011 survey found that 4.1 per cent of the sample belonged to Nurcu groups, the vast majority adhering to that of the neo-Nurcu Fethullah Gülen.[2]

From the 1970s, further fissions occurred over politics and over ownership and amendments to the text of the *Risale-i Nur*. Today, the four predominant groups are, on the one hand, the Copyists, who have largely kept together over the years and supported the AKP, and, on the other, three heirs to the Readers tradition—the *Yeni Asya* (New Asia) group, with a newspaper long critical of the AKP; the İstanbul Group with its Hizmet Foundation and Envar printing house; and the *Yeni Nesil* (New Generation) group. The last two have focused more on issues of teaching and faith, and appreciate Erdoğan for buttressing Islam.

These vicissitudes have left the Nur movement so fragmented that no single fraction can claim pre-eminence over the mantle of Nursi. Indeed, most of the splits were led by men hallowed for closeness to their saint. Six decades after his death, almost all of these have passed away, leaving their heirs with further challenges.

In the early argument over script, it was mainly the conservatives who sided with the Copyists. Their leader was Hüsrev Altınbaşak, a calligrapher who refused to use modern typesetting machinery. Relations between the two wings were initially cordial, but broke down when a pressure cooker sent by a Reader exploded in Altınbaşak's kitchen—an attempt, he considered, on his life. Before he died, he established the Hayrat Foundation, to raise "more knowledgeable, virtuous, moral, and patriotic people." His fellow Copyists, considering this task needed books, established a printing press in Isparta, which, with a 14,000-square-metre plant, has grown to describe itself as one of the largest publishers of the *Kur'an* in the world.

The Copyists have prospered. They insist on the primacy of Ottoman Turkish in propagating Bediüzzaman's words, and their books elegantly present these. Altınbaşak favoured cooperating with the ultra-nationalist MHP, but generally the Copyists have prioritized their relations with the state. In 1995, the Hayrat Foundation signed an agreement with the Ministry of Education to carry out courses in the Ottoman language. These activities received fresh impetus in 2012 when the Ministry, perhaps seeking to establish a counterweight to the Gülen movement (see Chapters 12–13), revived this programme, two years later extending it to morality lessons throughout the country. A later protocol extends the link to state dormitories and Turkey's Yunus Emre cultural centres abroad. The Copyists' foundation organizes *Kur'an* courses in Turkey and Islamic education in countries from sub-Saharan Africa—Burkina Faso, Niger, and Sudan—to Afghanistan, and from London and Berlin to Kuala Lumpur. Between 2008 and 2013, the Copyists organized annual symposia on the *Risale-i Nur*; no female participant was evident in the promotional video after one such event. Their commercial interests include a small chain of markets in İstanbul selling *helal* foods and products.

However, the majority of the community has followed the Readers, the Nurcu "brothers" who held authority and power through reading and interpreting Nursi's writing in the *dershane*. For some, such activities were enough in themselves, but the group initially agreed that they had to correct overall attitudes towards religion, and that for this a printing house and journal were necessary.[3]

The Readers then launched a series of short-lived weekly titles. The last of these, *İttihad* (Unity), was closed after the military intervention of March 1971, but by this time a group led by Zübeyir Gündüzalp and Mehmet Kutlular had started publication of the daily, *Yeni Asya*. The paper thrived during the next decade, supporting Erbakan's National Salvation Party, and contributing deputies to it from 1974 to 1977. However, considering a general amnesty proposed by the party would benefit the left, it switched its support to Demirel's Justice Party, seeing this as better representing the traditions of the Democrat Party, the Nurcus' previous haven.

Meeting in May 1980, the General Consultative Meeting of the Nurcu had called on the *ağabey*, the respected close students of Nursi, to act in harmony. However, the coup that September proved to be a further dividing factor. A group led by the influential Mehmet Kırkıncı argued that Demirel, who had been excluded from politics by the generals, had now fulfilled his historical function. This group lauded General Evren as "the Commander of the Faithful," and three years later threw in its lot with Turgut Özal when he became prime minister.[4]

Most of the Readers, however, maintained their loyalty to Demirel. *Yeni Asya* was vocal in its criticism of the generals, and was duly banned. Its publishers immediately launched another newspaper, *Yeni Nesil.* Publication of *Yeni Asya* was then re-allowed, but the Nurcus decided to transfer the rights of *Yeni Asya* to *Yeni Nesil* and to continue publication of the second. *Yeni Nesil*, in its own words, followed a policy of "legal and logical" criticism of the generals' closure of political parties, Evren's random pronouncements on religion, and a ban on headscarves. Its issue censuring the generals' draft constitution led to it being closed for a year—during most of which the Nurcus continued to project their ideas through *Tasvir* (Portrait), a defunct newspaper that they temporarily resuscitated.

The *Yeni Nesil* group was vocal throughout the 1980s, generally attacking Özal's ANAP and giving unstinted support for Demirel. On 3 January 1990, Kutlular, other leading writers of *Yeni Nesil*, and almost all the staff of the group's magazines found themselves at the door. The owners of the newspaper wanted to "adjust the dosage" of criticism of Özal.[5] Those thrown out then started their own newspaper, in less than a fortnight reviving the title *Yeni Asya*.

Three decades later, these two factions continue to make their mark.

The rump *Yeni Nesil* group adopted a more nuanced approach to Demirel, tending towards Erbakan and the parties that were heirs to his National Outlook. Their stand did not resonate within the Nurcu community, and publication of the newspaper ended around 1992. However, its Moral FM long continued broadcasting, supporting the National Outlook and, eventually, Erdoğan as the continuation of that. Further, this group has been one of the most effective of the bodies promoting the saint's work. Its activities include publishing works by and on Nursi at its *Sözler Neşriyat*; a student scholarship programme; and a series of events organized by its *İstanbul İlim ve Kültür Vakfı* (İstanbul Foundation for Science and Culture), a foundation set up in 1979 by Mustafa Sungur, Mehmet Emin Birinci, and Mehmet Nuri Güleç (Fırıncı). The foundation has held a dozen symposia on Said Nursi in İstanbul, and others in Ukraine, the Mediterranean, and Asia. It has maintained respectful relations with the AKP. Its chairman, Said Yüce, worked for the president when the latter was mayor of İstanbul and was an AKP deputy from 2015 to 2018.

Fırıncı was one the Nurcu leaders to visit Erdoğan and reiterate Said Nursi's calls for reopening Ayasofya to prayer and for state printing of the *Risale-i Nur*. With the ability of the Nurcus to work more openly—and the state's willingness to differentiate between mainstream followers of Said Nursi and the proscribed followers of Fethullah Gülen—many Nurcu are happy to support the AKP. The day before the first round of voting in the presidential elections of May 2023, the head of the *Diyanet* attended a reading from *Risale-i Nur* in Sakarya.

The main continuing exception is the *Yeni Asya* group, which has been consistent in its vehement opposition to the various National Outlook parties and to Erdoğan as a continuation of that tradition. It backed the challengers to Erdoğan in the 2014, 2018, and 2023 presidential elections.

It supported Demirel through his terms as prime minister and president, its publishing house printing his speeches and regularly interviewing him for its quarterly magazine, *Köprü Dergisi* (Bridge Journal). Its newspaper, *Yeni Asya*, started the 2000s with a daily circulation of under 10,000, built this up to exceed 50,000 between 2011 and 2015, but has since slipped back to linger under 10,000.

Kutlular, publisher of the paper, was no stranger to controversy.[6] He long denounced the Ergenekon trials (see next chapter) as a sham and the 2016 coup attempt as a product of the same clandestine forces. The paper's criticisms of Erdoğan's government and its continuing publication of impudent cartoons have led to a deluge of lawsuits. In early 2020, its publication manager, Kazım Güleçyüz, and its responsible editor and cartoonist, Halil İbrahim Özdabak, received prison sentences of 20 and 19 months respectively. On appeal, they were acquitted.

Yeni Asya has an active news website, operates Bizim Radyo, publishes a clutch of magazines of which the most influential remains *Köprü Dergisi*, and runs one of the major operations distributing the works of Nursi, *Yeni Asya Neşriyat*. Its *Risale-i Nur* Institute has arranged over a dozen congresses on Bediüzzaman's work since 2004. It runs Euronur, an association for Nurcus in Europe. It also has a charitable foundation, active, not least in cataract operations, in Africa, and works with the Australia Light Foundation.

Spreading—and changing—the word

The differences between the Nurcu fractions should not mask the continuing cohesion created by the communal study meetings carried out week in and week out throughout the towns of the country. These *ders*, or lessons, are simple—a reading from *Risale-i Nur*, a discussion of the reading led by the most knowledgeable person present, a long tea break for developing friendships, a second reading by a young Nurcu from Nursi's *Lahikalar*, and a concluding reading from the *Kur'an*.[7] These usually take place in the evening, with those on Saturday given particular weight.

The setting for these meetings has evolved over the years. Initially, they would take place in the homes of the clandestine copiers of Nursi's works. Later, specially designated apartments were established. Today, most *dershane* have retained their modesty, though in some larger towns one better-furnished apartment is occasionally to be found, intended to assist recruitment. Radio and television were long banned. Over time, rooms for students have started to be provided.[8]

There are now several thousand of these *dershane*. In 2022, the Copyists' Hayrat Foundation claimed to have at least one association running *sohbet* in each of Turkey's 519 sub-provinces (*ilçe*). At least as many *dershane* follow the *Yeni Nesil* Group, but rather less the *Yeni Asya* group. "With us being known for criticising the AKP, people are frightened of being identified with us, particularly in small communities," one member of *Yeni Asya* said in August 2021. In all, there may be between three and six thousand Nurcu discussion circles. These figures exclude the discussion groups run by the Gülen movement until its closure in 2016.

Their focus on their master's texts rather than the *Kur'an* sets the Nurcus apart from other Islamic groups in Turkey and is valuable in building a sense of community. The *dershane* also encourage business cooperation between participants.

Sustaining these *dershane* and the millions of those seeking the teachings of Nursi has fuelled a substantial printing industry. Nursi himself nominated a group to supervise publication of the *Risale-i Nur*, and it became customary within the Nurcu movement to obtain permission from this group in order to publish the work. Publishers were expected to meet Nursi's stipulation that 20 per cent of the income generated from publication would be allocated to scholarships for students of his work.

In April 2014, the government, seeking tools to use against the Gülen movement, decided to curtail its revenue by ruling that only *İhlas Nur Neşriyat* and *Envar Neşriyat* had the copyright for *Risale-i Nur*. That November, it went further, decreeing that the copyright of all the works of "Sait Okur (Bediüzzaman Said Nursi)" would be transferred to the *Diyanet*.[9] The *Diyanet* then authorized the six main non-Gülenist publishers to print up to 150,000 volumes a year. Publishers visited in August 2021 said that this situation was causing them no hindrance.[10]

From early on, some editions began to make amendments to Nursi's original words, with the addition or removal of words, sentences, and even paragraphs. Sometimes these changes reflected instructions from Nursi himself, though a number seemed designed to attune the works with the prevailing nationalist ethos. Disputes between publishing houses were often settled not by the courts but by non-official *Shari'a* courts, which would arbitrate or settle differences. At least some publishers welcomed the involvement of the *Diyanet,* arguing that supporters of Gülen were publishing distorted versions of Nursi's works.

The Kurdish dimension

The issue of textual integrity had become particularly contentious as the eruption of the PKK separatist group brought the question of Kurdish identity onto the national agenda and revived discussion of what Said Kurdi, as Nursi had originally been named, stood for.

Some early editions of the *Risale-i Nur* removed references to Nursi's Kurdish origins and to the Kurds—instead referred to as 'peasants,' 'people from the east,' or 'tribes'—and pruned Nursi's comments on the political regime of Turkey. Concerns that this distorted Nursi's teaching caused M. Sıddık Dursun (Şeyhanzade) from Bingöl and İzzettin Yıldırım from Ağrı to start their own publishing house, *Tenvir* (Illumination), in the early 1980s.

Şeyhanzade and Yıldırım then launched a magazine, *Dava* (Struggle), and what they called the *Med-Zehra* movement. Their approach was to build on Nursi's Kurdish origins, not to support separatist nationalism, but rather to underline his message that the Kurds and the Turks were inseparable brothers in the Islamic community. This spirit lay behind Nursi's dream of a University of the East, the *Medresetü-z Zehra,* and their breakaway took its name from this.[11]

Dava was first published in 1989, and early issues saw Med-Zehra criticizing other Nurcu groups, particularly *Yeni Asya*, because of their involvement in day-to-day politics. The magazine argued that political parties were a byproduct of European philosophy, and that involvement in politics prevented the Muslim from focusing on his or her true mission, which is to make Islam the dominant force in all areas of life. In *Dava*'s view, Nursi avoided use of the term democracy because rules created by humans prevent the rules of God from being fully realized. Şeyhanzade would later write that his aim was to make the *Shari'a* the dominant law of Islamic societies, with the *Risale-i Nur* being the best guide to achieve this goal; he would call for re-establishing the Caliphate.[12]

For ten years, Şeyhanzade had close relations with Fethullah Gülen, falling out over distortions by Gülen's followers of the texts of *Risale-i Nur*.[13] But Şeyhanzade's more serious difficulties resulted from the intensification of the struggle between the PKK separatists and the army after 1992, and the killing and torture by the state of its opponents. This caused him to publish a series of articles criticizing state policies. For him, the problems for the Kurds dated back to the Ottoman Empire, and, as the Ottoman Empire was not founded on the basis of race, nor on the basis of justice and equality, it permitted repression of the Kurds. In his view, these problems worsened during the republican period because of what he considered the underlying element of racism within the Turkish Republic. He argued that, in a true Islamic order, every nation or ethnic group should have the right to speak and be educated in its own language.

Come 1993, *Dava* started publishing reports from the human rights organization, *Mazlum-Der*, on incidents in the Kurdish region. Şeyhanzade wrote that he was shocked by what he was seeing. From this point on, *Dava* put more emphasis on its distinctive Kurdish identity and interpreted Islam in a more nationalist manner. This won it widespread support in the east and south-east of Turkey as well as in Ankara and İstanbul, according to one political scientist in 2001.[14]

Dava continued publication until 2002, with Şeyhanzade generally keeping his distance from the state and from other Kurdish groups. In 2015, the movement denied that it was supporting the pro-Kurdish HDP (People's Democratic Party), saying it had never supported any party. Şeyhanzade died in 2017. He was succeeded by a council of four or five, who, as of 2024, had limited resonance.

In around 1990, Yıldırım and a group looking for a more nationalistic line broke away from Med-Zehra and established what has since been known as the Zehra Nur group. Two years later, they launched the magazine *Nübihar* (Spring) in Kurmanji Kurdish and a publishing house with the same name. "This magazine was like a breath of fresh air to Kurdish publishing," ran one recent comment. "Because he was expressing the truth of Kurdistan, the literary products of a thousand years of the Kurdish language simply and beautifully, with Islamic concerns but without Islamism, in Kurdish but not making Kurdish politics."[15] Yıldırım also funded the Kurdish nationalist magazine, *Yeni Zemin* (New Foundation), published in 1993 and 1994.

These activities and those of the group's Zehra Education and Culture Foundation (*Zehra Eğitim ve Kültür Vakfı*) angered members of the security forces. Yıldırım himself was kidnapped by the Kurdish Hezbollah at the end of 1999, his tortured corpse being found a month later. There was always the suspicion that the deep state (see next chapter) was involved.[16] Zehra Nur also angered the Gülen movement, and it seems no coincidence that the years 2005–2014 when the Zehra foundation was closed were those when the Gülen movement dominated the police and judiciary. In recent years, it has opened schools in Ankara (Batıkent), Bingöl, and Van, sought to revive Nursi's dream of a university in Van, and campaigned for the use of Kurdish in schools and public life.

Zehra Nur is the most active of the Nurcu movements in the homeland of Nursi himself—and continues to disturb the establishment by failing to join in the prevalent obeisance to the memory of Atatürk. For its part, the Med-Zehra group has a support base among religious Kurds, both in predominantly Kurdish cities, and also in cities with large Kurdish migrant populations. The group supported the AKP during its "Kurdish opening" of 2009 to 2015.

Aczmendi—the antinomian fringe

While the various wings of the Nur movement have generally sought to work within the bounds of parliamentary politics, one figure distorting the teachings of Nursi decided that a frontal assault on the system was required. This was Müslim Gündüz, one of thirteen children of a hospital worker, whose take-no-hostage approach appalled secular Turkey in the 1980s and 1990s.

Gündüz dressed himself like Said Nursi, adopting Kurdish robes, a long beard, and a staff. Surrounded by other *Aczmendi* (The Humble Servants) and dressed in denial of all to which the new Republic aspired, he would appear in the streets of his native Elazığ, a conservative town in eastern Anatolia, and rail against the heathen religion of Kemalism. He appeared to welcome controversy and was often on the front pages of a horrified mainstream press, attacking the core values of the republican regime. "Its God is Mustafa Kemal and its prophet is İsmet İnönu. Democracy is godless. So is secularism," he told *HBB* television channel in June 1996. He would usher in the rule of the *Shari'a*, and the armed forces would not have the strength to stop him.

The State Security Court sentenced Gündüz to two years' imprisonment for his 1996 television appearance, a conviction overthrown by the European Court of Human Rights in 2003. By this time, he had other concerns. Six months after the *HBB* broadcast, he had again been in front of the television cameras, but this time half-dressed and accompanied by a 22-year-old woman. The police had broken down the door of a Kadıköy apartment and found the two together.[17] Gündüz and his acolyte, "Cinci Hoca" Ali Kalkancı, received two-year sentences for crimes against chastity and honour.[18] In this period, he also received a 50-month sentence for establishing an illegal organization. He was then sentenced to a 30-year prison term for seeking to overthrow the constitutional order. Freed under the general amnesty of 2000, in 2004 he was again arrested, this time accused of terrorism, not being acquitted and released until 2008.

The raid on Gündüz won one of Turkey's highest television programme ratings ever. It also destroyed the momentum of his movement, leaving it crippled though not dead. The tone of his trajectory is evidenced by his officiating at the funeral service of Mirzabeyoğlu, the man who set up the militant İBDA-C group (see Chapter 9).

Probably his main contribution to Islam has been that of so horrifying the generals that he became part of their self-justification for the soft coup of February 1997, the "fine tuning of democracy," as one general would describe it, which, counter to its perpetrators' aspirations, was to trigger the events precipitating the rise of Erdoğan.

12

GÜLEN AND FIVE DECADES OF GUILE

In the post 9/11 anguish, Washington was looking around for a Moslem voice for tolerance and dialogue and the Gülen movement appeared to fit the bill. As a senior U.S. diplomat told me in those years: "It seemed almost too good to be true."

Suzy Hansen, writer, interviewed in 2024.

Hiding in plain sight

In 2011, the polling company Konsensus shed a rare light on the reach of the religious orders. Its findings indicated a national membership of around 3 million and that nearly two thirds of these followed Fethullah Gülen. Far behind came the Süleymancı, Menzil, and 'Nakşibendi' communities—multiple answers were allowed—then Erenköy and İsmailağa.[1] A second survey that year indicated that the orders could have as many as 5 million members and that one quarter of these were members of, or felt close to, the Gülen community.[2]

Gülen has long lived in self-exile in Pennsylvania, 100 kilometres west of Newark Liberty International Airport. A visitor in 2015 recalls: "his head was bowed, and he moved with a hesitant shuffle, more resembling a pensioner awakening from his afternoon nap than the patriarch of a global organization. He had a large, pale head, an expansive nose, and eyes freighted by enormous sacks."[3] But his impact on those he encountered can only be described as mesmerizing.

Two Turkish presidents, Turgut Özal and Abdullah Gül, came under his sway, as did three prime ministers, Çiller, Ecevit, and—for a long time—Erdoğan. In Özal's case, the attraction was probably based on a common desire to advance Islam; Özal helped Gülen develop his network of schools in the Turkic republics of Central Asia. With Ecevit, the linkage is more shadowy. However, for Gül, Çiller, and Erdoğan, the interactions seem opportunistic. Gülen could mobilize and deliver support, not least through his newspapers and television stations, while his evident closeness to power added to his lustre and assisted his disciples as they implemented a stunningly orchestrated infiltration of the traditional pillars of the Republic.

Bracing Gülen's prestige was the position he had staked out for himself in a world anguished by al-Qaeda and successor groups such as ISIS. From the late 1990s, Gülen launched calls for interfaith dialogue, and Western chancelleries were quick to identify him as an apostle of tolerance and Islamic enlightenment. For NATO governments and Western think tanks, Gülen seemed to offer a new way forward for dealing with the complexities of Islam. Western academics jumped on the bandwagon. From 2000 to 2015, writers and publishers competed with their portraits of the philosopher saint's achievements.

Yet, even three months after the failure of the Gülenist coup of July 2016, when a group of "Gülen scholars" met at the University of Utah to discuss how they had so misjudged their hero, their tergiversations continued the airbrushing from history of the evidence of his designs littering his career. This evidence is clearly set out in the 80-page indictment of Gülen prepared in 1999 by the Ankara prosecutor, Nuh Mete Yüksel. The latter did not feature in the Utah discussions, being overlooked, as he is in most of the adulatory international literature on Gülen.[4] But Yüksel—like all those who crossed the ambitious and vindictive cleric—deserved better than the character assassinations and prejudiced prosecutions which were their common fate. First, it is worth considering what gave Gülen his allure.

The preacher's paternal family came from Ahlat on the shores of Lake Van, long a cauldron of conflict between Armenians and Kurdish Muslims, Sunni and Alevi, and occupied by the Russians from 1915 to 1918. In his book *Küçük Dünyam* (My Small World), Gülen describes how his great-great-grandfather, Halil Ağa, a hereditary landowner, was known as Kurt Halil, and that it was as exiles that his family moved to Korucuk, near

Erzurum, where he was born. In that book, he gives his date of birth as 10 November 1938, the fateful day on which Atatürk died.[5]

Erzurum is a conservative area, fiercely nationalist after three occupations by Russian forces, and studded by *tekke*. It was—and is—a centre of Islam. Gülen's great-grandfather had been a respected scholar, and his father was committed to the Nakşibendi tradition. While still in his teens, he also came across Kadiri teachings and, aged around twenty, the writings of Nursi, being particularly struck by the latter's concept of positive action.

Gülen qualified as a state *imam*, and worked for three years in Edirne and Kırklareli near the Bulgarian border. There, he participated in a series of activities contesting communism and Darwinism, also reading the works of Kısakürek, the nationalist Nurettin Topçu, and the more discursive Sezai Karakoç.[6] He was transferred to İzmir in 1965, becoming director of a *Kur'anic* school attached to the city's Kestanepazarı Mosque. He started summer camps to teach Islamic sciences to male high school and university students. These camps attracted the attention of the authorities and, after the 1971 military intervention, a martial law report described him as the leader of one of "the most dangerous of the destructive and divisive organizations" advocating a theocratic state in Turkey.[7] He was found guilty of infringing Article 163 of the Penal Code. However, after seven months in prison, he returned to the cadres of the *Diyanet*, serving as *imam* in Edremit and Manisa, before taking up post at Bornova Merkez Camii in İzmir in 1976.

He proved a charismatic preacher, with an emotional delivery that impressed those who attended his mosque and the coffee houses that he would visit. His sermons in Bornova became renowned. One description by a journalist, writing under a pseudonym and with probable poetic licence, captures the mood:

> The mosque was overflowing with people from all over Turkey. Fethullah *Hoca* would preach with tears in his eyes, and the congregation would cry with him. People in different corners of the mosque were shouting 'Allah' for everyone to hear, throwing themselves to the ground. At the rostrum, Fethullah *Hoca* was humiliating himself, crying, sometimes passing out, being sobered and fainting, sometimes throwing the *Kur'an* saying 'I am helpless, I am nothing, let them cut off my head'... people threw themselves to the ground, shouting to the congregation: 'I saw our Prophet. I swear to God, he was sitting next to our teacher' and then went to Fethullah *Hoca* and burst into tears.[8]

Gülen's acolytes proved effective at raising funds from the devotees of these ceremonies. With these funds, he established "safe houses" called *Işık Evleri* (Lighthouses), homes for poor students from out of town as they pursued their studies and in which the elders in charge ensured firm discipline and an Islamic environment. Before long, he started dormitories for high school and university students, next adding schools to help teenagers prepare for the nationwide university entrance exam. At that time, only one tenth of would-be entrants to universities were accepted.

As Gülen's influence began to show up in other cities, he attracted increasing attention from senior figures of the Nur movement, not least as he was a supporter of Erbakan. In 1977, the *Yeni Asya* group printed a number of his talks in a book entitled *Hitap Çiçekleri* (Flowers of Oratory). Neither this gesture nor visits from influential Nurcus won him over, and he continued his own course, underlining the separation in 1979 by launching a monthly magazine, *Sızıntı* (Fountain). Soon, it was not Nursi's writings that were the focus of this publication, but the pronouncements of Gülen himself.

The 1980 coup was followed by a further arrest warrant, only rescinded in 1986, three years into Özal's rule. During this time, he continued his activities, in apparent full sight of the authorities, using audio cassettes to disseminate his ideas in the form of sermons, publishing these sermons, and continuing the buildout of his classroom network. He developed a close relationship with Özal, who supported his educational activities. In 1986, he launched the daily newspaper, *Zaman* (Time). As its first editor, he employed Fehmi Koru, previously foreign editor of the İskenderpaşa order's weekly, *Islam*. He is not known to have married.

The year 1996 saw the launch of the Islamic banking operation, the Asya Finance House (later Bank Asya). The future presidents, Gül and Erdoğan, held the ribbon for Çiller, then deputy prime minister, to cut. Gülen was standing close by. For Gülen, the bank gave him and his fellow "neo-Nurcus" a further facility for reaching out to businessmen and industrialists in Anatolia, and they responded, joining and financing his *Hizmet* (Service) movement. By this time, his followers in business had begun to group together in professional associations and in 2005 launched TUSKON, the Turkish Confederation of Businessmen and Industrialists. This flourished, with Erdoğan and other leading AKP figures proving regular speakers at its events. In 2013, TUSKON had 180 affiliated associations. A sociologist who researched the movement wrote that Gülenists generally gave between 5 and 20 per cent of their income to the movement's projects; she met one businessman who gave an annual 3.5 million USD.[9]

Linking his activities were Kaynak Holding, which handled his commercial interests, and the Feza Media Group of his media operations. None of the companies were formally controlled by Gülen or had any direct link with him. A Gülen spokesman explained: "As with all Gülen-inspired projects, Gülen simply provides inspiration, motivation, vision, and some guiding and overarching principles."[10] By this time, *Zaman* had become the largest-circulation paper in the country, with a peak printing of 960,000 in March 2012.[11] It was the centrepiece of the formidable media group supporting Gülen, which comprised three other newspapers—*Today's Zaman*, *Bugün* (Today), and *Millet* (Nation/People)—eight television channels led by Samanyolu (Milky Way) and Kanaltürk, and a handful of radio stations. Gülen had become a power in the land.

The first decade of the century proved a halcyon period for his influence in his country, and abroad too his honour was high. The collapse of the Soviet Union created openings in Central Asia which he, with the support of Özal, had been quick to exploit. He signed his first agreement in Central Asia in 1992 and by winter 1996–1997 had 148 affiliated schools abroad with 26,532 students. His movement grew to become a useful adjunct to Turkish foreign policy, setting a Turkish flag in its schools in over 100 countries—in the U.S. alone, it had 199 charter schools in the academic year 2016–2017—while the movement's businessmen supported the country's opening to Africa and other regions of the Third World.

Committing himself to promoting interfaith dialogue, he built up an impressive international network, meeting with Pope Benedict, Ecumenical Patriarch Bartholomew, and various chief rabbis. To a Western world shocked by the 9/11 attacks and ISIS, he appeared as an example of tolerant Islam, a symbol of Islamic enlightenment, appealing to the many seeking to enable a dialogue between two seemingly clashing civilizations.

However, the preacher himself was now in self-exile. In 1999, he had fled Turkey, establishing himself in Saylorsburg, a rustic hamlet near the Delaware River, at a farm now called the Golden Generation Chestnut Camp Retreat Center. The move, prompted by a warning of impending prosecution by the sedulous Yüksel, did little to diminish his status at home, and helped him raise his profile abroad. Apart from continuing to extend his school network, he reached out to other religious communities, not least with his annual Friendship Meals at the Waldorf Astoria in New York during meetings of the U.N. General Assembly.

Whatever the secularists in Turkey may have thought, Erdoğan and the AKP obviously appreciated him. Erdoğan visited him in May 2000. Abdullah Gül, then foreign minister, attended one of the Friendship Meals in the early 2000s, and in September 2007, Erdoğan, this time as prime minister, met him, as did Senator Hillary Clinton (to whose subsequent election campaign Gülen contributed 250,000 USD). In September 2008, Gül, now president, was the main speaker at his annual dinner, with Ali Babacan, foreign minister, also attending—as did Robert Mugabe of Zimbabwe. In September 2013, Ahmet Davutoğlu, then foreign minister, visited Gülen in Pennsylvania, as he had on at least one other earlier occasion.

At home, Gülen's interests coincided with those of Erdoğan, with both concerned at the intrusive role of Turkey's military. In April 2007, after four years of rumbling discontent with the AKP, the armed forces tried to block Gül from becoming president. Their intervention in the Grand National Assembly's elections—a partisan statement published on the website of the Turkish General Staff—caused Erdoğan to call elections. Running a campaign calling for civilian-led democracy, Erdoğan increased his share of the vote by one third to 46.6 per cent, a shocking rebuff to the commanders. The new Assembly was quick to approve Gül as president. Erdoğan then pushed through the constitutional amendments required to lift the ban on women wearing the Islamic headscarf in universities and public offices.

The Constitutional Court blocked this last initiative, and the secularists looked to the court to curb Erdoğan's wider efforts. The court's prosecutor charged the AKP with attempting to undermine secularism. In July 2008, the prosecutor won his case—by ten votes to one—but, by a hair's breadth, he failed to have the party closed: six members of the eleven-strong court voted for the party's closure, one short of the seven required for a binding decision.

It is to the subsequent years that many trace the switch in Erdoğan from reformist to autocrat and the start of his trajectory from advocate of democratic rights, EU membership, and improved governance to increasing authoritarianism.[12]

This trajectory required a frontal assault on potential opponents, and Gülen—with his own history of problems with the military—was to prove an unsparing ally. His newspaper, *Zaman*, gave its backing to the AKP in the municipal elections of March 2009 and then supported him through the parliamentary debates in spring 2010 and the referendum on revisions in the constitution that September.

The revisions affected twenty-six of the 196 articles and temporary provisions in the constitution. A number of these changes aimed at aligning Turkey to the governance systems of the EU, membership of which was still proclaimed as a government priority. But other changes reduced controls over the executive. Particularly important were those that terminated the military's traditional immunity from civilian law. The Chief of General Staff and the commanders of the land, sea, and air forces became liable for trial by the parliament's High Court. For earlier generations of republicans, this last provision was *lèse majesté*. Chiefs of General Staff considered themselves not as just above the law but as the law itself. In earlier times, they would avoid NATO meetings in which they would be treated as lower in protocol than the country's defence ministers.

Equally striking were the changes to control of the judiciary. The High Council of Judges and Prosecutors (*Hakimler ve Savcılar Yüksek Kurulu*, HSYK) was brought under tighter government control. As Rıza Mahmut Türmen, a former judge on the European Court of Human Rights and later CHP deputy, wrote at the time: "Fifty per cent of the changes are concerned with the judiciary. This means that the authorities have a problem with the judiciary."[13] So, indeed, it would prove.

A quasi-Platonic "saintly charisma"

Gülen was a prolific speaker and writer. Apart from his well-publicized sermons, he wrote the lead editorial in his monthly magazine, *Sızıntı*, and between 1982 and 1996 published one book every twenty-eight weeks. His publications were not commentaries on Said Nursi's work but collections of his own thoughts and preaching. His ideas are thus well known, and it is easy to see that his appeal was not only because of his oratorical derring-do but also because of the ideas themselves.

On the key issues of the time such as secularism, the Kurdish question and whether women should be allowed to wear headscarves in state settings, his was a soft and conciliatory voice. His language was one of inclusiveness and tolerance, emphasizing co-existence with other cultures while inspiring his listeners that, together, they would be able to construct a new and more powerful Turkey. Like Said Nursi and the İskenderpaşa and Işıkçı movements, he emphasized the importance of science. For him, the split between religious education and modern scientific knowledge was at the core of modern alienation and nihilism. Yet, rather than encourage critical debate, he stressed the benefits of obedience to those who taught in his schools, and to the state. He combined all this with a resolutely nationalist message. For him, Islam was an integral element of Turkish culture, and individuals who built their life round Islam were contributing to building the strength of the Turkish nation. It was a timely message, and it resonated among small businessmen and traders in Anatolia, as well as in İstanbul and Ankara.[14]

Until the access to power of the AKP, writings about the Gülen movement tended to give as much weight to the educational, commercial, and media presence that Gülen had developed as to his teaching. However, as his profile rose, academics began to find increasing qualities in his message. One work published in 2013 referred to the "saintly charisma" of Gülen, and described the *Hocaefendi* (the term used within the *Cemaat*, as his movement was often termed) as "an exemplary model with an ascetic lifestyle; an extraordinary teacher; a source of benevolent power; an intercessor; and a selfless altruist who sacrifices for the welfare of others. Gülen believes that the task of a *Hocaefendi* is to guide and lead the spiritual awakening of his people."[15]

Far from being restricted to religion, Gülenism had now become a political philosophy, contributing to the Islamization of nationalism and "the articulation of the synthesis between local sociopolitical conditions and the universal principles of Islam." In this optic, the importance in Islam of pursuing knowledge is emphasized, and Gülen lauded for the priority he gave to education by example, that is by the sober discipline, dress and conduct of his teachers. His followers "are bound together by the quasi-Platonic vision of raising what Gülen has termed a 'golden generation.'"[16]

Despite a major expansion of university education, only one quarter of applicants were being accepted, and many parents, anxious for their children's future, turned to private cramming courses, also termed *dershane*. These courses flourished, with commentators describing them as "super money makers" that were "spreading like rabbits." By the academic year 2009–2010, there were 4,193 such courses, with 1,174,860 students. One analysis in 2013 concluded that one quarter of high school students in general and 61 per cent of those in their last year attended such courses.[17]

The extent of Gülen's presence in this system became clear in 2016 when, after the coup attempt, the authorities closed 934 schools and 109 dormitories for "membership, affiliation or contact with the Fethullahist Terrorist Organization [*Fethullahçı Terör Örgütü*, FETÖ]."[18]

In parallel with this was an unremitting public relations campaign led by the Journalists and Writers Foundation (*Gazeteciler ve Yazarlar Vakfı*, GYV). This was established in 1994 as a counterforce to the (secularist) Society of Journalists of Turkey (*Türkiye Gazeteciler Cemiyeti*). Gülen was the GYV's Honorary Chairman, though, as with his financial and media operations, eschewed legal responsibility.

The GYV's annual award ceremonies in the 1990s attracted the top politicians in the country, including Demirel and Erdoğan. Winners of its Tolerance Awards for 1995 included Erdoğan; Hayrettin Karaca, leader of the environmental movement, TEMA; the singer, Barış Manço; and various journalists. The award jury included the film star, Hülya Koçyiğit, and the composer, Zülfü Livaneli, the main opponent of Erdoğan in the 1994 İstanbul mayoral election. One American journalist considered the GYV "the Gülenists' unofficial P.R. firm" and described how it capitalized on her joining a visit to Adana.[19]

The GYV launched three platforms to promote international understanding. The first, the Intercultural Dialogue Platform, "served as a platform for dialogue [with] organizations affiliated with the *Hizmet* Movement in Europe."[20] The second was the Dialogue Eurasia Programme, which worked in former Soviet republics, and the third, and most active until it too was closed after the coup attempt, was the Abant Platform. Named after the lakeside hotel where it held its first meeting in 1998, it staged thirty-four "Conferences for Dialogue."

A number of Islamists criticized Gülen's calls for interfaith dialogue. One such critic was Molla Muhammed Doğan, leader of a Nurcu splinter group, who faced a remorseless counterattack accusing him of supporting ISIS. This started on the Gülenist Samanyolu TV and culminated in the planting of bombs by police officers—all of whom would later be imprisoned as followers of FETÖ. A second critic was *Cübbeli* Ahmet of the İsmailağa community who found himself targeted by a CD purporting to show him involved in sex, and led to his arrest on accusations, later dismissed, of trafficking women. There are claims that this too was organized by Gülenists.[21] Indeed, while in public Gülen was a humble cleric, others have described a very different private persona. He was "vain, megalomaniac, demanding total obedience," according to Ahmet Keleş, his *imam* for Central Anatolia until 2005.[22]

But others appreciated the way that Gülen's followers had energized Muslims. "They are playing an important role in bridging Turkey with the outside world and helping internationalize the country... While the Gülen community was becoming global, it also helped others to become global as well," wrote Kenan Çamurcu, a journalist, Islamic cultural adviser to various municipalities, and weightlifter.[23]

A frequent academic response was hope; Yavuz, for instance, noted that the followers of Gülen seek to compare him:

> with hallowed Western intellectuals such as Kant, Sartre, and Habermas and not with Muslim thinkers like Ghazali, Rabbani, or Ibn Rushd... what is taking place in Turkey is the paradoxical Islamization of secular society and the internal secularization of Islamic thought. A new form of piety is under construction, unshackled from traditional and literalist Islamic terminology and references. Consequently, I would argue that the movement is one of the main forces for the modernization of the Turkish state and society with further profound implications for other Muslim countries.[24]

In the arteries of the system

Nuh Mete Yüksel, chief prosecutor at the State Security Court in Ankara in the late 1990s, was stocky and pugnacious. In 1998 and 1999, he ordered the arrest of the mayor of Ankara, Melih Gökçek , for tender irregularities, launched a case against Erbakan, and interrogated Abdullah Öcalan, the PKK leader seized by the Turks in Kenya. He also started an investigation into Gülen's penetration of the security forces.

Concerns over Gülen had become a national issue. In June 1999, in two cassettes broadcast on ATV, a secular channel, Gülen set out a strategy of penetrating the judicial and financial control systems of the country. The commitment to sedition was complete—an extraordinary message and delivered in unequivocal detail. In the first tape, dressed in almond-coloured robes and a white prayer cap, he shifts in an armchair as he tells his followers that the spread of their friends in the judiciary, civil service, and other vital institutions "should not be seen in terms of them as individuals. They are our guarantees of our future in those units," adding,

> They are the pulse of our existence, the assurance of our existence. And, if those present are not able to preserve their presence, we will have some trouble in protecting those who follow in the way we try to protect them now... In other words, we will not be able to march to the future with that establishment in the same way as we do with the judiciary and the civil service... Going forward without making your presence felt is very important for our future... going forward, wandering in the arteries of the

> system… Our friends will march towards the future inside the system. So they need to know and discover the weak points of that system. They have to overcome them.
>
> It is very important to protect our friends in that or the other office. Let us not live another Algeria, Syria, Egypt… Until there is a balance of forces, I personally prefer the route of spreading my own ideas, conquering and subduing everywhere to my system of thought. In particular, our friends as civil servants should not indulge in heroism. It would be superfluous… Sometimes even running away from the enemy is a very important manoeuvre.[25]

The quality of this recording indicates it was taken by a hidden camera. The second tape is shot from close up, with Gülen this time standing, dressed in conventional clothes, as usual eschewing a tie, and speaking to a microphone. In this recording, he extols the particular virtues of his network of "camouflaged" *Işık Evleri*, as they carry on functions carried out by Islamic bodies in earlier times. Again, he urges patience and caution:

> Until you reach the right moment, when you can take the world on your back, until you have the strength to carry it, until you have in your hands that which represents such strength, until you have got the power of constitutional institutions on your side, every step is too early.[26]

Gülen sought to dismiss the two videos as a faked montage, but even his followers were nonplussed. The journalist, Fehmi Koru, by 1999 at *Yeni Şafak* (New Dawn), called for Gülen to provide a "more proper, more convincing and more detailed explanation," but, he continued, "Trying to eliminate Gülen, following attempts to close the Virtue Party (*Fazilet Partisi*, FP), is just like dissipating a perfect opportunity that can only be found once in 500 years"—the opportunity in Koru's view was to establish religion-state relations on a sound platform and to ensure the twenty-first century was the century of the Turks.[27]

Others sought to dismiss the whole incident, for instance describing it as part of "a sensationalistic character assassination against Gülen and his movement;" Yavuz continued, "Gülen had learned a painful lesson that obsequiously catering to the center of military power can breed contempt as much as it does forbearance."[28]

The background to Yüksel's investigations is, however, far more sinister.

Public denunciation of Gülen's infiltration of the security services dates back to at least 1986. That December, *Nokta* magazine disclosed that thirty-three students from Kuleli Military High School, sixteen students from Bursa Işıklar Military High School, and seventeen students from İzmir Maltepe Military High School had been expelled from their schools because of their affiliation with Gülen, and up to 100 students had been served warnings. Similar steps were taken in schools that trained non-commissioned officers. The investigations revealed that those expelled had been specially prepared for the exams in the *dershane* affiliated to the *Cemaat*, and the situation of some students initially disqualified from military high schools had been "arranged."[29] Neophytes were provided with exam answers, ensuring both their entrance into the streams feeding the future leaders of these bodies and their future loyalty. *Star* newspaper reported instances of this at the Kuleli academy in 1991 and in the security services that year.[30]

In this period, only one in forty Islamist officers was expelled, according to Nurettin Veren, a close aide of Gülen until breaking with him in 2005. In Veren's description, the remainder constituted underground sleeper cells, often presenting their first salaries to Fethullah Gülen and bringing him the swords they received on graduation.[31]

In 1998, the Ankara Police Chief, Cevdet Saral, had requested the then prime minister, Mesut Yılmaz, for permission to investigate *Cemaat* penetration of the police. Yılmaz refused, saying that, as Ecevit, then deputy prime minister, liked the work of Gülen, for him to authorize the investigation could destroy his coalition. In January 1999, the National Security Council, responding to an article in the newspaper, *Aydınlık* (Daylight), requested the Ministry of Interior to investigate Gülenist penetration of the security police. The General Directorate of Security appointed three inspectors who, blocked by the intelligence, the organized crime, and anti-terrorism sections of the General Directorate of Security, asked Saral for support.

Saral and his assistant, Osman Ak, set to work. Despite being refused permission to raid the Intelligence Department, they soon completed a 79-page report listing 130 members of the *Cemaat*. This was sent to the inspectors on March 18. Three days later, Gülen left the country, a fugitive again, but evidently with continuing tendrils.

The prosecutors' report was entitled "*The Işık tarikat/Fethullahism*." Saral concluded that the *Cemaat* had started targeting students in the Police Academy as early as 1978. He argued that the Gülenists had received a fillip when Özal's ANAP came to power in 1983 and, with a shortage of sympathisers in the bureaucracy, were happy to turn to the *Cemaat*, with its well-educated, modestly dressed, and obedient cadres.

The politicians also appreciated the support their children received from Gülen's schools.

Among the findings of Saral and his team was that in 1991 the General Director of Security had caught the *Cemaat* cheating in the draw for places in important police units and, vainly, requested the prosecution of those involved. Saral and his colleagues concluded, "considering some of the state institutions it aims to seize, and that it aims to take full control of these and that those developed in *Işık Evleri* may invade the management of these institutions, we have in front of us a crime admitted in their own words." The writers noted that their next report would be on the finances of the Gülen movement.

That report was never written as at this point a tape from a tea room in the Ankara Security Police was distributed to the newspapers, alleging that Saral and Ak had been illegally tapping the telephones of 963 figures, including the president, prime minister, politicians, and businessmen. Saral and Ak were suspended, not being cleared until three years later. Their investigation had been derailed. The ball was left with Yüksel.

He had launched his investigation into Gülen that February and eighteen months later presented his indictment accusing Gülen of establishing and running an illegal organization. In the next two years, he repeatedly pressed for the arrest of Gülen, but in autumn 2002 he was taken off the case. That summer, he had gained another adversary, Erdoğan. Yüksel wanted the party leader arrested for threatening public order for proclaiming that sending untrained twenty-year-old youths to fight terrorists was "causing their murder." He had also indicted Erdoğan on charges of corruption in municipal tenders and of conspiracy to overthrow the secular order.[32]

With such enemies, Yüksel was soon having to struggle to save his career. The terror squad of the security police fortuitously found a five-minute cassette of him making love in an Ankara lawyer's office. He was removed from his post.[33] Two decades later, asked about Gülen's long march through the institutions of Turkey, he was to regret only indicting the Fethullahists for setting up an illegal organization: "I should have made the charge attempting to overthrow the constitutional order. That was their purpose."[34]

Ergenekon and Gülen's sense of justice

Now widely referred to in Turkey under the sobriquet of FETÖ'cü (members of FETÖ), the followers of Gülen earlier had several labels. To many, they were simply the *Cemaat* (or community). Gülen himself preferred other terms: "Even though some call it the 'Gülen Movement,' I prefer to call it sometimes 'Service-*Hizmet*,' sometimes 'the Movement of Volunteers,' sometimes the 'Souls Dedicated to Humanity'..."[35]

The ATV cassettes had shown the ambiguity of these values.

The early 2000s were a perilous time for the critics of Gülen and his neo-Nurcu movement. Professor Necip Hablemitoğlu, who had been one of the ATV studio panelists who argued the tapes showed Gülen was trying to set up a religious state, was shot dead outside his house.[36] A second commentator, Haşmet Atahan, was sued by Gülen for damages.[37] Yüksel himself remembers how his friends told him not to get involved: "At that time, becoming a follower of Fethullah was a means of winning promotion within the state, within politics, within trade."[38]

A senior American government official told the journalist Hansen in 2010 that, while at first the movement seemed benevolent, "it became clearer they had penetrated the intelligence apparatus of the Turkish National and that they were using it for some purpose, clearly for wiretaps and leaks to newspapers;" Bill Park of King's College, long contributing to the Gülen-funded Turkey Institute in London, commented:

> There has been, or is now, a long march through the institutions... Even in places like the foreign ministry, it seems that Gülenists are starting to appear. What a lot of people tell me, in a way that I am starting to believe, is that they set up parallel structures within government institutions.[39]

The conviction that his followers had established themselves in the police meant that many critics of Gülen and his ally, the AKP, bit their tongues when discussing politics on the telephone. They were not wrong so to do. In April 2007, the Turkish Security Directorate had been given a blanket permit to monitor and record all communications in Turkey including mobile and landline telephones, SMS text messaging, e-mail, fax, and internet communications.[40] Two years later, Minister of Justice Mehmet Ali Şahin stated that "as far as we know" it was not 70 million people whose communications had been monitored but 70,000. The Information Technologies and Communications Authority (*Bilgi Teknolojileri ve İletişim Kurumu*, BTK) warned that, apart from three legally constituted listening centres, other illegal means of tapping telephones existed.[41] The various leaks that occurred in the press in this decade indicated that these security activities were under the control of the *Cemaat*.

With both Gülen and Erdoğan having a common enemy in the old elites, there was much to draw them together. After AKP's election victory of July 2007 and even before the Constitutional Court decision of autumn 2008, the two leaders appear to have gained confidence—and it is to this period that dates the Ergenekon case that convulsed Turkish daily life as it developed into a frontal assault on critics of Islamic politics.

The case had started in June 2007 after the discovery of a crate of grenades in the loft of a house in a shanty town in the Ümraniye district of Asian İstanbul. It rapidly developed into one of the largest and most controversial judicial investigations in recent Turkish history. By the time of his first indictment of July 2008, the prosecutor, Zekeriya Öz, had had eighty-six people arrested in a series of dawn raids. As one researcher wrote: "... the motley collection of eccentrics, conspiracy theorists, criminals, racists, nationalists, former soldiers and journalists and their friends and acquaintances who were now behind bars all appeared to be staunch advocates of Atatürk's brand of secular nationalism;" each, the prosecutor concluded, was part of an organization called Ergenekon.[42]

The name is that of a remote valley in the Altay mountains of Central Asia where nationalist legend has it that, after a defeat, Turkic tribes were trapped for four centuries before a blacksmith melted the mountain and created a passage through which a grey wolf led the Turks to freedom.

Further arrests and indictments followed, with other cases being blended into the original one. After five years of hearings, seventy-nine of the accused were found guilty, with seventeen of them receiving life sentences, including the former Chief of Staff, İlker Başbuğ, and five other generals, one of them, Kemal Yavuz, apparently not forgiven for appearing on the ATV programme criticizing the Gülen cassettes. However, times were changing. From late 2013, Erdoğan and Gülen were at open war, and early 2014 saw a purge of many Gülen supporters from key roles in the police and judiciary.

It seemed that for Erdoğan, the case, which had dominated the headlines for five years, had served its purpose, with the commanders seemingly reduced to the role of bystanders in Turkey's body politic. The case was unwound, the sentences quashed, and a retrial saw the prosecutor withdraw all charges. By November 2018, the only people on the run were the first two prosecutors in the case, Zekeriya Öz and his successor, Fikret Seçen, both of whom fled Turkey in 2015. A month after his flight, there was a photograph of Öz on Instagram in front of a Bugatti Veyron, a car costing 1.5 million USD or more.

In its initial flush, the Ergenekon trial was welcomed by many, including critics of Erdoğan, as a chance to shed light on what is generally termed the deep state. This term has been used for several decades to refer to ultra-conservative armed groups working outside the normal command structures of the country's military. The original groups were run by a unit founded in 1952 and long operational under the name *Özel Harp Dairesi* (Special Warfare Department). The ÖHD was part of the NATO "stay-behind network" conceived by the U.S. as cells to mobilize resistance in the event Turkey should be overrun by the Warsaw Pact. The Turkish cells have been connected with the pogrom against the Greeks of İstanbul in 1955. General Sabri Yirmibeşoğlu, the right-hand man of General Kemal Yamak who headed the unit, said these events "were the work of the Special Warfare Department. They were magnificently organised. They achieved their purpose. I ask you, were they not magnificently organised?"[43] The events, now known as the 6–7 September, led to between eleven and fifteen people being killed, up to 300 wounded, and as many as 200 women raped.

ÖHD was part of what is now generally termed Operation Gladio, the name of the Italian branch of this malign network. ÖHD was funded by the U.S. until about 1974.[44] As Jenkins writes:

> ... the involvement of the ÖHD networks in the factional violence of the 1970s did exhibit what were to remain the defining characteristics of Deep State activity over the following decades; namely, not a highly centralized and tightly controlled campaign directed by a cabal of senior figures but a culture of immunity in which individuals and small groups were able to operate with almost complete autonomy against targets they knew others in the ÖHD-created networks regarded as enemies of the Turkish state...[45]

The rise of the PKK from the late 1980s was matched by a proliferation of gangs and groups in the south-east and in areas with large Kurdish populations such as İstanbul. Hundreds—more probably thousands—of suspected PKK members and sympathizers were assassinated. Some groups became involved in narcotics trafficking, protection rackets, and the fixing of state contracts. Others began to shift their attention to the perceived threat to the secular state posed by the growing religious communities.

But public attitudes were changing, with the turning point for many Turks being the Susurluk incident of 3 November 1996. In this, a speeding Mercedes crashed, killing three of the four passengers—Hüseyin Kocadağ, a former deputy head of the İstanbul police; Abdullah Çatlı, on Interpol's Red Notice list for murder charges; and Gonca Us, a former beauty queen. The surviving passenger, Sedat Edip Bucak, was leader of a Kurdish clan and an MP from the True Path Party. The boot contained two Heckler &

Koch MP5 submachine guns, five handguns, ammunition, and a silencer. Çatlı had been used by the Turkish state to target members of the Armenian Secret Army for the Liberation of Armenia (ASALA), whose attacks had resulted in the deaths of 46 people, including Turkish diplomats, and injured 299.

Subsequent parliamentary investigations into the bizarre alliances between these passengers ran into the traditional obfuscation but "transformed the Deep State from a whispered suspicion to a revealed reality."[46] However, those who hoped that the Ergenekon case would shed light on this pervasive underworld had their hopes dashed as soon as the first indictment was published. This was prodigiously long—1,455 pages and annexes—tortuous, self-contradictory, and imprecise. One sentence lasted for over eight pages, including extracts from wiretaps of telephone conversations with 26 people, yet contained nothing of substance. In the prosecutor's view, Ergenekon was an organization responsible for virtually every act of politically motivated terrorism in modern Turkish history. But the indictment produced no evidence that this ubiquitous, almost omnipotent organization had ever existed, let alone that any of the accused had any link with it.[47]

In parallel with the Ergenekon spectacle, a further 500 people found themselves subjected to similar arrest, judicial harassment, and acquittal in the other show trials of those years. The accused included generals, public prosecutors, journalists, activists in secular non-governmental organizations, and motley officers and would-be assassins. The most prominent case was the *Balyoz* (Sledgehammer) trial, named after the title given to a coup preparation exercise allegedly carried out by the armed forces in 2003. In January 2010, the newspaper *Taraf* (Side) claimed to have received a suitcase containing electronic files and documents. Its publication of this material led to court proceedings being launched against 365 officers. In a country where generals had long projected themselves as untouchable, the photographs of dawn arrests in military compounds were shocking—and an irreversible confirmation of the diminished role of officers who in 1997 had openly orchestrated a public relations blitz against the government of Erbakan.

The *Balyoz* trial saw the heads of Turkey's First Army, the fleet, and the air force at the time of the alleged *Balyoz* exercise receiving twenty-year prison sentences and 321 other officers prison terms of six to eighteen years. The trial had been rushed through by local standards, being completed twenty-six months after the prosecutor delivered his 96-page indictment.

But, as with Ergenekon, the fall from Erdoğan's favour of Gülen's *Cemaat* gutted the proceedings. In June 2014, the Constitutional Court ruled that the case should be reheard. An İstanbul court found that at least two of the computer discs adduced as evidence were faked and expressed strong doubts over the others. The case was dismissed.

Other cases that opened in 2010 and 2011 but subsequently fell by the wayside included:

- The Poyrazköy case, launched after the discovery of a cache of weapons in this fishing village at the head of the Bosphorus. This was combined with two initially separate indictments—one for planning the assassination of admirals and the second the "cage plan" for political terrorism and assassinations of Eastern Orthodox, Armenians, Kurds, Jews, and Alevis. Details of these too were published by *Taraf* newspaper. After five years of hearings, all eighty-five accused were acquitted.
- The arrest and trial of the Erzincan prosecutor, İlhan Cihaner, and thirteen others for organizing a "terrorist organization." Cihaner, apart from targeting İsmailağa, had also probed the Gülen movement. In November 2015, the Supreme Court acquitted all the accused.
- The OdaTV case against Soner Yalçın and other journalists, arrested in February 2011 as they prepared to broadcast footage showing police officers involved in the Ergenekon investigation apparently planting evidence. This case was expanded to include the authors of three books describing the growing penetration by the Gülen movement of the state—Hanefi Avcı, a former police chief, Nedim Şener, and Ahmet Şık. The prosecutor eventually withdrew charges, and in April 2017 the case was dropped.

As Jenkins presciently commented in 2013:

> ... the evidence—including confessions—that a cabal of Gülen's followers are behind cases such as Ergenekon, Sledgehammer and the Izmir Spying Ring is now so extensive as to be irrefutable... the severity of the Ergenekon sentences has focused international attention not only on the case itself but also on the alarming gap between the Gülen Movement's rhetoric and the practices of some of its members.[48]

13

COUP AND PURGE

This uprising is a great gift from God. Why is it a gift from God? Because, with our armed forces needing to be absolutely clean, this is an opportunity for cleansing them.

President Erdoğan, 16 July 2016

The belated divorce

The relationship between Gülen and Erdoğan dates back to at least the 1990s. There are photographs of the two together during Erdoğan's term as mayor of İstanbul—in his office, at the wedding of the footballer Hakan Şukur on 15 August 1995, at the press awards at the Çırağan Palace Hotel arranged by the GYV on 4 January 1996, and at the opening of Asya Finans on 24 October 1996.

As Erdoğan struggled to overtake his original mentor, Necmettin Erbakan, his relationship with Gülen was critical. Gülen's *Zaman* and television stations supported him and his fellow reformists in their sparring inside Erbakan's Virtue Party in 1999 and 2000, and contributed to Erdoğan's own election victory in 2002.

With Esat Coşan, his long-term spiritual guide, having died in February 2001, it would have been surprising if Erdoğan did not discuss his political plans with Gülen and seek reassurances of media support during the six months before he launched his AKP.[1] Certainly, he was quick to receive the backing of Gülen's *Cemaat*. As *The New Yorker* reported:

> 'The Gülenists saw an opportunity,' İbrahim Kalın, an Erdoğan aide, told me. 'We were newcomers. When our party came to power, the only thing it had was the support of the people. Our party did not have any access to state institutions—no judiciary, no security forces.' Gülen, with his supporters in the bureaucracy, was an appealing ally.

This support was not trivial. Even by the 1990s, Gülenists accounted for 40 per cent of the police in Central Anatolia and 20 per cent of the judges and prosecutors, according to Ahmet Keleş, then the movement's "*imam*" for Central Anatolia, but since 2005 a vociferous critic.[2]

The Gülen media solidly supported Erdoğan in his early years in office, not least during his struggles with the army and the Constitutional Court. Those years, Erdoğan seems to have been content to let the *Cemaat* build up its presence in the police and judiciary. Indeed, in the early days of the Ergenekon trials, he embraced the investigations as being similar to those of the *Mani Pulite* (Clean Hands) process that rattled Italy in the 1990s. "Yes, I am the nation's prosecutor," he proclaimed in July 2008 in answer to accusations that he was interfering in ongoing trials. The constitutional changes of 2010 allowed the Gülenists to consolidate their hold among judges.

Contributing to his increasing self-confidence was the resignation in May 2010 of Deniz Baykal, the truculent leader of the opposition. A cassette had appeared of Baykal in a hotel room in Antalya with a scarcely dressed party aide. A *Zaman* journalist was to later state that Gülen supporters in the police had shot this.[3] A year later, in the run-up to the general elections of June 2011, nine further tapes appeared aimed at creating embarrassment for Erdoğan's main rival for conservative votes in the general election, the ultra-nationalist MHP.

The first public difference between Erdoğan and the ambitious Gülen came not over domestic issues but over relations with Israel. In 2009, Erdoğan had denounced the Israeli Defense Forces' invasion of Gaza and the killing of around 1,400 Palestinians. In May 2010, the *Mavi Marmara*, a Turkish relief ship, joined a flotilla carrying aid to the beleaguered territory. The ship was attacked by Israeli security forces in international waters and nine Turks killed. As Turkey united in condemnation of this, Gülen wrote an article in the *Wall Street Journal* criticizing the convoy for not having been agreed with Tel Aviv.

More fundamental was the incipient struggle for power in Ankara. Gülen's media outlets had supported Erdoğan in the constitutional referendum, and Gülen now pressed for an enhanced presence in the AKP itself. As the vice chairperson of the AKP responsible for candidate lists later said:

> After the constitutional referendum in 2010, the Gülenists became the most powerful force in Ankara. Moreover, the government relied more on the Gülenist networks outside Turkey than on the Turkish embassies. We totally depended on their media, TV stations, and networks in and outside the country in order to get something done. They became aware of their power, and we received a list of names that Gülen wanted to be parliamentarians in the [June] 2011 elections. He asked for 52 seats in electable positions. This angered Erdoğan.[4]

The demand came at a sensitive time. Erdoğan had announced that he intended to amend the constitution after the elections, strengthen the powers of the president, and replace the incumbent, Abdullah Gül. Gül, who had the support of the Gülen movement, had publicly opposed such changes.

The rise of the *Cemaat*'s strength within the state machinery had thus come to represent a challenge to Erdoğan's own power. This was made clear in two further incidents. The first was in September 2011, when tapes were published of telephone calls between Hakan Fidan, then deputy undersecretary at the prime ministry, and leaders of the proscribed PKK. The country's National Intelligence Agency (MİT) had been meeting with the PKK in Oslo. That Turkish officials were talking with a group the state deemed terrorists shocked many nationalists. The origin of the leaks was unclear, but as one journalist asked: "With this last cassette, is the *Cemaat* reminding him of its strength?"[5]

Five months later, a prosecutor now considered a supporter of Gülen summoned Fidan to testify on these talks, calling him not as a witness but as a suspect. By this time, Fidan had been promoted to head of MİT, making the investigation a direct attack on the prime minister. Erdoğan took personal responsibility for the talks, refused to allow Fidan to testify, enacted a law to protect him, and carried out another shuffle of security chiefs and prosecutors.[6]

By this time, listening devices had been found in Erdoğan's home and office in Ankara. As one deputy chairman of the AKP later said:

> I was in Ankara when they discovered the listening devices in Erdoğan's house. Erdoğan was terrified. He knew everything—all his legal and illegal dealings were now in the hands of the Gülen movement. This was a major shock and since then he has never been able to sleep comfortably as he is obsessed with how to eliminate the Gülen movement.[7]

In 2013, the gloves came off. That summer, Erdoğan and Gülen clashed over the government's brutal response to protesters' occupation of Gezi Park in İstanbul, with Erdoğan infuriated by Gülen's question of whether "a shopping centre is worth a single drop of blood." Erdoğan appears to have decided to curb the *Cemaat* by cutting its revenue from the *dershane*. Suggestions of closing these schools mounted, and in November Erdoğan announced on television his intention to address the unfairness they caused in the education system.

For the *Cemaat*, that was a step too far. Two weeks later, Turkey awoke to learn that in a dawn raid, prosecutors had arrested officials and high-profile businessmen known to be close to the AKP as well as the sons of three ministers and an Iranian gold trader. A total of seventy-one prominent figures were rounded up to face accusations of fraudulent tenders, bribery, and irregular trading in gold.

This judicial coup of December 17 seemed to confirm the hold of the *Cemaat* over sections of the judiciary and security services. Fuelling the flames were tapes released of telephone calls in which Erdoğan purportedly instructs his younger son, Bilal, to distribute funds stashed in his apartment. Erdoğan claimed the tapes were fabricated and, after a flurry of headlines that would have ended the career of a lesser person, picked himself off the canvas and carried through the wholesale transfer of the judges and police officers involved.

He survived this round, those who had hunted him became hunted, and the public seemed content to accept his denial of the accusations.[8] His AKP increased its vote in the municipal elections of March 2014. While campaigning, Erdoğan taunted Gülen, asking: "What did you want that you did not get?"

Through the summer of 2014, Gülenist schools throughout the country were subjected to police inspections; the student intake that autumn was reported to be only half of that in the previous school year. Scores of Gülen-run hospitals had their contracts with the state social security organization revoked.[9] The year 2015 saw a further escalation of tension. In January, police detained some twenty people suspected of illegally eavesdropping on Erdoğan and other senior officials; local media said the move was aimed at the "parallel structure," the term Erdogan used to refer to Gülen's supporters in the state machinery. In February, the Turkish Deposit Insurance Fund (TMSF) took control of Bank Asya (as Asya Finans had been renamed), and the prosecutor launched charges against Gülen and—alleged for the first time—the existence of FETÖ, claiming it was operating a parallel state.

Over the summer, the focus of these investigations was broadened. In October, the courts attacked another Gülen ally, Akın İpek, alleging his gold and media operations had been financing FETÖ and appointing an administrator to them. Four months later, the administrator closed these media operations, the police raiding the television stations, Kanaltürk and Bugün TV while on air, and shuttering *Bugün* and *Millet* newspapers. In parallel, the authorities curtailed the transmission rights of Samanyolu and twelve other televisions stations and radios under the *Cemaat*'s control. They then took over Zaman itself, continuing its publication under their nominee. On 26 May 2016, the Gülen movement was formally added to Turkey's list of terrorist organizations.

Coup and aftermath

The showdown between the Gülenists and Erdoğan came two months later. On 15 July, military officers, many of them fearful of being expelled from the armed forces for their links with the *Cemaat*, rebelled. Calling themselves the Council for Peace in the Homeland, they seized the Chief of General Staff, Hulusi Akar, and pressed him to sign a declaration supporting their coup. He refused, restraints on him being temporarily eased when, in the heat of the turmoil, he asked to say his evening prayer. Brigadier General Hakan Evrim, commander of the Akıncı airbase, the plotters' centre, told Akar: "If you wish, we can have you talk with our opinion leader, Fethullah Gülen."[10]

The rebels closed the two Bosphorus bridges and temporarily gained control of the main İstanbul airport.[11] Turkish Airforce F-16s strafed the presidential palace, the Grand National Assembly, and the headquarters of the police special forces and of MİT in Ankara, and broke the sound barrier low over İstanbul, cracking windows by the Golden Horn. But the rebels failed to capture the president. Bizarrely, they did not learn until midnight where he was staying, and, even before their helicopters set off to his south coast hotel, Erdoğan was already on board the presidential Gulfstream IV, flying from Dalaman to İstanbul, with the pilot masking his flight as Turkish Airlines Flight 8456.

The plotters had seized the state broadcaster, TRT, just after midnight, but failed to close other television channels or the mobile telephone network. Their proclamation had scant impact as ten minutes after it Erdoğan appealed via FaceTime through the opposition-owned CNN TV to his followers to come to the streets and airports. Crowds of citizens overwhelmed the rebels, and crucial commanders in İstanbul rallied to the president. The rebels' attempt to take control of the Special Forces Command in Ankara had also been foiled. After circling over İstanbul for around fifty minutes, Erdoğan landed just after 03:00. The coup was effectively over. The government claimed 250 people had died and 2,100 had been injured.[12]

Contributing to the coup's failure was that the plotters were forced to act five hours earlier than intended. At 14:45 that fateful Friday, an army pilot presented himself at MİT revealing plans to attack the agency. At 16:21, MİT telephoned the General Staff saying that three helicopters had been prepared for illegal activities, and at 18:00, Hakan Fidan, the head of MİT, briefed Akar. The general ordered all military planes to return to base and confined military tracked vehicles to barracks. It was these orders that caused the plotters to trigger the putsch which they had been discussing since January.[13]

The attempt was quickly condemned by opposition parties, President Putin and Chancellor Merkel, and, less vigorously, the EU. It was disavowed by Gülen himself around midnight, Turkish time, in terms that he largely reiterated in the *New York Times* on 26 July:

> I have been advocating for democracy for decades. Having suffered through four military coups in four decades in Turkey—and having been subjected by those military regimes to harassment and wrongful imprisonment—I would never want my fellow citizens to endure such an ordeal again. If somebody who appears to be a *Hizmet* sympathizer has been involved in an attempted coup, he betrays my ideals.[14]

Four weeks later, he called for an international commission to investigate the coup. He said he had been "living a reclusive life in self-exile in a small town in the United States for the last 17 years" and deplored the "smear campaign and suffering under state oppression for the last three years in the hands of a politically-controlled law enforcement and the judiciary" to which the *Hizmet* movement had been subjected.[15]

While the rest of the country was still reeling from the events, Erdoğan had sensed the opportunity they gave him to crush the Gülen movement.

Up to this point, the armed forces had been spared the purges that had affected Gülen supporters in the police and judiciary. But within days, the witchhunt was nationwide.

On 21 July, the government declared a state of emergency—for an initial ninety days, subsequently extended—and on 23 July it announced the organizations connected with FETÖ that it was proscribing. Its initial list, of fifty-eight pages, was impressive and included thirty-five health institutions, 934 schools, fifteen universities, 109 student dormitories, 1,229 foundations and associations, and nineteen trades unions. Included were TUSKON, the business confederation, and the Journalists and Writers Foundation, which had hosted Erdoğan twenty years before, as was—an example of the mills grinding finely—the Struggle against Mobbing Association.

This first decree was followed by eleven similar decrees targeting individuals, one with nineteen lists of people totalling over 800 pages. Together, these set out the human cost of Gülenry, or at least a part of it.

The government initially discharged 149 of the country's 325 generals and admirals, as well as 1,099 officers of lower rank and 430 non-commissioned officers. By April 2017, 5,688 members of the armed forces had been listed as dismissed, as had 5,609 members of the gendarmerie and 20,743 members of the security police. Also losing their posts were 3,704 professors and other university teaching staff, 31,198 teachers employed by the Ministry of Education, and 1,952 members of the *Diyanet*. Certainly, some of those dismissed may have been penalized for other views the government found distasteful, but the vast majority were tainted by their association with the *Cemaat*—and, to judge from the *Official Gazette*, there was hardly a single significant state institution that had not been contaminated. Decree 672 of 1 September 2016 dismissed individuals from over 90 institutions.

By the end of 2016, 3,549 judges and prosecutors had lost their jobs.[16] Two of these were members of the Constitutional Court who would receive sentences of around eleven years for membership of FETÖ. The figures indicate that the government considered nearly one third of the judiciary to be Gülenists.

In July 2021, the Ministry of Interior reported that the authorities had detained 312,121 and arrested 99,123 individuals on grounds of alleged affiliation with the Gülen movement. Of these, the courts had convicted nearly 30,000 people, and another 70,000 were in prison awaiting trial. More than 130,000 civil servants had been dismissed or suspended. More than 100 persons had been subject to forcible rendition from abroad, according to a report by several U.N. rapporteurs in May 2020.

The government also shut Samanyolu and 15 other television stations; 23 radio stations; *Zaman*, *Taraf*, and 43 other newspapers; 15 magazines, including *Sızıntı* and *Nokta* (Point), a prominent radical weekly; and 29 publishing houses. As the months passed and the government used the state of emergency provisions to tackle other opponents, the number of closed media outlets rose to over 170, and the number of non-governmental organizations to over 1,500. The authorities also seized businesses deemed to have been financing FETÖ. By the end of 2019, some 1,100 corporations with an annual turnover of over 7 billion USD had been taken under state control.[17]

In their investigations into supporters of the coup, the authorities considered two factors as proving culpability—having an account with Bank Asya and having the ByLock messaging application installed on one's phone. The first factor penalized citizens who had, for instance, opened an account with the bank recommended by İstanbul Municipality in order to pay utility bills. The second also jeopardized many with no connection with the coup. ByLock had been launched in April 2014 and downloaded 600,000 times before its founders closed it down in April 2016. It had been in the top 500 apps in 41 separate countries.[18] However, it was the chosen means of communication of a number of the identified plotters, at least up to March 2016 when they switched to Eagle IM and WhatsApp. According to a senior official, tracking of ByLock data started in May 2015 and exposed close to 40,000 undercover Gülenist operatives, including 600 ranking military personnel.[19] In December 2017, Deutsche Welle reported that of roughly 215,000 ByLock users in Turkey, around 23,000 had been detained. At this point, Turkish authorities agreed that almost half the people who had been prosecuted for having ByLock on their smartphones would have their cases reviewed.

Apart from those killed or wounded during the coup, the human cost of the insurrection lives on. By 2021, over half a million people had been arrested or lost their jobs. Any significant institution designed to act as a check or balance to executive power had been cowed or subjected to newly appointed loyalists. And, what had started as an operation focused on the *Cemaat* had broadened to include supporters of Kurdish rights, of human rights in general, and many critics of the regime. For Erdoğan, it had indeed been a gift from God.

Gülen's legacy

The Grand National Assembly set up a Commission Researching the Development of the FETÖ Coup. This started work with a burst of enthusiasm and public expectation, and parts of a first draft of its report were leaked to the press on 22 December 2016. At that time, the report was 936 pages long, but by June 2017 it had been trimmed to 637 pages. Over twenty pages of extracts from the main report were released by Reşat Petek, the AKP's President of the Commission, on 15 May 2017. But the official account remains missing in action.

As of the eighth anniversary of the coup, the Commission's report still had to be discussed by the Assembly. The opposition argued that the draft report whitewashed alleged AKP failings before the coup, and produced its own 450-page document entitled *The Predicted, Unprevented, Controlled and Exploited Coup*.

Much still remains unexplained about what ended as a cluster of mutinies rather than a clearly planned seizure of power. As *The Economist* wrote in 2020: "The official version, in which Gülenist sleeper cells in the armed forces awoke to take over the country all on their own, seems as watertight as a teabag."[20] Neither the proclamation issued by the rebels in the short period during which they controlled state broadcasting nor any document released since makes clear what they intended to do or who was to be their leader.

A dozen trials have been held. Of the 471 brought to trial in connection with the events at Akıncı airbase, around 400 were found guilty. Among those, each receiving the most severe penalty of seventy-nine "aggravated" life sentences were four civilians: Kemal Batmaz, convicted as Gülen's representative responsible for the air force; Nurettin Oruç, convicted as responsible for the gendarmerie; Harun Biniş, responsible for the plotters' communications; and Hakan Çiçek, found guilty of being responsible for General Staff officers and having the coup plan approved by Gülen. The airbase's security cameras show the first three of these mingling through the night with the rebels.

Separated from those sentenced were Gülen himself and five other fugitives, including the man often referred to as the *imam*'s representative for the air force, Adil Öksüz. He had travelled to the U.S. 109 times between 2002 and 2016 to meet with Gülen, with at least two visits to the U.S. and the rebels' centre at the Akıncı airbase in the weeks before the coup. He was arrested the morning after the coup walking away from the airbase through fields. Brought before a magistrate, he was released and promptly fled abroad, being later seen in Germany. For this intriguing leniency, the magistrate received a nine-year prison term, sentenced himself for membership of FETÖ.

The most striking element of all summaries is the absence of evidence directly linking Gülen to the coup. Apart from one rebel's description of Gülen as their "opinion leader" on the date of the coup, interviews with arrested officers do not seem to have secured details of the preacher's involvement—and this despite alleged use by interrogators of "severe beatings, electrical shocks, exposure to icy water, sleep deprivation, threats, insults, and sexual assault."[21]

This morass of imprecision is a fertile breeding ground for conspiracy theories. Apart from casting the blame on Gülen himself or on groups of his threatened officers, there have been suggestions that Erdoğan himself was involved, either through learning of the coup plans but allowing them to go ahead or, even, of initiating them with the agency of Öksüz. To date, evidence for an instigated coup, a controlled coup, or a "seduced coup" is at best circumstantial, with the allegations saying more about those who make them than what may have happened.[22]

For most observers, as for those running the trials, there are no doubts of the prime role of followers of Gülen. For years they had acted with impunity. Once the AKP came to power, dismissals of alleged Gülenists from the armed forces stopped; in the previous two decades such dismissals had averaged twenty per year.

Seemingly precipitating the coup was that in August 2016 the authorities were planning to act against the *Cemaat*, with the focus expected to be on a list of 1,774 officers sent to the Chief of General Staff on 4 January that year. Ahead of the review, and indeed due the day the coup was to take place originally, the deputy chief prosecutor of İzmir had ordered the arrest of several hundred suspected followers of the *Cemaat*. For many officers, it was thus a case of now or never. Of the 1,774 officers on the January list, 1,668 took part in the July coup attempt.[23]

Had they succeeded, they would have been at war with swathes of the country's 650,000-strong armed forces and many of its citizens.

Systematic cheating in exams; recurrent character assassinations; abuse of authority; replacement of a judicial system based on law and a police system based on public ethos with ones based on loyalty; assembly of fake evidence for the Ergenekon and Balyoz trials—a leader cannot be held responsible for every act of his followers.[24]

However, Gülen's statements broadcast by ATV in 1999 are clear. He was interested in power, and the subsequent record indicates that he was prepared to use any means to achieve it. Despite this, even today, many remain in spellbound denial of the democratic unacceptability of a movement committed to penetration of the key institutions of Turkey, routinely resorting to calumny and fraud, and subject to zero accountability.

If you look for Gülen's birthplace of Korucuk in a recent map of Turkey, you will not find it. In October 2016, the local municipality, responding to villagers who wished to lessen the stigma of having reared the rebel cleric, expunged the place's name, changing it to commemorate a soldier who had just died in Syria, Şehit Burak Karakoç.

By any standard, Gülen's is a remarkable trajectory, from this small village—even today only 65 households—to a mass following, penetrating almost all the key institutions of Turkey, controlling a media empire, developing schools and universities in over 150 countries, and gaining the support of businesses with almost $10 billion turnover. For many Turks, such an organization could not have been built without foreign support, with his ally sometimes alleged to be the CIA or Israel's Mossad. No evidence of such links has ever been produced.

In 2024, even after all that has been learnt about him, some remain bewitched. As Hüseyin Gülerce, until 2014 a close aide of Gülen, explains: "Fear of God has been replaced by fear of Gülen. The love of the Prophet has been replaced by an unconditional commitment to Gülen as the '*İmam* of the universe', 'the expected righteous person'... Why does no member of FETÖ repent? Because no instructions have been received from Gülen."[25]

He broke the career of many, and, perhaps more than any other person, facilitated the rise of the man who is now his arch foe. In the course of this rise, he corrupted the structures of law and justice in Turkey, reducing the judiciary and police to tools of power. Not just the coup (to which Gülen has yet to be formally linked), but Gülen's machinations throughout half a century are Erdoğan's gift from God. No man could contribute more to the decay of democracy. Indeed, as the president struts the stage, it must be a daily mortification for Gülen to consider his munificent contributions to the unfettered power of his nemesis.

PART FOUR

HARVEST—MONOCULTURE

You can change political power through elections... But cultural hegemony cannot be generated through the ballot box... The heroes of 15 July were youngsters. They love their motherland and nation. They fought the putschist traitors. Those were not the Gezi Park youngsters. They were on the streets for the flag and prayer.

President Erdoğan's speech to the annual general meeting of the Ensar Foundation, 2017

Brought to power by a population weary of earlier politicians, Recep Tayyip Erdoğan has developed his offer with the times. Starting with policies aimed to ease Turkey's accession to the European Union, he has since doubled down on religion and nationalism. He has swept aside the checks and balances that constrained his predecessors, helped by a symbiosis with the redefined religious orders, drawing on them to staff the state machinery and being boosted by their votes. With or after him, the religious orders will be there, mediating, as they did for half a millennium, between state and citizen, and contouring the future of Turkey.

14

THE NEW TURKEY

This throne on which you are seated, do you owe it to the unanimous agreement and full consent of the Muslims, or to the violence you have used against them, abusing your strength and your power?

The question of an unknown Sufi to the seventh Abbasid Caliph, al-Mamun (r. 813–833)[1]

Erdoğan and strategic depth

Five weeks after surviving the coup, Erdoğan dispatched Turkish troops into Syria. It was the first time in ninety-eight years that the Turks had fought in the Arab lands they had ruled for a full four centuries. This time, the incursion appeared aimed to bolster Erdoğan's prestige at home as well as advance Turkey's interests abroad. It allowed him to present himself as leader of a nation rather than just of a faction that had narrowly escaped being overthrown. It fitted with Ankara's determination to limit the resurgence of the Kurdish fighters as they drove ISIS forces out of eastern Syria. It aimed at establishing a *cordon sanitaire* in Syria between Turkey and the Kurdish fighters. It was intended to curb the flow of refugees from the civil war; between mid-2015 and mid-2016, registered refugees had doubled to 2.9 million people. And it won Turkey a seat at the diplomats' top table, establishing a new level of dialogue with Russia on regional issues.[2]

The Turkish president's beating of the nationalist drum was well timed. He had just returned from St Petersburg where his 'dear friend,' Vladimir

Putin, whose forces controlled Syrian airspace, had agreed to give his troops cover. And he appreciated that in many ways, the country faced the most favourable international environment since the Second World War. It may not have been the most stable of times, but Cold War confrontation had given way to a multipolar world. The years since the collapse of the Berlin Wall had seen Russia much diminished and, for Ankara, the West was in decline. The U.S., floundering in Iraq and Syria, was no longer prepared or able to impose its former influence on the region, and Western Europe had lost the vigour that it had before the Eurozone crisis. The EU, in any case, had long prioritized its economic offer, and, since March 2016, had been beholden to Erdoğan to restrain refugee flows to Europe. Greece, a formidable lobbyist in earlier years, was now an also-ran.

Facing no regional competitor, Turkey seemed better placed than at any time during the life of the Turkish Republic. To some, it faced fewer external threats than in the nineteenth century, when Britain, Russia, and France lopped off its limbs; than in the eighteenth, when it was obliged to give Russia access to the Black Sea; and than in the seventeenth, when it was disputing the Balkans with the Holy Roman Empire and its eastern borders with Iran. The resulting self-confidence underpinned the abrasive approach that Erdoğan began to adopt as he covered his earlier near-green mantle with the vivid red flag of his nation.

As Turkey has lurched from one confrontation to another, it has become increasingly hard to recall the AKP's original framework for Turkey's role in the world. This was to be a policy of "zero problems with neighbours" and was to be based on the elegant principle of "strategic depth." That last phrase had been the title of a book published in 2001, and the book's author, Professor Ahmet Davutoğlu, rose giddily in the AKP hierarchy—from adviser to Erdoğan, to ambassador, foreign minister, and then, for twenty-one months, prime minister.[3]

Initially, developing relations with the West had seemed as important to Erdoğan as to his predecessors. Previous governments had committed Turkey to membership in the European Union, and Erdoğan started by surfing the same wave. Two years after his party came to office, the EU agreed to the launch of membership negotiations, and Turkey committed itself to continuing its democratic and regulatory alignment with the community.

For both sides, the commitment involved a certain hesitancy. Turkey was not only a Muslim country but also as large as France and with major economic and social issues. After only two years, the EU froze talks on eight of the thirty-five chapters of discussion. The proximate cause was

Turkey's refusal to end measures against the Greek Cypriots, just admitted to the EU as Cyprus. Three years later, Cyprus was to block a further six chapters. Further, in 2005 and 2006, the leaders of Germany and France had changed, and neither Angela Merkel nor Nicolas Sarkozy favoured Turkey becoming a full member of the community.

This partial spurning was a devastating blow to those who looked to European values to underpin the country's secular future and caused a collapse in popular support for accession to the EU. In 2007, over half of the country had a favourable opinion of the EU. By 2014, the share had halved, and two thirds of Turks considered it unfavourably.[4] Indeed, the EU was not alone in attracting Turks' disdain. China, Brazil, NATO, the U.S., Russia, Iran, and Israel were even less popular.[5] Then, as so often, the Turks considered their only friend to be the Turk. That Ankara should thus switch to a less accommodating policy towards Brussels was no surprise.

Those years, Russia, Turkey's enemy for four centuries and a dozen wars, seemed defanged. The U.S. still talked the talk of regional influence, but its limitations had emerged after the invasion of Iraq in 2003. Washington deployed troops and materiel to Turkey in preparation for opening a northern front against President Saddam Hussein, but Turkey's Grand National Assembly just failed to cast the majority vote required to authorize U.S. use of Turkish territory. The resulting U.S. pique encouraged Turkish questioning of the country's role in the newly multipolar world.

In his time, Özal had shifted Turkey towards a more global engagement while İsmail Cem, foreign minister from 1997 to 2002, was to argue: "If Turkey is to become a country that matters in the world, it first has to embrace its past as an imperial power and to engage with its immediate neighbourhood."[6] Davutoğlu's call for building on the past thus fell on fertile ground.

In his words:

> Turkey's strategic depth rests on its geographical and historical depth. Our long history provides us with a unique set of relations with countries and communities all around us. Our geostrategic location in the midst of a vast geography, on the other hand, places us in a position to relate to and influence the developments that are key to the future of the world. So the question is not achieving the strategic depth, but using it for regional and global peace. This requires us to engage with the countries with which we share a common past and geography in a way that will promote our shared interests and create a mutually beneficial framework for cooperation and dialogue.[7]

The history is that of the Ottoman Empire, whose four-century control of the Arab world is so often neglected in accounts of the Middle East. Some commentators suggested that Erdoğan was aspiring to a neo-Ottoman role. For Davutoğlu, this was misrepresentation. "The key word defining Turkey's relations with the Arab countries is not 'hegemony,' but 'mutual cooperation;'" rather, he argued, Turkey would gain security in its region through engagement rather than disengagement, through working with countries in its regions to help them solve their problems.[8] He also championed Turkey's commitment to democracy. In 2009, he proclaimed to EU ambassadors, "We are cognizant of the fact that our democracy is our biggest soft power."[9]

The 1990s had seen Turkey reach out to the newly emergent states of the Balkans and Central Asia, harking on their shared Turkic heritage. With Erdoğan, Turkey started thinking globally, its foreign policy matched by the adventurous entrepreneurialism of Turkey's private sector. A particular focus of outreach were the countries to Turkey's south, with AKP Ankara targeting investment from and trade with these countries. While scant investments were attracted in the early years, the share of the country's exports to countries from the Organization of Islamic Cooperation (OIC) doubled, as did the share of imports from those countries and from "other Asia" (largely China).[10] All these gains were at the expense of trade with the EU.

Turkey's approaches were reciprocated, not least by Saudi Arabia. King Abdullah made visits in 2006 and 2007, the first by a Saudi ruler for four decades. Emine Erdoğan, wife of the Turkish leader, joined the effort, linking hands with the wives of rulers from Damascus to Doha. All this went with a readiness to condemn Israel, not least for its killing of Palestinians in Gaza in 2008–2009 and of Turks on the *Mavi Marmara*.

This policy of playing the good neighbour to the Islamic world, combined with changes inside Turkey, caused Turkey's star to rise. King Abdullah and Muammar Gaddafi awarded Erdoğan medals. The canny traders in the main Cairo date market named their most succulent varieties after him—and their most shriveled ones after President George W. Bush. The country's businessmen were welcomed.

In much of the West too, Erdoğan was still a poster child, in the anguish of the post-9/11 world being embraced as a modernizing Islamic leader. Politicians in the West presented the country as a role model that seemed to marry Islamic belief with parliamentary structures and embody one route for combining religion and the Western sense of modernity.

The U.S. overcame its irritation at Ankara's not allowing use of its territory for the invasion of Iraq. Oil and gas from Azerbaijan started flowing through Turkey in 2006, weakening Moscow's hold over its former fiefdom. The U.S. think tanks were fulsome. President Barack Obama included Erdoğan among the five world leaders with whom he had been able to forge 'bonds of trust.'[11] Turkish soap operas glittered on screens from Cairo to the Caspian and the Balkans. Aspirations for soft power had become reality.

The green mantle of proselytization

Activism abroad

For the AKP, the 'common past' in many countries of Davutoğlu's strategic depth involved a culture in which the Ottoman Empire represented the *Dar al-Islam*, the territory of Islam, and its rule involved submission to the Caliph as the successor of the Prophet. Integral to Turkey's new outreach was recourse to this shared Islamic heritage, the projection of which became an inherent component of the AKP's foreign policy.

Demirel had taken Turkey into the OIC in 1969, and in the 1990s Erbakan had backed an Islamic Common Market and launched the D-8 Muslim counterpart to the then G7 of the developed world. With Erdoğan, this reach to global Islam gained new impetus. This involved a number of initiatives. Some of these were modest, such as attempts to promote a regional free-trade area encompassing Turkey, Jordan, Syria, and Lebanon. Others were more ambitious, not least suggesting that Turkey could act as arbitrator between the Shiites of Iran and the Sunni Arab states.[12] All would be dashed by the mounting political storms of the region.

Erdoğan's government was quick to embrace Hamas after it won the 'free and fair' elections in Palestine in 2006 and was an early supporter of the Arab Spring. For Davutoğlu, the revolutions of that time were creating regimes with a social legitimacy that had previously been lacking, and would enhance their stability.[13] With the Arab Spring often bringing to power supporters of political Islam, this led to suggestions that, rather than being neo-Ottoman, Turkish foreign policy was now neo-Islamic.

In much of this, Erdoğan was following close to Erbakan, whose funeral drew what has been described as "a who's who of the global Islamist movement;" participants included the Hamas leader, Khaled Meshaal, and the Muslim Brotherhood's former spiritual guide, Mohamed Mahdi

Akef. The Turkish prime minister feted the downfall of President Hosni Mubarak. Visiting Cairo, he was greeted by adoring crowds like a rock star before giving a thunderous speech to the Arab League, positioning himself as the unrivalled champion of Palestine, and insisting that a Palestinian state was "not an option but an obligation." Davutoğlu himself made six visits to Mohamed Morsi's short-lived government. When U.S. aid to the new government faltered, Turkey stepped in, contributing over 1 billion USD to the beleaguered regime. General Abdel Fattah al-Sisi's overthrow of Morsi and the Muslim Brotherhood outraged Ankara. It was soon to claw back its aid.

The funds provided to Morsi were part of a major increase in the country's overseas aid programme. Between 2004 and 2011, official aid totaled 6 billion USD, ten times the figure for the previous eight years. Turkish entrepreneurs added a further 4 billion USD in direct investments, and non-government players also became significant. Much of this was to the countries constituting Turkey's 'strategic depth,' but suddenly Turkey was ubiquitous, from the Muslim countries of Asia and the Middle East to Africa and Latin America.

Prominent in this was the country's aid body, TİKA, the Turkish Cooperation and Coordination Agency. Initially, the Turkish foreign ministry and TİKA tended to emphasize the nationalist element of Turkish culture, leaving the *Diyanet* to plough a lonely furrow. With the arrival to power of the AKP, TİKA added the promotion of religion to its remit.

TİKA was supported by the semi-governmental Turkish Red Crescent (the Turkish counterpart of the International Red Cross), the *Diyanet*, and, from 2007, the Yunus Emre Institute, a cultural institute on the lines of the British Council. They were joined by bodies set up by Turkey's religious communities, in particular the Aziz Mahmut Hüdayi Foundation (Erenköy order), Cansuyu (in the tradition of Erbakan's *Milli Görüş*), Hayrat (Nurcu Copyists), *İlim Yayma* Association (Erenköy-İskenderpaşa), and the IHH Humanitarian Aid Foundation, organizer of the aid convoy stormed by Israel. Until the mid-2010s, the Gülen movement was also prevalent.

From developmental projects to mosque and tomb repair, and water projects to sacrificial lambs, the range of activities was, and remains, impressive. The year 2010 saw the establishment of the Public Diplomacy Coordinatorship. Davutoğlu's aspirations for soft power had now become institutionalized.

Leadership and votes of the diaspora in Europe

A major thrust of Turkey's projection of the Islamic spirit is among the Turkish diaspora in Western Europe, which numbers between 7 and 12 million ethnic Turks—measurements in different countries are inconsistent.[14]

Initially the state and private sector were in competition. The Süleymancıs were the first to proselytize among the guest workers who flooded into Germany from the 1960s, being followed by Erbakan's *Milli Görüş*, their network spurred by Erbakan's time in the country after the 1971 military intervention, by Saudi support, and by the Nurcus, who set up a printing press in West Berlin. By 1980, these three communities controlled most of the mosques serving the Turkish communities in Germany and the Netherlands. The *Diyanet* was virtually absent, lacking a legal basis for operating abroad, battling with the Ministry of Foreign Affairs for access to the funds for promoting Turkey's cultural heritage that Atatürk had envisaged they would share, and dependent on contributions by local groups in Germany.[15] The Gülenists too were scarcely evident, starting low-key activities in the 1980s and never developing the profile in Europe that they had elsewhere.[16]

After the 1980 coup, the generals decided they needed to strengthen the role of the *Diyanet* abroad, as they had at home. Tayyar Altıkulaç, the entrepreneurial director of the body, reached an agreement for the Muslim World League in Saudi Arabia to pay the salaries of *Diyanet imam*s in Europe. This led to outrage from Kemalists, and was scrapped. More durable was a protocol with the foreign ministry authorizing the *Diyanet* to establish and fund foundations abroad. Özal continued this approach.

By 1990, the directorate had 800 religious personnel abroad and in 2000 this figure reached 1,110.[17] The *Diyanet* rarely publishes breakdowns of its figures, partly because France and Germany set limits on the number of religious personnel that it may appoint, which the *Diyanet* circumvents by making 'short-term' appointments. However, a survey published in 2002 found that the *Diyanet* controlled half of the 1,769 mosques and local 'cultural associations' in Germany and the Netherlands, its reach equal to that of all the other religious communities combined.[18]

Over the years, the nature and needs of the Turks in Europe have changed. The initial guest workers were sustained by 'the myth of return,' the idea that they would earn and save, and then return to their families in Turkey. A generation later, the focus was on reunification, with wives and children coming to join their breadwinner. The share of women among the emigrants rose from about one third in 1973 to nearly one half by 2010.

The early Islamic communities set up amongst these often maginalized groups focused on helping them fulfill the ritual obligations of Muslims. The *Diyanet* aimed to prevent opposition forces from exploiting their religious needs and mobilizing them against the interests of the Turkish Republic. Over time, the *Diyanet*'s mosques developed into community centres, offering *Kur'an* courses and Islamic lessons, but also staging language classes and training programmes, sports events, and local festivals. One researcher noted in its festivals Turkish food; games for children; martial arts shows; book stands; pony rides; conferences given by invited speakers; 'Islamic music'; whirling dervishes; and even grand prizes, such as a car.[19]

Official Islam has long advanced the Turkish-Islamic synthesis, with the AKP elevating the Islamic component of this, and, with increasing assertion, presenting this and nationalism as the natural and dignified elements of a Turk's identity. Visitors were struck by the importance that *Diyanet* mosques gave to national holidays and historical anniversaries, celebrating them, for instance, with competitions in reciting the country's national anthem. The emphasis on nationalism reflected the new zeitgeist of the Turkish-Islamic synthesis. This diluted support for groups such as the Grey Wolves and other movements linked to the MHP.

With the AKP in power, Turkish officials abroad were encouraged to reach out beyond the communities under the control of the *Diyanet* to the other Turkish communities too, not least the *Milli Görüş* groupings and the network of schools run by the Gülen movement. Elsewise, the AKP intensified rather than changed the nature of Ankara's proselytizing in Europe. The number of religious personnel sent abroad doubled, reaching 2,059 in 2019. Training programmes were instituted and stiffer education criteria introduced. *Diyanet* staff would often be better grounded in Islam than those running the mosques of the religious orders. Many had language training, half frequently paid for by France and Germany.[20] The *Diyanet*'s religious counsellors gained a status within the country's embassies that was previously begrudged them.[21]

The *Diyanet* also launched a theology programme for students from abroad at Ankara University and added a programme for Values Education and Virtuous Youth, targeted to build up to 3,600 students (including ones from countries outside Europe) in 2023.[22]

Quality, funding, and the legitimizing role of the state—all these mean that the *Diyanet* now has a dominant position among the Turks' scattered religious communities. For their part, in 2020 *Milli Görüş* and the Süleymancıs each had one fifth of the mosques and 'cultural' associations of the Turks in Germany and the Netherlands, and the Gülenists less than one tenth. A similar balance applies in France.

From being seen as a blot on Turkey's image in Europe, the Turkish communities began to become appreciated as a potential component of the country's projections of its influence. In 2010, the government established a Directorate for Turks Abroad and Related Communities. The guest workers were, in effect, upgraded to a diaspora, with the aspiration that this diaspora could prove as useful to Ankara as the Greeks of the U.S. had earlier been to Athens—and perhaps serve as a counterweight to the collective efforts of the Armenians to promote remembrance of their losses in 1915 as a genocide.

As the last decade advanced, Erdoğan paid increasing attention to this diaspora, speaking at large rallies in Cologne in 2008, 2010, and 2014, and Düsseldorf in 2011. His speeches remain notorious for his urging German-Turkish children to learn Turkish first and German second, an admonition outraging the German authorities. But it resounded well among the Turks abroad. In 2014, he gave them the right to vote in Turkey. Two thirds of them supported him in that year's presidential election, as did three fifths in 2023.

In all this, DİTİB, the *Diyanet*'s foundations in Europe, beyond their role of identity maintenance, have become a parallel diplomacy machine of the Turkish state, seeking to become the representative of European Islam. Initially, this Turkish model of Islam was welcomed, or at least condoned, by some European governments as an alternative to Salafism and Wahhabism.[23] But, as the *Diyanet* has become instrumentalized by the AKP and begun to play a role in policing the diaspora, the welcome has faced questions. In 2018, the Austrian government decided to shut down seven mosques and deport sixty *imams* financed by the *Diyanet* and their families. The government, a nationalist and conservative one, cast the *Diyanet*'s activities as outside the framework of moderate Islam. Erdoğan proceeded to portray this decision as the preliminary steps in a crusade against Islam, reflecting "the employment of ethno-religious elements first in the domestic realm and then, in a boomerang-like fashion, in Turkey's foreign policy."[24]

Revival in the Balkans

A focus for use of this new power was in the Balkans, an area central to Turkish history and identity. One fifth of the Turkish population is of Balkan origin, and so integral are the Balkans to the Turkish sense of self that one writer, noting Ankara's membership of the Balkan Pacts of 1934 and 1957, has commented, "Turkey is not back to the Balkans. It is a Balkan country and has never, even figuratively speaking, left the region."[25]

Around 9 million Muslims live in the Balkans, with these forming the majority of the population in Albania and Kosovo, half the population in Bosnia and Herzegovina and one third of that in Macedonia.[26] They are deeply fissured by history, language, doctrine, and culture. As one study describes the variegated result:

> 'Being Muslim' is often a very local affair and only one of many identities, i.e. national, ethno-linguistic (and... those of class and gender)... At the same time, a layer of institutional and doctrinal persuasion is apparent (expressed in the historical orientation towards Istanbul's religious authorities, the prevalence of the Hanafi school and the presence of *tarikats*), permeating most of the region's Muslim communities.[27]

All this means that attitudes towards Turkey and the Ottoman Empire range from general dismissal among the secular elites of Albania, to ambiguous scepticism in Bosnia, and to high levels of sympathy in Kosovo and Macedonia.

Turkey appears to have been caught off guard by the wars of Yugoslav succession, and it was the Salafis and Wahhabis who moved in first. In Albania, religious foundations from Saudi Arabia and the Gulf funded the reconstitution of the life of the Muslim community, while handouts and services provided by missionary foundations were evident in Bosnia, Kosovo, and Macedonia.[28]

During the war of 1998–1999, Serbian forces particularly targeted the mosques, the *medrese*, and the *şeyh* themselves. In that war's aftermath, the Saudi Joint Committee for the Relief of Kosovo and Chechnya sent 388 'religious propagators,' setting up at least thirty *Kur'an* schools and around 100 primary and secondary schools.[29] The Saudis also built a number of mosques, of an austerity at odds with the intricate ornamentation of Ottoman mosques. But with the Sufi brotherhoods surviving and forming a popular template for religious life, Salafism faced challenges. As Rexhep Boja, former Mufti of Kosovo and later Kosovar Ambassador to Riyadh, said in 1999: "Albanians have been Muslims for more than 500 years and they do not need outsiders to tell them what is the proper way to practise Islam."[30]

With the 9/11 attacks, these Balkan Salafists became the target of suspicion from Western security analysts, who considered them as recruiting agents for al-Qaeda and Islamist terrorists. The Saudis and Qataris slashed their financial aid to the area, bringing the 'Wahhabi intermezzo' to an end. But a number of studies have underlined that the Salafist message had failed to resonate in an area long characterized by its rich diversity of Islamic practice, ranging from the Alevi rituals of Albania's prevailing Bektaşi dervishes to the numerous Halveti, Kadiri, Rifai, and other *tarikat* that had survived the repressions of Tito. In Kosovo alone, the association of dervish orders grouped 126 lodges and 50,000 members in 1984, and in 1998 claimed 100,000 members.[31]

The Saudi retreat from the Balkans came at a time of faltering Europeanization and the absence of regional competitors. Turkey's state agencies were well placed to push an integrated religious and political agenda. Davutoğlu himself had been involved in the area through friendships he made with Bosnians while teaching at the International Islamic University in Malaysia in the early 1990s. In October 2009, he told an audience in Sarajevo:

> We desire a new Balkans, based on political values, economic interdependence and cultural harmony. That was the Ottoman Balkans. We will restore these Balkans. People call this 'neo-Ottoman'. I don't point to the Ottoman state as a foreign policy issue. I emphasize the Ottoman heritage. The Ottoman era in the Balkans is a success story. Now it needs to come back.[32]

In the first few years of the AKP, trade with the Balkans quadrupled, Turkey's contractors flourished, and overall aid exceeded 70 million USD per year. TİKA and other Turkish agencies "changed the architectural landscape of the Western Balkans—Ottoman mosques, neglected during Yugoslav times, destroyed in the violent conflicts of the 1990s or disfigured by Saudi-financed reconstruction projects, have once again become the iconic and proud reminders of the Ottoman heritage of the region."[33] The *Diyanet* began to shape how Islamic unions in the Balkans interacted with one other and with the Islamic world. And Turkey's religious orders reached out to their counterparts, funding the restoration of dervish lodges. Erenköy started publishing the works of Osman Nuri Topbaş in Balkan languages, and the Süleymancıs were active with their

Kur'an courses. The *İlim Yayma* Association led the establishment of a university in Sarajevo.

During these years, an integral component of this outreach was the Gülen movement, which picked up *medrese* and schools abandoned by the Saudis and Gulf countries. By 2010, Gülen had over twenty schools and two universities in Albania, Bosnia and Herzegovina, Kosovo, and Macedonia.[34] In 2011 and 2012, his *Kimse Yok Mu* (Is Nobody There?) Association led the list of Turkey's NGO aid donors. In TİKA reports printed after the Gülen-Erdoğan confrontation, the association's name disappears. Management of his schools abroad became an issue, and after the 2016 coup attempt, teachers featured among the hundred or more Turkish nationals subjected to forced rendition for alleged FETÖ links. Many of the renditions seemed to have a transactional nature. One from Albania was followed by the release of aid for the 2019 earthquake. Seven from Moldova were followed by Turkey agreeing to boost trade and to fund a 10-million-euro renovation of the country's presidential palace.[35]

By this time, it had become clear that the secular and modest Turkey that had been welcomed two decades earlier was now carrying out at home what one political scientist has described as "a pragmatic ethno-nationalist, coercive Sunnification of state identity." Abroad, it was no longer a neutral player but was instrumentalizing Ottoman nostalgia as one of its policy tools to spread its influence. Some considered this more aggressive, reactive and somewhat more religious approach the correct policy under contemporary regional and global conditions. But one Albanian former minister argued that, especially after 2010, with its pro-Islamist ideas, its aggressive tone towards the EU, its reactive political strategies, and its authoritarianism, the AKP's Turkey started to lose both influence and prestige in the region.[36]

Brandishing the flag

New Turkey

It was for his first presidential election that Erdoğan campaigned on the theme of a New Turkey (*Yeni Türkiye*), using the term for the renewal of the nation he said was taking place under his watch. The birthday of this New Turkey was 27 August 2014, the day before he took over as president, and the term has since become familiar throughout the country, hammered home by Erdoğan in what sometimes seem like daily speeches throughout the years.[37]

The New Turkey involves a change in language and a change in mindset. Gone are the days of looking to the West for alliance and reassurance. The New Turkey no longer seeks the safety of the pack but has chosen the role of lone wolf. Dr İbrahim Kalın, long Erdoğan's chief aide and head of the country's intelligence agency since June 2023, describes it as a "valued isolation," echoing Britain's nineteenth-century "splendid isolation" as it eschewed alliances. Today, the country seeks respect rather than friendships, recasting the alliances it once had as transactional relationships. Turkey's Atlanticists have lost out to its Eurasians.

In part, the change was a response to the checks the AKP had faced. EU accession, de-escalating Iranian nuclear tensions, reaching out to Assad, brokering peace between Israel and the Palestinians, siding with the Arab Spring uprisings, talking with the PKK, supporting negotiations over Nagorno-Karabakh and Cyprus—by 2015, the AKP's multilateralism had demonstrably failed in every case. By contrast, other powers were employing hard power in Turkey's neighbourhood, and Turkey realized that it was equipped to match them.

Revamping its power projection meant integrating a military approach into its diplomacy, and that has been the inherent characteristic of the New Turkey. It has set up bases for its troops in Afghanistan (until 2021), Albania, Iraq, Libya, Qatar, Somalia, and Syria. It has expanded its network of military agreements, providing training to over thirty countries. It has entered into industrial defence partnerships with Malaysia, Pakistan, and Ukraine. It has built up its defence industry, becoming renowned for its drones but also producing a host of other items; its arms exports in 2023 totalled 5.5 billion USD. It has developed its military doctrine to integrate new sensors and weapons. And—perhaps most critically—it has united behind a risk-tolerant political will in foreign affairs.

This is not the policy of a rogue leader but a geopolitical strategic culture, which one U.S. commentator considers rooted in "a long historical memory and an extreme trust deficit;" in his analysis, the 1920 Treaty of Sèvres is a far more potent and durable cautionary tale than Western equivalents such as appeasement in Munich or defeat in Vietnam.[38]

The change is substantial. For the second half of the last century, Turkey was the south-east flank of NATO. Today, it is also a regional power in its own right, economically forceful and militarily significant, and integral to all discussions of its neighbourhood.

Erdoğan, never slow to sense an opponent's weakness, has shown he is determined to make the best of the improved environment. Stiffening his back has been his far-from-unassailable situation at home. A slowing economy has increased his vulnerability. His recent electoral victories have been aided by—and perhaps depended on—depriving his opponents of fair campaigning and polling conditions. To consolidate his position, he has allied with Devlet Bahçeli's MHP, formally linking with it in the 2017 referendum and the elections of 2018, 2019, 2023, and 2024. It was Bahçeli who was at his side when he led the faithful at the reopening of Ayasofya Mosque to worship. He seems to have little trouble in accommodating Bahçeli's nationalist demands in foreign policy.

Erdoğan has stuck to his lathe where support for the Muslim Brotherhood is concerned. This caused a protracted confrontation with the government of General al-Sisi in Cairo. It also so upset Saudi Arabia that in October 2014 the latter joined the campaign to block Turkey becoming a non-permanent member of the U.N. Security Council. The rift between Ankara and Riyadh widened after Mohammed bin Salman (MBS) took over as Crown Prince in March 2017. That June, Erdoğan castigated the blockade of Qatar launched by MBS as "inhumane and against Islamic values," while in March 2018, MBS accused Turkey of trying to reinstate the Islamic Caliphate and described the country as part of a "triangle of evil" along with Iran and hardline Islamist groups. Riyadh then launched a partial boycott of Turkish television programmes and goods. Erdoğan appears to have been appalled by the Saudis' murder in their İstanbul consulate of the journalist, Jamal Khashoggi, his officials for several weeks leaking the macabre details of the gruesome attack. It took four years for *raisons d'état* to cause the estranged leaders to embrace afresh.

Strutting in Syria

Erdoğan's continuing support for Egypt's Muslim Brotherhood can be linked to the religion-driven policies evident in earlier AKP years. Such policies were also initially evident in Syria, the issue which has progressively come to define Turkey's role and vulnerabilities. Here, as elsewhere, the past decade has seen a shift, with nationalism eventually displacing religion as the main force motivating the Turkish leader.

Post-Ottoman Syria has rarely felt close to Turkey. Resentment over Turkey annexing the Hatay region in 1939 lives on, while from the 1950s onwards Damascus disdained Ankara as a pawn of the West. Erdoğan came to power during a brief thaw in relations. In 1999, Hafez al-Assad expelled

Abdullah Öcalan, the leader of the Kurdish rebellion in Turkey, from his villa in the Syrian capital. The two sides were content to forget the Turkish threats that had precipitated the Syrian president's decision, and in 2004, Erdoğan visited Damascus to sign a free-trade agreement with Hafez's son, Bashar. Natural gas connections were planned, and the two leaders' wives began to be seen hand in hand.

The last known photograph of the two first ladies together dates to January 2009 when they joined in condemning Israel's assault on Gaza. But then something went terribly wrong. Some have suggested that oil, or rather natural gas, was to blame, with Erdoğan being angered by Syria's preferring a natural gas pipeline from Iran to his favoured link with Qatar. Another hypothesis is that Assad was infuriated by Turkey's support for Islamic rebels in his country. More probable is that, as the Arab Spring of 2011 weakened Washington's certainties in the Middle East, Obama decided to step up U.S. pressure on Damascus, and Erdoğan considered this an opportunity to win favour in Washington while enhancing Turkey's influence in its region.

At this point, a convoy of Turkish pilgrims returning from Mecca was attacked in Syria and two people wounded. Some witnesses said the assailants wore the uniforms of Syrian soldiers. Erdoğan started denouncing Bashar al-Assad. "Just remove yourself from [the presidency] before shedding more blood, before torturing more, for the welfare of your country, as well as the region," he declaimed in November 2011.

In one analysis, Erdoğan appears to have allowed Turkey to become a highway for weapons to the opponents of Assad. "By the summer of 2012, a freewheeling feel had taken hold along Turkey's border with Syria as the Gulf nations funneled cash and weapons to rebel groups—even some that American officials were concerned had ties to radical groups like Al-Qaeda."[39] Obama signed off on CIA support for this in early 2012, and in 2013 authorized lethal assistance. In one report, this involved the CIA coordinating training and arms supplies, with funding by Qatar, Saudi Arabia, and Turkey.[40] The recipients were a motley bag, including the al-Nusra Front and other al-Qaeda- and ISIS-influenced bands.

Obama hesitated about involving the U.S. military, but in August 2012 described any regime use of chemical weapons as a 'red line' that could trigger such intervention. By mid-2013, there had been a dozen such incidents (a few of them clearly initiated by opponents of Assad). Then, in the early hours of 21 August 2013, at least eight and possibly twelve rockets carrying sarin hit Eastern Ghouta, a rebel area south-east of Damascus. Estimates of the death toll range from nearly 300 to 1,729. Obama ordered a 'monster' retaliatory air strike, but at the last moment backed down, either because Russia had brokered a deal for the destruction of Syria's chemical weapons, or because evidence about the attackers was inconclusive.

To this day, a debate rages on the origins of the sarin. When Erdoğan and Hakan Fidan, then his intelligence chief and since June 2023 his foreign minister, met with Obama three months before the Ghouta massacre and raised earlier use of chemical weapons, Obama refused to let Fidan talk, telling him: "We know what you are doing with the radicals in Syria."[41] That same month, the police arrested thirteen men in Adana on charges of supplying chemical weapons to al-Qaeda. In a 130-page indictment, the thirteen were accused of attempting to purchase fuses, piping for the construction of mortars, and chemical precursors for sarin.

Ankara continued relations with radical Islamist groups long after these were condemned by the West. It was not until eighteen months after the U.S. had denounced al-Nusra Front as a terrorist organization that Ankara did so too. Instead, Turkey continued to prioritize toppling Assad while other countries had switched their focus to combatting the al-Qaeda-affiliated jihadist groups in his country. It also appears to have found the al-Nusra Front a convenient partner to counter the YPG, the People's Defence Units, the Syrian ally of Kurdish rebels in Turkey.

Turkey's aid appears to have been substantial. One lorry stopped in Adana province on 1 January 2014 was found to be carrying over 80,000 bullets and mortar shells, according to the newspaper *Cumhuriyet*. A second *Cumhuriyet* report detailed seizure of a truck at Akçakale border post "loaded with 10,000 detonators and 290,000 meters of explosive primers."[42] In August 2015, the newspaper *Bugün* printed video stills of what it said was the transfer, under the observation of Turkish border guards, of weapons and explosives from Turkey to ISIS. *Bugün* alleged that transfers had been continuing on a daily basis for two months. The authors of the first *Cumhuriyet* story were arrested and one, Can Dündar, was sentenced *in absentia* to twenty-seven years in prison for espionage and aiding the Gülenist FETÖ. The second paper, *Bugün*—part of a pro-Gülen group—was seized by the state and closed down after the 2016 coup.

By this time, Putin had sent troops to shore up Syrian forces and had started upgrading Russia's air and naval bases in the country; Tartus was then Russia's only overseas naval base. Russian planes coordinated with

U.S. flights against their shared enemy of ISIS. However, on 24 November 2015, a Turkish F-16 shot down a Russian Su-24M bomber. The Russian president said he considered declaring war, but instead launched days of abuse against Erdoğan and his family, accusing them of benefitting from the sale of oil from ISIS-controlled regions. He also imposed a range of sanctions against Turkey.[43]

It was not until seven months later that Erdoğan expressed regret. Three weeks after his climbdown came the coup attempt of 15 July, and Putin was one of the few to ring the beleaguered president to offer help. Erdoğan's subsequent visit to St Petersburg not only led to his sending Turkish troops to Syria but also to a visit by Putin to sign the inter-governmental agreement for the TürkStream pipeline, a project dear to the Russian president for reducing Gazprom's dependence on Ukraine. This halcyon period between the two countries survived the murder of the Russian ambassador to Ankara, and culminated in Erdoğan announcing in 2017 that Turkey would buy Russia's S-400 air defence system. The purchase was a clear refutation of Turkey's cooperation with NATO and a confirmation of the depths to which U.S.-Turkish relations had sunk.

Russia and Turkey still had different aims in Syria. It was only after an apparently tart telephone call from Putin in late 2016 that Erdoğan pulled back from describing Assad as a 'killer' and calling for his removal.[44] By this time, it had become apparent that the security of Turkey's invasionary forces depended on Russian air and diplomatic cover. Through 2017 to 2019, such cooperation was in place, but early in 2020 Ankara received a reminder of its vulnerability. Syrian attacks led to the deaths of at least forty of its troops and to Turkey being forced to abandon a dozen of its seventy 'observation posts.' Erdoğan visited Moscow for redress, but received short shrift. Instead, he was obliged to help Russia control the southern quarter of the rebel-held Idlib region.

The relationship on the ground continued to prove fractious, yet in 2020 Erdoğan still felt sufficiently self-assured to arm Moscow's opponents in the Libyan civil war and to step up his presence in the Caucasus, risking ruffling Moscow's feathers by supporting Azerbaijan's reconquest of much of Nagorno-Karabakh. It may be that, for Putin, these were small irritants compared to the damage that Erdoğan had wreaked in NATO's south-eastern flank. But it was hard to say the same of Turkey's supplying armed TB-2 drones to Ukraine and its support for Ukraine's membership of NATO.

Wrestling with Washington

In 2021, Erdoğan had to wait ninety-three days before the new U.S. president, Joseph Biden, telephoned, a call to warn that he would the next day remember "all those who had died in the Ottoman-era Armenian genocide", the first U.S. president so to do.[45] China and Russia initially headed his agenda, and did so until Putin's invasion of Ukraine upended the balances in Europe developing since the fall of the Berlin Wall.

Prior to the invasion, Turkey was on the defensive in the U.S. The state Halkbank is charged with 20 billion USD of breaches of U.S. sanctions on Iran, with Erdoğan implicated by one state witness.[46] The Turkish president's insistence on proceeding with the purchase of Russia's S-400 missile system had led to Turkey's suspension from the programme to produce the next generation Lockheed Martin F-35 stealth fighter aircraft and to federal sanctions against the officials heading its Defence Industry Directorate. Meanwhile, the U.S. Congress, also concerned at Turkish military overflights of Greece, was blocking delivery of the communication kits required to fit Turkey's ageing General Dynamics F-16 fighters for modern combat.

The Russian invasion allowed Erdoğan to push himself forward as a key figure in mediating with Putin over issues such as grain exports. NATO's subsequent wish to add Finland and Sweden to its members required overcoming the veto that Turkey exercised. Before ending his veto, Erdoğan had the two applicants step up measures against those Turkey classes as terrorists and the U.S. agree to deliver the F-16 upgrades.

By spring 2024, he had achieved these aims, but his enemies in Washington continued to fulminate at Erdoğan's praise for Hamas, his refusal to condemn its October 2023 massacre of over 1,200 Israelis and hostage-taking, and at evidence of Turkey facilitating breaches of international sanctions on arms supplies and oil trade with Russia.

Muting Europe

A parallel rebalancing has taken place with the European Union, with Turkey moving from prospective partner to frosty neighbour. The inward focus of the EU after the Eurozone debt crisis contrasted with the growing self-confidence of Turkey and its increasing insouciance. Erdoğan's rows with Germany and the Netherlands ahead of the 2014 presidential elections showed that domestic politics had become more important than the diminished carrot of accession to a Christian club.

At this point, Turkey was the supplicant, but the Syrian crisis provided it with a consummate bargaining chip: the ability to influence refugee flows to Europe. Disruption from Syria to Afghanistan had led to Turkey receiving a flood of asylum seekers. By the end of 2014, it hosted 1.6 million registered refugees, more than anywhere else in the world, with most of them being from Syria. The number doubled in 2015, and this despite the horde who transited its territory to Europe. That year, Syrians made up the bulk of 1 million refugees who entered the EU, and half of them did so by crossing the six miles from Turkey to Lesvos in the northern Aegean. In October alone, 135,063 refugees came to this lauded island, around 100 overcrowded and perilous rubber dinghies crossing each night, local fishermen doing their best to save them from the rocks.

Ankara saw this as an opportunity to revive its process of accession, and, in exchange for curbing the refugee flows, called for revitalizing talks on membership. In the end, it settled for 3 billion euros in aid, subsequently increased to over 9 billion euros, and improved visa rights. The issue of visas was to founder, but the balance of power had changed. Europe now needed Turkey.

The following years saw relations go from stressed to worse. In 2017, the AKP's efforts to campaign among the Turkish communities of Germany and the Netherlands led to a diplomatic crisis with both countries. Erdoğan and three of his ministers were refused permission to hold rallies in Germany, and his foreign minister, Mevlüt Çavuşoğlu, was forbidden to land in the Netherlands. The president accused Germany of 'Nazi-style' tactics and described the Dutch as 'Nazi remnants.'[47] The next years saw Turkey's navy in collision with that of Greece and preventing an Italian vessel from drilling off Cyprus. The country's oil company drilled wells in areas claimed by Cyprus, and 2020 saw rows with France and Germany over their naval vessels' search of Turkish-controlled vessels en route to Libya.[48] Macron's policies towards Islam showed he "needs treatment on a mental level," Erdoğan decried that October.

An incident involving 25,000 would-be migrants massing at the Pazarkule border gate with Greece had made Turkey's point in Brussels, and response to Erdoğan's provocations was limited to restricting investment funding and sanctions against senior bureaucrats.[49] In March 2021, the European Council received a Commission report setting out a litany of Turkey's "threatening actions and disparaging rhetoric; and assertive Turkish interventions in most of the surrounding regional conflicts." [50] The EU's political masters set these aside, preferring to talk of 'enhanced cooperation' provided Turkey did not resume illegal drilling. The subsequent visit to Ankara by the presidents of the European Council and Commission saw human rights downplayed.

Come the Ukraine crisis and EU concerns over Turkey's lax approach to sanctioning Russia have been mitigated by the value of Ankara's diplomatic efforts during the conflict. The regular reports by the European Commission on developments in Turkey continue to paint a bleak picture of democratic backsliding, evidenced not least by Turkey's continuing refusal to release the leader of the pro-Kurdish HDP, Selahattin Demirtaş, and the philanthropist Osman Kavala as required by the European Court of Human Rights.

In November 2023, the Commission reminded its political masters of the "considerable evidence of Türkiye's territory being used to divert sanctioned goods to Russia" and criticized Turkey's policies in connection with Cyprus as undermining chances for a solution to the island's problems, blocking EU-NATO cooperation and endangering civilian air traffic. It referred to "the grave domestic human rights and rule of law situation" and pointed out Turkey's divergences with the EU over designation and condemnation of Hamas. It called for further steps towards constructive engagement. "Efforts to bridge the key differences with Ankara must continue."[51] The subsequent EU summit, as often before, decided to defer the issue. As for the European Council meetings of March and June 2024, their conclusions do not even mention Turkey.

A place in the sun

Russia's invasion of Ukraine has quickened Turkey's regaining what it considers its rightful place in the sun. Western sanctions and international isolation have left Moscow increasingly reliant on Ankara. "One hand washes the other. Both leaders need each other," Hüseyin Bağcı, who heads the Foreign Policy Institute in Ankara, told the *Financial Times* in November 2022. This relationship has survived Turkey supplying drones to Ukraine. It is a component of Western hopes for an eventual settlement of the devastating war.

Turkey has morphed from a country content with soft power to one brandishing hard power, tempered in decades of conflict against the Kurdish rebels and backed by a formidable domestic arms industry. For Turkey's nationalists—and they are many—the country's re-emergence as a regional power is vindication of the lessons of Ottoman history, that the Turks can expect no favours from abroad and that foreigners are fair-weather friends who betray Turkey whenever it suits them. For these, Erdoğan's New Turkey is not a question of coming of age, but of regaining a status which obsequiousness to the West had long denied it.

Such a message is inherent in Nakşibendi teaching, with its worldview tempered by British and French depredation of Muslim India. This message has resonated among the followers of the various *tarikat*, almost all Halidi, who have risen to rule Turkey. Erdoğan's skill has been taking advantage of these orders to mobilize followers and support, and then blending this teaching with nationalism. He has instrumentalized this into the policies that make Turkey the power it has become. It is popular among the Turkish public, rarely providing the parliamentary opposition with room for criticism. As the historian Hugh Thomas wrote in another context: "... politicians are the expression of public moods which are the masses' collective dreams."[52] For the opposition, there are no votes in challenging this.

The default style of the New Turkey is assertive, confrontational, and likely to continue as such. The suave Western-style diplomats of Turkey's post-war foreign ministry have been replaced by a generation that acts first and does not apologize. Davutoğlu's world of zero problems with neighbours has given way to self-interest. In this, no treaty is sacrosanct. In 2017, Erdoğan shocked Greece by questioning the Treaty of Lausanne. In 2021, he classed 104 admirals who called for respect for the Treaty of Montreux on the Turkish straits as putschists. He has long flouted key principles of the U.N. Law of the Sea.

For Erdoğan and his team, isolation has been valued rather than daunting, but the rewards of recent years have their risks. Such squalls could develop in Syria, where Turkish troops are particularly dependent on the cover provided by Moscow. As the Ukraine crisis has showed, the relationship with Russia is enmeshed and multi-dimensional—but that with the U.S. also has its risks.

The country already faces curbs on arms sales from Britain, Canada, Finland, France, Germany, and the Netherlands. And it can expect further confrontations with Washington. There, Erdoğan has few friends, not least because of his scorn for Israel and Sisi's Egypt, and his dialogue with Tehran. Penalties for past breaches of U.S. sanctions and future sanctions on Turkey's defence industries are possible. The extent to which such sanctions will hinder sales of the drones that have come to symbolize Turkey's hard power is unclear. Some lingering dependence on foreign technology may remain in power and transmission systems, as well as microelectronic and sensor components. This dependence impacts the production of drones and of engines for tanks and the country's vaunted TAI Kaan airplane programme.[53] This is the country's next-generation fighter and, following disputes with the U.S. over the F-35, has gained importance. The first Kaan prototype was able to carry out its maiden flight in March 2024, powered, as a holding solution, by a General Electric F110 engine: Rolls-Royce had balked at the technology transfer terms demanded for the joint venture in Turkey planned to produce engines for the Kaan programme. That said, Turkey has become markedly more self-reliant. In the 1980s, imports from abroad accounted for one third of military procurement. In the past decade, this figure was down to 5 per cent. Indeed, some role reversal seems under way. As the U.S. Ambassador to Ankara wrote in early 2024:

> Türkiye's ongoing defense sector transformation—from drones and high-tech components to engines and artillery shells—is integral to the U.S. defense supply chain and the strength of our NATO alliance... In Texas, the Department of Defense is building three munitions lines purchased from a Turkish defense firm. By next year, an estimated 30% of all 155 mm rounds made in America will come from these Texas factories, thanks to the U.S.-Türkiye defense partnership.[54]

Erdoğan's New Turkey promises the end of what he perceived as Turkey's subservience to external forces; the country's rise as a global power; and a determination to defeat internal and external foes bent on hindering its progress.[55] His "valued isolation" frees Turkey to balance its partnerships and maximize its opportunities. In his new vision, the country will become "one of the ten great states in the world."

Erdoğan has worn down U.S. support for the Kurds. His hardline approach to the accession of Finland and Sweden served his purpose. The longer the Ukraine crisis continues, the more it seems that Erdoğan has ensured a Turkish geopolitical veto in his region. How this will survive the Israeli-Hamas conflagration remains to be seen.

15

ERDOĞAN REGNANT

No one can be a Muslim until he governs his greed.

Bahâeddin Nakşibend (1318–1389)

The pious generation

It was for reciting a poem that Erdoğan was condemned to prison, in 1999 serving four months for inciting religious hatred. The words that led to his conviction were:

> The mosques are our barracks, the domes our helmets, the minarets our bayonets, and the faithful our soldiers...

The poem he cited was commended by the Ministry of Education, and the prison sentence only enhanced his lustre among those who had earlier supported the young politician to become mayor of İstanbul. A convoy of several kilometres accompanied him to detention in Thrace. Four years after this, he was prime minister.

In 2012, confident in power, he declared his aim of creating a "pious generation." It is a theme to which he has frequently returned, for instance in 2019:

> With God's will, a pious youth and a pious generation will be raised in your hands. If we succeed in this, with God's permission we will not then see addicts and thieves in town centres, on streets and in markets, or we will

> minimize them. We will not see alcoholics... it is my belief that in a country in which there is a pious generation all moral values will instantaneously take a huge upswing and a nation will come into being that loves one another, not out of interest or for office or position, but for God.[1]

The president's personal commitment to this mission is evidenced in his family's cooption of the elements surrounding the grand Süleymaniye complex. These, long the pinnacle of the Ottoman judicial and teaching system, now house part of Ibn Haldun University, an establishment with an interesting tale. Its establishment followed a donation in April 2012 of $99,999,990 to a foundation set up by Recep Tayyip Erdoğan and which, that August renamed TÜRGEV (the Turkey Youth and Education Service Foundation), subsequently endowed the university. Bülent Arinç, deputy prime minister, confirmed TÜRGEV's receipt of the donation, while Haluk Koç, spokesman of the CHP, alleged that the funds had come from an account entitled Royal Protocol "probably of Middle East or Saudi origin," being transferred to the bank account of Necmettin Bilal Erdoğan and five minutes later transferred by him to the account of the foundation with Vakıfbank.[2] Two months later, the İstanbul Municipality granted a zoning permit for a magnificent site on the flanks of the Bosphorus that King Abdullah, then Crown Prince, had bought in 1984. Arzu Akalın, Chairperson of TÜRGEV, denied a connection between the donation and the zoning permit: "Was such a donation made to TÜRGEV? Yes it was. But is the change in the zoning plan something that took place with the involvement and request of TÜRGEV? Those making such allegations need to put forward something. They can't because there is no such thing."[3]

The university opened its doors three years after the Saudi munificence. Bilal Erdoğan has long been deputy chairman of its board of trustees.

Ibn Haldun is one of a dozen universities set up by foundations with a conservative persuasion. These can draw on a student flow increasingly influenced by the *imam-hatip* system. During Erdoğan's two decades in office, registrations in such schools have risen by twenty times to 1.3 million students in the 2022/2023 academic year, over one in ten of the students in secondary education. There has also been a quadrupling of attendance at *Kur'an* courses.

Such students have clearly embarked on a pious route, with the state and private dormitory system underpinning this. The Turkish word for these dormitories, *yurt*, evokes communal memories of the Turks' ancestors who came to Anatolia with their tents. These dormitories are not a simple place to sleep, but of an all-embracing nature. "For the

Süleymancı, the Gülenists and the Nurcu, these dormitories and the associated *dershane* are actually *tekke*. The young do not go there just to sleep but they live together, eat together, practise Islam together and that's how they learn it."[4] Lessons in memorizing the *Kur'an* are integral to the group's activities.

The *Kur'an* courses—in an Arabic that few comprehend—take place throughout the country. A minority have sessions teaching rudimentary Arabic or providing an initial commentary on the Prophet's words. Three quarters of these courses are operated by foundations, associations, and bodies registered with the Ministry of Education, but subject to limited supervision.

Nation and family

For Erdoğan, the revival of Ayasofya as a mosque was "the greatest dream of our youth." Proclaiming the step, the president quoted at length from the speech in which his mentor, Kısakürek, exhorted the nationalist youth of the 1960s:

> Ayasofya must be opened. To keep Ayasofya closed is to attract the curses of thirty million Turks on this soil and of thirty billion Turks united in anger in the heavens above. Keeping Ayasofya closed is a crime equivalent to cursing God, to spitting on the *Kur'an*, to throwing Turkish history into the toilet, to defiling Turkish chastity, and selling the Turkish homeland… Sealed shut by hearts sealed by God, Ayasofya will open like the hearts of the pious youth of Turkey, which they attempted to seal but could do nothing to stop their flow swelling from day to day.[5]

For Erdoğan's generation, carrying through the dream of their idol was a sacred obligation. Ayasofya had been the central locus of Turks religion for nearly five centuries. Its revival was a matter of Turkey's sovereign rights.

In 1994, Erdoğan had been at the side of Erbakan as the latter raised a crowd to its feet, shouting, "We will meet in Ayasofya." For Erdoğan and many believers in Turkey, being deprived of the right to pray in this great symbol of faith was a national humiliation. That he waited until 2020 to correct the wrong is more of a surprise than that he finally acted. The Orthodox Patriarchs of Constantinople and Moscow expressed dismay. Their voices and the muted concerns of the opposition in Turkey were drowned out by the acclaim from Erdoğan's supporters and the major religious orders in the country.

Restoring Justinian's legacy to its Ottoman status was also "an expression that we, as the Turkish Nation, Muslims and all humanity, have new messages for the world," Erdoğan proclaimed that day, underlining that it was part of a larger design. As one historian comments:

> As self-proclaimed architect of the 'New Turkey', Erdoğan inscribes his rule in the space of the metropolis of Istanbul in the form of large-scale infrastructural projects (the third Bosphorus Bridge, Istanbul Airport and, currently, the Istanbul Canal). These projects stand for the modern, future-oriented vision of New Turkey. However, it would not be New Turkey, if it would not connect this futurism with an anchoring in Ottoman past and Islamic tradition.[6]

A further component of this vision is the president's new mosque dominating the Anatolian flank of the lower Bosphorus. The Çamlıca Mosque has a footprint larger than Ayasofya, a broader and higher dome, six soaring minarets, and a massive entrance courtyard. In non-pandemic times, 63,000 worshippers can gather there. By mere metrics, Erdoğan has surpassed Justinian.

Construction started in 2013, disregarding objections that the site was a protected green area, one of the perilously few remaining in İstanbul. It was opened six years and 67 million USD later, now often being frequented by the president when he is in İstanbul on a Friday. One such recent afternoon, the presence of a protest control vehicle and some hundred police in the street with others sitting languidly in a café showed that he was expected. Arrivals to the mosque were greeted with a harangue from the *mihrab* about the blood and strength of Turkey's armed forces. There were over 1,000 worshippers present when Erdoğan entered, many rising to take his photograph. His arrival was well after the hour for the prayer, but only stimulated the orator to new levels of enthusiasm. The practised rituals of the prayers were a relieving calm.

Mosque-building is a virtue in Islam, and Erdoğan may well have had in mind the saying attributed to the Prophet: "Whoever builds a mosque for Allah—though it be the size of the ground nest of a sandgrouse—Allah will build for him a house in Paradise." With the opening of a further İstanbul mosque at Taksim Square in May 2021, Erdoğan seems to be assuring himself of a compound in the hereafter.

Also of religious merit is education, and that is the declared aim of the half-dozen or more foundations that the leader and his children have developed. Apart from endowing the Ibn Haldun University, these foundations provide scholarships, promote appropriate values in education, give school meals to over 25,000, set up and operate over 150 dormitories, teach Islamic design, and encourage sports such as archery. The foundations linked to the family include:

- Ensar (Auxiliaries of the Prophet) Foundation, originally founded in 1979.
- TÜRGEV (the Turkey Youth and Education Service Foundation), dating back to 1995. Apart from Ibn Haldun University, this focuses on supporting women.
- *Okçular* (The Okmeydanı Spot and Education Foundation), founded in 2012.
- *İhsan ve İrfan* (Human and Learning Foundation), founded in 2012.
- TÜGVA (the Turkey Youth Foundation), founded in 2013.
- TURKEN in the U.S., founded in 2014.
- KADEM (The Women and Democracy Foundation), founded in 2015.
- T3 (the Turkish Technology Team), founded in 2017.

A related association is TOGEM (the Social Development Centre), initiated by Emine Erdoğan, the president's wife, in 2005 and long run by her sister-in-law, Saadet Gülbaran.[7] Working closely with these is the *İlim Yayma Vakfi*, of whose board of trustees Bilal Erdoğan, the president's second son, has long been chairman. This too has a university, named after the academic Sabahattin Zaim.[8] All these foundations have been classed as being of public benefit and awarded exemption from taxes.

The foundations have distinguished themselves by nimble property work. In 2015, Ensar gained control of an Armenian school in Üsküdar from the local municipality. By this time, TÜRGEV had taken over the grand Ottoman stone building for relics of the Prophet as well as a large property at Mevlanakapı, İstanbul.[9] It was soon to rent the prestigious religious schools at the Süleymaniye mosque complex, adding these to 726,000 square metres of treasury land at Başakşehir on the western fringes of İstanbul, where zoning regulations were changed to its favour.[10] These last two assets are used by Ibn Haldun University.

For its part, TÜGVA won rights over a park area under the ancient Byzantine walls of the city, and in less than a month had the park reclassified to house its headquarters. Like TÜRGEV, TÜGVA also took over a number of the Gülenist dormitories when they were seized in mid-2016.

By this time, the *Okçular* foundation was in charge of a large open area once belonging to a dervish lodge. In similar vein, in 2015, the *İlim Yayma Vakfi* took over the Ottoman Veterinary College and land earmarked for Marmara University for its own university.

Nor are the family's activities limited to Turkey. In Manhattan, TURKEN, a joint venture of Ensar and TÜRGEV, has developed a prime site at 300 East 41st Street to house a 21-storey cultural centre and student housing. TURKEN is offering student accommodation in seven further U.S. cities, and spent 2.5 million USD for the 81-acre Rope-a-Dopes estate in Michigan of the late Muhammed Ali.[11] As of 30 June 2020, its assets totalled 63 million USD. Its IRS filing for the previous year recorded zero expenditure on scholarships or affordable housing. A parallel initiative, TURKEN Foundation UK, has opened female student housing in London, runs lecture programmes, and has hosted Recep Tayyip and Bilal Erdoğan at *iftar* dinners. Ensar has described TURKEN's activities as being to counter the influence of Fethullah Gülen among the Turkish diaspora. Indeed, at home too, many of the activities targeted at the young may have been to challenge the momentum of the Gülenists.

The investment funds required for this panoply of activities are large. Apart from the Saudi donation of 2012, other known benefactors are the Torun brothers, Mehmet and Aziz, a football friend of the prime minister. In December 2017, the brothers' gas distribution company, Başkentgaz, paid 7,925,000 USD to Ensar for the construction of dormitories, routing these funds via Turkey's Red Crescent Organization.[12] Ensar forwarded them on to TÜRGEV.

In the opposition's view, many businessmen winning state contracts have been encouraged to contribute to these foundations. Lost in the confused reporting after the 17 December 2013 probe was that the prosecutors were also targeting TÜRGEV, Bilal Erdoğan, and his father.[13] Three months later, Sezgin Tanrıkulu, deputy chairman of the CHP, asked whether a naval vessel tender had been cancelled on the instructions of Erdoğan and "whether the changes were made deliberately in order to increase the tender price that was originally envisioned as 800 million euros, and whether 200 million of 400 million euros—which was made up of the increase in the tender price—was transferred to TÜRGEV as a donation."[14]

Substantial sums appear to have been needed abroad. TURKEN in the U.S. received 79 million USD in the five years to 30 June 2019. The donors are not identified.[15] In October 2020, an opposition deputy called for an investigation into whether funds earned by Eti Maden, the boron exporter owned by the Turkey Wealth Fund, were being diverted to TURKEN. Haluk Gani, the general manager of Eti Maden's U.S. subsidiary, was also secretary general of TURKEN.

Some of the funds required to operate these wide-ranging activities come from the state budget. In 2019, for instance, the Ministry of Education paid dormitory owners TL600 (100 USD) per month for each student, while the owners charged a similar amount to the students' families.[16] These figures indicate operating budgets for TÜRGEV and TÜGVA of a combined 35–40 million USD per year.

A regulatory change in 2014 allowed them and other non-governmental organizations to provide services to state *imam-hatip* schools. In 2016 and 2017, the Ministry of Education signed protocols with TÜRGEV and TÜGVA and with Ensar, recently in court over abuse in one of its dormitories.[17] The İstanbul Municipality, under the control of the AKP until mid-2019, was generous, paying Erdoğan-linked foundations 56 million USD up until the end of 2018.[18] The new CHP mayor would have nothing to do with this practice, taking back control of five dormitories financed by the municipality, and cancelling budgetary transfers. He has also sought, with less success, to unwind some of the property transactions in their favour.

TÜRGEV has been able to generate some fresh funds from provincial development agencies, which are under central government control, and has become a significant beneficiary of funds from the European Commission.

These foundations have made a contribution. They have restored part of the fabric of the country's Ottoman heritage, having fallen into ruin since the orders that ran the lodges and *medrese* were banned. They have caused learning again to resonate in the teaching rooms of the once revered *medrese* of Süleymaniye and the mosque of Mehmed the Conqueror. They have helped tens of thousands to further their education. They have also helped Erdoğan to reach out to the young of Turkey more successfully than his party's own youth movement.

During its first decade, the AKP scarcely had an explicit youth policy. It was only in 2011 that this began to develop, with the launch of a new Ministry of Youth and Sports (*Gençlik ve Spor Bakanlığı*) signalling an increased political interest in the youth. The next year saw Erdoğan's talk of the 'ideal young person carrying a computer in one hand and a *Kur'an* in the other.'[19] This process appears to have been driven by a need to combat the influence of Gülen and intensified by the wish to marginalize the Gezi Park generation of youth protesters. The ensuing policy draws on the traditional role of civil society in the Middle East of acting as charitable service providers, using these also to enhance the legitimacy of Erdoğan's regime.

TÜGVA has played a central role in this, using a mixture of indoctrination, extra-curricular training, service provision in the education sector, street activism, and humanitarian work. By 2019, it claimed 150,000 members. Its recruitment has been bolstered by the summer courses it runs for the Ministry of Education. In 2023, in İstanbul alone, 238 schools were allocated for its summer courses focused on *Kur'an* courses and sports activities. It also runs summer camps mobilizing youth in what have earlier been described as "rituals of thraldom for the state." Lecturers there hallow Abdülhamid II and the Gallipoli campaign during the First World War as indication that Turkey is a nation under constant attack.[20] The message is clearly xenophobic, and it is this spirit that underlies the ruling culture of the early 2020s, involving, as it has, Erdoğan's new alliance with the MHP.

As one of TÜGVA's founders wrote in 2018:

> The 'Sacred and Nationalist youth' described by [Kısakürek] is today's 'Native and National Youth'... It means protecting this flag, this homeland, and the values of this homeland. ... It means not being led, ruled, and the puppets of enemies from outside this homeland. It is to feel all the troubles of the *ummah* as deeply if they were taking place in one's own home. It is to struggle to the limits of one's strength to solve these problems.[21]

Bilal Erdoğan used TÜGVA's resources to campaign on his father's behalf in the critical constitutional referendum of 2017. The foundation's bulletin for that year notes that it mobilized 30,000 people throughout the country, with photographs showing its members marching with the president's son at their head.

Absent from all this is the president's eldest child, Ahmet Burak Erdoğan. Burak has developed into a ship owner, running a company trading under the names MB Denizcilik and Manta. As of February 2021, it had a fleet of ten dry-cargo vessels.[22] He has kept a low profile ever since a car accident in May 1998 killing the singer Sevim Tanürek. A medical certificate exempted him from military service.

Erdoğan has long experience with the courts. He spent seven months in prison in 1980–1981, one week in 1989 and four months in 1999. He was also fined in 1986 for building on protected land. But the system has acquitted him on charges of illegal profiteering, defaming the army, and numerous counts of peculation while mayor of İstanbul.[23] By the end of 2022, over 50,000 people (fifty-three of them aged twelve to fourteen) faced lawsuits for insulting him or the state, while as of mid-2024, the system kept figures like Demirtaş and Kavala in prison.

Social engineering

The AKP started as a radical, populist movement. It promised "a new and dynamic political will to start the economical development movement; to correct the improper distribution of income; to eradicate poverty; to eliminate disgruntlements [sic]; which is unifying, embracing, ensuring social peace, providing trust between institutions and the citizens."[24]

Growth there has been, and some reduction in poverty, but the main characteristic of the AKP's rule has been instrumentalizing the state. Indeed, the gains in poverty have in part been achieved by a social welfare budget comparable to that for defence for handing out to the needy and potentially supportive.

In general, living standards have improved, but on most measures of life quality, Turkey underperforms all thirty-eight OECD countries except Chile. For those with jobs, the work-life balance is affected by high levels of informal employment, extremely low and declining unionism, and strikingly poor occupational health and safety.[25] Turkish employees work at their main jobs longer than those of any other OECD member except Colombia. One third of employees work over fifty hours a week.

Unemployment averaged 9.4 per cent in 2023. Employment rates for women and the most vulnerable groups are the lowest in the OECD. The share of youth not in education, employment, or training is double the OECD average. Social insurance cover is low, being available to only 37 per cent of the population in 2019.[26] However, health indicators are generally good. During the two decades of the AKP, the number of physicians per thousand people has increased by one third and those of nurses and midwives by one half. Life expectancy has increased by five years, and mortality rates during birth and of children aged one to five have fallen by more than a half.

Inter-regional disparities are large: in İstanbul, average household income is nearly three times higher than in south-eastern Anatolia, the highest regional gap among OECD countries. Similarly large regional differences are observed with respect to educational attainment, access to broadband connection, and life expectancy.

All in all, the AKP's growth model is thus far from inclusive. Indeed, as it has benefitted businessmen close to the government and the small to medium-sized traders of Anatolia, it has led to a striking concentration of wealth. Between 2005 and 2014, the share of assets owned by the richest 1 per cent of the population rose from 41 per cent to 54 per cent.[27] In income distribution, Turkey is now less equitable than all OECD countries except Chile and Mexico.

The party's model has been conservative, rather than liberal or redistributive. This was masked in its first years when the economy was still under the tutelage of an IMF programme and the government aspiring to membership in the EU. But, initially with some hesitancy and then full-bloodedly, the AKP has been reducing checks on political involvement in business. The once autonomous authorities regulating banking, energy, telecommunications, and other key sectors have been brought under ministerial control. The Public Tender Law has been defanged. The powers of the state audit board have been slashed, and the Central Bank's semblance of autonomy shredded. The main state banks—Halk, Vakıflar and Ziraat—have become tools of the government.

Particularly privileged has been a clique of construction companies that have risen together with the AKP. A study of public sector tenders between 2004 and 2011 showed that companies directly connected to the party won 40 per cent of public construction and service tenders while members of the secular TÜSİAD, which represents companies contributing 50 per cent of value added in Turkey and 80 per cent of foreign trade and of corporate tax revenue, won only 10 per cent.[28] The respected Koç Group was openly targeted, though, together with other household names such as Sabancı and Eczacıbaşı, eventually established a *mode de vie* with the new masters.

Openly gaining from the change in regime, some first making their mark when Erdoğan was mayor of İstanbul, have been the AKP's new tigers who have fed on the projects of the state-owned Mass Housing Fund, TOKİ; the £5-billion new airport for İstanbul; prestige ventures such as the new presidential palace; and massive investments in motorways and high-speed train networks. Still on the president's agenda in 2024 was construction of a 45-kilometre canal to link the Black Sea and Marmara Sea, a plan which appalls many, including İstanbul's mayor, Ekrem İmamoğlu, bankers concerned over Turkey's bloated debt, and environmentalists worried about the threat to western İstanbul's water table. Its price tag is estimated at 65 billion USD.

Where governance is concerned, between 2013 and 2023, Turkey fell sixty-two places in Transparency International's annual survey of perceptions of corruption. It is a signatory of the OECD Anti-Bribery

Convention of 1997, but has yet to fulfil commitments to the EU over cooperation on tax affairs. Turkey has also slumped in ratings of rule of law and press freedom. To Erdoğan's critics, the New Turkey is a kleptocracy married with the collapse of the rule of law.[29] It is a far cry from the AKP's founding proclamation: "One of the main principles of our Party is the proverb, 'Unless everyone is free, no one is free.'"[30] As for the press, 90 per cent of the media is now owned by groups loyal to the government, though Turkey has ceded its title as the world's worst jailer of journalists.[31]

The quest for power and money aside, Erdoğan has also advanced a retro approach to the environment. His government has no plans to reduce power generation from coal and has adopted a minimalist approach to issues of climate change and the abatement of greenhouse gases.

Schooling remains inadequate at all levels, with public expenditure per student the lowest in the OECD. Classes teaching Sunni Islam are now compulsory in public schools despite rulings against the practice by the European Court of Human Rights and the Council of State. Darwinism has long been under threat from anti-evolution conservatives. The new school curriculum introduced in 2017 led to "the removal of the theory of evolution in favor of a theological explanation for the creation of the world; the inclusion of 'jihad', as an essential concept of 'our religion' [Islam]; and Pan-Turkist notions."[32]

Where gender issues are concerned, Turkey ranked 127th out of the 146 countries rated in the World Economic Forum's *Global Gender Gap Report 2024*.[33] The OECD links the problem to the low participation rate of women in the work force, one of the fifteen lowest in the world. Half the women who have jobs are only employed informally.

Of particular concern is violence against women. In a 2014 survey, 37.5 per cent of women complained of suffering violence during their lifetime, twice the average of Mediterranean Europe, according to the WEF.[34] Each year around 300 women die in such violence, but 2018 was particularly deplorable. The graphic artist, Vahit Tuna, mounted an installation in İstanbul's Kabataş of women's shoes—one pair for each of the 440 victims killed that year.

Giving campaigners some hope was Turkey's adherence to the Council of Europe Convention on preventing violence against women. Signed in İstanbul in July 2011 and since known as the İstanbul Convention, this was rapidly ratified by Turkey. However, in 2020, AKP deputies started voicing calls to withdraw. In spring 2021, Erdoğan issued a presidential decision cancelling Turkey's membership of the convention that it had briefly vaunted. Attacks on lesbian, gay, bisexual, and transgender communities were central to his 2023 electioneering, as was his well-worn mantra: "Family is sacred to us—a strong family means a strong nation."

Erdoğan and the Kurds

In the macho Turkey of the 2020s, it is hard to remember that during most of his career Erdoğan sought an accommodation with the country's Kurds. In 1991, as İstanbul head of Refah Party, he presented a paper to his party leader, Erbakan, stressing the need for education in the Kurdish language and calling for establishing local parliaments. The paper dismissed national security concerns surrounding Kurdish identity claims. It blamed Kemalist secular nationalism for creating the problem and suggested Islamic brotherhood as the alternative.

Kurds were prominent amongst his colleagues as mayor of İstanbul and later as prime minister. In his early electioneering, he proclaimed, "The Kurdish problem is not the issue of part of the population but rather it's the problem of the entire nation! It is my problem." This approach morphed into his Kurdish Initiative of 2009 and the Peace Process of 2012. During this, he announced that he would open negotiations with Abdullah Öcalan, the imprisoned PKK leader. He even stated: "A powerful Turkey should not fear a federal system."

All this came to an end in 2015. The pro-Kurdish HDP declared it would not trade the peace process to advance Erdoğan's quest for a strong presidency. In the elections that June, the AKP lost its majority in the Grand National Assembly. Erdoğan turned to the nationalists for support, abandoning what was left of his opening to the Kurds. Violence broke out. Erdoğan won back control of the Assembly.

Since then the pro-Kurdish HDP has been demonized, its leaders arrested while prosecutors seek to close it, and the party forced again to change its name, which as of mid-2024 was the Peoples' Equality and Democracy Party, DEM. Contesting Kurdish attempts to take control of north-east Syria has proved one of Erdoğan's key priorities, bringing him into protracted dispute with the U.S.. Vilifying Kurdish terrorism was a central theme of his nationalist drumbeat during the 2023 elections.

16

THE CENTURY OF TÜRKİYE

> *We will bring about the Century of Türkiye for the mothers whose hearts are racing for the future of their children and the dreams their fathers have for them. We will bring about the Century of Türkiye by meeting the expectations of our youth in all fields, from technology to art, from sports to environment. We will bring about the Century of Türkiye by fortifying the bridge we built from the past on the basis of our national and spiritual values with humanitarian and moral pillars. We will bring about the Century of Türkiye, making our country one of the ten great states in the world in politics, economy, technology, military, diplomacy and all fields.*
>
> President Erdoğan, 28 October 2022

Centenary

The first earthquake of 6 February 2023 came in the early hours of the morning. It lasted a sickening eighty seconds. The second one caught survivors salvaging for clothing and food from their shaken homes to combat the icy Anatolian chill. The earthquakes were among the most brutal in the Levant for 400 years. The official death toll exceeded 50,000 for Turkey and 8,000 for Syria. Actual deaths may have been in six figures; surveys carried out after the Marmara earthquake of 1999 indicated that official figures captured only half the losses.

That previous earthquake had underscored Turkey's seismic vulnerability at the zone of collision between the Eurasian, African, and Arabian geological plates. But a quarter of a century later, the government was unprepared, and its response was dismal. The civil authorities were overwhelmed. For the first thirty-six hours—critical for saving lives—the military were excluded from playing a role. The Minister of Interior had insisted that his AFAD, the Disaster and Emergency Management Directorate, should manage the situation alone.

Aid convoys piled up as AFAD wilted in the face of the catastrophe. Aid teams arriving in the disaster zone and asking where to go were greeted with a shrug. Shelter and blankets were urgently needed, yet three days after the disaster, the state relief agency, Kızılay—managed by members of the Menzil order—was holding 2,000 tents in its warehouses and refusing to release them unless paid.

Erdoğan's response was to threaten rather than comfort. He took a day longer than the opposition to visit the stricken cities and then declared martial law in the area. Three weeks later, he asked for forgiveness from the citizens of Adıyaman for the inadequate support. By then the opposition was accusing him of direct responsibility for the deaths. It pointed to his amnesty for the owners of buildings that failed to meet safety standards. For Erdoğan, this amnesty had "solved the problems" of 144,556 people from Kahramanmaraş and 205,000 from Hatay. These numbers, proclaimed before the 2018 elections, were in line with those afflicted in 2023 when 97,000 homes were completely or severely damaged in Kahramanmaraş and 156,700 in Hatay.

Despite all this, his ratings held up. And so it was to prove in the elections that May. In the ten of Turkey's eighty-one provinces most affected by the devastation, his share of the vote in the first round of the presidential election was 56.4 per cent, only marginally down from his previous showing.

It should have been an easy run for Erdoğan, entrenched in power and controlling the media and state machinery. The 2017 referendum had reshaped the country's governance, ending Turkey's 70-year commitment to parliamentary democracy and ushering in a system where the president alone exercised executive authority, with unsupervised power to appoint and dismiss ministers and high officials. He (or she) could remain head of a party, dissolve the Grand National Assembly, and issue presidential decrees without laws for the Constitutional Court to review.

This change had been assured via a knife-edge vote, a 51.4 per cent majority won in circumstances that could hardly have been more contentious. The referendum had been staged with the post-coup state of emergency still in force. Observers from the Organization for Security and Cooperation in Europe and the Council of Europe had other complaints too, including violence against opponents of the government and lopsided media coverage. It was, they concluded, "an unlevel playing field... The dismissal or detention of thousands of citizens negatively affected the political environment... late changes in counting procedures removed an important safeguard."[1] This last point was the most egregious. Halfway through the counting process, the authorities allowed the inclusion of unstamped ballot papers. The opposition contends that these totalled a potentially decisive 1.5 million votes.

It was thus a visibly shocked Erdoğan who shuffled onto the balcony of the president's Bosphorus palace in Tarabya in the small hours of 17 April 2017 to announce Turkey would be changing to the autocratic presidential system he had sought. His tone, while testy, seemed to indicate that even he had doubts as to whether he had won.

The changes came fully into effect with the 2018 elections. In these, Erdoğan allied with the MHP, the two securing 57 per cent of the seats in the Grand National Assembly. Erdoğan himself, ensconced in his grandiose $615-million new governing palace, was now not only political *reis* (leader) of the country but also chairman of the newly created Turkey Wealth Fund, adding to his powers control of Turkey's oil and natural gas companies, Turkish Airlines, the İstanbul Stock Exchange, and one quarter of the country's banking assets.

But with this untrammelled mastery came the launch of a giddy profligacy that would empty the country's coffers. Up to 2018, AKP governments had financed Turkey's dash for growth by allowing its current account deficit to rise. From then onwards, the government started drawing on the nation's foreign exchange reserves. Erdoğan appointed his son-in-law, Dr Berat Albayrak, as Minister of Finance, and the latter dutifully acted on Erdoğan's conviction that interest, together with exchange rates and inflation, constitute "the devil's triangle." As inflation took off, he thus embarked on slashing interest rates rather than raising them. For the IMF and the international markets, which each year roll over around 200 billion USD of Turkish debt, such policies were eccentric, if not voodoo.

The cost of defending the Turkish lira rose. After spending an awe-inspiring 140 billion USD to protect the currency, the country's net foreign exchange reserves fell to a negative 50 billion USD.[2] By November 2020, family links could no longer protect the haughty son-in-law, who overnight moved from heir apparent to scapegoat. Erdoğan brought in a new economic team, but the policies continued, with interest rates brought down as inflation soared to 85 per cent in the year before the election. Come 2023 and, as further funds were spent propping up the Turkish lira, net reserves tumbled to their lowest level ever, a negative value of 65 billion USD. In five years, the Turkish lira had lost three quarters of its value against the U.S. dollar. The rating agencies were appalled, grouping this G20 country with Cambodia, Mongolia, Montenegro, Nicaragua, and Uganda as "highly speculative" and with a negative outlook. As 2023 continued, pre-election generosity morphed into austerity. By mid-2024, net reserves and the country's rating had improved, but inflation was still over 60 per cent.

In the elections, the opposition stressed the need to rebuild the country's institutions and called for *helalleşme* or mutual forgiveness, a word with the emotive appeal of use on deathbeds or before battles or long separations. The state of the economy gave Erdoğan's opponents ready ammunition, and they were buoyed by an opinion poll finding that for 56 per cent of Turks the economy was the main problem.[3] But they had to contend with Erdoğan's cornucopia of pre-election hand-outs—a jump in pensions, striking subsidies in natural gas and electricity prices for households, boosts to the minimum wage and civil servants' salaries, hiked up social security payments, and free internet for students.

On the ground, concern over the economy seeped away. For most members of the religious communities, the privileged access of their community to the state machinery was more important. When Kemal Kılıçdaroğlu, the opposition leader, sat down with a largely AKP audience for a four-hour television session, this showed scant interest in the economy, unemployment, tackling poverty, social justice, or rebuilding the shattered finances of the country. With the state TRT continuing to shroud him, it was one of the rare occasions when Kılıçdaroğlu could reach a mass audience. Indeed, the interview attracted 25 million views in the three days after it was broadcast. But the audience's concerns were terrorism and national survival.[4] And it was on these visceral issues—and the equally emotive "threats" to family values of the LGBTQ community and refugees—that Erdoğan had focused.

This mix was central to the New Turkey, which he launched in 2014 with his vision of a nation of "flag and prayer." And it inspired the holistic rhetoric of his new Century of Türkiye, the galvanizing panoply of dreams that he launched in Ankara's largest hall on 28 October 2022.

The next year would mark the 100th anniversary of the emergence of the Republic from the rubble of the Ottoman Empire, and that October afternoon Erdoğan set his stamp on the second hundred years: "The designs of the imperialists on Turkey have never been lacking... Instead of relying on the superiority of the national will, our country has wasted its golden years in the hands of the administrations that remained under the control of the forces of tutelage." Atatürk, Menderes, Özal—they had tried to create democracy and development in an independent country, and been blocked. His party's own twenty years had not been passed in a rose garden without thorns: "All the apparatus of the imperialists, tutelageists and putschists at home and abroad have been unleashed on us."

Reopening Ayasofya to prayer was a symbol of this casting off of tutelage, and his Century of Türkiye the golden prospect to which Turks could aspire: "Our country has come to the position that it is not a follower but one that is followed." He continued: "We are the only country that makes sincere efforts for peace by establishing equitable, moral and fair relations with all parties at a time when wars, conflicts and tensions are escalating around us."

His Century of Türkiye has seventeen themes, the number corresponding to the sixteen Turkic states commemorated in the president's coat of arms plus the Republic. These themes range from the practical to the moral, including strength and compassion, justice and peace, success and sustainability, education and the digital world.

Some 10,000 people had been assembled to hear his rousing words, and these set the tone for his protracted re-election campaign. Religion, nation, the family—these resonate in a country where near jingoism is inherent in the education system and sedulously fanned by a loyal media. In the elections of May 2023 and March 2024, his party won 36 per cent of the vote and its ally, the MHP, and other overtly nationalist and religious parties around 20 per cent of the vote. To call the Turkish electorate conservative is to mask its underlying passions.

As for Erdoğan, with a steep fall in the votes of the AKP and MHP—down from 50 per cent of the vote in 2019 to 40.5 per cent in 2024—he is increasingly reliant on the two new partners he welcomed in March 2023. The first is Hüda Par, a Kurdish Sunni Islamist party, usually associated with the Kurdish Hezbollah, a group encouraged by the Turkish military to counter the PKK terrorist group and assassinating some 500 PKK members in the 1990s. The party wants restrictions on the freedom of religion and worship to be lifted, adultery criminalized, and religious marriages to be recognized. Its poor vote, only 0.6% in 2024, means it may be less listened to than the other ally from 2023, the New Refah Party.

This is named after the Refah Party which carried the pro-Islamic vote from 1983, brought its leader Necmettin Erbakan to the prime ministry and was then banned in 1998. New Refah won a striking 6.2% of the vote of March 2024. It is headed by Fatih Erbakan, son of the mercurial Necmettin, who has a less controlled message than his father ever did—fundamentalist but also anti-vaccine, advocating the abolition of laws protecting women from violence, and arguing that fourteen-year-old children are suitable for marriage. And he is now a pivotal figure in the country's politics.

Addressing his followers from his party's balcony on the night of the 2024 elections, Erdoğan gave a mollifying promise to listen to the message of the elections. But the lessons that he draws may be about what he needs to do to retain power, not those required to reduce the continuing polarization of his country.

Erdoğan and his heartland

Erdoğan's open recourse to religion goes back to at least January 2012, when he told an AKP meeting: "There is the raising of a pious youth. [...] do you expect from us, from the AKP, which has a conservative identity, to raise an atheist generation? [...] We will be raising a conservative democratic generation, loyal to the historical values and principles of the nation, and the fatherland."[5]

Prior to this, the party had done little to revive religious education. In 1997, the generals had required that *imam-hatip* middle schools be subsumed into an extended schooling system, and it was not until the 2012–2013 academic year that secondary school students were again allowed to join these schools. To many, that marked the launch of Erdoğan's programme for his "pious generation." Indeed, in the next six years, the numbers of those enrolled in religious education went up to 2 million—0.6 million in *imam-hatip* middle schools, 0.8 million in *imam-hatip* lycées, and 0.7 million in mushrooming *Kur'an* courses. There was also a surge in the number of pilgrims to Mecca; since Saudi Arabia caps visitors during the holy month, the rise has been in *umre*, the minor pilgrimage in other months, to almost 500,000 people per year before COVID-19 limited travel. (See illustration 29.)

The *Diyanet* has facilitated this growth in pilgrimage, playing a more active pastoral role, with its share of the budget increased. Erdoğan first appointed as its head a co-student from the *İmam-Hatip* School in Fatih, Ali Bardakoğlu, replacing him in 2010 with Mehmet Görmez, who encouraged cooperation of the *Diyanet* with the Gülen movement. A year after the coup attempt, Görmez was succeeded by Ali Erbaş, one of his deputies. It was with Erbaş, sword in hand, that Erdoğan reopened Ayasofya as a mosque.[6] All of these have eschewed reference to Atatürk in the Friday sermons distributed by the *Diyanet*, even when the Friday falls on the anniversary of the death of the Republic's greatest statesman.

With official Islam long on his side, Erdoğan has also capitalized upon his relations with the religious orders. He has tirelessly cultivated these formally illegal communities, assiduous in his respect for their elders, visiting their *şeyh*, and attending the funerals of leaders who have passed away. This commitment has assured him the electoral support of almost all the major orders of the country—the main exceptions being the Süleymancıs, some fractions of the Nurcus, and, from 2014, the Gülenists. Apart only from a wobble by İskenderpaşa, the others have mobilized their followers on his behalf through almost all the three presidential elections, seven general elections, five local elections, and three constitutional referenda held since 2002—and been amply rewarded in visibility and patronage.

The religious orders have proved a source of the disciplined manpower that Erdoğan's party could not supply. This was evident at the beginning as he sought to mould the institutions of central and local government to his will. It was also evident after the 2016 coup attempt. With the purging of Gülenists, the Menzil community in particular began to fill their place, not least in the armed forces and security services. "From Pennsylvania to Menzilvania" runs a doggerel referring to Gülen's place of residence in the U.S..

This order's pervasive infiltration of the judiciary is portrayed in *Metastaz* (Metastasis), a book as graphic as its title.[7] The *tarikat*'s influence is also reported in the Ministry of Interior and in particular in the Ministry of Health. In the early years after the AKP came to power, it made space in that ministry for other groups such as the Fethullahçı, Süleymancı, İskenderpaşa, Hak Yol, and Nurcu.[8] As the 10-year term as minister of Professor Recep Akdağ advanced, these other groups were squeezed out, and in January 2013, Erdoğan appointed his school companion, Dr Mehmet Müezzinoğlu, to the ministry with the apparent mission of curbing the pro-Menzil excesses.[9] The new minister faced a hostile bureaucracy that stalled his efforts. Three years later, Akdağ returned to his earlier post. In 2018, Erdoğan turned to his personal doctor, Dr Fahrettin Koca. Reportedly, the latter's task was to increase the influence of İskenderpaşa. Six years later, a figure reported as close to Menzil was again put in charge of the Ministry.[10]

Helping Erdoğan lure the orders to his cause were three factors. First was the sense of him as a fellow Nakşibendi, educated in the *Kur'an* and its enduring values. Second, most of them were masonic in their approach to power, happy to work alongside politicians to advance the interests of their members and increase the size of the crumbs which fell their way. And third was the weakening of the leadership of these often imperious communities. The rise and fall of Gülen we have considered above. The Süleymancı and İskenderpaşa lost their charismatic leaders just as the AKP began its rise. Erenköy found itself attacked for its commercial alliances. İsmailağa still has to put behind it the muted struggle for succession to Ustaosmanoğlu. The main Menzil community has been particularly riven by splits following death.

The orders and Islam, present and future

The challenges lived by Erdoğan and his regime have come to be a test for the orders as well. The state has filled a number of the gaps that had long drawn families into their gravity field. As public profession of piety becomes the norm, the orders have less to offer the individual, at least where ritual is concerned. The line separating conservative and secular lifestyles remains, while believers are adopting a more selective approach to Islam. "Twenty years ago, a youngster who wanted to be religious would have looked for a guide and tried to do what he was told," Etyen Mahcupyan, an adviser to a former AKP prime minister, says. "But now that youngster wants to redefine Islam for himself, and no guide can do that."[11]

Such comments do not capture the multiple levels on which the orders make their mark.

Islam in the Ottoman Empire was rich, deep, and variegated. The bookish and often learned *ulema*, the Sufi orders with their mystical traditions, the urban intellectuals, the craftsmen and tradesmen of the towns with their vestiges of the medieval guilds, the rural communities—each followed different forms of Sunni Islam, and lived and interacted with their Alevi brethren and with Armenian, Greek, and Jewish minorities.

A century of the Republic has reduced the range of Islam on offer. The *Diyanet* follows a narrower course than did the *şeyhülislam* and imperial *medrese*. The prayer leaders and preachers of the country are now civil servants, their Friday sermons often dictated by Ankara. The intellectual debate on Islam is limited, even if some intellectuals have begun to enrich the field, not least Sezai Karakoç, who argued the rich collective conscience of Muslims is leading to a rebirth of Islam; Hayrettin Karaman, whose knowledge of the legal aspects of Islam helps address which sociocultural innovations may be embraced by Muslims; İsmet Özel, who focuses on how the culture of Islam is carried on by collective memory; and İsmail Kara, who has systematized the key trends in late Ottoman and republican Sunni Islamic thought.[12]

The Sufi orders too have a narrower cultural offer. Throughout the long centuries of the Empire, mysticism was an integral component of Ottoman Islam, sheltering under its wings a number of heterodox traditions drawing on the distant cultural roots of the shamanistic Turcoman tribes. Many dervish lodges were centres of erudition and instruction. The leading Sufis were widely trained and read. They drew on the Islamic theosophers of the past such as Ibn Arabi. Poetry was central to their culture. Rumi's *Mesnevi* was a celebration of love for the divine and earthly creation, and figures such as Rumi's near contemporary Yunus Emre and, almost half a millennium later, Niyazi Misri and Galip Dede show the abiding vigour of this love—and tolerance—in the Sufis' world. The dervish orders were a central part of a world of spiritual quest. Their rituals were open to believers of all classes, with the orders often acting as a mediating force between the privileged and the less so.

Descriptions of their shuttering by the Republic tend to focus on the pillaging of their treasures of centuries. But the moral loss has also been incalculable, and it is on this that modern thinkers tend to focus.

For Kenan Gürsoy, a professor of philosophy, Sufism "has aesthetics, philosophy, a spiritual side. But this side has been slowly lost. That is where our problem lies." His own roots trace back to that world. His grandfather was a respected Ottoman intellectual and educationalist who in his forties became a prominent Rifai. For Gürsoy himself, earlier Erdoğan's ambassador to the Vatican, today's religious communities are "the fruits of degeneration and a decadent society... There is confusion and distress in our civil and economic life. These communities are the fruit of the mixing up of everything—pedagogy, philosophy, administration. We suffer from alienation from our culture."[13]

The traditional Sufi values of tolerance have been edged off the stage by the intolerant message of the Nakşibendis. It was with this message that Erdoğan conquered the craftsmen and townsmen of Anatolia, and, blended with nationalism, it is continued by the party that has led Turkey since 2002.

The transition from the protean and versatile Islam of Ottoman times to the more homogeneous blend of today needs to be borne in mind when looking at the state of religion in the country. But, at least where numbers are concerned, Islam is flourishing. Nearly three fifths of Turks consider themselves 'very' or 'extremely' religious. This was the finding of a study published in 2007 by TESEV, the Turkish Economic and Social Studies Foundation, a solidly based İstanbul NGO. In this, 59.3 per cent of respondents classed themselves in these terms and a further 33.9 per cent as religious.[14]

This study was carried out three years after AKP had come to power. The same two academics had carried out a similar study seven years earlier.[15] In the earlier survey, the share of very and extremely religious individuals was a mere half of the figure researched in 2006.

Much had changed between the surveys. Turkey was no longer reeling from the military soft coup of 1997 and rampant inflation and, in the early days of the AKP, was a more tolerant society with a perspective of membership in the European Union. Had the share jumped because Turks had altered in response to these, because they now felt free to express their true feelings, or because they felt peer pressure to overstate their religiosity? Probably a mixture of all three.

Subsequent research has confirmed the importance that Turks give to Islam in their identity. A survey carried out by the *Diyanet* in 2013 saw 87.5 per cent of respondents class themselves as religious or considerably religious. It also found nearly 70 per cent of the respondents express full or partial appreciation of religious organizations and communities—while also favouring state monitoring of these.[16] Four years later, and with the dust settled after the pro-Gülen coup, another survey recorded one fifth of respondents saying they were or had been linked to a *cemaat* or *tarikat*.[17] A third survey, carried out in 2018, found that parents ranked free summer schooling in *Kur'an* courses and foreign languages as equal, with both far preferable to sending their children to sports schools, computer courses, or summer camps.[18]

İsmail Kara, one of the most creative of recent Turkish commentators on religion, is encouraged by the growing number of younger people attending mosques for the Friday midday prayers and by the improved debate at home. In his opinion, there has been a rise and diversification of education levels in religious families—and this despite the "deeply negative correlation" between the growth of religious members of universities, intellectual life, and the media, and their contributions to Islamic thought.[19]

For him, through the twilight of the Ottoman Empire, İstanbul surpassed Cairo as the intellectual centre of the Muslim world. Those years, it was on the shores of the Bosphorus rather than of the Nile where the debate raged on how the faith should tackle the challenges—material and scientific—from the Christian West as Britain, France, and Russia hacked away at the *Dar al-Islam*.

The founders of the Republic weakened Turkey's links with its Muslim past, not least when they abolished the Caliphate and vaulted from the Ottoman alphabet to a Latin-based one. Those years, Western historians of the Middle East, supporting Europe's post-World War I narrative, played down the region's Ottoman dimension, as did Arabic writers. Kara comments that, despite the title, almost all the figures in Albert Hourani's *Arabic Thought in the Liberal Age, 1798–1939* were Ottoman citizens.

Kara sees religion in Turkey within the larger context of Islam in the world, arguing "all of the problems and issues that produced and maintained the conditions for the emergence of Islamism, especially those of colonialism, occupation, and Orientalism, still exist and continue to shatter the lives of many Muslims."[20] He thus finds it natural that Islamist parties should have developed in Turkey.

As the surveys cited above show, the hold of religion was already strong before the AKP took the country's helm. The conventicles had kept the flame of Islamic learning alive through the early republican period, and the *tarikat* were crucial after the 1950s when they helped poor and more pious new emigrants to the cities. Their activities strengthened conservative and later Islamist political groups in the indigent urban fringes, transforming Turkish bureaucracy and business communities during this process. In this period, their role in stabilizing society was welcomed by the central authorities, but today the orders are suspect to the state for challenging its monopoly of religious education and yet tolerated when they look to bodies such as the *Diyanet* to reassure them of their legitimacy. It is, as Kara describes it, an equivocal situation with the orders both opponents and beneficiaries of the system in a symbiotic yet mutually distrustful relationship between the state and religious communities.

For Kara, the Gülen movement is an aberration. In his view, its members:

> began to establish branches and initiated activities with encouragement from bigger Cold War political forces in Central Asia, the Balkans, and

> former Soviet Republics. They were blessed by the support and protection of various political authorities both within Turkey and internationally... especially from the US and England... They assumed that their global spread and influence was due to their own efforts and strategic genius, denying the fact that the sources of that power belonged to others' encouragement and promotion.[21]

The past half century has seen modern communication tools creating a new relationship between *şeyh* and disciple. The mass linking of Menzil penitents with their *şeyh* is only one instance of the mechanization of these relations. The Internet too has impinged, with 45 per cent of Turks describing this as their main source of religious knowledge.[22]

Today, the orders act as some counterbalance to the centralizing authority of the *Diyanet* and Erdoğan's Ankara. In this netherworld between politics and religion, the world of Sufi spirituality is often relegated to the background. Erenköy's Osman Nuri Topbaş offers a calming voice of religious reassurance, and other preachers, not least Cevat Akşit, have their followers. But as the years go by, many of the orders seem led less by the pedagogical zeal that inspired their founders than by financial imperatives. This is as true of Menzil with their business empire as the Süleymancıs who eschew commerce but run a fundraising operation of callous efficiency.

Fuelled on the steroids of social media and gorged on Mammon, several orders have taken commercial shapes which no history of their development in Islam foresaw. It is approaching a situation where Islam needs to be saved more from some of its prominent practitioners than from the state.

Most of these communities have been active again in Turkey for three times the period that Erdoğan has been in power. A number, some treated in the annexes, have fallen aside, reduced to irrelevance or racked by scandal. But they are the living heirs of a tradition that has created a sense of brotherhood and sisterhood for the faithful for over a millennium and addressed the dilemma at the heart of Islam, as of every religion: the need to bridge the gap between the believer and his god.

The orders were an inherent part of the Islam that the Turkish tribes brought with them from Khorasan. They were central to the practice of faith by thirty-six Ottoman Sultans and six centuries of their subjects. And they protected the faith during the brief years of early republican secularism. For a generation, they were on the defensive, but the past half century has seen them regaining their traditional role as a core component of Sunni religious culture in Turkey and its daily practice. The politicians who have ruled the country for the last three generations have embraced these religious communities, few more so than Erdoğan himself.

He took office in a pluralistic parliamentary democracy, with a free press, variegated television, and a relatively independent judiciary. He has switched the country to a presidential system, less French or American than Putinesque. Its ethos is that of the xenophobic generation of the poets of his youth. Its symbols are the prayer, the flag, and the drone.

This New Turkey has the Nakşibendi orders as its bedrock. They were rife before him. They are pervasive today, their social base broadened, their structures resilient, their presence as ubiquitous as the Sufis of previous centuries. Whatever happens to Erdoğan, they and their millions of adherents will be there to shape his legacy and to colour the contours of post-secular Turkey.

ANNEXES

ANNEX A
ALEVIS AND BEKTAŞIS

Alevis in the New Turkey

The paradox of the Ottomans was that, while they were among the most faithful servants of Sunni Islam, a large proportion of the population maintained a form of Islam at fierce divergence with the ruling orthodoxy.[1]

Today, the Alevis constitute the second-largest belief community in Turkey, an integral part of the humanity if not the governance of the country. They account for between one sixth and one tenth of the population of Turkey, yet they are treated by the state almost as if they do not exist.[2] The *Diyanet*, whose 130,000 personnel include all the mosques' preachers, and the Ministry of Education, whose 900,000 teachers enforce compulsory religious lessons, understand only Sunni Islam of the Hanefi school.

For a brief period, it seemed that Erdoğan's Turkey might follow a more tolerant course towards a community itself characterized by a religious tolerance forged through centuries as a minority. But, as Erdoğan has doubled down on his New Turkey, so he and the Turkish state have turned their back on the Alevis.

Three decisions by the European Court of Human Rights in 2015 and 2016 confirm the Alevis' beleaguered status. The court found that compulsory religious lessons with a Sunni curriculum must be converted to selective lessons and be taught with egalitarian curricula, that the Alevis' *Cemevi* are places of worship and must be treated with rights equal to those provided to other places of worship, and that all belief groups should be accorded a legal identity with state funds divided between all of them. In the more than eight years since these judgements, scant progress has been made on implementing them.

It is all a far cry from the expectations with which the Alevis greeted the formation of the Republic. Equality in a secular country has proved a pipe dream. Instead, current policies appear designed to promote assimilation of the Alevis. Over time, the CHP has become open to the Alevis, yet the party knows it has to tread carefully; in 2006, one quarter of Turks did not want someone from a different sect as a neighbour.[3] That its most recent candidate for the presidency, Kemal Kılıçdaroğlu, the party's leader from 2010 to 2023, was an Alevi broke uncharted ground.

Turkey's Alevis share with Iran's Shiites respect for the imamate of the *Ahl-al Bayt* (the People of the House), the designation in Islam for the family of the Prophet, particularly his daughter Fatimah, her husband Ali (who was also the Prophet's cousin), and their descendants. The Alevis consider their approach to Islam broader than that of the Shiites who, they contend, believe that the *Kur'an* is only narrowly open to interpretation. As Doğan Bermek, chairman of the Alevi Philosophy Centre, ADO, says: "Alevis do not fear God but only bear love for him. They do not believe in paradise or hell but an infinite circulation until one reaches the status of perfection and reunion with where the believer comes from."[4]

The Alevis do not have mosques but centres of gathering and worship known as *Cemevi.* They differ from Shiites (and Sunnis) in the lower importance they give to the *hajj* and to regular prayers (generally three times a day in the case of the Shiites; five times a day for the Sunnis). They allow use of alcohol, but not to the extent of troubling others. They do not require women to be covered, and allow them to participate fully and unveiled in their ceremonies. They believe in single marriage but allow *muta* (second and temporary) marriage.

They argue that Alevism may be little known as a result of its continuous exclusion by Sunni commentators but is a third interpretation of Islam, to be set beside Sunnism and Shiism, and differentiated from them. That said, Alevis' beliefs and practices are sufficiently heterodox to be almost as heretical for the Shiites of Iran as for the orthodox Sunni of Turkey.

Entry to the community requires introduction by one of its elders. This will often be a *dede*, the local leader, and every *dede* is affiliated with one of the *ocak*. These, the prime social structure of Alevis, constitute a link to the traditions of the original Turcoman settlers. Their head is considered endowed with a sacred lineage. The site of the *ocak* is fixed—the word also has the meaning of hearth and recalls ancestors' gatherings around a fire—but the adherents may roam. Affiliation tends to be hereditary and often follows, though is not restricted by, tribal links.

Today, there are six main *ocak* and some fifty smaller ones, and until the rise of the *tarikat* and *cemaat*, the *ocak* were the largest faith-based subgroups in the Republic. They constitute a hidden power, but the relative neglect of their activities by Turkey's press and politicians reflects their general unwillingness to act outside the spiritual sphere and their lack of success in creating an assembly to voice political demands. The leading *ocak* include the Ağuçan (Ağuiçen) of Dersim and Amasya, Baba Mansur (Mazgirt in Tunceli province), Sarı Saltık (Hozat, Tunceli), and Zeynel Abidin (Mineyik, Malatya).

The modernization of Turkey has not been kind to the Alevis. They were generally supportive of the Young Turks. In 1921, some Kurdish Alevi tribes in the Koçgiri region east of Sivas rebelled, being ruthlessly suppressed by Mustafa Kemal's nationalists. However, most Alevi tribal leaders backed the new state, including during the *Şeyh* Said rebellion of Sunni Kurds. In the 1930s, the Kurdish Alevis again came into the cross-sights of Ankara through their hostility to taxation and, in particular, to the 1934 law allowing the forced relocation of people to promote cultural homogeneity. As the decade advanced, so did resistance in the Kurdish Alevis' heartland in the massif between Sivas and Lake Van.

In early 1937, one chieftain, Seyid Riza, convened an *ocak* gathering at the Alevi shrine at Halvori on their sacred Munzur River. The subsequent Dersim rebellion lasted six months. The government invited Riza to peace talks, only to hang him, his eighteen-year-old son, and five others. The military killed between 13,160 purported rebels (the official figure) and 40,000 (a possibly exaggerated estimate from the 1940s).[5] The death toll was at least ten times that at Guernica and twice that at Srebrenica, but there has been no Picasso or international tribunal to perpetuate awareness.

After the Second World War, with the advance of industrialization and the lures of Western consumerism on ever more pervasive display, the flow from village to city became a flood. This social convulsion was quick to unleash political turmoil. Alevi migrants—in the cities of Turkey as well as the embryonic diaspora—were often radicalized by the Republic's creed of secularization, the pressures for assimilation in their new environment, and the calls for social justice resonating through Western Europe in the 1960s.

For a brief period after the 1960 coup, the new rulers considered establishing an office for non-Sunni denominations within the *Diyanet*. This idea did not last long, and subsequent years saw the Alevis' position worsen.

In October 1966, they launched their own party, the Unity Party (from 1969, the Turkey Unity Party, TBP). This won 2.8 per cent of the vote in 1969 and eight seats in the Grand National Assembly, but by 1977 it had disappeared from the Grand National Assembly.

In the clashes of the 1960s and 1970s, the Alevis became identified with the left, and were targeted by the para-state. Attacks by militant youth of the Nationalist Action Party led to 111 deaths in Alevi communities in Kahramanmaraş in 1978 and 57 deaths in Çorum in 1980. Further killings of Alevis took place in 1993 in the arson of the Madımak Hotel in Sivas where 33 died, and the shootings and police violence in the Gazi District in İstanbul costing 23 lives in 1995.

Demirel, prime minister from 1991 to 1993 and then president, was among those concerned that pro-Sunni policies were threatening the social fabric. He gave support to what has since been a significant if controversial spokesman for the Alevis, the CEM Foundation (the *Cumhuriyetçi Eğitim ve Kültür Merkezi Vakfı*—Republican Education and Cultural Central Foundation).

The Bektaşi order—coopted, then hobbled

Invigorating Turkish Alevism through the centuries was the Bektaşi order of dervishes. This is one of the great *tarikat*, dating back to the heroic years of the first Ottomans, inspiring the Sultans' Janissaries in their victories and regicides, and surviving persecution in the early nineteenth century to imbue the Young Turks. Its adherents were from high and low and found throughout the Empire.

Today, the Bektaşis are the main Sufi movement in Albania, but are much diminished in the Republic they had helped foster. The proscribing of their activities in the 1920s led to the suppression of their gatherings and the pillaging of their sanctuaries, not least of the treasures at the complex tracing back to Haci Bektaş himself.

This once revered shrine has now been restored, and every August admirers of the thirteenth-century saint gather for a festival in his honour. This had some early eccentricities, including a motorcyclists' wall of death, but has began to gain a more established profile. At the turn of the century, Ecevit visited it as prime minister to announce policies favouring the poor.

A few years later, Erdoğan made his own visit, a move he repeated in 2022. But the Bektaşis' own festival has recently been displaced by one sponsored by the Ministry of Culture and Tourism, while a dispute continues over leadership of the order in Turkey.

This has two leaders. One, known as *Çelebi*, is hereditary, dating back to the time of Hacı Bektaş Veli, with a line of incumbents claiming spiritual succession to the thirteenth-century saint, taking over direction of the *külliye*, and being recognized by the village groups of Alevis as their spiritual authority.[6] The second is the *Dedebaba*, elected by the *dede* whom the various Bektaşi communities had themselves elected.[7] The *Dedebaba*, usually but not always unmarried, lived in the Hacibektaş complex, often sharing this uneasily with the *Çelebi*. The appointment of the *Dedebaba* needed confirmation by the Ottoman administration—and this petition had to be sent by the *Çelebi*, giving the latter a degree of authority.

The *Dedebaba* at the time of the formation of the Republic was Salih Niyazi, a figure appreciated by Mustafa Kemal who, despite the closure of the *tekke*, for over a year tolerated the conventicle that Niyazi ran at a hotel in Ankara. In 1930, Niyazi moved to Albania, home of a particularly vibrant Bektaşi community who elected him as their leader. For over a decade, he was accepted as the spiritual leader of the Bektaşis worldwide. But in 1942, he was murdered in his *tekke* by the Italians, and his successor died shortly after, committing suicide after killing a communist official who had come to arrest him.

A group of the order's members, meeting in Cairo in 1949, chose the Albanian Ahmed Sırrı Baba to take on the role of leader. Sırrı Baba was invited to Turkey and met with President Celal Bayar. Just as Menderes was preparing to allow Sırrı Baba to settle in Hacibektaş, Kemalists struck back, arresting him for holding an *Ayin-i Cem* in İstanbul.

He was exiled back to Egypt and, shortly after, with the seizure of power by Nasser, was to lose the protection of Kings Farouk and Zog, his revenue, and his *tekke* in its splendid cavernous dwellings in the Mokattam hills behind the citadel.[8] Diabetes led to the amputation of one of his legs. Alone with his family and receiving occasional visiting Bektaşis, he died, probably early in 1963, and the order in Egypt with him.

The Bektaşis have revived in post-communist Albania. The Bektashi World Centre in Tirana claims that their *Kryegjysh*, Arch-leader—Edmond Brahimaj, Baba Mondi (b. 1959)—is the head of the worldwide Bektaşi community. This claim is accepted by the Pope and a number of world leaders. In 2015, Erdoğan joined Baba Mondi in cutting the ribbon for a reconstructed mosque near Tirana.

Most Turkish Bektaşis reject the Albanians' claims, but are divided over who is the current *Dedebaba*, one pole following a *dede* in Ankara and the other one in İzmir. This division has weakened the movement, dimming the lustre of the celebrations each August at Hacıbektaş.

The hereditary *Çelebi* continue to play a role in the Alevi community, the heads of the Ulusoy family asserting a status comparable to the leaders of the main tribal *ocak* of the country. Not many Bektaşis share this sense of their importance, and the family too is split, with two branches of it uneasily sharing the title of *postnişin* at Hacibektaş.[9] Neither has the prestige or personality to answer the quest of some Bektaşis for a leader.

Today, the main Bektaşi groups take the form of cultural associations drawing on the rich literary and musical traditions of the Bektaşis. Such associations generally keep their distance from the state, with the main exception to this being the CEM Foundation. This was founded by İzzettin Doğan, the *dede* of the Ağuçan *ocak,* whose father, Hüseyin Doğan (1902–1983), was respected by successive generations of Ankara politicians. The son has proved less adroit.

Of lasting impact is Doğan's delayed filing of the three dossiers that would later lead to the judgements of the European Court of Human Rights in the Alevis' favour. Doğan held these back for seven years so that, by the time the European judgements were handed down, Erdoğan had already ended his opening to the Alevis. "If we had had those judgements in our hands in 2008, we might have been able to push through some durable improvements in the Alevis' status," according to Bermek.[10]

With the Alevis progressively crushed by the country's Nakşibendi enterprise, their main hope thus remains the CHP. "This keeps promising and not delivering. The Alevis keep wanting to believe in it. They have nowhere else to go."[11] In the advancing monoculture of AKP's Turkey, their future seems frail.

ANNEX B
OTHER ORDERS

It is not only Khorasan but Anatolia whose product is saints. Researching this book, I encountered over 150 religious orders that have been active since the vain attempt to ban them a century ago.[1] Some orders, such as the Hazneviyye, are of recent presence in Turkey, arriving with the refugees from the Syrian civil war. Others have managed to retain a continuity with the past, sometimes being invigorated by *şeyh* from the Balkans as they have fled persecution in the Ottomans' former European territories for the relative calm of republican Turkey.

The table overleaf summarizes the current situation of the twelve *tarikat* that dominated the *tekke* of İstanbul before their suppression in 1925.

Various other orders exist in pockets, for instance the contrarian Melamis, clandestine even under the Ottomans. The orders portrayed below have the more significant activities.

1. The Halvetiyye and their active offshoots

In the summer of 2019, I was a guest in a dervish lodge in the Levent district of İzmir, an area of parasol mulberry trees and low stucco houses retaining the early-twentieth-century style and charm of the old port city. The prayers there were led by the 30-year-old Hüdayi Yayıntaş, scion of a family which, after eight generations as Halveti *şeyh* in Ottoman Rumelia, fled south in the 1950s. His grandfather, Ali Alaeddin Yayıntaş, had headed the Derbent *tekkesi* south-east of Skopje, a rich and influential lodge in Ottoman times. Ali Alaeddin encouraged local Muslims to leave Tito's

Table 2. The Tekke of İstanbul

Order	Tekke in İstanbul		Current state of tarikat
	1889–1890	1920	
Nakşibendiyye	63	95	Has a dominant presence through the various sub-orders active today.
Halvetiyye	13	69	Some current branches, invigorated from the Balkans.
Kadiriyye	58	65	The *asitane* maintains the order's traditions. Its main appeal is in the Kurdish-populated regions of the country.
Rifaiyye	35	40	Limited family and popular activity.
Sa'diyye	23	34	No longer active.
Celvetiyye	22	31	Spiritual heritage ended in 1946. Erenköy has coopted its assets.
Sünbüliyye*	22	26	Led the state funerals of assassinated Mahmud Şevket Paşa and Said Halim Paşa but is no longer active.
Şabaniyye*	25	24	No longer active.
Bektaşiyye		14	Continues to be important to the Alevis, particularly as a cultural tradition, but has a divided leadership.
Cerrahiyye*	14	12	Has a limited intellectual following, mainly in İstanbul.
Uşşakıyye*	5	6	Has developed a teaching network.
Mevleviyye	5	5	Promoted by the Ministry of Tourism. The Çelebi family invokes its tradition, seeking to access its assets.
Other	21	29	
Total	306	450	

Sources: 1889–1890 *Mecmua-i tekaya* by Bandırmalızade Ahmed Münib Efendi, *İslam Ansiklopedisi*, Vol. 5/II, 1977. 1920 (date assumed) Enver Behnan Şapolyo, *Mezhepler ve Tarikatlar Tarihi*, Türkiye Yayınevi, 1964, p. 472.

* signifies sub-order of the Halvetiyye

Yugoslavia for Aegean Turkey. Eighteen thousand people are reputed to have followed his call, and he came to join them in 1957, dividing his time between fruit farming and proselytizing. His son, Hasan Şükrü, set up the İzmir lodge.

The Levent district is higher than the port below, attracting summer breezes, and is an area populated by refugees. All of the men praying with Hüdayi in the *semahane* were from such families. Most had married into fellow refugee families.

I first met Hüdayi when travelling in Kosovo with Hasan Şükrü, one of the most active Halveti *şeyh* of modern times. In April 2019, he led forty of us to a seminar in Yakova, the third largest city in Kosovo. The trip took in a Rifai lodge in Skopje, the Halveti lodge where Hüdayi had been training, and a number of other spiritual gems that had survived the Kosovo war.[2] There were speakers from thirteen universities, with their topics ranging from mystic thought in the Balkans to U.S. experiments showing the value of Sufism in repairing brain damage.

The Halvetiyye were one of the four major Sufi orders in the Empire, active through the centuries, with the main order and its sub-orders accounting for at least one quarter of the 450 *tekke* in İstanbul at the time of the First World War. Seventeen of the thirty-six Ottoman Sultans had links with the order.[3] It had a reputation for the strictness of its training. It emphasized self-renunciation and retreat (*khalwa*).[4] It also had a reverence for leaders with power, a characteristic that may well have endeared it to the palace.

The order appeared in the area of today's Azerbaijan in the wake of the Mongol invasions of the thirteenth century, then being brought by Turcoman tribes to Anatolia. From there, the Ottomans carried it into Syria, Egypt, the Hijaz, and Yemen. In the mid-eighteenth century, it was probably the most influential order in Egypt, and it remains a force from Africa to Asia, with a broad appeal in Asia Minor until well into modern times and in the Balkans up to today. For all this, its origins are obscure, being linked more to the mystical traditions of the Melamis than to any original teacher.

In the fifteenth century, its devotees spread its teachings in Crimea, while a particularly gifted group went to Amasya, then a town of influence amidst the largely nomadic population of Anatolia. It was here that Mehmed the Conqueror had sent his eldest son, Bayezid, to learn the rudiments of government. Bayezid became close to the Halveti *şeyh*, Cemâl-i Halvetî.

When the young prince succeeded to the throne, the Halvetiyye were elevated to a prominence that was to last for over two centuries.

Şapolyo reports that all nine Sultans ruling from 1640 to 1774 had sympathies for the Halvetiyye or its offshoot, the Cerrahiyye. Of the forty-eight appointments between 1621 and 1685 to the coveted positions as preachers of the Friday prayers at the main imperial mosques, nineteen were followers of the order.[5]

The order was characterized by frequent splitting. Its two most durable sub-orders were the Cemaliyye and Ahmediyye. The Cemaliyye, named after the *şeyh* of Bayezid, were long a force through their branch, the Sünbüliyye, who four centuries later led the state funerals in Young Turk İstanbul and had offshoots in Egypt, the Hijaz, Yemen, and North Africa, where they contributed to resistance against the French.

The three offshoots of the Halvetiyye most active in Turkey today are all of the Ahmediyye tradition, often called the Middle Way of the Halvetiyye. One branch followed Hasan Hüsameddin el Uşşakı, becoming known as the Uşşakıyye. The main lodge of this branch is still operating, with its current head being Muhammed Hikmet Dağlıhâfız Önem, an energetic proselytizer. As of early 2024, his foundation claimed to be operating ten *Kur'an* courses, to be providing food each day to 3,500 people in Gaziantep and İskenderun (presumably largely to Syrian refugees), and to have branches "in every region of Turkey," and student dormitories. It opened an online radio in 2012. Visited in 2021, it said it had built mosques in two African countries and brought drinking water to villages in half a dozen others.

Further Uşşakı communities can be found in the Aegean, while the order also has a traditional presence in the villages west of Çorum. There, the most active group was that following Eyüb Fatih Nurullah Sağban, who had wrestled for Turkey in the 57-kg category. In 2019, Nurani TV claimed the community had *dergah* in 22 of Turkey's 81 provinces as well as one in Germany. However, in June 2021, Sağban received a ten-year prison sentence for raping a twelve-year-old girl. The future of his community is uncertain.

A further order drawing on the Ahmediyye tradition is the Cerrahiyye, which has made good use of its cultural heritage to establish a presence among actors, musicians, and other İstanbul celebrities who have frequented the lodge named after Nureddîn Muhammed el Cerrahi in the Karagümrük district of old İstanbul. Contributing to the Cerrahiyye's recent revival was Muzaffer Ozak, an *imam*, bookseller, and writer who raised the tradition's standing in Turkey and used its music and poetry to spread its word in Europe and New York. The current head is the singer Ahmet Özhan. In April 2015, *Geredemiz*, a local newspaper, asserted that the Cerrahi had 5,000 members in Turkey and 30,000 in the world. When Özhan's predecessor died in September 2022, Erdoğan attended his funeral, but the Cerrahis appear as a marginal, if colourful, force.

2. The Kadiriyye—a grand tradition

At Erbakan's *iftar* for fifty-one religious leaders in January 1997, at least six participants were from branches of the Kadiri order. Most forcible of these was Professor Haydar Baş, a tireless campaigner until brought down by COVID-19. Baş set up the Independent Turkey Party (BTP), a youth organization, five television stations, and three magazines. He was mainly active in the Trabzon area of the Black Sea, with a message based less on religion than on respect for Atatürk, the Turkish armed forces, and constitutionalism. His party won 49,297 votes in the November 2015 general elections. He did not participate in the elections three years later.

The other Kadiri *şeyh* who dined with Erbakan were more typical of the traditions of the once great Kadiri order. These included Galip Hasan Kuşçuoğlu, who was a charismatic preacher, largely in Ankara, where a mosque is named after him, and who is now buried in a seaside complex west of İstanbul. His successors, (the late) Hacı Ali Yetkinşekerci and Atıf Uzunömeroğlu, continued the Kadiris' *zikir*, their disciples surrounding them in the traditional coffee-coloured *hirka* of the Kadiris. The Galipçis claim activities in fifteen or more provinces. They have tended to keep close to the AKP.

A more modest approach is adopted by the family occupying the lodge on the slopes of Cihangir, İstanbul, that served as *asitane* of the Kadiris for three centuries and now attracts an educated congregation. The incumbent, Eren Erkmenkul, describes rebuffing attempts by politicians to take advantage of the Kadiris' prestige, arguing that parties come and go, but the Kadiris continue. Other Kadiri centres are more worldly, that in Elazığ then headed by Cemil Evliyaoğlu receiving Erdoğan before the 2016 referendum.

The order continues its penetration of the mountainous reaches of the Kurdish-populated regions. Here, it has been in conflict with the Nakşibendis since at least the time of el-Bağdadi. The Barzani family, dominating the post-Saddam government of the Kurdish Region of Iraq, is Nakşibendi. The other great sheikhly family of the region, the Talabani, has traditionally been Kadiri.[6]

3. The Mevlevis and Neo-Mevlevis—whirling for God and money

Graceful and haunting, the whirling dervishes are to many the quintessential Sufis, their mysticism based on culture, music, and tolerance. It is the reed flute that launches their *sema*, as their ceremony is known, and, properly performed, it is an enduring catharsis for the soul. Hints of this can still be felt at the performances staged today for tourists as they have been for seventy years.

The Mevlevis were one of the great orders of the Ottoman Empire. Their source of inspiration is Celaleddin-i Rumi, a thirteenth-century poet who lived in the Seljuk capital of Konya from 1231 to 1273, the years of its pre-Mongol zenith through those as vassal to the Mongols.[7] The death of two intimate soulmates inspired his epic, the *Masnavī-ye Ma'nawī* (*Mesnevi* in Turkish), a poem of some 27,000 lines that causes him to resonate as one of the world's most-read poets, and the *Divan-ı Kebir* (Great Work), often named *Dīwān-i Shams-i Tabrīzī*, whose 44,281 lines honour the first of his intimate companions. The *Divan* begins with his meeting Shams, continues through the latter's disappearance—possibly thrown in a well by Rumi's son—and ends with verses probably written when Rumi was mainly composing the *Mesnevi*. "In Rumi's retelling of love's trials and joys, Shams is not a simple human being, nor even a guide in the manner of the prophets. Rather, he is the actual, living embodiment of the true beloved, who is God Himself."[8]

Rumi's legacy evolved into an order that would captivate Ottoman dignitaries for six centuries. This "was an aristocratic, intellectual, and cultural fraternity, finding its following and patronage in the classes corresponding to these terms."[9] It established around 130 *tekke* throughout the Empire, including in Athens, Belgrade, Baghdad, Cairo, Mecca, and Tabriz. One listing records fifteen *asitane* authorized to ensure disciples the training and the 1,001 days of *çile*, the ordeal of isolation through which each neophyte had to pass on his route down the mystical path required to become one of the order's *dede*. Three of the later Ottoman Sultans were among its many courtly adherents.

November 1925 was a particularly bleak month for the Mevlevis. On the 30th of the month, the Grand National Assembly voted to close all their lodges and ban their order and its ceremonies. A fortnight earlier, their leader, Abdülhalim Çelebi, died in circumstances that still remain unclear. The death followed two decades during which the head of the order, the *Makam Çelebi*, had changed five times. Abdülhalim himself had been sentenced to exile by the nationalists, rehabilitated, then accused of collaboration with the British. Despite all this, he became a deputy president of the First Grand National Assembly. Family lore has it that it was the evening after making a request to Mustafa Kemal for compensation for grain supplied to the nationalist armies that he fell from his balcony in the Pera Palas Hotel. The official cause of death was a heart attack.

Abdülhalim's successor, İzbudak, served the Republic well as a deputy in the Grand National Assembly. His memoirs clearly state that Abdülhalim had been the last *Çelebi* and stake no claim to have continued the tradition.[10] Despite this, some latter-day Mevlevis have tried to claim legitimacy as the descendants of Abdülhalim. But there is no evidence that any of his descendants was ever nominated as a successor or went through the strict training and ritual seclusion of the Mevlevis. To many, after twenty-two generations and over six centuries of grandeur, the famed *Çelebi* tradition was broken and the Mevlevi Order consigned to history.

With the opening of the Turkish economy from 1980, the great world brands began to jostle for their place in the local market. And here one of the most reputed names was that of Mevlana. As ambitious bureaucrats and devoted musicians and dancers revived the saint's cultural heritage, so the value of the brand began to become clear. Abdülhalim's descendants seem to have been late in appreciating this, not establishing the International Mevlana Foundation (UMV—Uluslararası Mevlana Vakfı) until 1996—and this in apparent response to the growing aura of the Mevlana Education, Culture and Art Foundation (MEKÜSAV—Mevlana Eğitim Kültür ve Sanat Vakfı), founded by some musicians in 1990.[11]

The current claimant to the title of *Makam Çelebi* is Abdülhalim's great-grandson, Faruk Hemdem. His education was secular and anglophone, culminating in a management degree from Marmara University. After administering the family's Hatay estate, he set up a travel agency in İstanbul, married a Swiss woman, and took Swiss citizenship. He later divorced, returned to Hatay, and married a Turkish woman. In 2005, he settled in the U.S., though soon returned. In this period, his eldest sister, Esin Çelebi Bayru, began running the UMV. Hemden has since taken on the role of its president and presents himself as leader of all the Mevlevis.[12]

This is no light claim. The Mevlevis not only shine abroad, but resonate through Turkish history for their contribution to Turkish culture. With the *ulema* banning study of Persian in the *medrese*, the Mevlevi lodges also became hearths for the study of this language. As İnalcık concludes his work on the early Ottoman Empire:

> Mevlevi-ism... was a major factor in creating classical Ottoman literature, which originally drew its main inspiration from Persian. In the eighteenth century, Mevlevis were in the first rank of Ottoman musicians and poets, but side by side with their deep influence on classical Ottoman art the Mevlevis, like the Bektaşis, created their own music and literature, entirely derived from Mevlevi tradition.[13]

Islam Ansiklopedisi says that the majority of composers of Turkish classical music were of Mevlevi background and that the order accounted for 220 of the 320 collections of *divan* poetry of Sufi origin.

Today's family members are cut from a different cultural cloth, and their spiritual heritage is not that seen during preceding centuries. Becoming a Mevlevi required long education and training from *dede* who themselves had also gone through this training. It also required spiritual preparation in a *tekke*. The dervish cells that visitors can see on Mevlevi lodges such as those at Galata and Manisa were not purely architectural elements but a central component of the function of the lodge, housing would-be dervishes for their obligatory ordeal of isolation.

Absent such an apprenticeship, Hemdem and his branch of the Çelebi family assert that blood ties alone give them the rights of leadership. As Bayru states of the *Makam Çelebi*: "This is a spiritual/family title. And thank goodness the biological line continues. And as long as this lineage continues, no one can dispossess us of this spiritual title."[14]

The importance of the family's assertions is clear. The title not only carries prestige, assuring the family a social and public status; it also underpins their claims for funding from the state and from UNESCO, which celebrated the 700th anniversary of Mevlana's death and 800th anniversary of his death. It has registered a number of Mevlevi terms and trademarks with the Turkish Patent Institute.

Less publicized, acceptance of the family's primacy opens the door to claims on the wealth of the Celaliye Foundation established by Rumi himself. The numerous Mevlevi properties sequestered in 1925 mostly belong to foundations subordinate to this foundation. Twenty per cent of the surplus of their annual income should go to the Çelebi family. The underlying assets, urban and rural, were vast. As of 2022, the family had finally won the court's acceptance of their *locus standi* as heirs to these rights though issues remained over which member was the current beneficiary.

The apparent distortions in tradition create the space for challenge, and by 2021 some eight figures had emerged to contest the family's legitimacy.[15] Of these, Hayat Nur Artıran is one of the first female *şeyh* for three centuries. As of March 2024, she had posted over twenty programmes receiving over 50,000 views on YouTube, the maximum being 307,000.

The famed *ney* musician Kudsi Erguner is critical of the spiritual loss:

> The fact of having known an important personality in the world of the tarikat, of being a relative, of knowing how to whirl, of playing the *ney*, of repeating a few beautiful words attributed to Mevlana, of wearing the Mevlevi robes, of believing one loves the Holy Mevlana, does not mean that one is Mevlevi... May God protect us all from spiritual evildoers who enslave people by imitating the words of the Saints.[16]

4. The Rifaiyye—an order for mortificants and the elite

In the past few decades, a number of *şeyh* have revived the tradition of the Rifai, the howling dervishes of yore whose self-castigation would macabrely attract nineteenth-century tourists. These include Ali Karaman in Zeytinburnu, Raik (Haznedar) Baba in Karagümrük, and İbrahim Baba in Kasımpaşa. In İstanbul, other *şeyh* preside over gatherings in Eyüp, in the Rifais' former *asitane* in Üsküdar, and at a former Rifai *tekke* in Kartal.

The Rifai practise protracted repetition of their prayers of remembrance, with their followers swaying together in their incantations, entering in or claiming a state of ecstasy. In this state, adepts may pierce themselves with skewers and knives, and subject their body to burning coals. The point is not to hurt oneself but to demonstrate that the rules of materiality can be overturned. When done correctly, there is no bleeding and no wound left afterwards. It is like a preview of Judgement Day, when we will all be raised up in our bodies although they long ago rotted away in the grave.

The order's inspirer was a twelfth-century mystic called Ahmad ibn 'Ali ar-Rifa'i (1106–1182). Until the fifteenth century, the Rifaiyye was the most widespread of all *tarikat*, then losing popularity to the Kadiris.[17] Where Turkey is concerned, the *Diyanet's İslam Ansiklopedisi* lists twenty-four branches of the Rifaiyye. Closure of the lodges where they trained their followers and performed their rituals hit them hard.

Their spiritual message was one of respect for the *Kur'an* and warmth to fellow humans, and it is this that has been propounded by the heirs of a late adept, the Ottoman official Kenan Büyükaksoy, often known as Kenan Rifai. In the West, the latter would have been termed a Renaissance figure. He was a director of education for the Ottomans and in the Republic. He then taught at a Greek Orthodox high school. He spoke half a dozen languages, embarking on learning English in his eighties. He appreciated Henri Bergson, and his friends included the leading poets and intellectuals of his time, not least Semiha Cemal, a translator of Plato and Marcus Aurelius who, before she died aged 30, had built a reputation as Turkey's first female philosopher.

His grandson, Kenan Gürsoy, a professor of philosophy and inspired choice as Turkish ambassador to the Vatican from 2003 to 2007, has long hosted cultural events at the family lodge in Fatih and runs philosophy workshops. His great regret is the loss of *tasavvuf* (Islamic mysticism) from the life of Turks today. Speaking in his library in 2022, he emphasized the importance of Sufi traditions, regretting how today's communities had distorted the role that they used to play.

One innovation of Kenan Rifai was to nominate a woman as his successor. This was Samiha Ayverdi, a writer on mysticism and Ottoman history, as well as author of nine novels and twelve memoirs. She in turn nominated a further woman, Cemalnur Sargut, to succeed her. Sargut is a tireless proselytizer of the Rifai message, attracting well-heeled supporters, and well followed on YouTube, where one of her talks had received 1.6 million views by March 2024. She has helped found institutes for *tasavvuf* studies in İstanbul, Kyoto, North Carolina, and Beijing. But she would be the first to admit that she and the Mevlevis' Hayat Nur Artıran are exceptions in the male-dominated world of the *tarikat*.

GLOSSARY

Turkish	Common alternative	Definition
Ağa	Agha	Honorific title, initially mainly used in the Sultan's entourage, later applied to large, often hereditary, land owners
Ağabey		Elder brother, used by Nurcu Movement to designate close students of Nursi (*Abi* is the İstanbul colloquial of this)
Asitane		A large or leading dervish lodge
Ayin-i Cem		The weekly ceremony of the Alevi
Baba		A leader of the Bektaşı community: earlier, a dervish who came to Anatolia with the Turkic tribes
Babagan		A leader elected by a local Bektaşı community
Biat	Bay'a(h)	Sufi oath of allegiance to a spiritual guide
Cemaat	Jemaat	An Islamic religious community; descriptive of most orders considered above; used by Gülenists for their movement
Cemevi		Community and religious centre of the Alevis
Cihad	Jihad	Religious endeavour, often used to denote War for the Faith

GLOSSARY

Turkish	Common alternative	Definition
Çelebi	Chelebi	Title given to heads of various dervish communities, particularly the hereditary heads of the Bektaşi and Mevlevi
Çile		The ordeal of retirement and fasting through which neophyte dervishes had to pass
Dârülislâm	Dar al-Islam	Abode of Islam—where Islam is the ruling religion
Dede		i. Grandfather ii. Title of heads of various dervish communities, particularly of the Bektaşi and of Alevi ocak
Dedebaba		The Bektaşi leader, elected by his peers
Dedegan		One from the (hereditary) chain of Bektaşi leaders
Dergah	Dargah	A Sufi convent, lodge, or shrine
Ders		Reading by a teacher or lesson
Dershane		Study centres, discussion schools, later cramming schools, particularly used by the Gülenists
Dönme		Convert, especially used to refer to the descendants of Jews who converted to Islam in the seventeenth century along with their messiah, Shabbatai Tsevi.
Evkaf (today vakıflar)		Pious foundations
Ezan	Adhan	Call to prayer
Fetva	Fatwa	Legal opinion issued by a religious authority
Fıkıh	Fiqh	Religious law
Hac	Hajj	The pilgrimage during the holy month to Mecca
Hadis	Hadith	Traditions on the sayings and actions of the Prophet
Hafiz		One who has memorized the whole *Kur'an*

GLOSSARY

Turkish	Common alternative	Definition
Hakikat	Hakkika	Imminent experience of (Divine) reality
Halife	Khalifa	Nominated deputy or successor
Halvet	Khwalat	Retreat or seclusion
Hanefi	Hanafi	One of the four major Sunni schools of Islamic jurisprudence
Hankah	Khan(a)qah	A religious cloister or Sufi centre
Haram		Forbidden by Islam
Hatip	Katib	Preacher or orator of the *hutbe*
Hatm-i hacegan	Khatm-i khwajagan	Concluding prayers of the masters
Hırka	Khirqa	A cloak, used to describe a dervish uniform
Hocaefendi		Respected religious teacher; used by followers of Kotku and Gülen to refer to their leaders
Hutbe	Khutba	The sermon delivered at Friday prayers and religious holidays
Iskat		The alms given on behalf of the dead as compensation for their neglected religious duties
İcazet		Authorization (by a *şeyh* of a disciple)
İlim	Ilm	(Religious) learning
İmam	Imam	Incumbent at a mosque, a leader in prayer
İrtica		Religious or political reaction
Kadı	Qadi	Judge
Kazasker, sometimes kadıasker		Chief military judge
Kelam	Kalam	Scholastic theology
Kızılbaş	Qizil-bash	Turkish term for red-hatted dervishes, generally applied to Shiites and Alevis
Kur'an	Qur'an	Quran, Kur'an, or Koran
Kurban		Sacrifice, sacrificial sheep
Kutup	Qutb	Axis or pivot, the head of a religious trend, e.g. Melamiyye

Turkish	Common alternative	Definition
Külliye	Kulliyye	Social complex
Makam		Ranking, in office, part of the title of leaders of the Bektaşi and Mevlevi
Marifet	Ma'rifa	Mystical knowledge of God
Medrese	Madrasa	Higher religious school
Mehdi	Mahdi	The Rightly Guided One who will appear at the end of times, the Messiah
Melâmet	Malamah	A state of humility, minimizing the importance of the self (rather than blame of oneself)
Mescid	Masjid	A small mosque
Mevlana	Mawlana	Our master, title for learned religious figure, especially Celaleddin-i Rumi
Mezar	Mazar	Shrine, tomb, place of visit
Millet		A component religious community of the Ottoman Empire
Minber	Minbar	The steps used as a pulpit in a mosque
Muharrem		The Alevis' commemoration of the martyrdom of the Imam Hüseyin
Murakaba/e	Muraqaba	Contemplation, meditation, entering a spiritual ecstasy
Musahib or musahip		Brother of the path, companion
Müceddid(iyye)	Mujaddid(iyye)	Renewer (of the faith), renewal (branch)
Müezzin	Muaddin or muazzin	One who calls Muslims to prayer
Müftü	Mufti	A (religious) lawyer authorized to issue an opinion, later, a state-appointed religious leader
Mürid	Murid	Aspirant or disciple
Mürşid	Murshid	Spiritual guide or mentor
Ocak		Hearth or fraternity such as a tribe
Pir		Elder
Pir Sani	Pîr-i Sani	Second founder

Turkish	Common alternative	Definition
Postnişin	Post-nishin	Head of a lodge (he who sits on a sheepskin)
Rabıta	Rabita	Union or connection (e.g. with a guide)
Seccadenişin		Head of a congregation, e.g. the Bektaşi Çelebi (he who sits on a prayer rug)
Selefi	Salafi	Predecessors, late-nineteenth-century reform movement
Sema	Sama	Spiritual concert of the Mevlevis, and ritual dancing of Alevis
Seyyid	Sayyid	Chief, lord, or (usually capitalized) descendant of the Prophet
Silsile	Silsila	Initiatic chain of succession
Sıddik	Siddiq	Eminently truthful, title given to Abu Bakr
Softa		Graduates from religious schools
Sohbet	Suhba	Fellowship, religious discussion and, often now, discussion group
Sünnet	Sunna(h)	The accepted customs of the Prophet
Şeriat	Shari'a	Islamic canonical law, the path to be followed
Şeyh	Shaikh	Master (of an order)
Şeyhülislam		The top religious post in the Empire, sometimes called the Mufti of İstanbul
Taç	Tadj	The half-conical dervish head gear
Takıyye (also takiye & takiyye)	Taqiyya	Precautionary dissimulation
Tanzimat		Reforms, often used to indicate the reform period from 1839–1876
Tarikat	Tariqa(h) (Pl. Turuq)	A way, used as a term for a religious order
Tasavvuf	Tasawwuf	Islamic mysticism, also known as Sufism; the Arabic word means being or becoming a Sufi
Tefsir	Tafsir	Exegesis on the *Kur'an*

Turkish	Common alternative	Definition
Tekbir	Takbir	The affirmation, *Allahu akbar* in Arabic, *Allahu ekber* in Turkish
Tekke	Tekkeh	A dervish lodge or monastery
Tevhid	Tawhid	Unity of God
Tevhid ibadet	Tawhid al-'ibada	Unified focus of worship
Türbe		Monumental tomb or shrine
Ulema	Ulama	Those trained in the religious sciences
Umre	Umra(h)	The pilgrimage to Mecca outside the holy month
Ümmet	Ummah	The (world) community of Muslims
Vahdet-i şühûd	Wahdat ash-shuhûd	Unity of witness, i.e. unity of being as a reflection, not an emanation, of reality
Vahdet-i vücûd	Wahdat al-wujûd	Unity of being
Vaiz		Preacher
Vakfiye		Founding deed of a *vakıf*
Vakıf	Waqf	Charitable or religious foundation
Vird	Wird	Repetition of the *Kur'an,* a phrase-patterned devotion
Zaviye	Zawiya(h)	Saint's tomb, small Sufi centre or monastery
Zekat	Zakat	The charitable alms prescribed in the Kur'an
Zikir	Dhikr	Spiritual exercise of remembrance or recollection

Arabic transliterations are mainly from Ruthven, pp. 425 ff., and Trimingham, pp. 300 ff.

NOTES

ACKNOWLEDGEMENTS

1. Svante E. Cornell, "The Naqshbandi-Khalidi Order and Political Islam in Turkey," Hudson Institute, 3 September 2015.

PREFACE

1. Recep Tayyip Erdoğan, AK Party Meeting to launch the Century of Türkiye, 28 October 2022.
2. See Chapters 12 & 13.
3. Şerif Mardin, "Islam in Nineteenth- and Twentieth-Century Turkey," *Religion, Society, and Modernity in Turkey*, Syracuse University Press, 2006, p. 269.

INTRODUCTION

1. Enver Behnan Şapolyo, *Mezhepler ve Tarikatlar Tarihi*, Türkiye Yayınevi, 1964, pp. 448–449.
2. Ekrem Buğra Ekinci, *Sürgündeki hanedan: Osmanlı ailesinin çileli asrı*, Timaş Yayınları, 2017.
3. Herein, the word *tarikat* is mainly used in its strict sense but occasionally as a generic term to cover both *tarikat* and *cemaat* that have developed from *tarikat*.
4. Fehmi Çalmuk, a biographer of Erdoğan, writing in *Hürses* on 19 July 2016, just after the coup attempt.

1. ABDÜLHAMID II

1. Cited in Madeline C. Zilfi, *The Politics of Piety: The Ottoman Ulema in the Postclassical Age (1600–1800)*, Bibliotheca Islamica, Minneapolis, 1988,

p. 227. Reprinted with permission of Persian Heritage Foundation and Dr Zilfi.

2. His formal title also listed all the shores of the Black Sea and some forty other domains from the Maghreb to Basra and from Tataristan to Abyssinia.
3. Article I of the Cyprus Convention stipulated that, if Russia attacked Ottoman lands, "England engages to join His Imperial Majesty the Sultan in defending them by force of arms." Britain repudiated this agreement in its Triple Entente with Russia, annexing the island at the outbreak of World War I.
4. Stanford J. Shaw, & Ezel Kural Shaw, *History of the Ottoman Empire & Modern Turkey, Vol. II Reform, Revolution and Republic: The Rise of Modern Turkey, 1808–1975*, Cambridge University Press, 1977, p. 113 and Benjamin Fortna, *Imperial Classroom: Islam, Education and the State in the Late Ottoman Empire*, Oxford University Press, 2002, pp. 4, 208 ff. & 220 ff.
5. In 1867, girls accounted for one third of students at the new secular elementary schools. From 1862, the government supported secondary education for girls, but it was not until half a century later that the first girls' high school was established. Shaw & Shaw, 1977, p. 112 and Niyazi Berkes, *The Development of Secularism in Turkey*, McGill University, 1964, pp. 176 & 387.
6. Gökhan Bacık, *Islam and Muslim Resistance to Modernity in Turkey*, Palgrave Macmillan, 2019, p. 135.
7. He is often referred to as Jamāl al-Dīn al-Afghānī or simply Al-Afghani.
8. J. Spencer Trimingham, *The Sufi Orders in Islam*, Oxford University Press, 1971, p. 126.
9. Hayreddin Kahraman, "Cemaleddin Efgani," TDV İslam Ansiklopedisi, 1994.
10. In 1889, Abduh received a khedival pardon which allowed him to return to Cairo. He became Grand Mufti of Cairo, publishing a modernist manifesto, and shaking up the al-Azhar religious school. He attracted febrile conservative criticism. Christopher de Bellaigue, *The Islamic Enlightenment*, Vintage, 2018, pp. 280–289.
11. Jacob M. Landau, *The Politics of Pan-Islam: Ideology and Organization*, Clarendon Press, 1994, pp. 15–21.
12. Ibid. The murder, in 1896, had indeed been carried out by a disciple of Efghani.
13. See Annex B 4.
14. Trimingham, 1971, p. 127.
15. Malise Ruthven, *Islam in the World*, 2nd edition, Penguin, 2000, p. 219 ff.
16. Trimingham, 1971, pp. 166 ff.
17. Richard Nelson Frye, "The Samanids," *Cambridge History of Iran*, Cambridge University Press, Vol. 4, 1975, pp. xi & 147.
18. S.H. Nasr, "Sufism," *op.cit.*, pp. 451–452, 456.

19. Shahab Ahmed, *What Is Islam? The Importance of Being Islamic*, Princeton University Press, 2016, p. 20.
20. Just before their suppression in 1925, the total may have been 450. Şapolyo, 1964, pp. 460–471 & 472.
21. Kemal Karpat, *Ottoman Population, 1830–1914, Demographic and Social Characteristics*, University of Wisconsin, 1985, p. 206.
22. Klaus Kreiser, "The Dervish Living" in *The Dervish Lodge*, ed. Lifchez, University of California, 1992 p. 49. Also Kreiser in *Les ordres mystiques dans l'Islam*, ed. Popović & Veinstein, ÉHESS, 1986.
23. John Kingsley Birge, *The Bektashi Order of Dervishes*, Luzac & Hartford 1937, p. 14, indicating the historian Prof. Köprülü as his source.
24. Erik J. Zürchner, *Turkey: A Modern History*, I.B. Tauris, 2003, p. 12.
25. Godfrey Goodwin, *The Janissaries*, Saqi, 1994, p. 87.
26. Cemal Kafadar, *Between Two Worlds: The Construction of the Ottoman State*, University of California, 1995, pp. 87–88, citing Topkapı Palace Archives. E. 5584.
27. Halil İnalcık, *The Ottoman Empire: The Classical Age*, Phoenix Press, 2000, p. 98.
28. The term used in Western Europe for the Ottoman government, often shortened to Porte.
29. See also Annex A.
30. Murat Çizakça, *A History of Philanthropic Foundations: The Islamic World from the Seventh Century to the Present*, Boğaziçi University Press, 2000, p. 2.
31. However, income from properties endowed in perpetuity was exempted from taxes. John Roberts Barnes, *An Introduction to Religious Foundations in the Ottoman Empire*, Brill, 1986, pp. 33–40.
32. Suraiya Faroqhi, *Der Bektaschi-Orden in Anatolien*, Vienna, 1981, p. 48.
33. Kreiser, 1992, pp. 49–50.
34. Halil İnalcık, *An Economic and Social History of the Ottoman Empire, 1300–1914*, ed. Halil İnalcık with Donald Quataert, Cambridge University Press, 1994, pp. 79–83.
35. Bruce McGowan in İnalcık & Quataert, 1994, p. 660, citing M.A. Ubicini, *Lettres sur la Turquie*, première partie, deuxième edition, Paris, 1853, p. 271.
36. Gönül Tankut, "Urban Transformation in the Eighteenth Century," *Mimarlık Fakültesi Dergisi*, 1:2, 1975, p. 262. (McGowan in İnalcık & Quataert, 1994, p. 712).
37. Barnes, 1986, p. 44.
38. Bahaeddin Yediyıldız, *XVIII. yüzyılda Türkiye'de vakıf müessesesi: bir sosyal tarih incelemesi*, Türk Tarih Kurumu Basımevi, 2003, p. 160.
39. Nazif Öztürk, "Evkāf-ı Hümâyun Nezâreti," *İslam Ansiklopedisi*, 1995
40. The Mevlevis' foundations were exempted "since the revenue of these is

given to the poor and to the dervishes for food." *Cevdet Evkaf*, No. 27168, C 1256/1849.

41. Charles MacFarlane, *Turkey and Its Destiny*, John Murray, 1850, p. 396, cited in Barnes, 1986, p. 118.
42. Perhaps to counter this, in 1882 the Porte transferred the revenues of all *vakıf* involved in education to the Ministry of Education. At the start of World War I, such revenues covered 80 per cent of primary school teachers' salaries. Çizakça, 2000, pp. 85–86.
43. The Sünbüliyye are normally classed as a sub-order of the Halvetiyye.
44. Ekrem Işın, "La Kadiriyye à İstanbul: Une vue d'ensemble," *İstanbul Ansiklopedisi*, Kültür Bakanlığı and Tarih Vakfı, 1993–1994, pp. 372–377, reprinted in *Journal of the History of Sufism*, 1–2, 2000: Special issue, "The Qadiriyya Sufi Order."
45. İsmail Kara, "Tarikat çevrelerinin İttihat ve Terakki ile munasebetleri," *Dergah*, 4:43, 1993, p. 14.
46. Cemaleddin had a strong sense of public service, insisting on opening the mosques to the wounded of the First Balkan War and cholera victims.
47. İrfan Gündüz, *Osmanlılarda Devlet-Tekke Münasebetleri*, Seha Neşriyat, 1983, p. 219. This assertion seems probable even if Gündüz cites a dubious authority in support of it.
48. İsmail Kara, 1993, p. 14.
49. Gündüz, 1983, p. 221.
50. M. Şükrü Hanioğlu, *The Young Turks in Opposition*, Oxford University Press, 1995, p. 56.
51. From September 1907 to July 1908, it termed itself the Ottoman Committee of Progress and Union (*Osmanlı Terakki ve İttihat Cemiyeti*). Herein the term CUP refers to the activities of both.
52. With the fall of Abdülhamid, Ebü'l-Hüda became a marked man. Interrogated on suspicion of atheism, sorcery, and use of snakes, he died while under house arrest.

2. THE YOUNG TURKS AND THE YEARS OF SIEGE

1. In *From Empire to Republic: Essays on the Late Ottoman Empire and Modern Turkey*, İstanbul Bilgi Üniversitesi, 2008, p. 172.
2. Halidé Edib Adıvar, *Memoirs of Halidé Edib*, Gorgias Press, 2004, p. 258, a reprint of the 1926 edition.
3. Sir Edward Grey to the British Ambassador in İstanbul, letters of 31 July and 11 August 1908 in *The Private Correspondence of Sir Gerard Lowther, British Ambassador to Constantinople (1908–1913)*, ed. Sinan Küneralp & Gül Tokay, Isis, 2018, pp. 14 & 17.
4. Feroz Ahmad, *The Making of Modern Turkey*, Routledge, 1993, pp. 33–34.

5. Zekeriya Kurşun & Kemal Kahraman, *İslam Ansiklopedisi*, 1994.
6. The date was 21 March 1325, according to the Rumi (near Julian) calendar then in application. The Republic formally introduced AD (now termed CE) at the end of 1925.
7. See Chapters 4 and 11.
8. Nader Sohrabi, *Revolution and Constitutionalism in the Ottoman Empire and Iran*, Cambridge University Press, 2011, p. 235.
9. Pears cites two earlier murders of persons connected with journals opposing the CUP. Edwin Pears, *Forty Years in Constantinople: The Recollections of Sir Edwin Pears, 1873–1915*, D. Appleton, 1916, pp. 274–275.
10. Francis McCullagh, *The Fall of Abd-Ul-Hamid*, Methuen, 1910, pp. 130–134.
11. Edib Adıvar, 1926, p. 280.
12. Sohrabi, 2011, pp. 224–225.
13. McCullagh, 1910, pp. 46–47.
14. Edib Adıvar, 1926, p. 278.
15. G.R. Berridge, *Gerald Fitzmaurice (1865–1939), Chief Dragoman of the British Embassy in Turkey*, Martinus Nijhoff, 2007, pp. 131–137 & chs. 5–6.
16. Hardinge to Lowther, 1 May & 29 June, 1909, F.O. 800/185A, cited in Ahmad, "Great Britain's Relations," *From Empire to Republic*, p. 156. Fitzmaurice later denied ever having intrigued against the CUP or having supported Kamil Paşa.
17. Bernard Lewis, *The Emergence of Modern Turkey*, Oxford University Press, 1968, p. 409.
18. Mustafa Ergün, *II. Meşrutiyet Devrinde Eğitim Hareketleri (1908–1914)*, Ocak Yayınları, Ankara, 1996, pp. 339–340.
19. Lowther to Sir Charles Hardinge, Permanent Under-Secretary at the Foreign Office, 19 May 1909, *Private Correspondence*, p. 117.
20. Benjamin C. Fortna, *The Circassian: A Life of Eşref Bey, Late Ottoman Insurgent and Special Agent*, Oxford University Press, 2016, p. 86.
21. Harold Nicholson to Vita Sackville-West, 12 June 1913, cited in James Lee-Milne, *Harold Nicholson, A Biography*, Archon, 1982, p. 59. Field Marshal Earl Roberts had been Britain's Commander-in-Chief of the Forces; Field Marshal Lord Kitchener was then British Agent in Egypt; and H.H. Asquith was prime minister.
22. Murat Bardakçı, *Mahmud Şevket Paşa'nın sadaret günlüğü*, Türkiye İş Bankası Kültür Yayınları, 2014, pp. 310–314.
23. Cihangir Gündoğdu, "The Anatomy of an Assassination: Assassination of Mahmud Şevket Paşa (11 June 1913)," thesis, Boğaziçi University, 2004, pp. 134 ff. Details of the finance flows are on pp. 147 & 152–154.
24. Cemal Paşa, *Anılarım*, İstanbul, Paraf, 2010, p. 40. See also pp. 31–32 & 122–123. Also, Berridge, 2008, pp. 182–184 & 200–203. Fitzmaurice left in February 1914, ostensibly because of a decline in his health.

25. Johann Bernstorff, *Memoirs of Count Bernstorff*, W. Heinemann, 1936, pp. 144–145; McCullagh, 1910, p. 47, and Dankwart A. Rustow, *Encyclopedia of Islam*, Leiden, Vol. II, 1965, p. 701.
26. Şükrü Hanioğlu *A Brief History of the Late Ottoman Empire*, Princeton University Press, 2008, pp. 203 ff. Italy soon joined the Sultan's enemies, as did Greece.
27. Bernstorff, 1936, pp. 197 & 156, cited in Feroz Ahmad, "The Dilemmas of Young Turk Policy, 1914-1918," *War and Collapse World War I and the Ottoman State*, ed. M. Hakan Yavuz with Feroz Ahmad, University of Utah Press, 2016, pp. 78 & 79.
28. Allied forces suffered 650,000 casualties on the Ottoman fronts. Hanioğlu, 2008, pp. 180–181. This author cites research that the Ottomans spent 9 billion gold French francs on the war, compared with around 240 billion gold francs spent by each of Britain and Germany.
29. Fanny Davis et al., *The Ottoman Lady: A Social History from 1718 to 1918*, Greenwood Publishing, 1986, p. 124.
30. Shaw & Shaw, 1977, pp. 305–308, and Nihan Altınbaş, "Marriage and Divorce in the Late Ottoman Empire," *Journal of Family History*, 2014.
31. İsmail Kara, 1993, p. 14.
32. Hanioğlu, 1995, p. 56.
33. Hanioğlu, 1995, pp. 49–50.
34. Turkey's only field marshals at this time were Fevzi Çakmak and Mustafa Kemal.
35. Letter of Rıza Tevfik Bölükbaşı to Ernest Edmondson Ramsaur Jr of 16 May 1941, cited in the latter's *The Young Turks: Prelude to the Revolution of 1908*, Princeton, 1957, n. 48, p. 113. Rıza Tevfik's grammar is left unchanged. Lewis (1968, p. 408) asserts that Musa Kazim was a Nakshibendi.
36. Hanioğlu, 1995, p. 54, and Bahaddin Veled Çelebi İzbudak, *Hatıralarım*, Türkiye Yayınları, 1946, pp. 48 ff.
37. Mustafa Kara, "Veled Çelebi İzbudak," *İslam Ansiklopedisi*, 2001. See also Annex B.
38. Jacob M. Landau, *Pan-Turkism in Turkey: A Study in Irredentism*, C. Hurst, 1981, p. 1. The Hungarian orientalist, Arminius Vámbéry, devoted a chapter of his *Sketches of Central Asia*, published in 1868, to the Turanians. He contended that, if the house of Osman had brought the Turkic peoples together, "a mighty Turkish Colossus might have arisen, certainly better capable of measuring itself with its great northern competitor than Turkey such as we see in the present day."
39. Ahmed Emin Yalman, *Turkey in My Time*, University of Oklahoma , 1956, pp. 34–35.
40. Gökalp wrote only two short essays on Pan-Turanism, neither of which contained a formulation of the ideology. He ceased to use the word 'Turan'

in his poetry after 1915. Niyazi Berkes, *Turkish Nationalism and Western Civilization: Selected Essays by Ziya Gökalp*, Columbia University Press, 1959, pp. 7–8. .
41. Ziya Gökalp, "Cemaat Medeniyeti, Cemiyet Medeniyeti," *Turk Yurdu IV*, No. 47, 1913, in Berkes, 1959, p. 103.
42. Ziya Gökalp, "An'ane ve Kaide," *Türk Yurdu*, IV, No. 39, İstanbul 1913, in Berkes, 1959, pp. 94–95.
43. Shaw & Shaw, 1977, pp. 302–303.
44. Ziya Gökalp, "Medeniyetimiz," *Yeni Mecmua*, No. 68, İstanbul 1923, in Berkes, 1959, pp. 270–271.
45. *Muasırlaşmak* is usually translated as "becoming contemporary."
46. Ziya Gökalp, "Üç Cereyan," *Turk Yurdu III*, No. 35, 1913, reprinted 1918, in Berkes, 1959, p. 75.
47. Ziya Gökalp, "Türkçülük Nedir?," *Yeni Mecmua*, No. 28, İstanbul 1917, in Berkes, 1959, pp. 284–285.
48. Ziya Gökalp, "Social Functions of Religion," *İslam Mecmuası*, III, Nos. 34 & 36, İstanbul, 1915, in Berkes, 1959, pp. 188–192.
49. Ziya Gökalp, "Turkishness and Religion," *Türkçülüğün Esasları*, Ankara, 1923, pp. 163–164, in Berkes, 1959, p. 301.
50. Ziya Gökalp, "State and Religion," *İslam Mecmuası*, IV, No. 48, İstanbul, 1916, in Berkes, 1959, pp. 202–213.
51. Idem.
52. Berkes, 1959, pp. 30–31.
53. The US ambassador at the time set the total as "nearly a million human beings." Henry Morgenthau, *Ambassador Morgenthau's Story*, Doubleday, 1918, p. 385. Estimates of the death toll range from under 0.5 million, the official Turkish view, to around 1.5 million, as some Armenians assert. Controversy also exists as to whether to term the massacres a genocide, as President Biden and several countries' assemblies have. Turkey argues the decision should be made by historians not politicians.
54. Hanioğlu, 2008, p. 181.
55. Ahmad, "The Dilemmas of Young Turk Policy, 1914–1918", *War and Collapse*, p. 80.
56. The Armistice of Mudros referred only to the "Bosphorus forts." A written undertaking by Calthorpe, the British signatory, said that the Triple Entente had no intention to dismantle the government or occupy Constantinople. The British justified their later takeover by citing article VII: "The Allies to have the right to occupy any strategic points in the event of any situation arising which threatens the security of the Allies." Bilge Criss, *Constantinople under Allied Occupation 1918–1923*, Brill, 1999, p. 1.
57. Recep Tayyip Erdoğan, 10 July 2020.
58. This treaty, signed on 10 August 1920, was never ratified by the Chamber

of Deputies. In March 1920, the British, disturbed by the rebellious stand of the many nationalists elected in December 1919, had the Sultan close the chamber.

3. FAITH AND SECULARISM IN THE NEW REPUBLIC

1. Andrew Mango, *Atatürk: The Biography of the Founder of Modern Turkey*, Overlook Press, 2004, p. 276 and Cemal Kutay, *Kurtuluşun ve Cumhuriyet'in Manevi Mimarları*, Diyanet İşleri Bakanlığı Yayınları, 1973, pp. 119–127.
2. Mango, 2004, p. 278.
3. Vahdeddin fled his palace, secreted in a British ambulance to board the waiting HMS *Malaya* at dawn on 17 November 1922.
4. Yalman, 1956, pp. 80–81.
5. Mustafa Kemal Atatürk, *The Great Speech (Nutuk)*, Atatürk Research Centre, 2005, p. 581. Refet Paşa's veneration for the Caliph caused him to be replaced after six weeks as the nationalists' representative.
6. Berkes, 1959, pp. 229 & 227.
7. Mustafa Kemal Atatürk, *Nutuk*, p. 674.
8. Mustafa Kemal Atatürk, *Nutuk*, pp. 673–674.
9. Talks at Lausanne had nearly broken down over British demands for the abolition of the Caliphate, at this point protected by Mustafa Kemal and his negotiators. It was only six weeks after Ankara abolished the Caliphate that the British Parliament ratified the Treaty.
10. Shamshad Ali, "Indian Muslims and The Ottoman Empire 1876–1924," doctoral thesis, Aligarh Muslim University, 1990, p. 220.
11. Yalman, 1956, p. 142.
12. https://www.alislam.org/khilafat/.
13. Safwat Hegazy, cited in Tom Robinson, "The Arab Spring that Wasn't," *Beyond Today*, United Church of God, 2 March 2013.
14. David McDowall, *A Modern History of the Kurds*, I.B. Tauris, 1996, p. 187, cited in Gareth H. Jenkins, *Political Islam in Turkey: Running West, Heading East?*, Palgrave Macmillan, 2008, p. 89.
15. Martin van Bruinessen, *Agha, Shaikh and State: The Social and Political Structures of Kurdistan*, Zed Books, 1992, p. 281.
16. Christopher de Bellaigue, *Rebel Land: Among Turkey's Forgotten Peoples*, Bloomsbury, 2010, p. 129.
17. De Bellaigue, 2010, pp. 132–133.
18. Cf. Van Bruinessen, 1992, pp. 265–305 and Kemal Kirişçi & Gareth M. Winrow, *The Kurdish Question and Turkey: An Example of a Trans-state Ethnic Conflict*, Frank Cass, 1997, pp. 103–105 of the Routledge Curzon, 2000 edition.
19. Van Bruinessen, 1992, pp. 298–299.

20. See Chapter 4.
21. Mustafa Kara, *Din, Hayat, Sanat açısından Tekkeler ve Zaviyeler*, Dergah, 1977, pp. 152 ff.
22. Server Tanilli, "Le Roman Nur Baba de Yakup Kadri Karaosmanoğlu," *Bektachiyya, Études sur l'ordre mystique des Bektachis et les groupes relevant de Hajdi Bektach*, ed. Alexandre Popović & Gilles Veinstein, Isis Press, 1995, p. 189.
23. İştar Gözaydın, "Religion, Politics and the Politics of Religion in Turkey," Dietrich Jung & Catharina Raudvere (ed.), *Religion, Politics and Turkey's EU Accession*, Palgrave Macmillan, September 2008, p. 166.
24. Interview with Maurice Pernot just before becoming president, cited in Mango, 2004, p. 396.
25. Some recent Turkish historians have begun to challenge descriptions of the *medrese*, *tekke*, and *tarikat* as having become degenerate, emphasizing their role as an integral part of Islamic tradition.
26. The original draft would have exempted the titles used by the Bektaşi and Mevlevi. Christos Retoulas, "Religion and Secularization in the 'Byzantine-Ottoman' Continuum: The Case of Turkish Secularism," doctoral thesis, University of Oxford Oriental Institute, 2010, pp. 342–362. Mustafa Kemal told his Minister of Education that the proposed bans were temporary: "Hamdullah Bey, come after fifteen years, I will make you the keeper of whichever shrine you want." *Hamdullah Suphi Tanrıöver ve Anıları*, ed. Mustafa Baydar, Menteş Kitabevi, 1968, pp. 171–174. A century later, Law 677 remains on the books, long broken with impunity, an indication of the inefficacy of administrative law when confronted with faith.
27. Fahri Maden, *Bektaşi Tekkelerinin Kapatılması (1826) ve Bektaşiliğin Yasaklı Yılları*, Türk Tarihi Kurumu Yayınları, 2013, pp. 143 ff.
28. Retoulas, 2010, p. 356.
29. Letter from İsmail Hakkı Kılıçoğlu, cited by Falih Rıfkı Atay, *Çankaya: Atatürk'ün Doğumundan Ölümüne Kadar*, Bateş, 1998, p. 31.
30. Şevki Koca in a letter of 8 November 2001: Retoulas, 2010, p. 276.
31. Annex A explores the Bektaşi order.
32. Retoulas, 2010, p. 282, citing Ali Fuat Cebesoy, *Bilinmeyen Hatıralar: Kuva-yı Milliye ve Cumhuriyet Devrimleri*, ed. Osman Selim Kocahanoğlu, 2001, Temel Yayınları, p. 298.
33. The early nationalist governments had little compunction on drawing on the substantial cash assets of the foundations. In 1954, the General Directorate of Endowments used the capital of the endowments to help establish the Vakıflar Bankası. At the end of 2023, the bank had assets equivalent to around 100 billion USD. Claims for compensation have usually foundered.
34. In *Official Gazette* numbers 63 of 6 March 1924 and 68 of 7 April 1924. Law

364 specifying "The religion of the Turkish state is Islam" is also found in two issues of *Official Gazette*, 40 and 41 of 4 and 7 November 2023.

35. Law 671 of November 1925.
36. Mustafa Kemal Atatürk, *Nutuk*, 2005, p. 713.
37. Mango, 2004, p. 436. At least three Nakşibendi *şeyh* were executed for related protests. Some demonstrators were sentenced by other tribunals, meaning the total is probably far higher—Jenkins, 2008, pp. 95–96.
38. These were incorporated in the 1924 Constitution by Law 3115 of 1937.
39. Halidé Edib Adıvar, *The Turkish Ordeal: Being the Further Memoirs of Halidé Edib*, Century, 1928, p. 188.
40. One of these was Rauf Orbay, a former general, who was sentenced to death but released after 10 years in gaol. After Atatürk's death, he re-emerged in political life, serving as Turkey's ambassador to London from 1942 to 1944. Another notable brought to trial was General Karabekir, who was acquitted, wrote his memoirs from seclusion, only to see them banned, and then, after Atatürk's death, became speaker of the Grand National Assembly.
41. Kısakürek, 1969, p. 158.
42. Yalçın Küçük, *Quo Vadimus-Nereye Gidiyoruz?*, Tekin Yayınevi, 1985, pp. 236–240.
43. Zekai Baloğlu, *Türkiye'de Egitim*, TÜSİAD, 1990, p. 6.
44. Berkes, 1964, pp. 479–486.
45. Jenkins, 2008, p. 84.
46. Colonel Emin Dirvana, formerly head of the president's cavalry guard, to author, 1983.
47. İsmet Bozdağ, *Kültür İhtilalimiz Bilinmeden Politika Yapılmaz*, Tekin Yayınevi, İstanbul 1999, p. 23.
48. Ziya Gökalp, "Fatherland (Vatan)," *Yeni Hayat*, İstanbul, 1918. Also Gökalp, "Turkishness and Religion," idem.
49. Berkes, 1964, p. 486.
50. Berkes, 1964, pp. 486–490 & Umut Azak, *Islam and Secularism in Turkey: Kemalism, Religion and the Nation State*, I.B. Tauris, 2010, pp. 56 & 190, n. 38.
51. It was not until the 1960s that the Second Vatican Council decreed that the Mass would be translated from Latin into vernacular languages.
52. Azak, 2010, pp. 49–50.
53. Azak, 2010, p. 58.
54. İsmail Kara, "Islam and Islamism in Turkey: A Conversation with İsmail Kara," *Maydan*, 2017, pp. 7, 10 & 18–19.
55. Nurullah Ardıç, *Islam and the Politics of Secularism: The Caliphate and Middle Eastern Modernization in the Early 20th Century*, Routledge, 2012, pp. 310 ff.
56. Susan Ritchie, "Postsecularization or Why We Have Never Been Secular," 20 July 2021. Text from author.

4. POST-WAR

1. A second future president, Turgut Özal, was probably near Demirel that day, according to Can Dündar, *Milliyet*, 10 September 2005.
2. Ahmet Hamdi Akseki, *Dini müesseselerimiz hakkında bir rapor*, Diyanet İşleri Başkanlığı, 12 December 1950.
3. Pilavoğlu himself was brought to trial in 1950, leading to protests by his followers, whom he claimed to number 40,000. He was later sentenced to 20 years' prison and exile to Turkey's Aegean islands.
4. *Zafer*, 4 June 1950, cited in Azak, 2010, p. 74. TBMM proceedings of 16 June 1950.
5. *TBMM Tutanak Dergisi*, 29 May 1950, Period 9, Vol. 1, p. 31.
6. Vatan, 7 December 1952.
7. "Başvekilin Konya Nutku," *Sebilürreşad*, 9:212, October 1956, pp. 179–182.
8. Azak, 2010, pp. 111–112.
9. Şerif Mardin, *Religion and Social Change in Turkey: The Case of Bediüzzaman Said Nursi*, State University of New York Press, Albany, 1989, p. 183.
10. Ahmet Akgündüz, *Arşiv belgeleri ışığında Silistre'li Süleyman Hilmi Tunahan*, 1997, pp. 93–94.
11. Notably Hamid Algar, "Said Nursi and the Risale-i Nur. An Aspect of Islam in Contemporary Turkey," *Islamic Perspectives—Studies in Honor of Sayyid Aba Ala Mawdudi etc.*, Leicester, 1979, pp. 313–333 and Mardin, 1989, especially pp. 147 ff.
12. Necmeddin Şahiner, *Bilinmeyen Taraflariyle Bediüzzaman Said Nursi: Kronolojik Hayatı*, Yeni Asya Yayınlarlı, 1993, pp. 264–265. This work is the source of many of the golden legends about Nursi.
13. Şükran Vahide (Fırıncı), *Islam in Modern Turkey: An Intellectual Biography of Bediüzzaman Said Nursi*, State University of New York, 2005, p. 13. Also Mardin, 1989, p. 77.
14. Şahiner, 1993, p. 103.
15. *Volkan* newspaper No. 90. In *Volkan*, he wrote under the name Said-i Kürdi. In later years, he—and particularly his disciples—would play down his Kurdishness.
16. Şahiner, 1993, p. 169.
17. *Bediüzzaman Said Nursi: Hayati-Mesleği-Tercüme-i Hali*, Yeni Asya Neşriyat, 4th reprint, 2004, p. 103.
18. Şahiner, 1993, pp. 182–183.
19. Caroline Tee, *The Gülen Movement in Turkey: The Politics of Islam and Modernity,* I.B. Tauris, 2016, p. 41.
20. Şahiner, 1993, p. 270.
21. The officer transporting the group to court later said he had been instructed to execute Nursi and his students en route. One of the arrested, Major Ahmet Asım Önerdem, died under interrogation. Vahide, 2005, pp. 216 & 201.

22. Vahide claims there were two attempts to poison Nursi during the period and further attempts in 1943. Vahide, 2005, pp. 250–251 & 257.
23. Between April 1944 and March 1960, the experts of the *Diyanet* were asked to investigate the works of Nursi 23 times, on each occasion concluding the works contained nothing against the law and showed no indication of an illegal *tarikat. Diyanet İşleri Reisliği Nurculuk Hakkında Ne Diyor?*, 1964, cited by Azak, 2010, p. 133.
24. Şükran Vahide, correspondence of 3 & 6 December 2020.
25. Vahide, 2005, p. 204.
26. Vahide, 2005, p. 322.
27. Ruthven, 2000, pp. 230–235.
28. It has recently been discovered that Ibn Arabi spent two decades in the Seljuk Sultanate of Rum. His stepson, Sadreddin Konevi, was a friend of Mevlana. His disciples and those of Konevi brought Ibn Arabi's teachings to the Ottomans, definitively shaping Ottoman Islam.
29. Ibn Arabi, *The Wisdom of the Prophets*, Aldsworth, 1975, p. 24, cited by Ruthven, 2000, p. 238.
30. Bediüzzaman Said Nursi, "The Thirty-Second Window of the Thirty-Third Word," *The Words, from the Risale-i Nur Collection*, tr. Şükran Vahide, Sözler Neşriyat, 1992, p. 272.
31. Mardin, 1989, pp. 231 and 222.
32. Mardin, 1989, p. 157.
33. Mardin, 1989, pp. 157, 219 & 221
34. Unsigned essay by Şükran Vahide, "About the Risale-i Nur" *The Words*, p. 750.
35. Hamid Algar, "The Centennial Renewer, Bediüzzaman Said Nursi and the Tradition of *tajdid* [*tecdit*, renewal]," *Journal of Islamic Studies* 12:3, Oxford Centre for Islamic Studies, 2001, p. 310.
36. Bediüzzaman Said Nursi, *Şualar*, p. 670, cited in Algar, 2001, p. 306.
37. Alison Clare Mermer, *Aspects of Religious Identity: The Nurcu Movement in Turkey Today*, 1985, Durham theses, pp. 419–420.
38. Necip Fazıl Kısakürek, *Son Devrin Din Mazlumları*, Büyük Doğu, 1969/2015, p. 265.
39. https://tunahan.org/en/his-life/his-mission-and-service/.
40. Reşat Öngören, "Süleyman Hilmi Tunahan," *İslam Ansiklopedisi*, 2012 and Akgündüz, 1997, pp. 47 & 58.
41. Akgündüz, 1997, pp. 71 and 73–74.
42. Kısakürek, 1978, p. 9, cited in Şerif Mardin, "Cultural Change and the Intellectual: Necip Fazıl and the Nakşibendi," *Religion, Society, and Modernity in Turkey*, Syracuse University Press, 2006, p. 247.
43. Kısakürek, 1978, p. 64.
44. A year after this distribution, the state changed position, ordering a collection of copies of the book for betraying military secrets. Atılhan was elected

president of the International Organization against Zionism, Communism, and Freemasonry in Munich in 1934.

45. Erdoğan had a copy. https://www.ynetnews.com/articles/0,7340,L-4507646,00.html.
46. Malatya now hosts a mosque, an *imam-hatip* school, and a youth association named after Kısakürek. Another mosque, in Tuzla, İstanbul, and a dozen other schools carry his name.
47. Abdurrahman Dilipak, *İhtilaller Dönemi*, Beyan Yayınları, 1991, pp. 133–138, cited in Soner Yalçın, *Kayıp Sicil, Erdoğan'ın Çalınan Dosyası*, Kırmızı Kedi Yayınevi, 2014, n. 1, p. 75.
48. Prosper de Barante, *De la littérature française pendant le dix-huitième siècle*, 1824, cited in Mardin, op. cit. p. 251.
49. http://blog.milliyet.com.tr/bir-genclik--bir-genclik--bir-genclik-/Blog/?BlogNo=350110.
50. Nicolas Cheviron & Jean-François Pérouse, *Erdoğan: Nouveau père de la Turquie*, Éditions François Bourin, 2016, p. 45.
51. These were the years after the MTTB had adapted its anti-communist militant nationalism of the 1960s—it was an immune protagonist in the Bloody Sunday attacks on leftists on 16 February 1969—to cluster around the cause of Islam. It started calling for Ayasofya to be reopened for prayer, and its three presidents from 1971 venerated the Nakşibendi *şeyh*, Mahmut Sami Ramazanoğlu, of what is now the Erenköy *tarikat* (see Chapter 8). The MTTB's president for 1976–1977 campaigned on the slogan of having a prayer room for every school.
52. Murat Ağırel, *Sarmal*, Kırmızı Kedi Yayınevi, 2020, pp. 83–84, citing Serkan Yorgancılar, *Akıncılar-İslami Gençliğin Yazılmamış Öyküsü*, Otorite Yayınları, 2016, p. 225.
53. *Cumhuriyet*, 7 December 2013, citing a report by the Gendarmerie Command of İstanbul to the National Security Council of 27 February 2004. Kotku had demanded the closure of the MSP's youth branches and called for Erbakan's resignation as party leader. Emin Yaşar Demirci, "Modernization Religion and Politics in Turkey: The Case of the İskenderpaşa Community," doctoral thesis, Manchester University, 1996, p. 257.
54. Mardin, Kısakürek, 2006, pp. 250 & 258. Italics in the original.

5. THE NAKŞIBENDIS

1. Hamid Algar, "A Brief History of the Naqshbandi Order" in Marc Gaborieau, Alexandre Popovic, and Thierry Zarcone (eds.), *Naqshbandis*, IFEA, Éditions Isis, 1990, p. 20.
2. See Annex B and Maden, pp. 382–383.
3. Ruthven, 2000, pp. 268 ff.

4. Şerif Mardin, "The Nakshibendi Order of Turkey," *Fundamentalism and the State: Remaking Polities, Economies, and Militance*, ed. Martin E. Marty & R. Scott Appleby, University of Chicago, 1993, p. 212.
5. Hamid Algar, "Devotional Practices of the Khalidi Naqshbandis of Ottoman Turkey," *The Dervish Lodge: Architecture, Art, and Sufism in Ottoman Turkey*, ed. Raymond Lifchez, University of California, 1992, p. 213.
6. Trimingham, 1971, p. 2. More recent writers prefer the terms renunciation or self-deprival rather than asceticism.
7. Ruthven, 2000, pp. 254–255.
8. Ömer Tuğrul İnançer, "Rituals and Main Principles of Sufism during the Ottoman Empire," *Sufism and Sufis in Ottoman Society*, ed. Ahmet Yaşar Ocak, Türk Tarih Kurumu, 2005, pp. 123 ff.
9. Ahmad al-Ghazali, *Bawariq al-ilma*, translated by James Robson in *Two Tracts on Listening to Music*, London, 1938, pp. 99–100, cited by Trimingham, 1971, p. 195.
10. Ruthven, 2000, pp. 255–256.
11. Trimingham, 1971, p. 199, where he notes that the Haidariyya, a Kalender group, used hemp and that later coffee became an essential aspect of all *zikir* gatherings.
12. Ibn Khallikan, Cairo, 1299, i. 95–96, written around 1256, according to Trimingham, 1971, p. 37.
13. Van Bruinessen, 1992, p. 236.
14. Mardin, 1993, p. 211 & Abd al-Majid al-Khani, *as-Saadat al-Abadiya*, Damascus, 1891, pp. 9–10, cited in Algar, 1992, pp. 213–214.
15. Algar, 1990, p. 119.
16. Trimingham, 1971, pp. 63–64.
17. Algar, 1990, p. 18.
18. Algar, 1990, p. 10.
19. Mehmed Fuad Köprülü, *Early Mystics in Turkish Literature* (Turkish 1918), ed. Gary Leiser & Robert Dankoff, Routledge, 2006, pp. 8–9.
20. Ahmet T. Karamustafa, "Origins of Anatolian Sufism" in *Sufism and Sufis in Ottoman Society*, ed. Ahmet Yaşar Ocak, 2005, pp. 78 ff.
21. Trimingham, 1971, pp. 203–204.
22. Algar, 1990, p. 20.
23. Algar, 1990, p. 22.
24. In his memoirs—one of the first by a ruling emperor—Babur writes of his family as having political kingship while Ahrar possessed spiritual monarchy. Algar, 1990, p. 25.
25. Hamid Algar, "İmâm-ı Rabbânî," *İslam Ansiklopedisi*, 2000.
26. *Maktubat* I, pp. 100–101, cited in Algar, 1990, p. 28.
27. Ruthven, 2000, pp. 274–276.
28. In recent times, most, if not all of these seminaries, have been well funded by

Riyadh. The Jamia Darul Uloom Haqqania in north Pakistan counts among its graduates Mullah Omar, former leader of the Taliban. Its director boasted that, whenever the Taliban put out a call for fighters, he would simply close down the *medrese* and send his students off to fight. William Dalrymple, "Inside Islam's 'Terror Schools,'" *New Statesman*, 28 March 2005.

29. The main Nakşibendi branch to suffer in the Ottomans' Golden Age was that following *Şeyh* Aziz Mahmud Urmevî. During the Ottoman campaign to recapture Baghdad, Urmevi's ability to attract 40,000 disciples caused Murad IV, askance at such power, to execute him. Cf. Algar, 1990, p. 124.
30. His original name was Diya al-Dīn Khalid al-Shahrazuri, with the *nesba* el-Bağdadi reflecting his frequent stays in that city.
31. Muhammad Hisham Kabbani, *Classical Islam and the Naqshbandi Sufi Tradition*, Islamic Supreme Council of America, 2004, p. 346.
32. Butrus Abu Manneh, "A New Look at the Rise and Expansion of the Khalidi Sub-Order," *Sufism and Sufis in Ottoman Society*, ed. Ahmet Yaşar Ocak, Türk Tarih Kurumu, 2005, p. 292.
33. Algar, 1990, p. 37.
34. Mardin, 1993, p. 213.
35. Ibn Taymiyya, *Siyasa Sharia*, tr. H. Laoust, Beirut, 1948, p. 172, cited in Ruthven, 2000, p. 171.
36. Natana J. DeLong-Bas, *Wahhabi Islam: From Revival and Reform to Global Jihad*, Oxford University Press, 2004, p. 84.
37. Dinimiz İslam, http://www.dinimizislam.com/detay.asp?Aid=1656
38. Reprinted in Fatih M. Şeker, *Osmanlılar ve Vehhabilik: Hüseyin Kazım Kadri'nin Vehhabilik Risalesi*, Dergah Yayınları, 2007.

PART THREE: FLOWERING

1. İrfan Özet, *Fatih Başakşehir, Muhafazakâr Mahallede İktidar ve Dönüşen Habitus*, İletişim, 2019, p. 62.

6. INDUSTRIALIZING TURKEY AND THE EROSION OF SECULARISM

1. Can Dündar, *Milliyet*, 5 December 2005.
2. The bans were only one example of the generals' abuses of human rights. Around 100 of their prisoners died from torture, a figure two orders of magnitude greater than those who perished in the cells of the Greek Colonels. The latter's regime was forced to resign from the Council of Europe. The West showed no such concerns over torture in Turkey.
3. Gözaydın, 2008, p. 163. The author pointed out that during the 1970s, Law 633 was partially suspended, describing as "one of the wonders of the Turkish

sociopolitical system, especially from a legal anthropological point" that an administrative unit as important as the *Diyanet* could subsequently operate without proper regulations. Idem, pp. 164 & 172.

4. Ahmet Erdi Öztürk, "Transformation of the Turkish *Diyanet* Both at Home and Abroad: Three Stages," *European Journal of Turkish Studies* [Online], 27, 2018, pp. 7 & 9.
5. Ersin Nazif Gürdoğan, *Görünmeyen Üniversite*, İz Yayıncılık, 1991, 7th edition, 2011, pp. 44–45.
6. Article 29 of the MNP programme.
7. Religious opinion was also split. As one leading Islamic philosopher wrote: "Before elections, they display themselves praying in well-known mosques with their dignitaries. ... This procession of delusion, which has turned the lodge sometimes into a factory chimney, other times into a gate of prosperity and politics, is today potentially the biggest threat to the religion of Islam." Nurettin Topçu, *Hareket*, VI/61-62, January–February 1971, cited in İsmail Kara, 2020.
8. Visiting Jeddah in spring 1979, Erbakan told Ahmed Zaki Yamani, Minister of Petroleum and Mineral Resources, that he had wished to call his party the Muslim Brotherhood, but the Turkish army would not have allowed this. Interview with Uğur Ergun, then First Secretary at the Turkish Embassy, in October 2021.
9. Yavuz, 2003, p. 208.
10. Behlül Özkan, "The Cold War-era Origins of Islamism in Turkey and Its Rise to Power," Hudson Institute, 5 November 2017.
11. Binnaz Toprak, "Religion and Politics," *The Routledge Handbook of Modern Turkey*, ed. Metin Heper, Routledge, 2012, p. 219.
12. Soner Yalçın, *Kayıp Sicil, Erdoğan'ın Çalınan Dosyası*, Kırmızı Kedi Yayınevi, 2014, p. 95.
13. Cited by Jenkins, 2008, p. 138.
14. On 15–16 March 1980, Evren ordered planning of a coup, and on 18 May the generals decided this should be carried out on 11 July. Formation of a new government caused the date to be deferred to 12 September. Tanel Demirel, "The Turkish Military's Decision to Intervene: 12 September 1980," *The Politics of Modern Turkey, Vol. 2: Political Institutions and Processes*, ed. Ali Çarkoğlu & William Hale, Routledge, 2008, pp. 331–355.
15. "Din Eğitimi, Laiklik ve Ötesi," *Nokta*, 26 March 1989. "12 Eylül'ün Din Raporu," *Milliyet*, 19 March 1989.
16. Yavuz, 2003, p. 70.
17. There are reports he served as head of *Kontrgerilla*, the Turkish "stay-behind" forces sponsored by the CIA to encourage resistance in the case of a communist occupation (see Chapter 12). Evidence of CIA involvement in the September 1980 coup is at best circumstantial.

18. *Atatürkçülük: Üçüncü kitap. Atatürkçü düşünce sistemi,* 2nd edition, Milli Eğitim Basımevi, 1964, pp. 223 ff.
19. Jenkins, 2008, p. 151.
20. As initially phrased in 1926, Article 163 focused on the use of religion by *şeyh* to mobilize armed rebellion, proscribing penalties of up to five years' imprisonment. In June 1949, the CHP broadened the focus of the article from the likes of followers of *Şeyh* Said to those of Said Nursi, with penalties of up to seven years' imprisonment. In January 1983, the generals increased the coverage of the article and its penalties.
21. Robert R. Bianchi, *Guests of God: Pilgrimage and Politics in the Islamic World*, Oxford University Press, 2004, p. 151.
22. Bianchi, op. cit., pp. 143–144.
23. Toprak, 2012, p. 220.
24. Necmettin Erbakan, *Adil Ekonomik Düzen*, 1991, p. 1.
25. Toprak, 2012, pp. 220–221.
26. Maside Ocak, interviewed in "28 Şubat Belgeseli 4. Bölüm," *32.Gün Arşivi*, broadcast 2012.
27. See Annex A.
28. This phrase was used by General Çevik Bir two weeks after the Sincan events. Bir was largely responsible for the establishment of the Western Working Group. In 2018, Bir was given an aggravated life sentence for his role in the "soft coup" of 1997. In August 2022, he was released from prison on health grounds.
29. *Altınoluk*, April 2011, p. 59.
30. *Economist*, 3 March 2011.

7. İSKENDERPAŞA AND THE RISE OF POLITICAL ISLAM

1. *Zakat* are the charitable alms prescribed in the *Kur'an*. Translation in Goodword Books, 2012.
2. "Cevat Akşit Hocaefendi'nin Hatıraları ve Mehmed Zahid Kotku Hazretleri," YouTube, 1 May 2017.
3. Korkut Özal, "Twenty Years with Mehmed Zahid Kotku: A Personal Story," *Naqshbandis in Western and Central Asia: Change and Continuity*, Swedish Research Institute in İstanbul, ed. Elisabeth Özdalga, Curzon, 1999, p. 166.
4. Gürdoğan, 2011, pp. 35 ff.
5. Korkut Özal, 1999, p. 166.
6. Korkut Özal, 1999, p. 162.
7. Mardin, 1993, pp. 222–223.
8. Algar noted these views after visiting Kotku on 10 January 1970. Algar, 1990, p. 136, footnote 3.
9. Yavuz, 2003, p. 207.

10. Interview with author Müfid Yüksel, 12 September 2020.
11. Mehmet Akkuş, "Mahmut Esat Coşan," *İslam Ansiklopedisi*, 2016. Coşan's name does not appear in the list of those preparing the 1983 report on National Culture.
12. Bacık, 2019, p. 137.
13. Esad Coşan, *Yeni Dönemde Yeni Görevlerimiz*, Seha, 1993, p. 163, cited in Yavuz, 2003, p. 143.
14. Bacık, 2019, pp. 164–167 & 195.
15. The Learning, Culture and Art Foundation (İLKSAV, *İlim Kültür ve Sanat Vakfi*), the Moral Culture and Environment Association (*Ahlâk Kültür ve Çevre Derneği*) and the Health Foundation (*Sağlık Vakfi*), which later morphed into TESA (*Türkiye Eğitim ve Sağlık Araştırma*) Foundation.
16. Ruşen *Çakır, Ayet ve Slogan*, Metiş, 1990. p. 27.
17. Çakır, 1990. p. 30.
18. Özet, 2019, pp. 64–66. Soner Yalçın, "İslam Dergisi'nin idealist gençlerine ne oldu," *Hürriyet,* 28 September 2008.
19. http://www.turktoresi.com/viewtopic.php?f=214&t=10224.
20. *Hürriyet*, 10 February 2001 and *Internet Haber*, 26 September 2019.
21. Soner Yalçın, 2014, p. 177.
22. Letter cited by Murat Bardakçı in *Hürriyet*, 11 February 2001.
23. As of 2013, the last public record identified.
24. The founding Secretary General of TESA was Zeki Agralı, once the right-hand man of Esat Coşan. *Tele 1*, 26 March 2020.
25. www.mecfoundation.org.au/qurban/organization-process/, figure not updated as of March 2024.
26. "M Nureddin çoşan hocaefendi," 16 January 2014, https://www.youtube.com/watch?v=6nAPfDAnQ4E.
27. Esat Coşan, "Şam Bölgesi'nin Halkı Helak olduğu zaman - 5.12.1993. 3. Hadis," 19 February 2018, https://www.youtube.com/watch?v=g5YDIB9TvZE.
28. *Cumhuriyet*, 7 December 2013, citing Gendarmerie report of 27 February 2004.
29. A number of instances of this are given by Barış Pehlivan & Barış Terkoğlu, *Metastaz*, Kırmızı Kedi Yayınevi, 2019, pp. 69–80.
30. Mustafa Öztürk, *Medyascope*, 22 December 2022.
31. "Cevat Akşit Hocaefendi'nin Hatıraları ve Mehmed Zahid Kotku Hazretleri," interview on YouTube, 1 May 2017.
32. Tayfun Atay, "The Reis Doesn't Care a Hoot for İskenderpaşa," *T24*, 25 March 2019.

8. THE TURKISH-ISLAMIC SYNTHESIS AND THE PATRICIAN ERENKÖY COMMUNITY

1. This, the normal translation of the name, misses the nuance in the word

Aydınlar, which tends to be used for those close to authority. By contrast, the word *entelektüel* connotes an independent-minded thinker, with an implication of Bohemianism.

2. Binnaz Toprak, "Religion as State Ideology in a Secular Setting: The Turkish-Islamic Synthesis," *Aspects of Religion in Secular Turkey*, ed. Malcolm Wagstaff, University of Durham Occasional Paper Series No. 40, 1990, p. 11.
3. Abdurrahman Dilipak, *Türkiye Nereye Gidiyor?*, Risale Yayınları, 1988, pp. 50–61, cited by Tanıl Bora & Kemal Can, *Devlet, Ocak, Dergah: 12 Eylül'den 1990'lara Ülkücü Hareket*, İletişim Yayınları, 1990, p. 152.
4. "According to Bennigsen, the most significant of the Sufi brotherhoods was a secret society called the Naqshbandiya, a Freemason-style fraternity closely tied to the elite of Turkey." Devin DeWeese, *Sufism in Central Asia: New Perspectives on Sufi Traditions, 15th-21st Centuries*, ed. Devin DeWeese & Jo-Ann Gross, Brill, 2018; Robert Dreyfuss, "The United States and the Birth of Islamism," *The Globalist*, 18 January 2006; Dreyfuss, *The Devil's Game: How the United States Helped Unleash Fundamentalist Islam*, Dell Publishing, 2006, pp. 253 & 14.
5. *Milli Kültür: Özel İhtisas Komisyon Raporu*, TC Başbakanlık Devlet Planlama Teşkilatı, October 1983, pp. 538–543.
6. Ibid, p. 527 and pp. 514–517.
7. Muharrem Ergin, A. Aydın Bolak and Süleyman Yalçın, *Milli Mutabakatlar*, Aydınlar Ocağı Derneği, 1984.
8. Toprak, 1990, p. 12.
9. Cf. Elisabeth Özdalga, "The Hidden Arab: A Critical Reading of the Notion of 'Turkish Islam,'" *Middle Eastern Studies*, 42/4, 2006, pp. 551–570.
10. Interview with Rasim Cinisli, former member of the consultative council of the Hearth, 10 August 2020.
11. Opening sentence of the IYC's slide presentation of its history, retrieved 22 July 2020 from IYC website. The plane tree was a symbol of the Ottoman dynasty.
12. Mardin, Islam, 2006, p. 276.
13. *Cumhuriyet*, 23 January 1955, p. 2.
14. *Aydınlık* newspaper on 20 March 2017.
15. It was not until 1990 that the Wahhabi *ulema* reasserted their control over religious policy.
16. *ANT*, issue 64, 19 March 1968, p. 4.
17. *İlim Yayma Cemiyeti ve Hizmetleri Kitapçığı*, year not specified, p. 12, cited by Ağırel, 2020, p. 142.
18. Uğur Mumcu, *Rabıta*, Gazi Kitabevi, 10th ed. 1993, p. 192. See below, Chapter 14.
19. Sabahattin Zaim, "Türkiye'nin ilk Sivil Toplum Kuruluşu İlim Yayma Cemiyeti," *İlim Yayma Cemiyeti Bülteni*, No. 12, Đikbahar, 2006, pp. 3–4. It

terms itself the first association to raise donations from the faithful for the sacrificial animals that form part of Muslim ritual celebrations. Such donations constitute an important source of revenue for many religious foundations.

20. Interview with Osman Acun, foundation officer responsible for relations with founders, 6 November 2019.
21. The house now serves as the Erenköy Mental Health Hospital.
22. Çakır, 1990, p. 56.
23. The previous General Secretary of MTTB was Devlet Bahçeli, head of the Nationalist Action Party (*Milliyetçi Hareket Partisi*, MHP) since 1997 and lately a political ally of Erdoğan.
24. Çakır, 1990, p. 60.
25. http://www.osmannuritopbas.com/osman-nuri-topbas-hocaefendi-kimdir.html.
26. Osman Nuri Topbaş, *The Secret in the Love for God*, p. 63, cited in Bacık, 2019, pp. 169–170. Also pp. 183 & 199.
27. Erkam Publications, 2013, p. 9.
28. The main websites of the Erenköy movement are http://www.osmannuritopbas.com/tag/erenkoy-cemaati and http://www.islamveihsan.com. Also http://www.evliyalar.net/musa-topbas-hocaefendi-k-s/.
29. Figures as of March 2024. His main X account was @osmannuritopbas, with @OsmanTopbasEN being an English account.
30. Yavuz, 2003, p. 14.
31. Çakır, 1990, p. 56. Also Barış Ermis, "Günümüz Dini Gruplarin Siyasetle İlişkisi (Altınoluk/Erenköy Cemaati)," thesis, Isparta, 2018, pp. 35 ff.
32. The Hüdayi Foundation's head, Ahmet Hamdi Topbaş, was named in the Panama Papers as having established a trading company, Twillett, and accused by *Birgün* newspaper of depositing funds collected for the foundation in Switzerland. A denial by Ahmet Hamdi Topbaş may be found at http://www.islamveihsan.com/tag/erenkoy-cemaati.
33. http://hudayivakfi.org/egitim-hizmetlerimiz.html, retrieved 23 October 2023 though dated 25 January 2018.
34. See also Chapter 14.
35. In 2007, the Ülkers' Yıldız Holding bought the Belgian chocolate manufacturer, Godiva, and in 2014 United Biscuits, Britain's leading biscuit company. The latter's brands include McVitie's, Jacob's, Twiglets, Penguin, Carr's, DeliChoc, Mini Cheddars, and Jaffa Cakes.
36. Abdullah Tivnikli, like Mustafa Latif Topbaş, had his assets temporarily frozen in 2013.
37. Published from 1986.
38. Cakır, op. cit., p. 60.

9. THE RISE OF THE PURISTS

1. Part cited in Çakır, 1990, pp. 60–61.
2. The suffix '-*cı*' implies a profession, for instance *tahtacı* is a person dealing in wood (*tahta*). Followers of Tunahan call themselves Süleymanlı, the suffix '-*lı*' meaning those who are with or follow. They consider the term Süleymancı to be deprecatory. Most literature about the community refers to them as Süleymancıs, and this term, without any sense of judgement, is used herein.
3. Almost all the rest are Alevis, whose course is reviewed in Annex A.
4. Kimberly Hart, *And Then We Work for God: Rural Sunni Islam in Western Turkey*, Stanford University Press, 2013, p. 214.
5. Hart, 2013, p. 215.
6. Interview with Hart, January 2020. For half a century, the Ministry of Education was involved in control of *Kur'an* courses. In 2012, full control of the courses and connected dormitories was passed to the *Diyanet*.
7. Hart, 2013, p. 198.
8. *Threat Evaluation of Reactionary Religious Groups*, a report purportedly by the General Staff, *Birgün*, 30 November 2016.
9. Yavuz, 2003, p. 147.
10. Zekayi Işın, a former branch director of the Süleymancıs in Germany, Veryansın TV, 2 January 2021. In 2012, they operated 274 cultural institutions and 48 mosques in Germany and the Netherlands alone, numbers then exceeded by the *Diyanet* but similar to those of the *Milli Görüş*: Ahmet Yükleyen, *Localizing Islam in Europe: Turkish Islamic Communities in Germany and the Netherlands*, Syracuse University Press, 2012, pp. 50 & 66.
11. "Konsensus Türkiye Gündemi Araştırması 'Cemaatler,'" *Habertürk*, May 2011. A report on "destructive and divisive currents" apparently printed by the army in 1982, says there were 300,000 Süleymancıs. Zekayi Işın, *Kim Bu Süleymancılar?*, Okuyorum Yayınları, 2001, p. 279.
12. One example is Yavuz, 2003, p. 145. He cites a number of historical sources, none of which appear confirmatory.
13. Işın, Veryansın TV, 2 January 2021.
14. These are listed at https://tunahan.org/en/his-life/his-mission-and-service/. These cover grammar, law, logic, and doctrine, with additional works at an advanced level.
15. Muslims in the Ottoman Empire and Turkey use the Hafs transmission (pronunciation and intonation) of the Aasim ibn Abi al-Najud reading of the *Kur'an*. Işın is scathing about Tunahan's teaching claims, Işın, 2021, pp. 19 & 55 ff.
16. Yükleyen, 2012, p. 99.
17. Hart, 2013, p. 219.
18. Ahmet Yükleyen, "Production of Mystical Islam in Europe: Religious

Authorization in the Süleymanlı Sufi Community," *Contemporary Islam*, No. 4, 2010, p. 277.

19. The building had long been condemned, with the municipality offering generous alternatives.
20. Kısakürek, 1969/2015, p. 263. İmam-ı Rabbani is the Turkish sobriquet for Ahmed-i Sirhindi, the renewer of Nakşibendism.
21. Articles 22 & 7 of Law 633 of 2 July 1965.
22. Ahmet Güner & Hakkı Karadeniz, "Türkiye'de Mezhep ve Tarikatlar," *Milliyet*, 17 May 1986, p. 6.
23. Çakır, 1990, pp. 126, 129 & 136.
24. Hayrullah Karadeniz's statement of 9 September 2016 in *İlk Kurşun*, 31 December 2018. This claim is also found in *Diyanet'in Tarikatlar Raporu*, ed. Oktay Yıldırım, Görev Kitap, 2019, p. 237.
25. Çakır, 1990, p. 133. Süleymancıs avoid public criticism of Atatürk, but in their private lessons some castigate him as *Deccal*, the Islamic equivalent of the Antichrist, according to Işın, Veryansın TV, 2 January 2021.
26. Şaban Sitembölükbaşi, "Süleyman Hilmi Tunahan—2," *İslam Ansiklopedisi*, 2012.
27. These blogs described Erdoğan as being a pawn of the CIA and the Israelis.
28. Pehlivan & Terkoğlu, 2019, p. 79.
29. This elevated title (*emîrü'l-mü'minîn*), first bestowed on Caliph Ömer, was used by Muammer Davran, responsible for the *cemaat*'s activities in Africa.
30. The most popular YouTube broadcast about Kuriş details an alleged plan of Erdoğan to have him replaced. Posted on 7 November 2019, by January 2023, this had attracted 516,000 views. Cevheri Güven, "Süleymancılar neden hedefte? Saray'ın Süleymancıların liderini değiştirme planının detayları."
31. This arrangement seems to have survived a year before it was shared with, or taken over by, the Ensar Foundation, one of the several foundations established by the Erdoğan family. The Erdoğan foundations are described in Chapter 15.
32. For the runoff, the necessary instruction by the 'İstanbul Secretariat' has found its way to the press. Işın, Veryansın TV, 2 January 2021 and *Aydınlık*, 13 June 2019.
33. "Türk Toplumunda *Cemaat Algısı Araştırması*," ANDY-AR Sosyal Araştırmalar Merkezi, 2011, reported by haber7, 6 April 2011.
34. Çakır, 1990, pp. 138–139, 136 & 129.
35. Interview with former regional organizer, December 2021.
36. Giving *zakat* is one of the five duties of a Moslem. For Süleymancıs in Germany, even going on holiday is subject to payment of a 'journey safety' levy.
37. Işın, 2021, p. 65.
38. Until 1983, the *cemaat* argued that the funds spent on *hajj* could better be used on charitable works. The İstanbul commercial register in September 2021 showed that Alihan and his elder brother, Hilmi Tuna Kuriş, were also

linked to three construction companies, an architectural company, and a shipping agency.
39. Cost from Işın, 2021, p. 67. In 2005, the Cologne tax authorities, less impressed, launched an investigation into 40 million euros of money laundering and tax evasion by the İKMB, causing it to have to close its branches.
40. https://www.youtube.com/watch?v=jzJxIhUE2fc.
41. Private communication of a professor at Bosphorus University.
42. Mahmud Ustaosmanoğlu, *Life Story of Hazrati Mahmud Effendi*, Ahıska Yayınevi, after 2013, pp. 16 & 20. In 2005, the number of Turks performing the *umre* were 42,109 more than those for the year before. In 2011, the increase was 29,391.
43. Ustaosmanoğlu, 2013, p. 59.
44. https://www.youtube.com/watch?v=dHYT0C6FIIU, http://www.hurriyet.com.tr/gundem/iste-tarikatin-merkezi-sokagin-adi-8868845.
45. Ustaosmanoğlu, 2013, p. 10.
46. Ustaosmanoğlu, 2013, pp. 9–10. A similar tale is told of Said Nursi's mother: Vahide, 2005, p. 8.
47. Çakır, 1990, p. 62
48. Çakır, 1990, p. 61
49. The Association website gave these numbers in mid-2020. As of March 2024, the numbers had not been updated.
50. https://www.iddef.org/kalici-eserler.
51. Tayfun Atay, 22 May 2015, http://www.cumhuriyet.com.tr/koseyazisi/282645/Cemaatlerde_hukumet_korkusu.html.
52. Çakır, 1990, p. 62
53. Çakır, 1990, p. 61
54. Cheviron & Pérouse, 2016, pp. 121–122.
55. Ustaosmanoğlu, 2013, pp. 62, 47 & 51–52.
56. Interview with Rıdvan Akar of CNN Türk, 4 March 2010.
57. Ustaosmanoğlu, 2013, p. 63.
58. *BirGün*, 24 November, 2023.
59. Ustaosmanoğlu, 2013, pp. 68–69.
60. *Cübbeli* Ahmet Hoca, "Oral Meselesi Hakkında Bilgi, Haram mıdır? Mekruh mudur?" YouTube, posted 15 July 2015.
61. Cihaner seems to have attracted this vindictive move not only for prosecuting the İsmailağa order but because he had opened a lawsuit against the Gülen Movement, accusing it of money laundering, espionage, and abuse of public sector entrance examinations. The prosecutor charging him was later thrown out of the judiciary for links with FETÖ and in 2019 received an 11-year prison sentence for these links.
62. Ustaosmanoğlu, 2013, p. 79.
63. Ustaosmanoğlu, 2013, pp. 68–69.

64. Prof. Mustafa Öztürk, "Turkey's Most Secular Structures Are the *Tarikat*," *Medyascope*, 22 December 2022.
65. Emine Bıçakçı, Medyascope, 1 May 2023.

10. MENZIL AND THE IŞIKÇIS

1. Goodword Books, 2012.
2. Saygı Öztürk, *Menzil: Bir Tarikatın İki Yüzü*, Doğan Kitap, 2019, p. 69.
3. Çakır, 1994, pp. 67–68.
4. According to the Dar al-Masnavi website, this poem is "is found in the same form in the quatrains of [Efdaluddin-i Kaşanı] (died 1274) and is related to a similar quatrain attributed to Abu Sa`id ibn Abi 'l-Khayr, died 1048."
5. Nafiz Ay, cited in Öztürk, 2019, p. 89.
6. Özet, 2019, pp. 129–133.
7. Aykaç, 2007, p. 66.
8. Aykaç, 2007, pp. 38–39.
9. Öztürk, 2019, p. 154.
10. Bilge Yabancı, "Work for the Nation, Obey the State, Praise the *Ummah*: Turkey's Government-oriented Youth Organizations in Cultivating a New Nation," *Ethnopolitics*, Taylor & Francis Online, October 2019, p. 2.
11. It also uses its Haşimî Training Institutions to spread the movement's message abroad. In Europe, the related UKBA assists the Turkish community, not least with funeral services. In October 2023, it had eleven representatives in six countries.
12. Ali Bayramoğlu, "İslami Kesim ve Temsil Krizi," *Yeni Yüzyıl*, 14 November 1995.
13. See previous chapter.
14. Öztürk, 2019, pp. 71, 92, 178 & 179.
15. Öztürk, 2019, pp. 146 & 170.
16. "Subject of the Month: The Non-ending National Struggle," *Semerkand*, Issue 231, March 2018, p. 41. This magazine is published in Turkish, Bosnian, German, and Arabic. Until June 2002, the editorials were written by Saki Erol, and since then mainly by Mübarek Erol, signing as Muhammed Mübarek Elhüseyni.
17. GENÇKONFED, 2017, cited in "Milli Dusunce, Yerli Uretim, Dogru Tercih." Also http://www.genckonfed.org.
18. https://aljazari.com.tr/tr/about-us/, visited 7 January 2023.
19. http://www.feyzdergisi.com/icerik/841/molla-seyyid-abdulbaki-hz-ile-muhammed-rasid-hz-hakkinda-roportaj.html.
20. Aydın Hasan, *Milliyet*, 30 May 2011.
21. Colonel Nuri Kureş, cited in Öztürk, 2019, p. 62.
22. Öztürk, 2019, p. 47.

23. Öztürk, 2019, p. 53.
24. Öztürk, 2019, p. 36.
25. Video of Fevzeddin Erol, posted on YouTube by Edip Yüksel, 12 May 2014. https://www.youtube.com/watch?v=1swmLB1h_Vs.
26. Aykaç, 2007, p. 62; also Öztürk, 2019, p. 36.
27. Öztürk, 2019, p. 46.
28. Öztürk, 2019, pp. 183–184.
29. Öztürk, 2019, p. 80.
30. Öztürk, 2019, pp. 205–206.
31. Abdullah İnce, "Yakın Dönem Türkiye'sinde Nakşilik-Siyaset İlişkisi," *Tarihten Günümüze Sufi-Siyaset İlişkileri—Sufism and Politics Past and Present*, ed. Salih Çift & Vejdi Bilgin, İslami İlimler Araştırma Vakfı, Ensar Neşriyat, 2020, pp. 674–675.
32. Cited in *Medyascope*, 26 July 2023.
33. Kısakürek questioned the authenticity of this certificate.
34. Bacık, 2019, pp. 140–141.
35. Bacık, 2019, pp. 161–163, 179–181 & 188.
36. Nazif Ay, "Işıkçılar arkasında hangi komutanlar vardı?," *Stratejik Güvenlik*, 25 April 2019.
37. http://huseyinhilmiisik.com/englife.htm. English edited by writer.
38. http://huseyinhilmiisik.com/englife.htm, last retrieved 17 August 2021.

11. THE APOSTLES OF NURSI

1. Nursi himself attracted less than six mentions per year from his death until Şerif Mardin's analysis of his teaching (Mardin, 1989) initiated a wider reappraisal of him. Cf. Azak, 2010, pp. 133–134.
2. Van Bruinessen, *Agha*, 1992, pp. 259 & 264; Yavuz, 2003, p. 151; and Konsensus, 2011.
3. Yavuz, 2003, p. 173.
4. This support for the Generals' Revolutionary Council (*Konsey*) means they are sometimes termed the *Konseyciler*.
5. Çakır, 1990, p. 92.
6. His statement that the 1999 Marmara earthquake was a "divine warning" led to a 276-day prison term—for which the European Court of Human Rights later ordered Turkey to pay him compensation.
7. The *Lahikalar* (Supplements), often published as part of the *Risale-i Nur* collection, contain Nursi's defence speeches in court, articles written by admirers, and his letters to disciples.
8. Mermer, 1985, pp. 173 ff.
9. Council of Ministers Decree 2014/7007, published 26 November 2014.

10. One said it was making copyright payments to the heirs of Bediüzzaman, not to the *Diyanet*. Editions published in 2020 and 2021 made no reference to the *Diyanet*.
11. Cf. "*Nurculuk*, Risale-i Nur ve Bediuzzaman Hakkinda Sorular ve Cevaplar," *Dava*, No. 70–71 (February–March 1996), p. 13, cited in Fulya Atacan, "A Kurdish Islamist Group in Modern Turkey: Shifting Identities," *Middle Eastern Studies*, 37:3, Taylor & Francis, July 2001, p. 113.
12. Issues of *Dava* from 1991 and 1995, cited in Atacan, 2001, pp. 120 & 125.
13. Interview with Ersin Çelik, *Gerçek Hayat*, 27 April 2007. In 2014, the heirs to the printing rights of *Risale-i Nur* obtained a court block on printing by a Gülen printing house. OdaTV, 16 April 2014.
14. Atacan, 2001, p. 112.
15. M. Xalid Sadînî, *Independent Türkçe*, 23 January 2020.
16. The Kurdish Hezbollah, termed Turkish Hizbullah, is described in Jenkins, 2008, pp. 185–195.
17. The apartment belonged to Hüseyin Üzmez, who had tried to kill Ahmed Emin Yalman in 1952 and then become a conservative journalist. In 2011, he was sentenced to thirteen years' prison for sexual abuse of a minor.
18. In 2009, Kalkancı received a 20-year sentence for operating a heroin laboratory in Büyükçekmece. The raid on his facilities uncovered 2 million tablets of Captagon, a pill often used by ISIS for giving chemical courage.

12. GÜLEN AND FIVE DECADES OF GUILE

1. The survey was of 3,000 adults: 6.2% said they had participated in *tarikat* activities, with higher figures for members of Erdoğan's AKP. This ratio is applied to those aged twenty and over to develop the total. "Konsensus Türkiye Gündemi Araştirmasi 'Cemaatler,'" *Habertürk*, May 2011.
2. This second survey was of 2,160 adults, carried out by Ömer Çaha et al., "Türk Toplumunda *Cemaat Algısı Araştırması*," ANDY-AR Sosyal Araştırmalar Merkezi, 2011. For subsequent surveys, see Chapter 16.
3. Dexter Filkins, "The Thirty-Year Coup," *New Yorker*, 17 October 2016.
4. The main organizer of the conference was the academic M. Hakan Yavuz. In 2013, he dismissed books by three authors imprisoned after criticizing Gülen as relying mainly on hearsay and reflecting "an alarmist view about the power and role of the Gülen movement in Turkey by those who have been tied to the Kemalist ancien régime, and are now witnessing their own power fade away." Yavuz, *Towards an Islamic Enlightenment: The Gülen Movement*, Oxford University Press, 2013, p. 227.
5. Latif Erdoğan, *Fethullah Gülen Hocaefendi: Küçük Dünyam*, AD Yayıncılık, 1995, re-issued 2006.
6. Yavuz, 2013, p. 34. He was a founder member of the revival of the Erzurum

branch of the Turkish Association for Combating Communism (TKMD), Ağırel, 2020, p. 107.

7. "*Teokratik develeti savunan örgütler yapılanması*," report to the martial law command, Ankara, 1972.
8. "Asiye Güldoğan," OdaTV, 19 July 2014.
9. Suzy Hansen, "The Global Imam: What Does the Leader of the World's Most Influential Islamic Movement Really Want?," *New Republic*, 10 November 2010.
10. Ibid.
11. *Zaman* distributed copious free copies.
12. Some commentators question whether a surgical operation on 26 November 2011 affected his character.
13. Rıza M. Türmen, *Milliyet*, 19 April 2010, and *Cumhuriyet*, 20 May 2010.
14. Yavuz, 2013, pp. 92 ff.
15. Yavuz, 2013, p. 75. The followers of Kotku also used the term *Hocaefendi* to refer to their preceptor.
16. Yavuz, 2013, pp. 58–59, 93 & 96.
17. Güngör Ergün, *Bugün Gazetesi*, 27 November 2013.
18. Various state-of emergency decrees with the force of law published in the *Official Gazette.*
19. Hansen, 2010.
20. Like the GYV, this was closed in Turkey after the coup, but continued in New York by the the Journalists and Writers Foundation, http://jwf.org/intercultural-dialogue-platform/2016/.
21. Soner Yalçın, *Sözcü*, 2 February 2014. See also Chapter 9.
22. Filkins, 2016. Keleş, now a professor of theology, has published a book describing the seven-level hierarchy of the Gülen Movement: Ahmet Keleş, *Feto'nun Günah Piramidi*, Destek Yayınları, 2016.
23. Yavuz, 2013, p. 20.
24. Ibid.
25. *Hürriyet*, 20 June, 1999, translations by author.
26. Ibid.
27. Fehmi Koru, 24 June 1999, *One Column Ahead*, TİMAŞ, 2000, p. 199.
28. Yavuz, 2013, p. 43.
29. Çakır, 1990, p. 104.
30. Later instances were in Düzce in 2008 and in university entrance exams. Yusuf Ziya Özkan, the head of the exam board from 2007–2011, says that FETÖ used two prosecutors to get data from his system, one being Zekeriya Öz of Ergenekon fame (see below). *Milli Gazete*, 27 March 2014.
31. Merdan Yanardağ, *Turkiye Nasil Kusatildi? Fethullah Gülen Hareketinin Perde Arkası,* Siyah Beyaz Yayınları, 2006.
32. *Cumhuriyet*, 8 October and 27 December 2002.

33. Soner Yalçın, 2014, pp. 197–201. The Ankara lawyer and a disciple of Gülen received 300,000 USD for entrapping Yüksel, Sabri Uzun, *İN*, Kırmızı Kedi Yayınevi, 2015, pp. 183–187.
34. Can Bursalı, *Independent Türkçe*, 19 February 2020.
35. Brian Knowlton, *Turkish Review*, 1:2, 2011, p. 52, cited in Yavuz, 2013, pp. 10–11.
36. In 2022, Nuri Gökhan Bozkır, a former officer, confessed to assisting in the murder. *Cumhuriyet*, 17 February 2022 and OdaTV, 10 June 2022.
37. The remaining two panellists would be targeted in the Ergenekon trials (see below).
38. Can Bursalı, *Independent Türkçe*, 19 February 2020.
39. Hansen, 2010.
40. *Vatan*, 2 June 2008.
41. *Hürriyet,* 26 April 2009 and *haber7com*, 9 December 2009.
42. Jenkins, 2009, p. 43.
43. Fatih Güllapoğlu, *Tanksız Topsuz Harekât*, Tekin Yayınevi, 1991, p. 104. Also Taha Kıvanç, *Yeni Şafak*, 7 & 8 September 2005 and Ağırel, 2020, p. 41.
44. Bülent Ecevit, *Milliyet*, 28 November 1990.
45. Jenkins, 2009, p. 18.
46. Jenkins, 2009, p. 24.
47. Jenkins, 2009, pp. 55–56.
48. Gareth Jenkins, *The Turkey Analyst*, 14 August 2013.

13. COUP AND PURGE

1. In 2002, the journalist Nasuhi Güngör wrote that Erdoğan had sought Gülen's opinion before forming the AKP—a report that, when mentioned by a presidential opponent in 2018, caused Erdoğan to launch a libel suit. Saygı Öztürk, *Sözcü*, 24 January 2020.
2. This and the excerpt including the quote from Kalın are from Dexter Filkins, "Turkey's Thirty-Year Coup," *New Yorker*, 2016.
3. "Asiye Güldoğan," OdaTV, 5 December 2019. In 2020, Gürsel Aktepe, accused of planning the sting, received a 27-year sentence for running the FETÖ "VIP telephone tapping service."
4. M. Hakan Yavuz, 23 February 2017, in Yavuz & Balcı, 2018, p. 41. In 2011, estimates of the 327 AKP deputies with links to Gülen's *Cemaat* ranged from thirty to sixty (Dexter Filkins, "The Deep State," *New Yorker*, 12 March 2012).
5. Soner Yalçın, OdaTV, 19 September 2011, cited in Yalçın, 2014, p. 231.
6. It was later suggested that Fidan may have been targeted because he was considered friendly towards Iran. *Taraf* accused him of sharing CIA reports with Tehran, and MİT of organizing murders, including of Hrant Dink, a

prominent Armenian journalist, in İstanbul in January 2007, and of three missionaries in Malatya three months later.

7. M. Hakan Yavuz, *Erdoğan: The Making of an Autocrat*, Edinburgh University Press, 2021, p. 222.
8. In March 2019, a court sentenced fifteen individuals involved in the corruption investigations to life imprisonment. There have been no reports of those originally targeted for corruption being arraigned.
9. Tee, 2016, p. 185.
10. *Sözcü*, 25 July 2016.
11. The third bridge over the Bosphorus was inaugurated a month later.
12. The subsequent Meclis report gives figures of 90 and 1,154, p. 326.
13. Ahmet Şık's articles in *Cumhuriyet*, December 2016, assembled in the reprint of *İmamın Ordusu*, Kırmızı Kedi Yayınevi, June 2017, pp. 15–81.
14. *New York Times*, 26 July 2016.
15. *Le Monde*, 11 August 2016.
16. On 5 May 2017, a further 107 were dismissed.
17. U.S. State Department Country Reports on Human Rights Practices for 2019 and 2021.
18. "Opinion on the Legality of the Actions of the Turkish State" by William Clegg Q.C. & Simon Baker, 2 Bedford Row Chambers, London, September 2017.
19. *Reuters*, 3 August 2016.
20. "Fethullah Gulen Shares Blame for Turkey's Plight," *Economist*, 13 August 2020.
21. The U.N. Special Rapporteur on torture on 27 February 2018 expressed alarm at "allegations that large numbers of individuals suspected of links to the Gülenist Movement or the armed Kurdistan Workers' Party were exposed to brutal interrogation techniques aimed at extracting forced confessions or coercing detainees to incriminate others."
22. Cf. Yavuz, 2021, pp. 230 ff.
23. Şık, 2017, pp. 19 & 29. The same author writes that 79 of the 192 officers promoted to brigadier general or above in the years 2011 to 2015 were arrested after the coup, as were 17 of the 40 who had become admirals, while a further five of the new admirals became fugitives. Idem, pp. 22 & 24–25.
24. The tax inspectors who crippled the opposition Doğan media empire in 2009 with tax demands of 4 billion USD were dismissed from their posts as FETÖ sympathizers.
25. Hüseyin Gülerce, *Star*, 18 July 2020; Gülerce was General Editor of *Zaman* until mid-2014.

14. THE NEW TURKEY

1. Macoudi, *Les Prairies d'Or*, tr. Barbier de Meynard, C. Imprimerie Nationale, 1873, Vol. VII, p. 40. (Translated from French by the author).
2. Sinan Ülgen of EDAM, speaking at a webinar on Syria, IFEA, 15 April 2021.
3. Ahmet Davutoğlu, *Stratejik Derinlik, Turkiye'nin Uluslararasi Konumu*, Kure Yayinlari, 2001.
4. Eurobarometer surveys of November 2007 and June 2014.
5. Pew Research Center, 31 October 2014.
6. Kerem Öktem, *Angry Nation: Turkey since 1989*, Zed Books, 2011, p. 170.
7. Ahmet Davutoğlu, *AUC Cairo Review*, 12 March 2012.
8. Davutoğlu, March 2012, op. cit.
9. Ahmet Davutoğlu at a meeting with EU ambassadors, 8 May 2009.
10. From 1969 to 2011, the OIC was named the Organization of the Islamic Conference.
11. Interview with Fareed Zakaria, *Time*, January 2012.
12. Ahmet Davutoğlu, "Turkey's Foreign Policy Vision: An Assessment of 2007," *Insight Turkey*, 10:1, 2008, p. 82.
13. Davutoğlu, March 2012.
14. Estimates for 2020 are Germany 4–7 million; Netherlands 1–2 million; France 1–1.5 million; and Austria and Belgium each 0.4–0.6 million.
15. Benjamin Bruce, "Governing Islam Abroad: The Turkish and Moroccan Muslim Fields in France and Germany," thesis at Centre d'études et de recherches internationales (CERI), Institut d'Études Politiques de Paris, 2015, p. 216.
16. In Germany, the *Diyanet* operates through two associations, both called *Diyanet İşleri Türk İslam Birliği* (DİTİB), and in the Netherlands through the *Hollanda Diyanet Vakfi*, all founded in the early 1980s.
17. Bruce, pp. 397–398.
18. Andreas Goldberg, "Islam in Germany," *Islam, Europe's Second Religion*, edited by T. Shireen Hunter, 29–50. Westport, CT, Praeger, 2002, p. 41, cited in Yükleyen, 2012, p. 52. In 2009, there were 2,600 mosques in Germany and 432 in the Netherlands, according to Stefano Allievi (ed.), *Mosques in Europe: Why a Solution Has Become a Problem*, Alliance Publishing Trust, 2010, p. 20.
19. Bruce, p. 526. His research was in 2011 to 2013.
20. Bruce, pp. 394 & 403–407.
21. Bruce, pp. 551–552.
22. *Değerler Eğitimi ve Erdemli Gençlik* programme, *Stratejik Plan 2019–2023*, updated 2020, *Diyanet*, p. 33.
23. Ahmet Erdi Öztürk, 2018, p. 9.
24. Ahmet Erdi Öztürk, *Religion, Identity and Power: Turkey and the Balkans in the Twenty-First Century*, Edinburgh University Press, 2021, p. 211.

25. Dimitar Bechev, "A Very Long Engagement: Turkey in the Balkans," *Another Empire? A Decade of Turkey's Foreign Policy under the Justice and Development Party*, ed. Kerem Öktem, Ayşe Kadıoğlu & Mehmet Karlı, İstanbul Bilgi University Press, 2009, p. 211.
26. Kerem Öktem, *New Islamic Actors after the Wahhabi Intermezzo: Turkey's Return to the Muslim Balkans, European Studies Centre*, University of Oxford, December 2010, p. 8.
27. Öktem, 2010, p. 17.
28. Öktem, 2010, p. 19.
29. Isa Blumi, "Political Islam among the Albanians: Are the Taliban Coming to the Balkans?," Kosovar Institute for Policy Research and Development, 2nd edition, June 2005, pp. 9 & 15.
30. Blumi, op. cit., p. 1. Nine tenths of the population of Kosovo are ethnic Albanians.
31. Gerlachlus Duijzings, *Religion and the Politics of Identity in Kosovo*, C. Hurst & Co, 2000, pp. 113–114.
32. Cited in Öktem, 2010, p.27.
33. Öktem, 2010, p. 31.
34. Öktem, 2010, p. 38. A third university, the International University of Sarajevo, was set up in 2001. Its founders included the president's friend, Remzi Gür, and two current founders of the *İlim Yayma Vakfı*.
35. Laura Pitel, "Erdoğan's Great Game: Turkish Intrigue in the Balkans," *Financial Times*, 14 January 2021.
36. Ahmet Erdi Öztürk, 2021, pp. 3–7.
37. Aslı Aydıntaşbaş, "The Turkish *Sonderweg*: Erdoğan's New Turkey and its Role in the Global Order," *IPC-Mercator Policy Brief*, February 2020, p. 3.
38. Colonel Rich Outzen, "Deals, Drones, and National Will: The New Era in Turkish Power Projection," *Policy Notes 108*, Washington Institute for Near East Policy, 9 July 2021.
39. Mark Mazzetti and Matt Apuzzo, "U.S. Relies Heavily on Saudi Money to Support Syrian Rebels," *New York Times*, 23 January 2016.
40. Seymour M. Hersh, "The Red Line and the Rat Line," *London Review of Books*, August 2014.
41. Hersh, idem.
42. *Cumhuriyet*, 29 May 2015, pp. 1 & 13, and 6 July 2015, p. 5.
43. Russia's exports of natural gas continued, but, for a period, construction of the Akkuyu nuclear reactor slowed down.
44. He also repaired relations with King Abdullah of Jordan who had accused Turkey of seeking a religious solution in Syria and of helping Islamist militias in Libya and Somalia.
45. As vice president, Joe Biden had said that Erdoğan "had intentionally supplied

or facilitated the growth of ISIL or other violent extremists in Syria." He later telephoned the Turkish leader to apologize.

46. In April 2023, the U.S. Supreme Court rejected the bank's plea for sovereign immunity.
47. The confrontations helped at the polls; two thirds of the diaspora's votes in the two countries supported Erdoğan's campaign to boost the powers of the presidency.
48. Turkey adopts a maximalist approach to delineating its exclusive economic zone, though it has not adopted the Blue Homeland (*Mavi Vatan*) concept launched by a rear admiral in 2006. That would split the Aegean, denying the eastern Greek islands and Crete rights to territorial waters or exclusive economic zones.
49. Turkey had just lost over forty soldiers in Syria; the state broadcaster, TRT, indicated the incident would also distract local opinion.
50. High Representative of the Union for Foreign Affairs and Security Policy, *Joint Communication to the European Council: State of Play of EU-Turkey Political, Economic and Trade Relations*, 22 March 2021.
51. Update on 29 November 2023 of High Representative's report of March 2021.
52. Hugh Thomas, *The Spanish Civil War*, Penguin, 4th Edition, 2012, Book One, section 12, p. 196.
53. In April 2021, Canada cancelled licences for export of sensors and targeting technology to the company. *Ahval News*, 12 April 2021.
54. Jeff Flake, *Deseret News*, 13 February 2024.
55. Aydıntaşbaş, 2020, p. 3.

15. ERDOĞAN REGNANT

1. Erdoğan on the 70th anniversary of the foundation of the Faculty of Theology in Ankara, *Daily News*, 9 November 2019.
2. Mustafa Çakır, *Cumhuriyet*, 9 April 2014.
3. Interview with Star TV, reported in *Yeni Şafak*, 29 July 2014.
4. Interview, January 2020, with Hart.
5. Necip Fazıl Kısakürek, "Ayasofya Hitabesi," 29 December 1965.
6. Markus Dressler, "The Reconversion of the Hagia Sophia: Silences against the Backdrop of AKP Nation-(Re-)Building," paper delivered at "The Conversion of Spaces and Places of Worship in Anatolia ADIP International Conference" organized by The Anatolian Religions and Beliefs Platform, 10 April 2021.
7. Issues on which Emine Erdoğan has campaigned include early education, education for girls and analphabet mothers, violence against children and their forced labour, reducing caesarean birth rates (unusually high in Turkey),

drug abuse, waste reduction, improved conditions for women in business, and the rights of Palestinians and Rohingya Muslims.

8. The related *İlim Yayma* Association led the establishment of a university in Sarajevo in 2001.
9. Canan Coşkun, *Cumhuriyet*, 13 September 2014 et al.
10. *Gerçekçi Haber*, 1 December 2018 and *Sözcü*, 19 December 2019.
11. The family of Muhammed Ali prevented Erdoğan from speaking at his funeral and refused to accept the president's gift of a part of the Prophet's shround from Topkapı Palace. Tolga Tanış, *Hürriyet*, 10 June 2016.
12. Interview of Mehmet Torun with Muharrem Sarıkaya on Habertürk, published in Sözcü, 1 February 2020.
13. Murat Yetkin, *Hürriyet Daily News*, 1 May 2014.
14. *Hürriyet Daily News*, 5 March 2014.
15. According to Form 990 reports submitted to the U.S. Internal Revenue Service. *Cumhuriyet*, 2 April 2020.
16. Aykut Küçükkaya, *Cumhuriyet*, 26 August 2019.
17. A teacher in Karaman was sentenced to 508 years' imprisonment for ten incidents of sexual abuse of boys aged nine to ten.
18. Five of the top six recipients of funds from the municipality had members of Erdoğan's family on their board.
19. Demet Lüküslü, "Creating a Pious Generation: Youth and Education Policies of the AKP in Turkey," *South-east European and Black Sea Studies*, 16:4, 2016, p. 2.
20. Yabancı, 2019, pp. 10, 11 & 15.
21. Suat Kır, former deputy chairman of TÜGVA, *Fikirname*, April 2018. Also Yabancı, 2019, p. 13.
22. www.mantaship.com.
23. Soner Yalçın, 2014, pp. 115, 135, 143, 155–165 & 198–199. Yalçın was sentenced to a fine for insulting Bilal Erdoğan in this book and required to pay damages.
24. *Development and Democratization Program* of the AKP, announced in 2001.
25. Ayşe Buğra et al. *Progress at Risk. The Case Study on Income and Social Inequalities in Turkey:* Boğaziçi University Social Policy Forum for UNDP's Regional Human Development Program, 2016.
26. Coverage of social insurance programmes, World Bank Development Indicators.
27. Credit Suisse Research Institute, 2014, cited in OECD, 2018, p. 56.
28. Esra Çeviker Gürakar, *Politics of Favoritism in Public Procurement in Turkey: Reconfigurations of Dependency Networks in the AKP Era,* Palgrave, 2016.
29. E.g. Yavuz uses the words kleptocracy and kleptocratic eighteen times in his *Erdoğan: The Making of an Autocrat*, Edinburgh University Press, 2021.

30. *Development and Democratization Program* of the AKP, 2001 and still proclaimed two decades later.
31. Between 2003 and 2019, Turkey was responsible for 465 out of 1,279 journalists arrested worldwide, according to the Committee to Protect Journalists.
32. Hay Eytan Cohen Yanarocak, "The Erdoğan Revolution in the Turkish Curriculum Textbooks," *IMPACT-se*, March 2021, p. 14.
33. *Global Gender Gap Report 2024*, World Economic Forum, p. 12.
34. *Research on Domestic Violence against Women in Turkey*, Hacettepe University, 2015, p. 86, and *Global Gender Gap 2020*, World Economic Forum, p. 344.

16. THE CENTURY OF TÜRKIYE

1. *OSCE/ODIHR Limited Referendum Observation Mission Final Report*, Warsaw, 22 June 2017, pp. 1 & 17.
2. Estimate by Goldman Sachs cited in *Financial Times*, 10 November 2020.
3. "Turkey's Pulse," Metropoll, a survey of 2,610 people from 1 to 3 April 2023.
4. Berkant Gültekin, "The Realities Confronted on Babala [TV]," *Birgün*, 27 May 2023.
5. Cited in Lüküslü, 2016, pp. 637–649.
6. Erbaş had served on the board of Gülen's GYV's Intercultural Dialogue Platform. He helped organize several of Gülen's events. The GYV and the Platform were proscribed in July 2016, as was a book publisher to which Erbaş had entrusted one of his books.
7. Pehlivan & Terkoğlu, 2019.
8. Öztürk, 2019, pp. 205–206.
9. Öztürk, 2019, p. 62.
10. İsmail Arı, *Birgün.net*, 2 July 2024.
11. Erasmus, *Economist*, 1 July 2019.
12. Mardin, Islam, 2006, pp. 291–293.
13. Interview by author, date January 2022.
14. Survey of 1,492 Turks aged over eighteen carried out for TESEV in April & May 2006. Ali Çarkoğlu & Binnaz Toprak, *Religion, Society and Politics in a Changing Turkey*, TESEV, 2007. TESEV received some funding from George Soros's Open Society Foundations. Other findings included that two thirds of the population believed sale of alcohol during Ramadan should be banned and working hours arranged according to the time of the Friday midday prayers; that 60% considered interest from money invested in banks a sin and disapproved of men and women sitting next to one another in intercity buses; and that 40% called for teenage girls and boys to be educated in separate classrooms.
15. Survey of 3,053 Turks aged over eighteen carried out for TESEV in February 1999. Ali Çarkoğlu, "Religiosity, Support for Şeriat and Evaluations of

Secularist Public Policies in Turkey," *The Politics of Modern Turkey, Vol. 4: Major Issues and Themes in Contemporary Turkish Politics*, ed. Ali Çarkoğlu & William Hale, Routledge, 2008, chapter 56.

16. *Türkiye'de Dini Hayat Araştırması*, Diyanet İşleri Başkanlığı, 2014, pp. 239, 220 & 222.
17. Mehmet Ali Kulat, *Türkiye'de Toplumun Dine ve Dini Değerlere Bakışı*, MAK Danışmanlık, 2017, p. 20.
18. *Hayat Tarzlar Araştırması*, KONDA, November 2019, p. 108.
19. This section draws on the various writings of İsmail Kara cited and his interviews with *Maydan* (24 October 2017) and Medyascope TV (20 June 2016 & 16 April 2020).
20. İsmail Kara, 2017.
21. Ibid.
22. Mehmet Ali Kulat, p. 18.

ANNEX A

1. Irène Mélikoff, "L'Islam Hétérodoxe en Anatolie: non-conformisme -syncrétisme -gnose," *Turcica*, Vol. XIV, 1982, p. 67.
2. Precise numbers do not exist, partly because the state rarely addresses the issue and partly because the practice of *takıyye* or dissimulation means that, even if it had, the results would be questionable. The figures here are based on the 2006 survey by Konda, *Biz Kımız?*
3. Çarkoğlu & Toprak, 2007, p. 49.
4. Doğan Bermek, email to author, 7 July 2019.
5. Nuri Dersimi, *Kürdistan Tarihinde Dersim*, 4th edition, Dilan, 1992 (1st edition Aleppo, 1952), p. 319. Kurdish sources often allege use of poison gas, but it is not confirmed elsewhere. Martin van Bruinessen, "Mullas, Sufis and Heretics: The Role of Religion in Kurdish Society," *Collected Articles*, Isis, 2000, p. 116.
6. The Mevlevis use the same title for their (also hereditary) leader.
7. The *Dedegans* were often closer to the state.
8. Frederick de Jong, "The Takiya of Abd Allah Al-Maghawiri (Qayghuzsuz Sultan) in Cairo," *Turcica*, Vol. XIII, 1981, pp. 242–260.
9. Elise Massicard & Benoit Fliehe, "Die Ulusoy-Familie in der republikanischen Türkei: Abstammungsgebundene religiöse Autorität und Versuche ihrer Transformation," *Ocak und Dedelik*, ed. Langer, Robert, PL Academic Research, 2013, pp. 133–157.
10. Bermek, interview, 5 September 2021.
11. Ibid.

ANNEX B

1. This number excludes personal cults set up by individuals to abuse their followers. Six such *şeyh* are portrayed in İsmail Saymaz, *Şehvetiye Tarikatı* (Carnal Order), İletişim, 2019. One operation set up just east of İstanbul gained its leader fifteen wives and lasted from 1981 until clashing with modernity—and sports journalists—in the aspect of Formula 1.
2. Eighteen *tekke* in Kosovo are described in Tuğçe Tuna, *Balkanlardaki Miras*, H Yayınları, 2013, as are others in Albania, Macedonia, and Montenegro.
3. Şapolyo, 1964, pp. 448–449.
4. Trimingham, 1971, p. 75.
5. Madeline C. Zilfi, "The Kadızadelis: Discordant Revivalism in Seventeenth Century İstanbul," *Journal of Near Eastern Studies*, October 1986, pp. 251–269.
6. The Kadiri and the Nakşibendi were the only orders Van Bruinessen found in Kurdistan. Van Bruinessen, 1991, p. 210. There is an International Qadiriyya Foundation in Bielefeld, Germany, http://www.ukav.net/eng/.
7. This is the spelling used in *İslam Ansiklopedisi*. Most Western writers prefer Jalal ad-Din Rumi. Mevlana (Mawlana) is an honorific.
8. Chittick, 2004, p. xi.
9. Trimingham, 1971, p. 74.
10. Ayşe Akyürek, "Neo-Mevleviye or the Emergence of a Brotherhood at the Confluence of Sufism and New Age in Contemporary Turkey, École Pratique des Hautes Études ," doctoral thesis (French), PSL, May 2021, p. 200.
11. Akyürek, 2021, pp. 188–189.
12. Akyürek, 2021, p. 179.
13. İnalcık, 2000, p. 202.
14. Akyürek, 2021, p. 182.
15. Chapters 2–5 of Akyürek, 2021, pp. 104 ff.
16. Cited by Akyürek, 2021, pp. 161–163.
17. Trimingham, 1971, pp. 38, 40.

BIBLIOGRAPHY

Apart from the works below, those interested are also recommended to consult the subject entries in *İslam Ansiklopedisi*, published online by Türkiye Diyanet Vakfı.

Introduction and origins—Chapters 1–2

Adıvar, Halidé Edib, *Memoirs of Halidé Edib*, Gorgias Press, 2004—original published by Century, 1926.

Adıvar, Halidé Edib, *The Turkish Ordeal: Being the Further Memoirs of Halidé Edib*, Century, 1928.

Ahmad, Feroz, *The Making of Modern Turkey*, Routledge, 1993.

Ahmad, Feroz, "War and Society under the Young Turks, 1908–1914," "Great Britain's Relations with the Young Turks, 1908–1914," & "The Kemalist Movement and India," *From Empire to Republic: Essays on the Late Ottoman Empire and Modern Turkey*, İstanbul Bilgi Üniversitesi, 2008.

Ali, Shamshad, "Indian Muslims and The Ottoman Empire 1876–1924," doctoral thesis, Aligarh Muslim University, 1990.

Atasoy, Nurhan, *Derviş Çeyizi*, İBB Kültür A.Ş. Yayınları, 2000.

Atatürk, Mustafa Kemal, *The Great Speech (Nutuk)*, translated and published by Atatürk Research Centre, 2005.

Bardakçı, Murat, *Mahmud Şevket Paşa'nın Sadaret Günlüğü*, Türkiye İş Bankası Kültür Yayınları, 2014.

Barnes, John Roberts, *An Introduction to Religious Foundations in the Ottoman Empire*, Brill, 1986.

Bellaigue, Christopher de, *The Islamic Enlightenment*, Vintage, 2018.

Berkes, Niyazi, *The Development of Secularism in Turkey*, McGill University, 1964.

Berkes, Niyazi, *Turkish Nationalism and Western Civilization: Selected Essays by Ziya Gökalp*, Columbia University Press, 1959.

Berridge, G.R., *Gerald Fitzmaurice (1865–1939), Chief Dragoman of the British Embassy in Turkey*, Martinus Nijhoff, 2007.

Berridge, G.R. (ed.), *Tilkidom and the Ottoman Empire: The Letters of Gerald Fitzmaurice to George Lloyd, 1906–1915*, Isis, 2008.

Bruce, Benjamin, "Governing Islam Abroad: The Turkish and Moroccan Muslim Fields in France and Germany," thesis, Centre de recherches internationales (CERI), Institut d'Études Politiques de Paris, 2015.

Bruinessen, Martin van, *Agha, Shaikh and State, The Social and Political Structures of Kurdistan*, Zed Books, 1992.

Cengizer, Altay, "The Policies of the Entente Powers towards the Ottoman Empire," *War and Collapse: World War I and the Ottoman State*, ed. M. Hakan Yavuz with Feroz Ahmad, University of Utah Press, 2016.

Clarke, Bruce, *Twice a Stranger*, Granta, 2007.

Çizakça, Murat, *A History of Philanthropic Foundations: The Islamic World from the Seventh Century to the Present*, Boğaziçi University Press, 2000.

DeLong-Bas, Natana J., *Wahhabi Islam: From Revival and Reform to Global Jihad*, Oxford University Press, 2004.

Findley, Carter Vaughn, *Turkey, Islam, Nationalism, and Modernity: A History, 1789–2007*, Yale University Press, 2010.

Fortna, Benjamin C., *Imperial Classroom: Islam, Education and the State in the Late Ottoman Empire*, Oxford University Press, 2002.

Frye, Richard Nelson, "The Samanids," *Cambridge History of Iran*, Vol. 4, Cambridge University Press, 1975, pp. 136 ff.

Gaborieau, Marc et al., *Naqshbandis*, Éditions Isis, 1990.

Goodwin, Godfrey, "The Dervish Architecture of Anatolia," *The Dervish Lodge*, ed. Raymond Lifchez, University of California Press, 1992.

Gökyiğit, Ali Nihat, *Doğa ve İnsan Sevdam*, ANG Vakfı, 2016.

Gündoğdu, Cihangir, "The Anatomy of an Assassination: Assassination of Mahmud Şevket Paşa (11 June 1913)," thesis, Boğaziçi University, 2004.

Hanioğlu, M. Şükrü, *A Brief History of the Late Ottoman Empire*, Princeton University Press, 2008.

Hanioğlu, M. Şükrü, *The Young Turks in Opposition*, Oxford University Press, 1995.

Hart, Kimberly, *And Then We Work for God: Rural Sunni Islam in Western Turkey*, Stanford University Press, 2013.

Heyd, Uriel, *Foundations of Turkish Nationalism: The Life and Teachings of Ziya Gökalp*, Luzac and The Harvill Press, 1950.

Holbrook, Victoria Rowe, "Modernism and Authenticity," *Festschrift in Honor of Walter G. Andrews—II, Journal of Turkish Studies 34/II*, eds. Cemal Kafadar & Gönül Alpay Tekin, Harvard, 2010.

İnalcık, Halil, *An Economic and Social History of the Ottoman Empire, 1300–1914*, ed. Halil İnalcık with Donald Quataert, Cambridge University Press, 1994.

İnalcık, Halil, *The Ottoman Empire: The Classical Age*, Weidenfeld & Nicholson, 1973. Page references are to the Phoenix Press edition of 2000.

İnançer, Ömer Tuğrul, "Rituals and Main Principles of Sufism during the Ottoman Empire," *Sufism and Sufis in Ottoman Society*, ed. Ahmet Yaşar Ocak, Türk Tarih Kurumu, 2005.

Jenkins, Gareth H., *Political Islam in Turkey: Running West, Heading East?*, Palgrave Macmillan, 2008.

Jong, Frederick de, *Sufi Orders in Ottoman and Post-Ottoman Egypt and the Middle East: Collected Studies*, Isis Press, 2000.

Kafadar, Cemal, *Between Two Worlds: The Construction of the Ottoman State*, University of California, 1995.

Kara, İsmail, "Islam and Islamism in Turkey: A Conversation with İsmail Kara," *Maydan*, 2017, https://themaydan.com/2017/10/islam-islamism-turkey-conversation-ismail-kara/.

Kara, İsmail, "Tarikat çevrelerinin İttihat ve Terakki ile münasebetleri," *Dergah*, 4:43, 1993.

Kara, Mustafa, *Din, hayat, sanat açısından tekkeler ve zaviyeler*, Dergah Yayınları, İstanbul, 1980 (extended edition of 1977 original).

Kara, Mustafa, "The Social and Cultural Activities of the Dervishes under the Second Constitution," *Sufism and Sufis in Ottoman Society*, ed. Ahmet Yaşar Ocak, Türk Tarih Kurumu, 2005.

Karamustafa, Ahmet T., "Origins of Anatolian Sufism," *Sufism and Sufis in Ottoman Society*, ed. Ahmet Yaşar Ocak, 2005.

Köprülü, Mehmed Fuad, *Early Mystics in Turkish Literature* (Turkish, 1918), ed. Gary Leiser & Robert Dankoff, Routledge, 2006.

Kreiser, Klaus, "The Dervish Living," *The Dervish Lodge*, ed. Raymond Lifchez, University of California, 1992.

Kreiser, Klaus, "Notes sur le présent et le passé des ordres mystiques en Turquie," *Les ordres mystiques dans l'Islam: cheminements et situation actuelle*, ed. A. Popović et G. Veinstein, Paris: École des hautes études en sciences sociales (ÉHESS), 1986.

Kuneralp, Sinan & Tokay, Gül, *The Private Correspondence of Sir Gerard Lowther, British Ambassador to Constantinople (1908–1913)*, Isis Press, 2018.

Landau, Jacob M., *Pan-Turkism in Turkey: A Study in Irredentism,* C. Hurst, 1981.

Landau, Jacob M., *The Politics of Pan-Islam: Ideology and Organization*, Clarendon Press, 1994.

Le Gall, Dina, *A Culture of Sufism: Naqshbandis in the Ottoman World, 1450–1700*, State University of New York Press, 2005.

Lewis, Bernard, *The Emergence of Modern Turkey*, Oxford University Press, 1961, 2nd edition 1968.

Lowry, Heath, *The Nature of the Early Ottoman State*, State University of New York Press, 2003.

Macfie, Alexander Lyon, *The Eastern Question 1774–1923*, Routledge, 2014.

Mango, Andrew, *Atatürk: The Biography of the Founder of Modern Turkey*, Overlook Press, 2004.

Mardin, Şerif, *The Genesis of Young Ottoman Thought: A Study in the Modernization of Turkish Political Ideas*, Princeton University Press, 1960.

Mardin, Şerif, "Islam in Nineteenth- and Twentieth-Century Turkey," *Religion, Society, and Modernity in Turkey*, Syracuse University Press, 2006.

Mardin, Şerif, "The Nakshibendi Order of Turkey," *Fundamentalism and the State: Remaking Polities, Economies, and Militance*, ed. Martin E. Marty & R. Scott Appleby, University of Chicago, 1993.

McCarthy, Justin, *Muslims and Minorities, The Population of Ottoman Anatolia and the End of the Empire*, New York University, 1983.

McCarthy, Justin, *The Ottoman Peoples and the End of Empire*, Arnold, 2001.

McCullagh, Francis, *The Fall of Abd-Ul-Hamid*, Methuen, 1910.

McMeekin, Sean, *The Ottoman Endgame: War, Revolution and the Making of the Modern Middle East, 1908–1923*, Allen Lane, 2015.

Nasr, S.H, "Sufism," *Cambridge History of Iran*, Cambridge University Press, Vol. 4, 1975, pp. 442 ff.

Norman, York A., "Beyond Jihad," *War and Collapse: World War I and the Ottoman State*, ed. M. Hakan Yavuz with Feroz Ahmad, University of Utah Press, 2016.

Ocak, A. Yaşar, "Kalenderi Dervishes and Ottoman Administration from the Fourteenth to the Sixteenth Centuries," *Manifestations of Sainthood in Islam*, ed. Grace Martin Smith, Isis Press, 1993.

Özal, Korkut, "Twenty Years with Mehmed Zahid Kotku: A Personal Story," *Naqshbandis in Western and Central Asia: Change and Continuity,* papers read at the Swedish Research Institute in İstanbul, ed. Elisabeth Özdalga, Curzon, 1999.

Parla, Taha, "The Social and Political Thought of Ziya Gökalp, 1876–1924," *Social, Economic and Political Studies of the Middle East*, Vol. XXXV, Leiden, E.J. Brill, 1985.

Paşa, Cemal, *Anılarım*, İstanbul, Paraf, 2010.

Ramsaur Jr, Ernest Edmondson, *The Young Turks: Prelude to the Revolution of 1908*, Princeton University Press, 1957.

Ruthven, Malise, *Islam in the World*, Penguin, 2nd edition, 2000.

Shaw, Stanford J. & Kural Shaw, Ezel, *History of the Ottoman Empire & Modern Turkey, Vol. II Reform, Revolution and Republic: The Rise of Modern Turkey, 1808–1975*, Cambridge University Press, 1977.

Sohrabi, Nader, *Revolution and Constitutionalism in the Ottoman Empire and Iran*, Cambridge University Press, 2011.

Toynbee, Arnold J., "Abolition of Ottoman Caliphate," *Survey of International Relations*, ed. Arnold J. Toynbee, Oxford University Press, 1927.

Trimingham, J. Spencer, *The Sufi Orders in Islam*, Oxford University Press, 1971.

Yılmaz, Coşkun (ed.), *II Abdülhamid: Modernleşme Sürecinde İstanbul*, Avrupa Kültür Başkenti, 2010.

Zilfi, Madeline C., *The Politics of Piety: the Ottoman* ulema *in the Postclassical Age (1600–1800)*, Bibliotheca Islamica, Minneapolis, 1988.

Incubation—Chapters 3–5

Abu Manneh, Butrus, "A New Look at the Rise and Expansion of the Khalidi Sub-Order," *Sufism and Sufis in Ottoman Society*, ed. Ahmet Yaşar Ocak, Türk Tarih Kurumu, 2005.

Akgün, Seçil, "Türkçe Ezan," *DTCF Tarih Araştırmalar Dergisi 13*, No. 24, 1980.

Akgündüz, Ahmet, *Arşiv belgeleri ışığında Silistre'li Süleyman Hilmi Tunahan*, OSAV, 1997.

Akgündüz, Ahmet, *Bilinmeyen bir dahi: Bedîüzzaman Said Nursi*, Bilge Yayıncılık, 2010.

Algar, Hamid, "A Brief History of the Naqshbandi Order" & "Political Aspects of Naqshbandi History," Marc Gaborieau et al., *Naqshbandis*, IFEA, Éditions Isis, 1990.

Algar, Hamid, "The Centennial Renewer, Bediüzzaman Said Nursi and the Tradition of *tajdid* [*tecdit*, Renewal]," *Journal of Islamic Studies*, 12:3, Oxford Centre for Islamic Studies, 2001.

Algar, Hamid, "Devotional Practices of the Khalidi Naqshbandis of Ottoman Turkey," *The Dervish Lodge: Architecture, Art, and Sufism in Ottoman Turkey*, ed. Raymond Lifchez, University of California, Berkeley, 1992.

Algar, Hamid, "Hâlid el-Bağdâdî," "Halidiyye," "İmâm-ı Rabbânî," & "Nakşibendiyye," *TDV İslam Ansiklopedisi*.

Algar, Hamid, "Said Nursi and the Risale-i Nur. An Aspect of Islam in Contemporary Turkey," *Islamic Perspectives—Studies in Honor of Sayyid Aba Ala Mawdudi etc.*, Islamic Foundation, Leicester, 1979.

Algar, Hamid, *Wahhabism: A Critical Essay*, Oneonta, NY: Islamic Publications International, 2002.

Ardıç, Nurullah, *Islam and the Politics of Secularism: The Caliphate and Middle Eastern Modernization in the Early 20th Century*, Routledge, 2012.

Azak, Umut, *Islam and Secularism in Turkey: Kemalism, Religion and the Nation State*, I.B. Tauris, 2010.

Bediüzzaman, Said Nursi, *The Words, from the Risale-I Nur Collection*, tr. Şükran Vahide, Sözler Neşriyat, 1992.

Bellaigue, Christopher de, *Rebel Land: Among Turkey's Forgotten Peoples*, Bloomsbury, paperback edition 2010.

Cheviron, Nicolas & Pérouse, Jean-François, *Erdoğan: Nouveau père de la Turquie*, Éditions François Bourin, 2016.

Demirci, Emin Yaşar, "Modernization Religion and Politics in Turkey: The Case of the İskenderpaşa Community," Manchester University, doctoral thesis, 1996.

Emre, Mehmed, *Üstadım Süleyman Hilmi Tunahan (k.s.) ve Hatıralarım*, Ankara, 2000.

Gökaçtı, Mehmet Ali, *Türkiye'de din eğitimi ve İmam-Hatipler*, İletişim Yayınları, 2005.

Gözaydın, İştar, "Religion, Politics and the Politics of Religion in Turkey," Dietrich Jung & Catharina Raudvere (ed.), *Religion, Politics and Turkey's EU Accession*, Palgrave Macmillan, September 2008, pp. 159–176.

Guni, Gurdas, *Scholars, Saints, and Sufis*, University of California Press, 1972.

Işın, Zekayi, *Kim Bu Süleymancılar?*, Okuyorum Yayınları, 2021.

Kara, İsmail, *Din ile Modernleşme Arasında Çağdaş Türk Düşüncesinin Meseleleri*, Dergah Yayınları, 2003.

Kirişçi, Kemal & Winrow, Gareth M., *The Kurdish Question and Turkey: An Example of a Trans-state Ethnic Conflict*, Routledge Curzon, 2000.

Krstić, Tijana, *Contested Conversions to Islam: Narratives of Religious Change in the Early Modern Ottoman Empire*, Stanford University Press, 2011.

Leezenberg, Michiel, "Religion among the Kurds: Between Naqshbandi Sufism and IS Salafism," *The Kurdish Question Revisited*, eds. Gareth Stansfield & Mohammed Shareef, Hurst, 2017.

Mardin, Şerif, "Cultural Change and the Intellectual: Necip Fazıl and the Nakşibendi," *Religion, Society, and Modernity in Turkey*, Syracuse University Press, 2006.

Mardin, Şerif, *Religion and Social Change in Turkey: The Case of Bediüzzaman Said Nursi*, State University of New York Press, Albany, 1989.

McDowall, David, *A Modern History of the Kurds*, I.B. Tauris, 1996.

Mermer, Alison Clare, *Aspects of Religious Identity: The Nurcu Movement in Turkey Today*, 1985, Durham theses, Durham University.

Ocak, Ahmet Yaşar, "Social, cultural and intellectual life, 1071–1453," *Cambridge History of Turkey*, Vol. 1, ed. Kate Fleet, Cambridge University Press, 2009.

Retoulas, Christos, "Religion and Secularization in the 'Byzantine-Ottoman' Continuum: The Case of Turkish Secularism," doctoral thesis, University of Oxford Oriental Institute, 2010.

Şahiner, Necmeddin, *Bilinmeyen Taraflariyle Bediüzzaman Said Nursi: Kronolojik Hayatı*, Yeni Asya Yayınları, 10th edition, 1993.

Şahiner, Necmeddin, *Son Şahitler Bediüzzaman Said Nursi'yi Anlatiyor*, Vols 1–5, Yeni Asya, 1980–1992.

Toprak, Binnaz, "Religion and Politics," *The Routledge Handbook of Modern Turkey*, ed. Metin Heper, Routledge, 2012.

Vahide (Fırıncı), Şükran, *Islam in Modern Turkey: An Intellectual Biography of Bediüzzaman Said Nursi*, State University of New York Press, 2005.

Yalçın, Soner, *Kayıp Sicil, Erdoğan'ın Çalınan Dosyası*, Kırmızı Kedi Yayınevi, 2014.

Yalman, Ahmed Emin, *Turkey in My Time*, University of Oklahoma, 1956.

Flowering—Chapters 6–13

Abu-Rabi, Ibrahim M. (ed.), *Islam at the Crossroads, On the Life and Thought of Bediuzzaman Said Nursi*, State University of New York Press, 2003.

Ağırel, Murat, *Sarmal*, Kırmızı Kedi Yayınevi, 2020.

Atacan, Fulya, "A Kurdish Islamist Group in Modern Turkey: Shifting Identities," *Middle Eastern Studies*, July 2001, 37:3, Taylor & Francis.

Atacan, Fulya, *Radical Islamic Thought in Turkey*, Bilkent University, 1990.

Aykaç, Sadiye Erol, *Seyyid Muhammed Râşid Erol*, Akış Yayınları, 2007.

Bacık, Gökhan, *Contemporary Rationalist Islam in Turkey: The Religious Opposition to Sunni Revival*, I.B. Tauris, 2021.

Bacık, Gökhan, *Islam and Muslim Resistance to Modernity in Turkey*, Palgrave Macmillan, 2019.

Basmacı, Sema, "The Intellectuals' Hearth and the Turkish—Islamic Synthesis: Nationalist-Conservative Balances Extending from the 1980s to the 2000s," M.A. thesis, Hacettepe University, 2009.

Bianchi, Robert R., *Guests of God: Pilgrimage and Politics in the Islamic World*, Oxford University Press, 2004.

Çakır, Ruşen, *Ayet ve Slogan*, Metiş, (originally published 1990).

Çalmuk, Fehmi, *Büyük Doğu'nun Atlıları*, Hoton Yayınları, 2018.

Demirel, Tanel, "The Turkish Military's Decision to Intervene: 12 September 1980," *The Politics of Modern Turkey, Vol. 2: Political Institutions and Processes*, ed. Ali Çarkoğlu & William Hale, Routledge, 2008.

DeWeese, Devin, *Sufism in Central Asia: New Perspectives on Sufi Traditions, 15th-21st Centuries*, ed. Devin DeWeese & Jo-Ann Gross, Brill, 2018.

Dreyfuss, Robert, *The Devil's Game: How the United States Helped Unleash Fundamentalist Islam*, Dell Publishing, 2006.

Dreyfuss, Robert, "The United States and the Birth of Islamism," *The Globalist*, 18 January 2006.

Erbakan, Necmettin, *Adil Ekonomik Düzen*, 1991.

Erdoğan, Latif, *Fethullah Gülen Hocaefendi: Küçük Dünyam*, AD Yayıncılık, 1995, re-issued 2006.

Ergin, Muharrem, Bolak, A. Aydın & Yalçın, Süleyman, *Milli Mutabakatlar*, Aydınlar Ocağı Derneği, 1984.

Ermis, Barış, "Günümüz Dini Gruplarin Siyasetle İlişkisi (Altinoluk/Erenköy Cemaati)," thesis, Isparta University, 2018.

Filkins, Dexter, "The Thirty-Year Coup," *New Yorker*, 17 October 2016.

Gürdoğan, Ersin Nazif, *Görünmeyen Üniversite*, İz Yayıncılık, 1991, 7th edition, 2011.

Güreli, Nail, *Gerçek tanık: Korkut Özal anlatıyor*, Milliyet Yayınları, 1994.

Hansen, Suzy, "The Global Imam: What Does the Leader of the World's Most

Influential Islamic Movement Really Want?," *New Republic*, 10 November 2010.

Jenkins, Gareth H., "Between Fact and Fantasy: Turkey's Ergenekon Investigation," *Central Asia-Caucasus Institute and Silk Road Studies Program*, John Hopkins University, 2009.

Jenkins, Gareth H., "The Fading Masquerade: Ergenekon and the Politics of Justice in Turkey," *Turkey Analyst*, 4 April 2011.

Kafeşoğlu, İbrahim, *Türk İslam Sentezi*, Aydınlar Ocağı, 1985.

Keleş, Ahmet, *Feto'nun Günah Piramidi*, Destek Yayınları, 2016.

Kepel, Gilles, *The War for Muslim Minds: Islam and the West*, Belknap Harvard, 2004.

Kırman, M. Ali, "Türkiye'de bir 'Yeni Dini Cemaat' Olarak bir Örneği, 'Süleymancılık,'" doctoral thesis, Ankara University, 2000.

Koru, Fehmi, *One Column Ahead*, TİMAŞ, 2000.

Kulat, Mehmet Ali, *Türkiye'de Toplumun Dine ve Dini Değerlere Bakışı*, MAK Danışmanlık, 2017.

Mumcu, Uğur, *Rabıta*, Gazi Kitabevi, 10th ed. 1993.

Özdalga, Elisabeth, "The Hidden Arab: A Critical Reading of the Notion of 'Turkish Islam,'" *Middle Eastern Studies*, 42:4, 2006.

Özet, İrfan, *Fatih Başakşehir, Muhafazakâr Mahallede İktidar ve Dönüşen Habitus* (*Power in the Conservative Neighborhood and the Transforming Habitus*), İletişim, 2019.

Özkan, Behlül, "The Cold War-era Origins of Islamism in Turkey and Its Rise to Power," Hudson Institute, 5 November 2017.

Öztürk, Ahmet Erdi, "Transformation of the Turkish *Diyanet* Both at Home and Abroad: Three Stages," *European Journal of Turkish Studies* [Online], 27, 2018.

Öztürk, Saygı, *Menzil: Bir Tarikatın İki Yüzü*, Doğan Kitap, 2019.

Pehlivan, Barış & Terkoğlu, Barış, *Metastaz*, Kırmızı Kedi Yayınevi, 2019.

Sitembölükbaşi, Şaban, "Tunahan, Süleyman Hilmi–2," İslam Ansiklopedisi, 2012.

Şentürk, Hulusi, *İslamcılık Türkiye'de İslami oluşumlar ve siyaset*, Çıra Yay, 2011.

Tee, Caroline, *The Gülen Movement in Turkey: The Politics of Islam and Modernity*, I.B. Tauris, 2016.

Toprak, Binnaz, "Religion as State Ideology in a Secular Setting: The Turkish-Islamic Synthesis," *Aspects of Religion in Secular Turkey*, ed. Malcolm Wagstaff, University of Durham Occasional Paper Series No. 40, 1990.

Umur, Mehmet Umur & Tanıl Bora, "Türk-İslam 'Masonları,'" *Yeni Gündem*, 22 February 1987.

Ustaosmanoğlu, Mahmud, *Life Story of Hazrati Mahmud Effendi*, Ahıska Yayınevi, after 2013.

Yabancı, Bilge, "Work for the Nation, Obey the State, Praise the Ummah: Turkey's Government-oriented Youth Organizations in Cultivating a New Nation," *Ethnopolitics*, Taylor & Francis Online, October 2019.

Yanardağ, Merdan, & Veren, Nurettin, *Fethullah Gülen Hareketinin Perde Arkası: Turkiye Nasil Kuşatıldı*, Siyah Beyaz Yayınları, 2006.

Yanmış, Mehmet, *"Yakın Dönemde" Kürtler: Kimlik, Din, Gelenek*, eKitap Projesi & Cheapest Books, 2017.

Yavuz, M. Hakan, *Erdoğan: The Making of an Autocrat*, Edinburgh University Press, 2021.

Yavuz, M. Hakan, *Islamic Political Identity in Turkey*, Oxford University Press, 2003.

Yavuz, M. Hakan, *Towards an Islamic Enlightenment: The Gülen Movement*, Oxford University Press, 2013.

Yavuz, M. Hakan, *Turkey's July 15th Coup: What Happened and Why*, ed. Yavuz & Bayram Balcı, University of Utah Press, 2018.

Yükleyen, Ahmet, *Localizing Islam in Europe: Turkish Islamic Communities in Germany and the Netherlands*, Syracuse University Press, 2012.

Yükleyen, Ahmet, "Production of Mystical Islam in Europe: Religious Authorization in the Süleymanlı Sufi Community," *Contemporary Islam*, No. 4, 2010.

Zelyut, Rıza, *Tarikat Kuşatmasındaki Türkiye: Halidi Cehennemi (Turkey under Siege from the Tarikat: The Khalidi Hell)*, Kaynak Yayınları, 2019.

Harvest—Monoculture—Chapters 14–16

Aydıntaşbaş, Aslı, "The Turkish Sonderweg: Erdoğan's New Turkey and Its Role in the Global Order," *IPC-Mercator Policy Brief*, February 2020.

Bechev, Dimitar, *Turkey under Erdoğan: How a Country Turned from Democracy and the West*, Yale University Press, 2022.

Benhaïm, Yohanan & Öktem, Kerem, "The Rise and Fall of Turkey's Soft Power Discourse: Discourse in Foreign Policy under Davutoğlu and Erdoğan," *European Journal of Turkish Studies*, 21, 2015.

Blumi, Isa, "Political Islam among the Albanians: Are the Taliban Coming to the Balkans?," *Policy Research Series, Paper 2*, Kosovar Institute for Policy Research and Development, 2nd edition, June 2005.

Buğra, Ayşe et al., *Progress at Risk. The Case Study on Income and Social Inequalities in Turkey*, Boğaziçi University Social Policy Forum for UNDP's Regional Human Development Program, 2016.

Çağaptay, Soner, *The New Sultan: Erdogan and the Crisis of Modern Turkey*, I.B. Tauris, 2017.

Cohen, Rachel S., "Biden's Pentagon to Keep Turkey Out of F-35 Program," *Air Force Magazine*, 5 February 2021.

Cornell, Svante E., "Erbakan, Kısakürek, and the Mainstreaming of Extremism in Turkey," Hudson Institute, 4 June 2018.

Davutoğlu, Ahmet, *Stratejik Derinlik, Turkiye'nin Uluslararası Konumu*, Kure Yayinlari, 2001.

Davutoğlu, Ahmet, "Turkey's Foreign Policy Vision: An Assessment of 2007," *Insight Turkey*, 10:1, 2008.

Dorroll, Philip, *Islamic Theology in the Turkish Republic*, Edinburgh University Press, 2021.

Dressler, Markus, "The Reconversion of the Hagia Sophia: Silences against the Backdrop of AKP Nation-(Re-)Building," delivered at "The Conversion of Spaces and Places of Worship in Anatolia ADIP International Conference" organized by the Anatolian Religions and Beliefs Platform, 10 April 2021.

Duijzings, Gerlachlus, *Religion and the Politics of Identity in Kosovo*, C. Hurst & Co, 2000.

Eroğlu, Zehra, "Turkish Foreign Policy towards the Balkans in the Post-Cold War Era," doctoral thesis, METU, 2005.

Goldberg, Andreas, "Islam in Germany," *Islam, Europe's Second Religion*, ed. T. Shireen Hunter. Westport, CT, Praeger, 2002.

Gringeras, Ryan, "Blue Homeland: The Heated Politics behind Turkey's New Maritime Strategy," *War on the Rocks*, 2 June 2020.

Güllapoğlu, Fatih, *Tanksız Topsuz Harekât*, Tekin Yayınevi, 1991.

Güngör, Nasuhi, *Yenilikçi hareket: yeni dünya düzeni ekseninde bir değerlendirme*, Anka Yayınları, 2002.

Gürakar, Esra Çeviker, *Politics of Favoritism in Public Procurement in Turkey: Reconfigurations of Dependency Networks in the AKP Era*, Palgrave Macmillan, 2016.

Hersh, Seymour M., "The Red Line and the Rat Line," *London Review of Books*, August 2014.

İnce, Abdullah, "Yakın Dönem Türkiye'sinde Nakşilik-Siyaset İlişkisi," *Tarihten Günümüze Sufi-Siyaset İlişkileri—Sufism and Politics Past and Present*, ed. Salih Çift & Vejdi Bilgin, İslami İlimler Araştırma Vakfı, Ensar Neşriyat, 2020.

Kara, İsmail, *Cumhuriyet Türkiyesi'nde Bir Mesele Olarak İslam 1*, Dergah Yayınları, 6th edition, 2014.

Lüküslü, Demet, "Creating a Pious Generation: Youth and Education Policies of the AKP in Turkey," *South-east European and Black Sea Studies*, 16:4, 2016.

Necipoğlu, Gülru, *The Age of Sinan: Architectural Culture in the Ottoman Empire*, Reaktion Books, 2005.

NEF, Conflicts over Mosques in Europe: Policy Issues and Trends—NEF Initiative on Religion and Democracy in Europe, 2009 Network of European Foundations.

Öktem, Kerem, *New Islamic Actors after the Wahhabi Intermezzo: Turkey's Return to the Muslim Balkans*, European Studies Centre, University of Oxford, December 2010.

Öktem, Kerem, Kadıoğlu, Ayşe & Karlı, Mehmet, *Another Empire? A Decade of Turkey's Foreign Policy Under the Justice and Development Party*, İstanbul Bilgi University Press, 2012.

Özcan, Gül Berna Özcan & Gündüz, Umut, "Energy Privatizations, Business-

Politics Connections and Governance under Political Islam," *Environment and Planning C: Government and Policy*, 33, 2015.

Öztürk, Ahmet Erdi, *Religion, Identity and Power: Turkey and the Balkans in the Twenty-First Century*, Edinburgh University Press, 2021.

Rubin, Michael, "A Comedy of Errors: American-Turkish Diplomacy and the Iraq War," *Turkish Policy Quarterly*, 13 April 2005.

Yanarocak, Hay Eytan Cohen, "The Erdoğan Revolution in the Turkish Curriculum Textbooks," *IMPACT-se*, March 2021.

Yüksel-Kaptanoğlu, İlknur et al., *Research on Domestic Violence against Women in Turkey*, Hacettepe University, 2015.

Annexes

Akyürek, Ayşe, "Neo-Mevleviye or the Emergence of a Brotherhood at the Confluence of Sufism and New Age in Contemporary Turkey, École Pratique des Hautes Études," doctoral thesis (French), PSL, May 2021.

Bermek, Doğan, "The Alevi Muslim Belief System and Its Rituals," communication, 16 July 2019.

Bilici, Faruk, "Alévisme et bektachisme, alliés naturels de la laïcité en Turquie?" *Islam et laicité: Approches globales et régionales*, ed. Michel Bozdémir, L'Harmattan, 1996.

Birge, John Kingsley, *The Bektashi Order of Dervishes*, Luzac and Hartford, 1937.

Brown, John P., *Dervishes or Oriental Spiritualism*, Trübner, London, 1868.

Bruinessen, Martin van, "Mullas, Sufis and Heretics: The Role of Religion in Kurdish Society," *Collected Articles*, Isis Press, 2000.

Çakır, Ruşen, "Political Alevism versus Political Sunnism: Convergences and Divergences," *Alevi Identity: Cultural, Religious and Social Perspectives*, ed. Tord Olsson et al., Swedish Research Institute, 1998.

Dedebaba, Bedri Noyan, *Bütün Yönleriyle Bektâşîlik ve Alevîlik*, Ardıç-Şahkulu Sultan Dergâhı, Vol. I, 1998.

Dersimi, Nuri, *Kürdistan Tarihinde Dersim*, 4th edition, Dilan, 1992 (1st edition Aleppo, 1952).

Faroquhi, Suraiya, "The Bektashis: A Report on Current Research," *Bektachiyya, Études sur l'ordre mystique des Bektachis et les groupes relevant de Hajdi Bektach*, ed. Alexandre Popović & Gilles Veinstein, Isis Press, 1995.

Gölpınarlı, Abdülbaki, *Mevlana'dan sonra Mevlevilik*, İnkilap, 2006.

Gölpınarlı, Abdülbaki, *Tasavvuf*, İstanbul, 2000.

Goodwin, Godfrey, *The Janissaries*, Saqi Books, 1994.

Kutay, Cemal, *Kurtuluşun ve Cumhuriyet'in Manevi Mimarları, Diyanet İşleri Bakanlığı, 1972*. ABM Yayınevi, 2013.

Maden, Fahri, *Bektaşi Tekkelerinin Kapatılması (1826) ve Bektaşiliğin Yasaklı Yılları*, Türk Tarihi Kurumu Yayınları, 2013.

Martin, B. G., "A Short History of the Khalwati Order of Dervishes," *Scholars,*

Saints and Sufis, Muslim Religious Institutions in the Middle East since 1500, ed. Nikki R. Keddie, University of California Press, 1972.

Massicard, Élise, "Alevi Critique of the AK Party: Criticizing 'Islamism' or the Turkish State," *The Turkish AK Party and its Leader: Criticism, Opposition and Dissent*, ed. Umit Cizre, Routledge, 2016.

Massicard, Élise, "Alevism in the 1960s: Social Change and Mobilization," *Alevis and Alevism: Transformed Identities*, ed. Hege Irene Markussen, Isis Press, 2005.

Massicard, Élise & Fliehe, Benoit, "Die Ulusoy-Familie in der republikanischen Türkei: Abstammungsgebundene religiöse Autorität und Versuche ihrer Transformation," *Ocak und Dedelik*, ed. Langer, Robert, PL Academic Research, 2013.

Mélikoff, Irène, *Sur les traces du soufisme turc. Recherches sur l'Islam populaire en Anatolie*, İstanbul, Isis Press, 1992.

Mélikoff, Irène, "Un Islam en Marge de l'Islam: L'Alévisme," *Au banquet des quarante*, İstanbul, Isis Press, 2001.

Subaşı, Necdet, "Anatolian Aleviism," *The Turkic Speaking Peoples: 2,000 Years of Art and Culture from Inner Asia to the Balkans*, ed. Ergün Çağatay & Doğan Kuban, Prestel & Prince Claus Fund Library, 2006.

Tuna, Tuğçe, *Balkanlardaki Miras*, H Yayınları, 2013.

Zarcone, Thierry, "Note Liminaire sur les Couvents Bektachis d'İstanbul," *Bektachiyya, Études sur l'ordre mystique des Bektachis et les groupes relevant de Hajdi Bektach*, ed. Alexandre Popović & Gilles Veinstein, Isis Press, 1995.

Zilfi, Madeline C., "The Kadızadelis: Discordant Revivalism in Seventeenth Century İstanbul," *Journal of Near Eastern Studies*, October 1986, pp. 251–269.

INDEX